TEACHERS OF HISTORY

Essays in Honor of Laurence Bradford Packard

Laurence Bradford Packard, Anson D. Morse Professor of History

Teachers of History

ESSAYS IN HONOR OF

LAURENCE BRADFORD PACKARD

EDITED BY *H. Stuart Hughes* WITH THE

COLLABORATION OF *Myron P. Gilmore*

AND *Edwin C. Rozwenc*

Essay Index Reprint Series

BOOKS FOR LIBRARIES PRESS
FREEPORT, NEW YORK

INTERNATIONAL STANDARD BOOK NUMBER:
0-8369-2164-X

LIBRARY OF CONGRESS CATALOG CARD NUMBER:
75-142644

PRINTED IN THE UNITED STATES OF AMERICA

Contents

Contents

III. PROBLEMS OF INTERPRETATION

TEACHERS OF HISTORY

Essays in Honor of Laurence Bradford Packard

[CHARLES WOOLSEY COLE]

Introduction:

Laurence Bradford Packard

Anson D. Morse Professor of History at Amherst College

LIKE the seminar, the *Festschrift* is an importation from the academic world of nineteenth-century Germany. Both in its homeland and in America, it has been published almost always to honor a revered teacher. But it typically has been written and edited by students who worked under such a professor in a graduate, Ph.D., seminar. The present volume is, quite possibly, unique in that it is designed to do homage to an *undergraduate* teacher by students whom he inspired to pursue the difficult but rewarding vocation of historian. The authors did their graduate work under others at divers universities. But without exception they look back to their classes with Professor Packard as sources of their motivation to become professionals in the field of history. It was from him that they acquired not only an understanding of what history is and what historical thinking is like at its best, but also a feeling of excitement about reading, teaching, and research in history.

Laurence B. Packard was born in Brockton, Massachusetts, in 1887. Whether he acquired his interest in history in the Brockton High School or whether he got it from the remarkable teachers under whom he worked as an undergraduate at Harvard is arguable. In any case, after receiving his A.B. degree at Harvard in 1909, he went directly on into four years of graduate work there. He was Rogers traveling fellow in

1

1911–1912. The Ph.D., somewhat delayed by the exigencies of teaching and of war, was conferred on him in 1921. His thesis dealt with the period of Louis XIV, a subject to which he returned when his *The Age of Louis XIV* (1929) joined his *The Commercial Revolution* (1927) in the Berkshire series, of which he was one of the editors. He enlisted in the army in the spring of 1917, was sent to Madison Barracks Training Camp, and emerged as a second lieutenant in the Adjutant General's Department. With its uncanny skill in choosing assignments for which the individual's preparation is seemingly inappropriate, the army then put him in charge of organizing the statistical section for the 78th Division at Camp Dix. He went into Philadelphia, bought the equipment which was lacking with his own money, and set up a personnel record system on cards long before the War Department realized how valuable such a technique could be.

Early in 1918 he was put in an intelligence section in the War De- -partment in Washington. From there he was sent as one of the intelligence officers on General Graves's expedition to Vladivostok. Thus he became one of the few historians who has actually done time in Siberia. After nine grim months, when the American forces were awkwardly poised between Japan and revolutionary Russia, he returned to the United States and was mustered out as a captain in time to take up his teaching in the fall of 1919.

Aside from some teaching done at Harvard in his graduate years and from visiting lectureships or professorships at Michigan, California, Harvard, Yale, Wesleyan, New York University, Smith, and Mount Holyoke, Professor Packard's career as a teacher falls into two major parts, that at the University of Rochester (1913–1925) and that at Amherst College (1925 to the present). People at Rochester still remember the breath of new life and vigor that he brought to the history department there with his introductory course in European history, and how he made a course in English history vital by explaining the origins of the war then raging in Europe. He later developed senior seminar work there and a course in Far Eastern history, and, as head of the department, reorganized the whole course offering.

Called to Amherst in 1925 as a full professor (he had achieved that rank five years earlier at Rochester), Laurence Packard again had an immediate impact. During his first year he offered History A (it became History 1 in 1928 and with only a brief intermission has been so known ever since), described as "Introduction to the history of contemporary civilization. A survey of the development of European civilization since the disintegration of the Roman Empire. *Elective for Freshmen.*" It now covers a longer span than when he first gave it, and a number of other teachers now work with him in giving it, though it is still fundamentally his course and his responsibility.

His other course was History 5: "Europe since 1871. A fairly detailed study of international diplomacy from 1871 to 1914, the military and diplomatic aspects of the Great War and the settlement of 1918–1920. *Elective for Juniors.*" Time and world events have evolved this course into the present-day History 49–50, "Two World Wars."

In addition to these two basic courses, Professor Packard, in 1926–1927, offered History 7: "An introduction to historical criticism; the 'Classics' of the historical method and a topical study of intellectual developments in the eighteenth and nineteenth centuries. *Elective for Seniors,*" which later evolved into History 9, "An introduction to historiography," and eventually into honors courses for both junior and senior years, with Professor Packard taking the seniors. In 1936–1937 he omitted History 5 and gave instead History 13: "Europe in the Age of Louis XIV. A reading knowledge of French requisite." In 1949 he offered History 45–46, "The Far East," and this last course, together with "Two World Wars" and "The Age of Louis XIV," have tended to be offered in successive years.

Thus both at Rochester and at Amherst, Professor Packard taught at three different levels—the elementary, the upper class, and the honors. The amazing fact is that at all three he has been equally successful. The freshmen he captures almost from the start by the quality of his lectures. The delivery is forceful and somewhat staccato, with emphasis given by both voice and gesture. Nobody has ever—nobody could have—fallen asleep in one of his classes. But delivery is only a part of the effectiveness. Each lecture is a work of art, beautifully formed, skillfully integrated. There is to each a lucid clarity that is sustained through the most tortuous intricacies of diplomatic negotiations or of military or political campaigns. Even beyond manner and context is the personality of the lecturer. Here is a man whose wide and deep knowledge of history has given him a contagious enthusiasm for the insights it can offer, the understanding of the world it can provide, the illumination it can shed on the complexities of modern life. When he is lecturing, Professor Packard somehow personifies the historical method at its most trenchant.

It is through the introductory history course at Rochester and at Amherst that Professor Packard has had his widest influence. Today, History 1 is required of all freshmen at Amherst, but in the earlier days, when there was no requirement, substantially the whole entering class elected the course, for the word was passed along by the undergraduates that this was a "must." The figures are startling. From 1925–1926 to 1953–1954, 6,154 students have taken Professor Packard's History 1 at Amherst. Exactly 55.9 per cent of all of Amherst's 9,152 living alumni have taken this course, and this does not include students now in college.

In addition, his advanced lecture courses have been elected by a very large portion of each successive class, whether they have dealt with one or two World Wars or the Far East. Thus, Professor Packard's position is unique in the long history of Amherst. He has taught more of its students than any other man. He has had most of them both at the elementary and at a more advanced level. He has influenced them profoundly not only by the impact of his ideas and of his personality, but also by giving them an understanding of what history can mean intellectually and a love for history itself.

Even more remarkable is the fact that each year Professor Packard has so influenced some of his students that they have chosen to go on to graduate study in history and to make history their life work. From his very first class at Rochester five men went on to graduate school in history, and three of them (Floyd Lear, Frank Nowak, and Dwight Salmon) took their Ph.D.'s in that field. At Amherst, the results of his teaching were no less striking. For example, a study of the Amherst Memorial Fellowships awarded for graduate work in the field of the social sciences from 1930 to 1946 showed that forty-four men received such grants. Of these thirty-one were in history, ten in economics, and three in political science. The figures are not all at hand but it is a safe guess that many more than a hundred of Professor Packard's students have gone on into graduate work in history. Some of them have strayed into other fields— the ministry, administration, government service, diplomacy, and business. But most of them are now teaching with distinction in schools, colleges, and universities from coast to coast and from the Rio Grande to the 49th parallel. Few men have ever made such a contribution to the recruitment of talent to their professions.

4

Introduction

It has been repeatedly noted, moreover, in such graduate schools as Harvard and Columbia that Professor Packard's students do extremely well and win far more than their share of honors and distinctions. They do well not only because they are able and excited about history but because they are well trained in the fundamentals of history and of the historical method. It is perhaps the most unusual thing about Professor Packard's teaching that he is superlative not only in the large lecture course but also in the senior seminar or honors course. The best of the students whom he attracted to history through History 1 or History 5 went on to major in history and to take with him the senior seminar in historical method and historiography or later the senior honors course that developed out of it.

In such a small class they see another Professor Packard. They may have realized what a scholar he is from their earlier work with him. They may know that he reads everything important in the fields in which he teaches, keeping abreast of new works that appear, as few teachers ever find time to do. They may even have heard that before offering a new course, like that on the Age of Louis XIV, though the field was already familiar to him, he had read or reread hundreds of volumes including the whole of Saint-Simon. But only in the give and take of a seminar can they realize how wide and deep are the veins of historical ore that he has mined, examined critically, and melted into historical wisdom.

They see him too in a new teaching role—rather different from the lecturer on the platform—full of ideas for papers and theses, eagerly attentive to material presented, sharply critical of sloppiness of work, method, or thought. By Socratic techniques he makes them see their own shortcomings. At the same time, his praise for a job well done is an academic accolade gracefully given. There is a tension and an excitement in Professor Packard's seminars, and no students are long in doubt that the materials they are dealing with and the methods they are employing are of the utmost importance. They work harder for him than most of them have ever worked before. He is intolerant of tardiness and laziness, though he can be almost gentle with honest, human shortcomings.

In the seminars, the students learn that history is not cut and dried, but subject to re-evaluation and reinterpretation. They learn how hard it is to establish a fact and how much harder to make a fact meaningful. They are introduced to the great historical thinkers of the past and the

5

types of problems that ever vex historians. When they go on to graduate school, they do well, for they have already been apprenticed to a master.

It is given to few men to teach in a classroom with the almost dazzling effectiveness of Professor Packard. It is given to few to teach in an advanced seminar with his skill, insight, and devotion. Those who can do both, as he does, must surely, in any generation, be numbered on the fingers of a single hand.

Those of us who as undergraduates have had the high privilege of working under Professor Packard offer him this volume as a symbol of our respect, admiration, and affection. We offer it, too, as professionals, to a teacher who has done so much through history to increase the understanding of the world of today.

Amherst, Massachusetts
December 10, 1953

» I «

INDIVIDUAL FIGURES

[MYRON P. GILMORE]

Fides et Eruditio:

Erasmus and

the Study of History

THE first work of Erasmus to appear in print was a letter in praise of a history of France and its author.[1] At the beginning of October 1495, Erasmus, who had recently arrived in Paris [2] to study for a doctor's degree in theology, was trying to make his way in the literary world. He appears to have introduced himself almost at once to Robert Gaguin, whose history, the *Compendium de origine et gestis Francorum,* was then being printed. There were some brief exchanges, of which we catch the tone from those of Gaguin's replies that have survived. Erasmus' flattery bought him an opportunity to insert his letter at the end of Gaguin's book before it was published and thus to reach the notice of the literary world through the established fame of the older scholar.

Robert Gaguin was then at the height of his reputation. Born in 1433, he had led a diversified life in which he distinguished himself in the church, in diplomacy, and in literature.[3] General of the Trinitarian Order, dean of the Faculty of Law at the University of Paris, he had frequently been employed by Louis XI and Charles VIII on diplomatic missions in Italy, Spain, and England. One of the purposes to which his order was devoted was the recovery of captives from the infidel, and

9

since the fulfillment of this aim also required expeditions abroad, he was able to combine his ecclesiastical with his secular missions. This active career in the service of church and state was balanced by a life of study and writing. His literary interests had been shaped by the influence of Italian humanist teaching. Although he knew little or no Greek, he tried in a variety of ways to apply in his own work the lessons of both form and content which he had learned from Latin history and literature. As a young man he had been a careful student of the *Aeneid,* and his own manuscript copy with his marginal notes survives. The vision of the destiny of Aeneas and the mission of imperial Rome took on an added meaning for a Frenchman in the royal service in the days of Louis XI and Charles VIII. Historians and publicists had endowed the first line of the French kings with a genealogy which also went back to Troy; in an age when the domain of the French crown had more than doubled in area and the first great expeditions to Italy in pursuit of the Neapolitan claim were preparing, it seemed that an imperial destiny opened also before the French monarchy.

The possibility of historical parallels, recurrences of the great deeds of the ancients, cyclical repetitions of typical situations, seems to have occurred to Gaguin although he never developed it into what we should call a philosophy of history. He had been one of the earliest collaborators of Fichet and Heynlin in the work of the Sorbonne press. The third work to issue from this press was an edition of Sallust. In it was printed a little poem by Gaguin on the rebellion and approaching ruin of Charles of Burgundy. The analogy is explicit between the conspiracy of Catiline and the revolt of a great noble against the French monarchy. A sense of the relevance of ancient history was also manifest in the works Gaguin chose to translate. In 1485 he translated into French the *Commentaries* of Caesar and in 1493 the *Third Decade* of Livy.

Twice Gaguin petitioned the crown to be named royal historiographer. In the first of these requests, addressed to the chancellor, he emphasized the fact that there had been no skilled writers of French history in Latin although there had been many who had written in the vulgar tongue. Accordingly, the reputation of the French with other nations had suffered. Only in a universal language could the great deeds of the French become a permanent possession. For patriotic reasons he urged the appointment of a qualified historian.[4]

In a second letter he pointed out the examples of virtue and glory, the triumphs over incredible adversity, that could be collected from the reign of Louis XI. He complained that no one had celebrated in literature the virtues of the French kings, who were not inferior to the Caesars. "Nicias and Alcibiades and Hannibal are glorious names but there are more effective examples from our own and not from an alien history." There is a justification not only for remote but also for recent and contemporary history. He pleaded with the king for a pension and suggested that the great history which he projected would not be written without pecuniary rewards. Aristotle was subsidized by Alexander and Virgil by Augustus.[5]

On neither of these occasions was the request granted, but Gaguin's devotion to the monarchy was proof against any disappointment. He went ahead with his history and worked on it for years without any subsidy. Had he been on the official payroll the result could hardly have been less critical of the growth of the French monarchy. *The Compendium de origine et gestis Francorum* was one of the first attempts to apply to the history of a modern people methods and conclusions derived from a study of the great historians of antiquity. The history was written frankly to prove the point that Gaguin had made in his letters that "there are more effective examples from our own history." Since this was the principle, the author had to be sure that his examples were effective, and the result was the glorification of the heroes of French history. The portrait of Charles VIII, who was then reigning, is hardly more realistic than that of the legendary Pharamond. This was the work, finally ready to appear in 1495, which was the object of Erasmus' praise. In spite of his ulterior purposes in composing the letter, Erasmus found it expedient to say something on the nature of history as well as on the character of the historian.

He begins by praising Gaguin's talents and motives. "No other motive than devotion to your country led you to undertake this task." This patriotism springs from a sense of piety that all can admire. The reputation of the French has not hitherto been equal to their virtue, and Italy has conquered in literature although not in arms. (It is to be remembered that this letter was being written at the time when Charles VIII was returning from the first Italian expedition and the impression made by the news of his original victories over the Italians was still fresh.) Erasmus even quotes a letter from the Italian humanist Filelfo to an earlier Charles of France to show that the French kingdom is inheriting the political succession of the Roman empire and will be the great bulwark of Europe against the Turk. In spite of her great political achievements and her historic destiny, however, France has hitherto lacked a Livy or a Sallust, and without a talented historian the greatest deeds will fall into nothingness. The purpose of history is to perpetuate the virtuous accomplishments of great men, and their fame will be higher in proportion to the genius of the historians who write about them. The two qualities which are especially to be sought in a historian are trustworthiness (*fides*) and learning (*eruditio*). Confidence in the integrity of an author adds a greater plausibility to his account of the course of events, and the genius of a really learned writer may make what is obscure illustrious and what is humble noteworthy; it may even add to the reputation of what is already famous. A historian, then, should combine learning and veracity with literary skill, and he finds his highest duty in the recording of the history of his fatherland. All these qualities Erasmus discovered of course in Gaguin, and the letter concludes with a brief summary of his life and a flattering elaboration on his intellect and character.[6]

It might have been supposed from the evidence of this first published work that Erasmus put a high value on the cultivation of historical studies according to Gaguin's plan and that he would follow in his own work the example of the model he alleged had made such an impression on him. In actual fact, however, Erasmus in his subsequent career and writing revealed very little interest in the kind of history he here praised so extravagantly.

In the first place, nothing was more antipathetic to Erasmus in his maturity than the celebration of the deeds and mission of a particular people in the European community of nations. He was attached to no national tradition, and we cannot imagine him writing a "national" history.[7] Although he probably knew several vernacular tongues, he always refused to use them either in speech or in writing and more than once got into trouble for this intransigence. He resisted every attempt by the national monarchs and even by the emperor to get him into their service, and he preserved his independence by living for the most part in the communes of the Netherlands, Switzerland, and Germany. Basel, Louvain, and Freiburg remained always more congenial to him than Paris, London, or Rome. It is true that he had a keen sense of the differences among the great national groups of the European world and his letters are full of sharp insights and observations on what we should call national characteristics.[8] This is apparent in a well-known passage of his most famous satire. Folly in the course of her oration recognizes among the forms of self-love the collective self-flattery of national groups:

> And now I see that it is not only in individual men that nature has implanted self-love. She implants a kind of it as a common possession in the various races and even cities. By this token the English claim, besides a few other things, good looks, music, and the best eating as their special properties. The Scots flatter themselves on the score of high birth and royal blood, not to mention their dialectical skill. Frenchmen have taken all politeness for their province; though the Parisians, brushing all others aside, also award themselves the prize for theology. The Italians usurp belles-lettres and eloquence; and they all flatter themselves that they alone, of all mortal men, are not barbarians. In this particular point of happiness the Romans stand highest, still dreaming pleasantly of ancient Rome. The Venetians are blessed with a belief in their own nobility. The Greeks as well as being the founders of the learned disciplines, vaunt themselves upon their titles to the famous heroes of old. The Turks, and that whole rabble of the truly barbarous, claim praise for their religion, laughing at Christianity as superstitious. And what is much more pleasant, the Jews are still awaiting their own Messiah, and even today hold on to their Moses with might and main. Spaniards yield to no one in martial reputation. Germans take pride in their great stature and their knowledge of magic.[9]

In the case of Erasmus, however, this kind of dispassionate observation of the differences among the claims of the great national groups at the beginning of the sixteenth century was not accompanied by the growth of any sense of allegiance. The scholar who looked back to the culture of antiquity and the piety of early Christianity was indifferent to the extravagant claims of the national monarchies. Like his friend More, but to an even greater degree, Erasmus was an internationalist; when he thought about contemporary politics at all he kept steadily before his eyes the interests of the *res publica Christiana* and not those of any one parochial group. In an age when nationalism was beginning its greatest triumphs both cultural and political, the foremost scholar of the age neither really understood nor approved it.

Erasmus had therefore no sympathy for modern national history, although this was the very basis of the work of Gaguin which he had pretended in 1495 to admire so much. Aside from nationalism, however, there was the broader question of the nature and value of historical studies. Here again there is a striking contrast with the phrases of 1495. Erasmus wrote a great deal and all his life on the subject of education, but his formal remarks about history are brief, scattered, and conventional.

In 1511, shortly after finishing the *Praise of Folly,* he composed and published the *De copia verborum ac rerum,* a work whose purpose may be described by saying that it was for the study of Latin in its day roughly an equivalent to Fowler's *Modern English Usage.* It supplied both schoolboys and intended authors with variations in vocabulary, grammatical usages, and tricks of style and rhetoric. As the result of his careful studies in the Latin language and literature for many years, it succeeded to the place previously occupied by Valla's *Elegantiae,* which Erasmus himself had regarded as indispensable for a writer. The *De copia* contains a few incidental comments about history. In discussing devices for increasing the interest and variety of narrative description, Erasmus commits himself to the use of imaginary direct discourse by the historian. If we do not know what was actually said on a given past occasion we are entitled to imagine what ought to have been said. This is the practice of the greatest of poets—Erasmus cites the speeches of Priam and Hecuba to dissuade Hector from going into battle, the appeal of Andromache, and Hector's reply. He continues: "Nor is there anything more admirable in the writers of history, for in the opinion of all it is permitted to historians to invent speeches for individuals." [10] This general rule is followed by an interesting reservation: Erasmus permits himself to doubt whether the same latitude is allowed to historians of Christianity, but he recalls examples from the lives of the martyrs where the practice of antiquity was followed. Except for raising this doubt Erasmus does not suggest departing from standard classical and humanist practice.

The great tradition of "invented" speeches had been inaugurated in Greek historical writing and was maintained and developed by the Romans and their successors. In Thucydides such speeches had served a genuinely dramatic purpose, but many of his successors made them occasions for dramatic flourishes and illustrations of their command of style.[11] In most humanist historical writing of the fifteenth century the device of imaginary direct discourse was used not only to conform to rhetorical rules but also to construct idealized portraits. In this way individual historical characters came to exemplify abstract virtues and vices and thus serve as material for moral instruction. A great gulf separated the purpose of this use of direct discourse from that of a realist like Guicciardini, who in his masterpiece which covered the years of Erasmus' mature life used the same rhetorical device to underline the ironic difference between what men said and what they did. Erasmus' position in the *De copia* is that of traditional humanism. Nor does he reveal any awareness of the possibility of a new dimension in historical writing of the kind which was emerging in the Italian realist school.

History conceived as philosophy teaching by example was the view Erasmus also adopted in other works when he had occasion to consider the place of history in education. In 1516 he wrote for the future Charles V the *Institutio principis christiani*. The emphasis is entirely upon the moral instruction of the young prince, and Erasmus appears to be very doubtful whether history has any real place in that instruction. History can in fact be dangerous. "A boy who is wild and impetuous by nature would easily be incited to tyranny, if without forewarning he should read about Achilles, Alexander the Great, Xerxes or Julius Caesar." Even worse than examples drawn from ancient history are the legends of King Arthur, "poorly done, stupid and fit for old wives' tales so that it would be more advisable to put in one's time reading the comedies or the poets instead of nonsense of that sort." [12] Erasmus recommended to the prince a course of reading which began with the *Proverbs* of Solomon, *Ecclesiastes,* and the *Book of Wisdom* and continued with the *Moralia* of Plutarch and the works of Seneca. Finally the studious prince was to come to Aristotle's *Politics,* Cicero's *Offices,* and Plato's *Republic.* Erasmus protests that he does not deny that a great fund of wisdom may be gathered from a reading of the historians, but unless they are read with discretion they may give counsel which will lead to destruction. Sometimes, however, bad examples may be turned to good. If historians are read selectively, the examples of very bad princes may by reaction incite to more good than those of mediocre princes. [13]

Elsewhere Erasmus repeated even more conventional views on the value of examples from history. In the *De conscribendis epistolis* he discussed the way history from the most ancient times down to the most recent can be utilized. [14] In a letter written in 1527 Erasmus advised a young German, Valentine Furster, to spend a large part of his time on ethical and historical writers because of the usefulness of the examples he could get from them. Livy, Tacitus, and Plutarch are especially mentioned.[15] But it is clear here as well as elsewhere that when historians and moral philosophers are mentioned together, the latter are preferred by Erasmus. Ancient histories are better than modern, and sacred history as revealed in the books of the Bible is infinitely above profane history. "Compare," says one of the speakers in the *Ciceronianus*, "Herodotus and his fables with Moses; compare the history of the creation and the exodus from Egypt with the fables of Diodorus. Compare the books of the Jews and Kings with Titus Livy who is often inconsistent with himself in his account of things—so far is he from a strict adherence to truth." [16] In any case the study of history whether sacred or profane is merely introductory to a greater purpose. It ought not to be rejected because it is the basis of allegory and leads us on to the discovery of a more abstract sense.[17] Eternal unchanging truth is hidden behind the temporal flux of the historical world.

On the basis of this evidence it would be easy to conclude that the intellectual interests of Erasmus were essentially unhistorical. He seems to have repeated the ordinary commonplaces of humanist discourse. Who would not agree that poetry, moral philosophy, and sacred history were to be preferred to secular annals? And if history had a function at all, what else could it be but that of philosophy teaching by example? Such attitudes were the product of considering history as so many pieces of historical literature—Thucydides, Livy, Tacitus, etc. Insofar as these judgments and opinions implied any general view at all of the nature of history, it was one founded upon classical and cyclical ideas. Human nature remained substantially unchanged; the same accidents could happen to individuals as to peoples again and again. In some expressions Erasmus seems almost to agree with Machiavelli's judgment on the repetitive course of human affairs. Certainly the view he most commonly expressed about the value of history seems far removed from the enthusiasm of the letter to Gaguin. Not only did Erasmus write no formal histories himself; what he said about them seems conventional and disappointing.

Yet such a conclusion would not be warranted. Side by side with his appeals to traditional humanist opinion, there exists in Erasmus' writings a different and much deeper understanding of the historical process.

Fides et Eruditio

Rarely expressed and then only indirectly, it is implicit in the aims and achievements of his whole scholarly career.

Like his conventional views on the value of historical studies, Erasmus owed this understanding in part to his Italian humanist predecessors, but it was also a specific product of his own genius. Viewed as a whole, the fusion of the individual and traditional elements in his thought produced a philosophy of history significantly related to the ideals of both the Renaissance and the Reformation.

The first element in that philosophy was a sense of perspective on the classical past. This had been one of the distinctive contributions of Petrarchan humanism, developed and refined by the scholarship of the fifteenth century. Historians of art have pointed out the importance of this phenomenon in the transformation of iconography. In medieval classical revivals there had usually been a sharp separation between plastic expression and literary tradition, so that Biblical personages appeared in classical dress and antique gods and goddesses as contemporary knights and ladies. Beginning roughly about the time of Petrarch, the new historical sense began to restore to a literary theme its proper historical content.[18] The same phenomenon was also manifest in the treatment of many literary and philosophical texts. In this development the study of legal texts was particularly important. The careful and continuing investigation of the meaning of certain terms in the great source collections of Roman law led ultimately to the discovery that although words remained the same they could stand for very different things at different times. There is a good deal of evidence to support the conclusion that a keen sense of the historical differences between the Roman world and the European Middle Ages first emerged among scholars of the law. Aided by increasingly refined philological techniques, they developed a novel awareness of a historical process in which elements of change and continuity were mingled; the result was a consciousness of perspective in time which had been missing in the Middle Ages.[19]

This realization—as yet incomplete—that various cultural characteristics "belonged together" in a given historical epoch was accompanied at the same time not only by a perception of the distance of such an epoch from the contemporary world but also by a sense of the "deadness" of the past compared with the living present. Men looked back on the glorious Roman past with nostalgia and with vain longing to establish a more intimate contact with the men and the ways of thought of this vanished age. This is the feeling voiced by Petrarch in the letters he addressed to the great authors of antiquity. In these characteristic epistles Petrarch spoke directly and frankly to Cicero, Livy, and others of his literary heroes as if he were writing to contemporary correspondents. But Petrarch himself knows that the tone of intimacy is only futile illusion, a trick of the imagination, imposed to create a more immediate sense of relationship with the classical past. In fact that past is dead; the experience of the Christian era lies between it and Petrarch's own day. It can be known through literature but not recreated. The whole attitude is perfectly illustrated in the epigraph of Petrarch's letter to Livy:

> Written among the living in that part of Italy and in that city in which you were born and were buried in the vestibule of the Temple of Justina Virgo and within sight of your very tombstone on the twenty-second of February in the thirteen hundred and fifty first year of Him whom you could have seen or of whose birth you could have heard if you had lived a little longer.[20]

The perspective of humanism extended from the eye of the fifteenth-century observer to the Greek and Roman past, but the civilization of the ancient world in the distance was bathed in an ever stronger and clearer light while the foreground was dark and the middle distance still more obscure. This attitude was accurately summarized by Leonardo Bruni, the chancellor and historian of Florence, when at the beginning of his *Commentary on His Own Times* he deplored the lack of information on the recent past in comparison with that which had been left by antiquity. "To me indeed the times of Cicero and Demosthenes seem much more familiar than those of sixty years ago. Those men cast such a great light on the periods in which they lived that even now after so long a time has elapsed these ages seem present before our eyes. But an incredible ignorance depressed and darkened the centuries which followed after." [21]

This was the view shared by many of the humanist historians of the *quattrocento* who were moved to write their histories largely because they wished to have their own times and the deeds of their great men live in the future in the same way as the Greco-Roman age and the heroes of antiquity had come down to them. Saved from the ravages of time, examples from the present, as Gaguin had pointed out, could be as instructive as those of the past. The fact that the remote past was so much better known than recent years was primarily due to its having been illuminated by literary genius. History and eloquence could therefore prevent the destruction by time of the great deeds of the present.

From this view of the purpose of historical writing there often followed the conclusion that the nature of the historical process was a repetitive pattern. All examples illustrated the same virtues and the same vices. Human nature was unchanging and the same accidents happened to different peoples. This was one current in humanist historical thought powerfully expressed in Machiavelli, and we have seen that Erasmus in some of his writing appears to share this view. Many humanists built themselves a dream world in which the word could be taken for the reality. This was conspicuously true of the so-called Ciceronians at the beginning of the sixteenth century. They prided themselves on purifying their vocabulary of any base modernisms and found their ultimate linguistic authority in the canon of Cicero's works. Although they managed to convince at least themselves that by applying the language of Cicero to the contemporary world they were bringing back to life the great age of Rome, they never perceived that they were dealing with language not life. The outcome of their cult ironically defeated their intention: instead of revivifying the past they turned Latin from a living to a dead language. In the general humanist tradition the Ciceronians exemplified the most limited view of the relationship between past and present and the most literal acceptance of the possibility of historical recurrence.

There was, however, in this tradition another and contrasting attitude toward history which emphasized the unique rather than the recurrent and the linear rather than the cyclical. The nostalgia of Petrarch himself, powerful as it was, did not yield to the illusion that an age dead and gone could be made to come to life again in its entirety. That element in humanist thought which emphasized the sense of historical perspective and the ineluctable and irrecoverable passage of time received continuous expression. Although Erasmus, as we have seen, was neither philosophical nor discursive on the subject of history, one of the best examples of the conflict between the two views is provided by his attack on the Ciceronians.

His dialogue the *Ciceronianus* was written in 1529. The conception of linguistic purity developed by Bembo and other Italians which maintained that one ought never to use a word which had not occurred in the corpus of Ciceronian writing seemed absurd to Erasmus, and he attacked it with spirit and irony. One passage is particularly relevant to the argument on history. Nosoponus, the character in the dialogue who defends the use of a pure Ciceronian language, is persuaded by his opponent Bulephorus to agree that language must be relevant to contemporary life. Bulephorus then asks:

> But can it be maintained that the situation of the present century is at all like that in which Cicero lived? On the contrary, religion, the empire, the magistrates, the government, laws, customs, ordinary pursuits and the very appearance of men have all changed.

When Nosoponus admits this, then Bulephorus wants to know how anyone can possibly demand in all things the use of the language of Cicero:

> Let the man who makes such a demand first give us back Rome itself as it once was, the Senate and the *curia,* the *Patres conscripti,* the equestrian order, the people divided in tribes and centuries; let him bring back the colleges of augurs and *aruspices,* the *pontifex maximus,* the *flamines,* and the vestal virgins, the aediles, the praetors, the tribunes of the *plebs,* the consuls, dictators, caesars, *comitia, leges, senatusconsulta, plebiscita,* statues, triumphs, ovations, supplications, shrines, temples and seats of the gods, the sacred rites, the gods and goddesses, the Capitoline, and the sacred fire; let him return the provinces, colonies, free towns, and allies of the master city. But indeed since the whole scene of human affairs has been overturned, who today can talk sensibly unless he uses language very different from that of Cicero? Wherever I turn my eyes I see all things changed, I stand before another stage and I behold a different play, nay, even a different world.[22]

In these words Erasmus seems to be thinking about history in a way that anticipates the historicism of a much later period. For many of his contemporaries there was between past and present a substantial continuity which extended not only to institutions but also to manners and customs and even to the details of daily life. Beyond the philological labors of a few scholars the concept of anachronism hardly existed. A Lorenzo Valla discussing the authenticity of the *Donation of Constantine* could urge among other arguments against it the fact that the document refers to the imperial crown whereas in reality in this period the Roman emperors wore a fillet and not a crown.[23] But this idea of what was historically "correct" had not begun to penetrate all realms of thought even among the intellectuals, to say nothing of the populace at large. Down through the eighteenth century historical characters appeared on the stage in contemporary costume, and people did not demand an "archaeological" correctness in the furniture of their historical dramas. Erasmus, on the other hand, at least when he wrote the passage quoted above, was arguing against anachronisms. The course of history was like that of a single life. "There is only one age in which you can learn," Erasmus wrote to a young student. "It will never come back." [24] Cicero lived in another world, immeasurably remote, and this world could not be recovered by the simple device of putting on blinders and agreeing to call things by their wrong names.

Yet if the past could not be thus recreated in its entirety it could at least be accurately known, and the provision of this knowledge was the chief task of the scholar. By his faithful erudition the important texts of the classical and the Christian tradition could be understood in their true historical context. In order to understand a text it was necessary first to purify it of the corrupting influences of time and error and, second, to apply to the reading of it a sound philological knowledge. Only in this way could the true meaning of sources be interpreted, and only through sources could history itself, whether of ideas or institutions, be understood.

This aim is the theme set forth in the prefaces to his greatest and most important work of scholarship, the *Novum Instrumentum*. Again and again Erasmus emphasized the necessity of a return to the sources. "He is no Platonist who does not read the works of Plato and no Christian, still less a theologian, who cannot read the Gospel." [25] In his *Methodus* and in the *Ratio seu compendium verae theologiae* he laid down principles for the study of the scriptural texts. These included not only mastery of the three languages, Latin, Greek, and Hebrew, and a knowledge of grammar and rhetoric, but also knowledge of nature. ("What will it profit you to utter a syllogism on the crocodile . . . if you do not know whether a crocodile is a kind of plant or animal.") [26] It was also necessary to know the institutions and customs of the society in which Jesus lived and taught. All this amounts to what we should call historical explication of a text, and this was the method essentially applied in the *Novum Instrumentum* and the editions of the Church Fathers.

Examples of the uses of this method which might be cited are many. The celebrated omission of the text of I John 5: 7, on the Three Heavenly Witnesses is only the most elementary application of the idea of establishing a text from the best manuscript tradition. The fact is that not one of the Greek manuscripts to which Erasmus had access contained this text and he was simply unable under these circumstances to include it. When challenged he agreed, perhaps rather hastily, to restore it if a manuscript authority were produced. One was forthcoming and Erasmus kept his promise and restored the text in the edition of 1519, although it now seems clear that the manuscript he was offered was forged for the occasion.[27]

In a still wider field, however, than that of a strict adherence to a manuscript tradition, Erasmus showed his grasp of a sense of history. The notes to the New Testament and the prefaces to the Fathers contain a wealth of historical analysis anticipating the achievement of a later age. Again and again he inquires into the precise meaning of a word in a passage and the sense of the passage in relation to its context. "I consider that this is the principal key to the understanding of scriptural difficulty, to investigate what he who speaks is thinking about, especially in the case of Paul, who is most free in disputation, rushing now hither, now thither, so that as Origen says, the reader hardly understands where he came in and where he is going."[28]

The fruit of this method is to be seen in a more extensive area in such productions as the discourse on the itineraries of St. Peter and St. Paul[29] and the *Life of St. Jerome*.[30] Here is historical reconstruction built on the sources, with full recognition of the differences that separate the ages of St. Peter or St. Jerome from Erasmus' own time in the sixteenth century. In announcing his method at the beginning of the *St. Jerome*, Erasmus rejects the miraculous as well as incredible feats of piety such as have been ascribed to subsequent saints. If examples of piety are to be related they are to be such as were known in the first age of the Christian Church. "Although the artisan can bring out the sparkle and lustre of any gem, yet no imitation ever attains the inherent quality of a gem. Truth has its own energy which no artifice can equal."[31] These expressions and others like them are as remote from the method which allowed the insertion of imaginary direct discourses as the achievement of Erasmus was from that of Gaguin. With such a work as the *Life of St. Jerome* we are already at the beginning of the principles of modern historical criticism.

The distance between the letter on Gaguin and the *Life of St. Jerome* does not wholly represent a progress from youth to age. In reality throughout the whole body of Erasmus' work there coexist two different views on history, each one owing much to his humanist predecessors but fundamentally incompatible with the other. The one was founded on the view that the chief function of history was to furnish examples of virtue and vice, that is, illustrations of timeless truths applied to the recurrent pattern of situations in which men found themselves involved. The other emphasized what could be learned from a unique historical evolution. The first was an essentially cyclical conception derived originally from the classical philosophers and historians. The second was a linear interpretation resting ultimately on the implications of the Christian religion. The difference between the two views may be crudely put by viewing it as centering on the point of departure. In the one a student went to history to find examples to illustrate truths derived from other sources, morality, religion, and philosophy. In the other he went to history to find out what truths could be elicited from it to apply to an understanding of morality, religion, and philosophy. When Erasmus talked about history in the abstract or as a part of an educational scheme, he tended to make use of the first or classical idea, but a whole lifetime of study of classical and Christian literature illustrated his adherence to the second. Like many great historians before and since, what he said *about* history was often singularly unrelated to what he did when he actually wrote history.

This dualism is apparent in his most comprehensive expressions on the subject of historical change and the relationship between past and present. He is constantly using the expressions *renovatio, restoratio, instauratio.* "It is a better thing to have restored than to have founded." "A genuine and purer literature will come to renewed life." ". . . three of the chief blessings of humanity are about to be restored to her." "Roman law and mathematics are restored." [32] At certain moments as in the spring of 1517 he appears to have anticipated the imminent return of a golden age almost in the spirit of Virgil's *Fourth Eclogue.* What was the nature of these renewals and restorations? We have already seen that in arguing against the Ciceronians Erasmus rejected the concept of a past which could be recaptured and imitated in its entirety. But if the stage was a different one and the play had never been performed before, it was still possible to hope that the characters might express intellectual and moral qualities of a height equal to or greater than those attained in great ages of the past. Amidst the fluctuations of historical circumstances and constantly changing institutions, learning and piety could be preserved from destruction by time, and the benefits of this achievement could be extended to an ever wider group. Insofar as this happened there would indeed be renewals of a golden age. If the process failed, ignorance and barbarism would be the result. The balance was a delicate one, and the optimism expressed by Erasmus in the years before 1517 was replaced by doubt and despair as he surveyed in his old age the effects of the Reformation.

At the basis of Erasmus' outlook on history was an emphasis on what could be accomplished by the rational faculties of man. His view of history was thus essentially dynamic. Erasmus did not merely postulate the appearance now and again of a timeless virtue in the chaos of men's affairs. The qualities which he so admired had themselves been the product of a slow historical growth in the history of mankind as they were in the history of the individual man. The wisdom of classical antiquity had prepared the way for Christianity. The Christian message was not in contradiction with the classical but in fulfillment of it. In the *Antibarbari* he defended the necessary connection between Christian charity and knowledge. "Without *scientia, caritas* is like a ship without a rudder." [33] This was not a doctrine of progress in anything like the modern sense. The modern doctrine as it was developed in the nineteenth century embraced both man and his environment. Not only was the nature of the individual man capable of steady improvement, but also the social and political institutions and the material circumstances which surrounded him were indefinitely perfectible. Erasmus was interested only incidentally in these institutional surroundings. There had been many stages and many different sets of scenery; unlike the theater, however, when the play was over the sets could not be used again. Erasmus participated in the first results of a genuinely historical outlook when he perceived how different from one another some of these scenes had been. But among the actors there was a certain continuity; there were lessons to be learned. History—the intellectual history of antiquity and early Christianity—showed the conditions for the intellectual and spiritual growth of man. As in time past there had been a development from learning to piety, from classicism to Christianity, so in time present learning could restore piety, and even more—as larger numbers of people profited from the methods of learning rightly understood, so the benefits of piety would be ever more widely distributed.

Fides et Eruditio

The proposition that there was a connection between piety and the right kind of education reflected the humanist belief in an aristocracy of intellect. Erasmus' educational treatises emphasized the training of that small number who were fitted by birth or intellect to assume positions of responsibility, the young nobleman, the Christian knight, even the future Charles V. If those who were to be the rulers of the world could but be given the proper education, the age of the philosopher kings would arrive. Yet it must also be remembered that the benefits of the new learning were not to be confined to those highly placed by birth or genius. The well-known remarks in the *Paraclesis* in which Erasmus affirmed his desire to have the ploughboy and the housewife know the gospel and recite the psalms, show that even in those of the meanest capacity Erasmus felt that knowledge was a necessary condition for piety.[34] He did not share Luther's belief that the simple unlettered peasant might be truly more pious than all the doctors. A program of education which was within the reach of human planning was thus to prepare the way for the greater triumphs of Christianity both within Europe and in the newly discovered lands which were being brought within the European horizon. In that educational program history as a formal subject was allotted but a small place, but the whole scheme nevertheless depended on Erasmus' conquest of the historical world of antiquity and early Christianity.

In the letter to Gaguin, Erasmus had declared that *fides* and *eruditio* were the two qualities most necessary for a good historian. Far more than the man he praised Erasmus had realized these qualities in the work of a lifetime. But in another sense and different from what he had intended, his choice of words was significant. Not only did he himself set standards in erudition and reliability but he proclaimed also his belief that *fides* in its religious sense depended on erudition, that the discovery of the significance of the Christian message and the restoration of piety were the products of historical research. The development of a historical consciousness has not always been accompanied by a growth in the sense of freedom or a feeling of confidence in the future; there are some in the modern world who have found the burden of history intolerable, and it has been said that the only logical conclusion to a complete historicism is existentialism. In the Renaissance the emergent sense of history was limited in scope and perhaps for that very reason it supported a confidence in man's capacity to rule his destiny. The thought of Erasmus marks a stage between the medieval lack of awareness of a different past and the later absorption of European thought in the concept of development from one stage to another. The balance between faith and erudition sustained a bright hope which, though tragically disappointed in Erasmus' own lifetime, persisted as an ideal and shaped the thought of subsequent generations on the relation of Christianity to time and the course of human history.

1. P. S. Allen, ed., *Opus epistolarum Des. Erasmi Roterodami* (Oxford, 1906 ff.), No. 45. This work will be hereafter cited as Allen followed by the number of the letter.

2. On the date of Erasmus' arrival in Paris see the discussion prefixed to Allen, 43.

3. For the biographical details in the following paragraphs on Gaguin, see L. Thuasne, ed., *Roberti Gaguini epistolae et orationes* (Paris, 1904), "Notice biographique," I, 6–168.

4. Thuasne, *op. cit.*, Letter 23.

5. *Ibid.*, 30.

6. Allen, 45.

7. See J. Huizinga, "Erasmus über Vaterland und Nationen," in *Gedenkschrift zum 400 Todestage des Erasmus von Rotterdam* (Basel, 1936).

8. See for example Allen, 103.

9. Erasmus, *The Praise of Folly*, translated by H. H. Hudson (Princeton, 1941), p. 61.

10. *Opera omnia De Erasmis Roterodami* (Leyden, 1703), I, 106 D. Subsequent references to this edition of the collected works will simply read *Opera* followed by the volume and column number.

11. See Sir Richard Jebb, "The Speeches of Thucydides," in *Essays and Addresses* (Cambridge, 1907), pp. 359–443. I owe this reference to Professor Hajo Holborn of Yale University, who was kind enough to read my essay in manuscript.

12. Erasmus, *The Education of a Christian Prince*, translated by Lester K. Born (New York, 1936), pp. 200–201.

13. *Ibid.*

14. *Opera*, I, 389 F.

15. Allen, 1798.

16. *Opera*, V, 470 C.

17. *Ibid.*, I, 998 A.

18. For a discussion of this phenomenon see E. Panofsky, "Renaissance and Renascences," *Kenyon Review*, VI (1944), 201–306; also the same author's *Studies in Iconology: Humanistic Themes in the Art of the Renaissance* (New York, 1939).

Fides et Eruditio

19. See Roberto Weiss, *Il primo secolo dell'umanesimo* (Rome, 1949), p. i.

20. Francesco Petrarca, *Le Familiari,* edited by V. Rossi (Florence, 1942), IV, 245.

21. Leonardo Bruni Aretino, *Rerum suo tempore gestarum commentarius,* edited by Carmine de Pierro, in the new Muratori, *Rerum Italicarum scriptores,* XIX, Part III, p. 423.

22. *Opera,* I, 992 C ff.

23. Lorenzo Valla, *On the Donation of Constantine,* translated by Christopher Coleman (New Haven, 1922), p. 107.

24. Allen, 1198.

25. Hajo and Annemarie Holborn, eds., *Des. Erasmi Roterodami Ausgewählte Werke* (Munich, 1933), p. 144.

26. *Ibid.,* p. 186.

27. See the discussion of this text in Preserved Smith, *Erasmus* (New York, 1923), pp. 165–166.

28. *Opera,* VI, 701 B.

29. *Ibid.,* 425–432.

30. W. Ferguson, ed., *Des. Erasmi Roterodami Opuscula* (The Hague, 1933), pp. 134–190.

31. *Ibid.,* p. 136.

32. For these expressions, see Allen, 384, 541, and 566.

33. *Opera,* X, 1718 F. Cited in R. Pfeiffer, *Humanitas Erasmiana* (Berlin, 1931), p. 13.

34. Holborn, *op. cit.,* p. 142.

[RALPH BOWEN]

The Education

of an Encyclopedist

ON OCTOBER 16, 1747, a very important decision was made by four Parisian booksellers—important to them because they were about to risk a large proportion of their capital in the publication of an encyclopedic dictionary in ten folio volumes. They had to select an editor-in-chief, and the minutes of their deliberations record that their choice fell on Denis Diderot.[1] Their decision was important in a much wider sense because the new editor turned out to be highly successful in realizing the aim of "changing the general public's manner of thinking"[2] which his *Encyclopédie, ou Dictionnaire raisonné des Sciences, des Arts et des Métiers* announced.

We can be reasonably sure that the publishers' decision was not lightly taken. A great deal of money was involved, and there were other than commercial risks to be run. Much would depend upon the character and capacity of the man chosen to direct the literary side of the enterprise. Two previous choices had, for one reason or another, been unfortunate. The first—a translator rather than editor—had been the Englishman John Mills, an adventurer and possibly something of a charlatan. His successor and the first editor-in-chief, the Abbé de Gua de Malves, though a man of sufficient learning, was apparently an eccentric visionary who proved utterly incapable of managing the practical side of the enterprise.[3] Now a third attempt was to be made; the *Encyclopédie* was to be entrusted to an obscure young man just eleven days past his thirty-fourth birthday, whose name had thus far appeared (in small letters and in second position) on the title pages of two not widely noticed translations from the English.[4] Hence the principal publisher, Le Breton, and his three associates—Briasson, Durand, and David l'aîné—must have had other grounds on which to base their choice.

To be sure, Diderot was not a total stranger to at least one of the associates—he had been employed by Briasson as a translator as early as 1743, and he had probably been introduced by the latter to Le Breton, who in 1746 was looking for someone to revise the unsatisfactory French version of Chambers' *Cyclopedia* on which Mills had been working before he and Le Breton came to blows and dissolved their agreement in 1745. Diderot had, together with D'Alembert, been employed by the associated publishers in a subordinate capacity during the editorship of the Abbé de Gua de Malves. But why was a young translator with only the slenderest of literary reputations chosen as editor-in-chief by the four cautious businessmen who were about to risk their fortunes on a venture as ambitious as the *Encyclopédie?* What else did they know about the man in whose hands they were placing so great a responsibility? What of his background and associations? What formal education had he received? What of his scholarly attainments?

It is fairly certain that Le Breton knew a great deal more about these things than we are ever likely to learn. Documentary evidence about Diderot's youth and early manhood is only slightly more abundant than the authenticated facts relating to the corresponding period of Shakespeare's life. As a young man he apparently kept no diary or, if he did, it has not survived. We have none of his letters before 1742. With one exception, and that of little value, he is not mentioned in the memoirs of persons who may have known him before 1741, the year he made Rousseau's acquaintance.[5] The records of schools he may have attended are believed to have disappeared. We are reduced to two biographical sketches written after Diderot's death—one by his daughter, Angélique de Vandeul,[6] and the other by his protégé and literary executor, Naigeon[7] (neither of whom is at all precise or circumstantial)—and to a surprisingly small scattering of autobiographical references in the twenty volumes of his collected works. This reticence is paradoxical, for Diderot, of all his contemporaries, would probably be thought by most people the least likely to be secretive about his own affairs.

Teachers of History

It is not easy to account for Diderot's silence about his youth, supposing his reticence to have been voluntary. So far as our knowledge goes his childhood was happy enough, and his few reminiscences about his school days are pleasant ones. Perhaps he looked back with no particular pride on the ten years of quasi-Bohemian existence in the Latin Quarter before his marriage in 1743, but this hypothesis is all but destroyed by the fact that it is chiefly his own testimony that gives any warrant for supposing that his morals left anything to be desired at that period. Indeed, it seems much more in character for Diderot to have paraded his own lapses from grace than to have concealed them. A more likely explanation is that—since he lived in a century before the advent of Freud—it simply did not occur to him that his early psychic history would be of profound interest to anyone.

But whether by design or negligence on Diderot's part, it is no easy task to reconstruct, even in part, the first three decades of his life. There is, moreover, a certain irony in the fact that we are virtually ignorant about the schooling of a man who was incontestably one of the Enlightenment's major educational theorists, and who was also without a doubt one of that century's most conspicuous practical advocates of the prevailing doctrine that through good education all good things are possible. He even seems to have gone out of his way to be tantalizing when, toward the end of his life, he wrote to Catherine the Great that he had drawn exclusively on memories of his own school days for his views about the proper aims and methods of public instruction: "These [ideas] have all been suggested to me by the defects of my own education." [8] He leaves the reader to infer what specific "defects" he had in mind; consequently the best account one can give of Diderot's own education is one that all too frequently rests on scantily informed conjecture.

The first years of Diderot's education—those occupying that presumably momentous interval between the cradle and the mastery of the three R's—may perhaps be briefly dealt with inasmuch as the salient facts about the family circle in Langres are common knowledge. His father, Didier Diderot, was a master cutler, as at least three of his immediate forebears had been before him. By all accounts he was a man of robust piety, kindly and generous by nature (though he could be stern and obstinate on occasion), honest to the core, and intensely proud of his craft, in which he seems to have excelled.[9] It is difficult not to conclude from allusions in more than one mature writing that his son Denis idolized him and tried more or less consciously all his life to be as good a man and as good a workman as he believed his father to have been.[10] Nor is it difficult to see a direct connection between the tradition of artisanship in which Diderot grew up and the enthusiastic sympathy for the mechanical arts exhibited by the editor of the *Encyclopédie*.

Since Denis probably did not begin attendance at the Jesuit Collège de Langres (now the Lycée Diderot) until November, 1723, just after his tenth birthday, and since only secondary education was offered there, he had presumably learned the elements of reading and writing either from a private tutor (of whom there were several in the town at that period) or in one of the *petites écoles* which provided primary education, some of them partly at municipal expense.[11] At any rate, at the age of seven and one-half he was able to sign his own name to the baptismal certificate of his baby sister Angélique.[12] Although it has been asserted (without evidence and in the teeth of some contrary indications) that the Diderot family was traditionally well disposed toward the Jesuits,[13] the father's decision to send Denis to the Collège de Langres can be amply accounted for on other grounds—its proximity, the fact that it catered for day students, and the absence of tuition fees.

Thanks to the patient researches of the late Chanoine Louis Marcel [14] one can form a fairly satisfactory idea of what the Collège de Langres was like during the five years when Diderot was there. The building appears to have been rather poor, and it had latterly fallen into disrepair; it was destroyed (together with the records of students) by a fire in 1746. There was, however, a fine chapel and a large hall where plays were performed, pictures and emblems displayed, and prizes awarded with elaborate ceremony. Diderot's class probably had between thirty and forty pupils in the year 1724–1725 when he was in the "fourth" class—actually his third year since the lowest class was the "sixth"— and his fellow students seem to have been mostly the sons of the lower nobility and higher bourgeoisie of the region, although there were a few who, like Diderot, came from prosperous artisan families. On the whole academic discipline seems to have been satisfactorily maintained, but on several occasions during Diderot's time the *corps de ville* had to be called out to deal with outbreaks of fighting. Diderot's name does not appear in any of the records of these incidents, but this fact does not prove that he was always a model of good conduct. In later life he still remembered some of his exploits with zest and liked to speak of his "forehead scarred by more than one stone from the sling-shot of a comrade." Deploring the effeminacy of some latter-day schools, he went on to recall how "two hundred children divided themselves into two armies. It was not rare for several seriously wounded ones to be carried home to their parents." And he boasted that on one occasion

my friends and I had the idea of tearing down one of the bastions of my native town in order to spend Holy Week in jail. Still, our parents used to admit that as far as they could remember they had never seen a happier brood of children. . . . I regret that an effeminate sort of education, pedantic and rigid, has taken the place of this training that developed healthy bodies and strong, courageous, free spirits.[15]

It may well be that Diderot entered with the same enthusiasm into the competitive activities of the classroom. The Jesuits made "emulation" one of their cardinal principles and arranged their classes so that each pupil of the "Roman" side was continually straining every nerve to give a better recitation than his opponent on the "Carthaginian" side.[16] Madame de Vandeul describes her father's scholastic triumphs under this regime, telling how he returned home one day after the annual distribution of prizes with many wreaths around his neck and his arms loaded with the books he had won.[17] It may be that her account is somewhat embellished,[18] but its substance is confirmed by the presence in the Musée de la Ville at Langres of a two-volume *Histoire de l'église du Japon* by the Jesuit Father Grasset, inscribed in Latin to "Dionysius Diderot" by his teacher, Father Léon-Dominique Couder. One volume was the second prize for Latin verse and the other was the second prize for Latin prose composition; both were awarded at a general convocation held August 3, 1728. Another certificate, also signed by Father Couder and dated the same month, attests that Diderot stood first in his class and that he received the notation "bene merenti" for his studies of Horace's *Odes*.[19] Diderot apparently continued his studies in Langres for one more year, but there is no further record of his achievements there. He must have done at least tolerably well, for we are told by a friend of the family that when he went to Paris—apparently in 1729— he carried with him letters of recommendation from his Jesuit teachers.[20]

Meanwhile it had evidently been decided by the Diderot family that young Denis would enter the church, for he received the tonsure from the hands of Monseigneur d'Antin, bishop-duke of Langres, August 26, 1726. His family probably hoped that he would be allowed to occupy the lucrative and dignified ecclesiastical post about to be resigned by one of his mother's brothers, the Chanoine Didier Vigneron. For reasons that are obscure, these hopes came to nothing; in 1728, at the uncle's death, his place was given to another candidate.[21]

This disappointment of the young "Abbé Diderot's" seemingly well-founded expectations in Langres was so close in time to his withdrawal —before he finished his final year—from the Jesuit Collège that one cannot help wondering if the two events were not more intimately connected. Did the Jesuits have anything to do with Diderot's failure to secure his uncle's canonicate, or did he believe this to be the case? Did his association with the Jesuits make him *persona non grata* with the cathedral chapter in a diocese where strong Jansenist sympathies had been recently widespread? There seems to be no way of knowing, but it does seem fairly certain that Diderot's desire to leave Langres was a very strong one, that he wanted very much to continue his studies in Paris, and that his father, after opposing the idea at the outset, finally gave in and made considerable sacrifices so that his son could achieve his heart's desires. There are good reasons for not accepting literally the highly dramatic account given by Madame de Vandeul [22] of Diderot's attempt one night to slip out of the house by way of a porte-cochere (it seems that the family residence never boasted an ornament of this sort [23]) in order to run away to Paris with a cousin his own age "to study with the Jesuits." An additional detail of her story—that a young Jesuit missionary had put this idea into the boys' heads—seems rather unlikely, especially since Denis was already a pupil of the order. Nor does it seem likely that Didier Diderot took his son to Paris "the next morning." But the indication that Diderot was ambitious to explore the wider horizons of intellectual life in the capital can probably be relied upon.

If the circumstances surrounding Diderot's exit from the Collège de Langres are obscure, the mysteries that envelop the next stage of his education are all but impenetrable. Nowhere in his published writings is there an unequivocal answer to the most important question: which school did Didier Diderot select for his elder son? [24] Madame de Vandeul and Naigeon both say flatly that it was the Collège d'Harcourt, the most ancient and one of the most illustrious of the eleven *collèges de plein droit* of the Faculty of Arts of the University of Paris. Both should have known whereof they spoke, and neither had any apparent motive for dissimulation on this point. Yet their testimony has been rejected not only by historians of the Jesuit Collège Louis-le-Grand [25] (who have been curiously eager to claim the free-thinking Diderot as a former pupil of that institution) but also by the erudite Chanoine Marcel.[26]

Now it makes a great deal of difference which of these contradictory assertions is correct—not so much because of any fundamental dissimilarities in methods or curricula, for in these respects the *collèges* of the University had modeled themselves very closely after the spectacularly successful system of the Jesuits—but because the Collège d'Harcourt was a center of Jansenist strength—that is to say, of intense opposition to all that the Jesuits stood for in religion, in society, and in politics. More than one episode in the subsequent career of Diderot the encyclopedist takes on a very different aspect depending upon which of the two theories about his studies in Paris one decides to adopt. Neither is susceptible of documentary proof, for the records containing the names of students of Louis-le-Grand at this period have "disappeared from the archives of the establishment," and a similar fate has apparently overtaken all the relevant registers of the *collèges* of the University.[27]

The main obstacle to accepting Madame de Vandeul's assertion that her father was enrolled at the Collège d'Harcourt is a passage in Diderot's anonymously published *Lettre sur les sourds et les muets* (1751) which seems to show that he was, on the contrary, a former pupil of Father Charles Porée, who had been Voltaire's teacher and who had achieved considerable fame as professor of rhetoric at Louis-le-Grand. This passage occurs in the course of a discussion of Racine's *Phèdre* in which Diderot takes issue with some remarks reported to have been made before the Académie Française by the Abbé de Bernis. Diderot says that

if at Louis-le-Grand they taught us to see all the beauties of this speech, . . . they did not fail to point out to us that it was out of place in the mouth of Theramenes, and that Theseus would have had good reason to stop him and to tell him: "Oh! Never mind my son's horses and chariot; speak to me of him!" . . . It is thus, the celebrated Father Porée went on to tell us, that Antilochus announces to Achilles the death of Patroclus. . . . It was in this fashion that the skilled rhetorician taught us . . . thirty or forty years ago.[28]

If one takes this statement at face value it seems to cast grave doubts on Madame de Vandeul's accuracy—doubts that are doubly puzzling since she must have been aware of the existence of this passage in one of her father's best-known writings. Why did she not at least take the trouble to notice it and to explain why she did not take it seriously? The most likely explanation is that she did know of the passage, but that she assumed it to be common knowledge that her father had deliberately inserted a number of false autobiographical clues, including the one in question, in order to conceal his authorship of the anonymously published *Lettre sur les sourds et les muets*. It is extremely difficult on any other hypothesis to account for the glaring chronological discrepancy in the last sentence of the passage quoted—"This is precisely what Father Porée taught us thirty or forty years ago." In 1751 Diderot was but twenty years out of school, and "forty years ago"—in 1711—he had not yet been born! Nor is it difficult to find other examples of deliberate mystification designed to prevent the police from attributing this work to the author of the somewhat similarly entitled *Lettre sur les aveugles,* for which Diderot had been imprisoned at Vincennes for three months in 1749. He dated his prefatory letter "de V[ersailles]" in an apparent effort to pass himself off as an habitué of the court; [29] he falsely claimed to know nothing about music; [30] for good measure he added a slur on his own acknowledged work, the *Lettre sur les aveugles,* a book which he describes as "pas trop bon." [31] He all but gives the whole game away in the last paragraph of his preface when he writes:

> I know in advance to whom my book will not be attributed; and I know very well also to whom it would surely be attributed if it contained more odd ideas, a certain amount of imagination, a good style, I know not what boldness of thought which I should be very sorry to indulge in, a show of mathematics, of metaphysics, of Italian, of English, and especially less Latin and Greek and more knowledge of music. [32]

Diderot was clearly well aware that he would be suspected of having written the book, and he was just as clearly determined to cover his tracks if possible. What better way to disarm suspicion than by seeming candidly to anticipate the grounds on which it would probably be entertained?

If we may conclude, then, that in 1751 Diderot was seeking to throw the authorities off the scent when he invited them to believe that the author of the *Lettre sur les sourds et les muets* was a former pupil of the Jesuits, the obvious corollary is that he did so on the assumption that the police knew that the editor of the *Encyclopédie* was not.

Teachers of History

There remains one other troublesome point in Madame de Vandeul's account of her father's schooling, one that has been taken to indicate that he was, after all, an alumnus of Louis-le-Grand. This is her assertion that "at the Collège d'Harcourt he formed friendly ties with the Abbé Bernis, already a poet and later a cardinal." [33] Now it is possible that the two young men became friends, since they were both physically present in the Latin Quarter as students of about the same age between 1729 and 1732, but it is known for certain that Bernis was in residence at Louis-le-Grand, where his brilliance had won him a scholarship. [34] Diderot's daughter, therefore, was either mistaken in her belief that the two boys were at the same school or, if she was correct on that score, she was mistaken in her statement that Diderot was at the Collège d'Harcourt. One flaw in this latter argument, however, suggests itself at once—Diderot may have met Bernis outside the precincts of their respective schools; in fact, Madame de Vandeul goes on to describe how "the two of them used to go to have dinner at six sous each at a nearby tavern, and I have often heard him [Diderot] enlarge upon the gayety of those meals." [35]

Another possibility is that Madame de Vandeul's memory for names may have played her false—her memoirs were not written until after her father's death—so that she may have confused Bernis with someone else. In a postscript to his Lettre sur les sourds et les muets Diderot explicitly denied that he had ever laid eyes on the Abbé de Bernis, [36] and the latter made no mention of Diderot in that part of his memoirs where he described (rather fully) his school days at Louis-le-Grand. [37] No other references to Bernis are to be found in Diderot's collected works, and there is no evidence that the two men were friendly in later life.

On the other hand, Salesses [38] has called attention to the fact that Diderot in his mature years maintained close relations with a number of former students and professors of the Collège d'Harcourt. With the Abbé Asselin, the principal, he is not known to have been intimate, but the Abbé was one of the few men of his cloth who expressed, even cautiously, sentiments favorable to Diderot during the crisis that overtook the Encyclopédie in 1752 in the famous affaire of the Abbé de Prades. The Abbé Basset, later a professor of philosophy and rector of the University in 1779, was probably a fellow student at D'Harcourt; Melchior Grimm, the man closest to Diderot during most of his adult life, repeatedly called the Abbé Basset "a long-standing friend of Diderot." [39] Diderot was certainly well acquainted also with Pierre Le Monnier, the astronomer and member of the Académie des Sciences who had formerly taught at D'Harcourt. One of Le Monnier's sons was a contributor to the *Encyclopédie*. Another of Diderot's friends, the Abbé Le Monnier, who also studied at the Collège d'Harcourt, may have been related to this same family; at least he came from the same region. According to Rousseau it was this Abbé Le Monnier who was present at the celebrated interview between Jean-Jacques and Diderot at Vincennes in 1749.[40] The materialist philosopher La Mettrie, whom Diderot knew well but did not like, was a former student of D'Harcourt and could have been there about the same time as Diderot. The philosopher and encyclopedist Boulanger, a member of the Baron d'Holbach's circle, to whose posthumous book Diderot contributed a biographical memoir, was a nephew of the orientalist Fourmont, who had taught at D'Harcourt. Vincent Toussaint, with whom Diderot collaborated as a translator and for whom he later made a place on the staff of the *Encyclopédie*, had studied around the year 1730 at D'Harcourt or at the Collège de Beauvais, the other main Jansenist center of the Faculty of Arts.[41] The Lieutenant-General of Police, De Sartine, who was a pupil at D'Harcourt a few years after Diderot's time, was described by the latter in 1774 as "my friend for the past thirty-five years." [42] Finally, in 1775 Diderot told of having been invited to attend a public exercise at the Collège d'Harcourt—and such invitations were as a rule given only to former students or patrons of the school.[43]

In contrast with these numerous ties to the Collège d'Harcourt, the indications are that in Diderot's circle of friends and acquaintances only a very few had associations with Louis-le-Grand. He seems to have had polite but distant relations with Turgot, Helvétius, and La Condamine, all of whom were former pupils of the Jesuits, and he came to know them only after his career was well launched. Another graduate of Louis-le-Grand, the journalist Elie Fréron, was the *Encyclopédie*'s bitterest enemy.

To add a further, and to my mind final, degree of corroboration to the thesis that Diderot's studies in Paris were carried on at the University rather than with the Jesuits, there is the following transparently autobiographical paragraph from the *Réfutation de l'ouvrage d'Hel-*

vétius intitulé "L'Homme," written in 1774 with no apparent view to publication and hence presumably free of distortion:

> Two parents who were neither poor nor rich had several children; they held education in high esteem, and in order to educate these children well they studied their natural aptitudes . . . and does that seem so unreasonable? They thought they observed in the older of the two boys a taste for reading and study. They sent him to the provincial *collège*, where he distinguished himself, and from there to Paris *to the classrooms of the University,* where his teachers could never overcome his disdain for the frivolities of scholasticism. They put into his hands textbooks of arithmetic, of algebra, and of geometry which he devoured. Carried on in the sequel to more pleasant studies, he delighted in the reading of Homer, of Virgil, of Tasso, and of Milton, but he always came back to mathematics just as an unfaithful husband, tired of his mistress, returns at intervals to his wife.[44]

It may be taken, then, as at least highly probable that Diderot was a student of the University of Paris and not of Louis-le-Grand. There is, however, a possibility that he did not remain at the Collège d'Harcourt during the entire course of his studies under the Faculty of Arts. His references to Dominique-François Rivard, who was for forty years a celebrated professor of mathematics and philosophy at the Collège de Beauvais, as "my former teacher" [45] lend substance to this conjecture, for Rivard never gave public lectures, and it is not likely that he taught at D'Harcourt, where there were several exceptionally able men in his field. Hence he could have been Diderot's teacher in a literal sense only if the latter had been enrolled at the Collège de Beauvais. There were plenty of precedents for students to transfer from one of the Jansenist *collèges* to the other. If Diderot did indeed attend the Collège de Beauvais, he might have studied under the great educational theorist and reformer Charles Rollin, author of the famous *Traité des études,*[46] which was written and applied there. Diderot's few references to Rollin in afterlife do not, however, lend any support to this hypothesis. Although he calls Rollin "the shining light [*aigle*] of the University of Paris," he seems to know him only through his book and takes issue rather sharply with many of the ideas contained in it.[47]

These facts barely suggest the possibility that Diderot may have studied briefly at Beauvais, though probably not under Rollin. But not even the strongest of these—Diderot's statement that Rivard was his teacher—carries full conviction, for it may only mean that he studied mathematics from Rivard's textbooks, which were introduced in the *collèges* of the Faculty of Arts around 1730. About all that can be inferred from the evidence at present available is that from the time of his arrival in Paris in 1728 or 1729 until 1732 Diderot was educated under Jansenist auspices, probably at the Collège d'Harcourt, but at any rate at the University of Paris.

Something that need not be inferred, for it is established by documentary evidence, is the fact that he received the degree of *maître-ès-arts* from the University on September 2, 1732. This is attested by an entry under that date in an official register discovered at the Bibliothèque Nationale by the late Chanoine Marcel.[48] The text reads: "*Anno Domini 1732 die secundo septembris graduatus fuit in artibus M[agiste]r Dionysius Diderot lingonaeus. Exp[edit] 5° septembris 1732.*" The entry also shows that Diderot took his degree at the normal time of year along with 185 others, including five from Langres, but in no case is there any indication of the *collège* at which the candidate had prepared. Diderot's name is not followed by the word "*clericus*" as are many of the other names, which doubtless indicates that he had abandoned his clerical status. This confirms the testimony of Taillefer, who reports that Diderot ceased to wear priestly garb after he left the Jesuits in Langres, a step taken not only with the approval but with the encouragement of his father, who "soon decided that his son was not born to be a priest. . . . Endowed with more sensibility than other men, and consequently more subject to the passions, young Diderot did not take long to let it be seen that he preferred liberty to fortune."[49]

One is naturally led to speculate about Diderot's reasons for taking the master's degree. Did he look forward to a teaching career? Or did he have ambitions to go on to higher studies in one of the University's three professional faculties (law, medicine, and theology)? The degree of *maître-ès-arts* carried with it the right to teach humanities and philosophy in secondary schools. It was also a prerequisite of admission to one of the higher faculties. Hence he may have had either or both of these possibilities in mind.

Whether either of them actually led to anything is another question, and one to which no certain answer can be given. For between 1732 and 1743, the year of his marriage, there is an almost total void in our knowledge of Diderot's life. About all the evidence available is the series of anecdotes—all hopelessly vague as to dates and circumstances —in Madame de Vandeul's memoirs. As appeared earlier in connection with Diderot's departure from Langres and with his choice of a school in Paris, her account is probably true in substance but not to be followed as literally as most of Diderot's previous biographers have done.

For example, she writes that "at the conclusion of his studies [at D'Harcourt], his father wrote to M. Clément de Ris, an attorney in Paris and his compatriot [of Langres] to take him [Denis] *en pension* and teach him law and jurisprudence. He stayed there for two years." She goes on to describe how her father soon grew disgusted with legal minutiae, how he spent the better part of his time studying Greek, Latin, and mathematics, "which he always loved passionately," and how finally, when informed of these lapses, Didier Diderot issued an ultimatum—his son must have an *état*, a station in life, and he offered him the choice between law and medicine. Denis found neither acceptable, to which his father replied that he might choose any profession that took his fancy provided only that he chose one promptly; otherwise he was to return at once to Langres. Not believing that his father would hold him strictly to this severe alternative, Denis ignored his father's injunction and continued his unproductive mode of life, exchanging the home of Clément de Ris for a furnished room and living from day to day on money from the sale of his personal effects. These funds he eked out by borrowing and by secret remittances from his mother, who economized at home and sent money to her son by the hand of a faithful serving woman, who, on three occasions, walked the sixty leagues from Langres to Paris and back. He also ran up debts which his father was finally obliged to pay, and he was not above resorting to a mild form of swindling if we are to believe a story about his dealings with the Carmelite Frère Ange. In this fashion, "abandoned to his own resources for ten years," Madame de Vandeul writes, he lived by a variety of expedients:

He taught mathematics; if the pupil was quick, with a good mind and a facile understanding, he taught him gratis; if he found him a dullard he did not return the next time. He got his pay in books, in furniture, in linen, in money, or not at all—and it was all the same to him. . . . He composed sermons: one missionary ordered six of them for use in the Portuguese colonies; he paid for them at sixty *écus* each. My father considered this one of his more successful transactions.[50]

Education of an Encyclopedist

Now this is all very well, and goes to make a story not without charm. So far as the main outlines are concerned, it is doubtless a reasonably faithful version of what Diderot had told his daughter about his life as a young bachelor on the Left Bank. By what we know of Didier Diderot's character from other sources (including some of his letters and his will), there is a ring of psychological truth in the description of his role, and it is not difficult to picture young Denis as headstrong in his eagerness to explore all the varieties of intellectual and other experience that might come his way rather than tie himself to a humdrum job. But the chronology is almost certainly mistaken, for Clément de Ris was not admitted to practice as an attorney before 1738 at the earliest, since he is first listed in the *Almanach royal* of 1739. Hence he could not have undertaken to initiate Diderot into the mysteries of contracts and inventories "at the conclusion of his [Diderot's] studies" in 1732.[51]

If, then, we suppose that Diderot's two years of nominal legal apprenticeship began only in 1738 or later, there is a mysterious period of at least six years to be accounted for. If he did not immediately turn to the law upon receiving his master's degree, what did he do? It is scarcely enough to say that he gave lessons in mathematics and wrote sermons to order, for this hardly sounds like a full-time occupation, or even one likely to keep body and soul together (especially if one takes at face value his daughter's account of how he was paid for his lessons). In fact, these occupations are precisely the ones traditionally resorted to by French university students who have to supplement scholarships or remittances from home. In order to write sermons, moreover, one would think that a student would have to be a little further advanced in his studies than Diderot was in 1732—the client would probably be most interested in having them written by a student in the Faculty of Theology. What evidence is there to suggest that Diderot may have used his master's degree as a passport to one of the higher faculties of the University?

In the first place, it appears that subsidies from Langres (in addition to those sent by Madame Diderot) continued to be forthcoming at least until Denis left the establishment of Clément de Ris, and perhaps even after that. This conclusion rests not only upon the word of Madame de Vandeul but also upon the following passage from a wil' which Didier Diderot drafted in 1750:

Vous scavez bien, vous, Diderot l'éné, les grandes dépenses que j'ay faictes pour vous depuis vingt ans que vous êtes à Paris. Si je suputais rien que ce qui est de ma connaissance, je vous ay envoyé plus de dix mille livres non compris ce que votre mère et votres soeurs vous a envoyés.[52]

Since Diderot's expenses at D'Harcourt must have been in the neighborhood of four or five hundred livres per year, or at most two thousand livres for four years, there is a tidy balance which must have been remitted after 1732.

Now assuming that Madame de Vandeul's account is reliable—except that she places the episode with Clément de Ris at least six years too early—and that Diderot's father became impatient about his son's professional future only when his legal studies proved disappointing, the conclusion may perhaps be drawn that Didier Diderot approved in principle of what his son was doing in the years between 1732 and about 1738. This is a clue which, taken in conjunction with Diderot's own reminiscences, leads to the conjecture that those six years, or a substantial fraction of them, may well have been spent at the Sorbonne in studies that would have led to a doctorate in theology.[53] Unfortunately this hypothesis is probably destined to remain one, for the admissions and examinations registers of the Faculty of Theology have disappeared without a trace. Still it is not so fantastic a notion as it may appear at first sight and can be supported by some interesting indirect evidence drawn chiefly from Diderot's later writings.

Let us begin with the elder Diderot's ambitions for his son. Naigeon asserts that Diderot's father wanted him to become "a reasonable theologian" and sent him to the Collège d'Harcourt "to prepare him for the study of theology."[54] Diderot himself seems to confirm this statement when he writes, in the *Salon* of 1767, "I came to Paris; I was going to get myself a fur-trimmed gown [*prendre la fourrure*] and install myself among the doctors of the Sorbonne."[55] He goes on to imply that it was only his marriage that upset these plans and forced upon him the drudgery of the *Encyclopédie*.

Concerning the intentions of Diderot *père* and *fils*, these indications are fairly convincing. But between intentions and realizations there is often less than perfect equivalence. What warrant is there for thinking that anything came of Diderot's ambition to become a doctor of the Sorbonne?

To begin with, it can be argued, as Salesses does, that the degree of *maître-ès-arts* required an arduous examination and that it was of little value except as a passport to the faculties of medicine and theology —it was not required for the Faculty of Law. Nowhere is there any indication that Diderot or his family seriously entertained the idea that he should study medicine—on the contrary he seems in his youth to have had a rather low opinion of the profession, if we are to rely on Madame de Vandeul's version of his reply to Clément de Ris—that "the physician's trade did not please him because he had no wish to kill anyone." [56] It is true that one of his early jobs as a hack translator, after his marriage, was James's *Medicinal Dictionary*, and that from his friendship with eminent doctors like Bordeu in later life he acquired a good deal of respect for the profession, together with some medical erudition, but he never figured as anything more than a highly gifted amateur in the field. By elimination, then, it can be inferred that Diderot went to the trouble of taking his M.A. in 1732 because he still had his hopes fixed on a career as a "reasonable theologian."

What, it may then be asked, would have prevented him from pursuing his theological studies? Not lack of money, for his father was in easy circumstances and was still willing to contribute to his son's support, all the more so since Denis would presumably have been doing exactly what his father most desired if he were studying at the Sorbonne. Perhaps the inclination was lacking? Perhaps, as Naigeon suggests, "mathematics had disgusted him with theology," and "he [had] shed the clerical garb which he had worn for several years." [57] The latter part of the statement corresponds to Taillefer's testimony already noted and is borne out by the fact that when he took his degree in 1732 he no longer styled himself "*clericus*." It may well be inadvisable, however, to follow the militant atheist Naigeon in his implication that Diderot had lost his faith so early in life, for it is plain that he was still a theist in 1745,[58] and on several different occasions between 1732 and 1743 he is represented in his daughter's *Mémoires* as being on the verge either of joining a monastic order or of entering a seminary to train for the priesthood. It is plain that on some of these occasions he was only pretending to be pious in order to get money, having no intention of carrying out his professed desire to enter the church. Still, the idea of a religious vocation seems to have been remarkably persistent, and one of his own avowals in a letter to Sophie Volland has a ring of sincerity:

I assure you that if the prior of the Chartreux had taken me at my word when, at the age of eighteen [that is, in 1731 or 1732], I went to offer myself to him as a novice, he would not have done me a bad turn. I would have employed a part of my time in shaping broom handles, in hoeing my little garden, and in observing my barometer.[59]

As late as 1740 his father seems to have had no doubts about the genuineness of his son's faith, for in that year he took out membership for him in a fraternity of St. Francis at Langres.[60] And when Denis came to Langres in late 1742 or early 1743 to get his father's consent to his marriage he brought a book of devotion to his father as a present.[61] All these considerations point to the desirability of placing a question mark beside Naigeon's implication that Diderot was already an unbeliever in his early twenties.

Nor does the phrase, "disgusted with theology," seem to represent fairly the attitude that was most characteristic of Diderot even in his mature years.[62] It would be more nearly exact to say that few subjects had stronger fascination for him.

It cannot, of course, any longer be seriously maintained that Diderot's many signed articles on theology in the *Encyclopédie* prove that he had a professional's knowledge of the subject, for there is too much evidence to show that these articles were not, for the most part, original compositions. More than half of those relied on by Salesses were drawn wholly or largely from various older dictionaries and compilations. Others were doubtless the work of trained theologians on the staff of the *Encyclopédie*—the Abbés Yvon, Pestré, Mallet, Morellet, and de Prades—and appeared without signatures after the real authors had abandoned the enterprise. These have been attributed to Diderot because his own articles—except for those he wrote in his editorial capacity, which are starred—were unsigned. Still others were the work of the Swiss Protestant pastor Polier de Bottens or of Diderot's man-of-all-work, the Chevalier de Jaucourt.[63] Joseph Barker is thus on firm ground in rejecting Salesses' argument from these articles, and one can only agree with the former that "these and the other theological articles by Diderot by no means prove that he had studied and digested the science of theology as a formal student at the Sorbonne; they prove merely that Diderot, like many other philosophers of his time, was sufficiently well-read on theological subjects to use works of reference intelligently." [64]

44

Another question arises, however, in connection with the role played by Diderot in the famous *affaire* of the Abbé de Prades's doctoral dissertation, which was first accepted with acclaim by the Sorbonne, then ignominiously repudiated when the Parlement of Paris and leading ecclesiastical dignitaries began to thunder against the systematic defense of natural religion which it was alleged to contain.[65] Public rumor and several journalists of the time were convinced that Diderot was the real author, and it is at least odd that he never offered a straight denial of these allegations. He left it to D'Alembert, in the preface to Volume III of the *Encyclopédie*, to deny in general terms any complicity of the editors in De Prades's escapade. Yet it would presumably have been easy for Diderot to point to the subtlety and compactness of the thesis and to the elegance of its Latin style, and to say: "How could I have written this thesis? Everybody knows that I never studied at the Sorbonne!" Perhaps too many people had knowledge that ruled out an alibi on these lines.

Finally, in the "Plan of a University for the Government of Russia," which he sent to Catherine the Great at her request, he did not suppress the faculty of theology, though she would doubtless not have been disturbed if he had done so. Instead he discussed its organization and the courses it should offer with great fullness and apparent ease,[66] while he was more brief in his treatment of the faculties of law and medicine and explicitly disavowed any special competence in those fields.[67]

Here, however, a difficulty arises, for in discussing the training of theological students he specified that a thorough knowledge of Hebrew would be an indispensable tool of their trade.[68] Can it be shown that Diderot himself possessed such a knowledge? Salesses believes that the evidence at least strongly suggests that he did, citing the following passage in which he argues that Diderot comes close to saying so explicitly: "At an early age I was nursed on the milk of Homer, of Virgil, of Horace, of Terence, of Anacreon, of Plato, and of Euripides, mixed with that of Moses and the prophets." [69] His command of Latin was certainly fluent, and he seems to have learned enough Greek to have read the authors mentioned in the original. He himself laid it down as an axiom that no piece of imaginative literature can be adequately rendered in translation.[70] So it is barely possible to infer that he meant to say, in the passage quoted, that he had read Moses and the prophets in Hebrew. Yet, the proof is far from decisive, and the inference is evidently a very insecure one.

Salesses also has called attention to Diderot's letter to his brother, the Chanoine Didier-Pierre Diderot, of November 13, 1772, which may contain a challenge to match the writer's Biblical learning: "Read your breviary, my good fellow, but I forbid you to read your Bible, whether in Greek or in Hebrew." [71] The challenge is supposed to be implicit if we assume the sentence to mean roughly the following: "I, the free-thinker, am familiar with the Bible in both the original Greek and Hebrew texts, while you are afraid to endanger your orthodox faith by reading any other text than the Vulgate." Yet the argument is not quite convincing, for Diderot may simply have meant to say, "The Bible itself contains powerful antidotes to bigotry."

Perhaps the only way of dealing with the difficulty is to leave the question open. Diderot may have had a fairly good knowledge of Hebrew, possibly acquired from studies at the Sorbonne, or he may have had only a smattering of the language picked up from his friends or from general reading. As for the bearing of this problem on the main question of whether or not Diderot went on after 1732 to the formal study of theology, it does not seem that the extent of his knowledge of Hebrew is necessarily crucial. He evidently did not complete his studies—the doctorate would have required at least five years of study after the M.A.—and Hebrew would probably not have been much studied in the first few years.

There is little else in the way of authenticated knowledge—or even of reasonably well-founded conjecture—about the formal education that helped prepare Diderot to be editor-in-chief and principal author of the *Encyclopédie*. We may therefore pause at this point to consider what he had learned that might be of use to him in that highly exacting role.

At first inspection it may appear that the only possible answer to this question is, "Not very much." Such, at any rate, was the answer that his co-editor, D'Alembert, whose education was not radically different, would presumably have given, for in his article "Collèges" he complained that

a young man, after spending ten years of his life in a *collège* [of the University]—years which should be counted among the most precious of his life—leaves school (assuming he has made the best possible use of his time) with a very imperfect knowledge of a dead language, with precepts of rhetoric which he should attempt to forget; . . . sometimes with very seriously misconceived ideas of his religious duties, but more commonly with so superficial a knowledge of religion that his faith succumbs at the first impious conversation or at the first reading of a dangerous book.[72]

But D'Alembert was probably somewhat soured by his bitterness about "the time I wasted in my childhood," and the severity of his often-quoted judgment needs to be tempered considerably. Not only was the kind of public education offered in the University of Paris the best that could be had at the time; it was by no means as narrowly confined to the study of a "dead language"—which was, of course, far from dead at that period—as D'Alembert implied. If he had said that it was almost entirely a *literary* education he would have been far closer to the truth and he would have singled out what was probably (considering the needs of the average student) the weakest point in the educational practice of the *ancien régime*—and one that has long survived it.

Yet for a man of letters, for a professional writer, it is difficult not to see precisely in this literary character of Diderot's education its strongest merit. Distasteful as he may well have found the years of unremitting application to the intricacies of Latin syntax and grammar, of endless exercises in the composition of quasi-Ciceronian prose and pseudo-Virgilian verse, the intellectual discipline was unquestionably one that could and did form habits of order, lucidity, and precision, that successfully trained young men in the conduct of the mind and in the use of language. Though these accomplishments, perhaps regrettably, are no longer universally regarded as the most important products of humanistic education, they were surely cardinal virtues for an encyclopedist. That Diderot possessed them is one of the most solid reasons for the contemporary efficacity and the lasting greatness of his *Encyclopédie*.

Nor was Diderot's formal education restricted to the ancient languages. It is generally known that the Jansenist educators of Port-Royal had very definite—and for their time novel—ideas on the desirability of teaching the mother tongue. This tradition had been carried over into the University, and by Diderot's time French grammar and the classics of French literature had won a recognized place in the curriculum.

Teachers of History

But we must probably look beyond the walls of the classroom to find the main sources of Diderot's extraordinary, almost universal, competence in the natural sciences. It is true that his introduction to mathematics and the beginnings of his enthusiasm for that discipline were part of his school experience. It is also highly probable that his studies both in Langres and in Paris had included some elementary chemistry and physiology, but we know that he felt it necessary to supplement his knowledge of those fields by following Rouelle's famous public lectures in chemistry for three consecutive years [73] and by reading the Swiss savant Haller's books on the human body. And when all is said and done, the formal part of his education could not have given him a very large part of that vast fund of general knowledge which he later displayed in his encyclopedic articles on science and technology. These were, of course, the most original and the most revolutionary feature of the *Encyclopédie*. In the very fields where his mature intellectual activity was to be the most significant, Diderot's formal schooling was the least useful to him—at least this is true if one thinks of information imparted.

It follows that the publishers of the *Encyclopédie* must have had reason to think that Diderot had devoted a good deal of time and energy to successful self-improvement in the fifteen years since receiving his master's degree. They may have known that part of that time was spent studying theology at the Sorbonne, if the hypothesis already proposed is not dismissed as altogether fanciful. Whatever else they may have known, there can be no question of reconstructing in detail the course of self-education that Diderot evidently undertook between his nineteenth and his thirty-fourth years. Those who know Diderot's early works even moderately well are surely well aware that he had read all the "great books" of his age—Hobbes, Newton, Locke, Bacon, Descartes, Gassendi, Bayle, Malebranche, Fontenelle, Montesquieu, Leibnitz, Spinoza, and Grotius, to name only the ones he most often referred to—and many, many more books that were not then and are not now considered great. He had access to at least one private library of great richness, that of the financier Randon de Boisset, in whose home, apparently, he was a private tutor for a short while (though this is disputed by Marcel on the ground that Randon de Boisset, a bachelor, seems to have had no children of his own). Diderot later wrote, somewhat cryptically, about Randon de Boisset, "I knew him when I was young;

it is not his fault that I failed to become a rich man." [74] When Jean-Georges Wille, the future *graveur du roi*, met Diderot as a fellow lodger in the Rue de l'Observance in 1740, the furnishings of the latter's entresol included "a handsome library." [75]

Besides his omnivorous reading one of the most important items in Diderot's program of self-education must have been the study of modern languages, for he learned both English and Italian during this period. His command of English was adequate not only for the translation of very difficult technical books like James's *Medicinal Dictionary* (in six folio volumes), but also for the composition of a short but very obscene narrative in English which he included (with continuations of the story in Latin and Italian) in his *Bijoux indiscrets*.[76] These two modern languages were, of course, the most important for a man aspiring to general culture in the mid-eighteenth century. The great days of Spain were past and German had not yet come to the fore. Diderot learned at most only a few words of Spanish and knew, he says explicitly, "not a word" of German.[77]

Beyond this there is very little that one can add. It would surely be interesting to know whether his interest in technology, in the mechanical arts and crafts, long antedated his association with the *Encyclopédie*, and one would like to know a great deal more about his scientific reading in the 1730's and 1740's. It would, for example, be of interest to know whether he was attracted to science as a result of his discovery of British empirical and sensationalist philosophy, or whether, on the contrary, his interest in science led him to Bacon, Newton, Locke, and Shaftesbury.

His relation to the continuing Jansenist controversy would be particularly important to establish with greater precision—his appointment as editor of the *Encyclopédie* had to be passed on by the venerable Chancellor d'Aguesseau, a staunch and pious upholder of Jansenism, and all publishing activity came traditionally within the purview of the University, where Jansenist influence was still powerful. Did Le Breton have reason to think that his prospective editor was *persona grata* in these quarters? He probably did, and Diderot has left more than one clue pointing to at least some youthful sympathy with the heirs of Port-Royal.[78] Very little, however, can as yet be said with any assurance on these matters.

It remains to take a final summary view of the agencies that can be identified as having contributed to the intellectual formation of the man who was to labor with might and main for the best twenty-five years of his life to produce the dictionary that was to "change the general public's manner of thinking."

As to Diderot's family background, there can be no question that his childhood was spent in an atmosphere of warmth and affection in a home where intellectual achievement was highly respected and where honest craftsmanship and moral uprightness were taught both by precept and by example. Indeed, although there is no indication of puritannical dourness, there is a color of moral earnestness, of conscious rectitude, even of moral rigor, in the characters both of Didier Diderot and of his elder son. In the father this fervent moralism suggests the possibility of Jansenist leanings, and it may not be altogether irrelevant to recall that the reigning bishop of Langres in the mid-seventeenth century had been one of the early partisans of the Port-Royal enterprise, so that it would not be surprising if his diocese had retained strong Jansenist traditions in the next generations. If Didier Diderot was a Jansenist, he may well have thought of the Jesuit school in which Denis spent his first years of study as a *pis aller,* only waiting until the boy showed unmistakable intellectual aptitude before sending him to a more acceptable—but more costly—institution in the capital.

At any rate, it is all but certain that young Diderot continued his education in Paris, not with the Jesuits at Louis-le-Grand, but in the Faculty of Arts of the University of Paris, probably at the Collège d'Harcourt and possibly later at the Collège de Beauvais. His closest associations in later life seem to have been with persons connected with these colleges of the University, and we have Diderot's own testimony, together with the recollections of his daughter and of his disciple Naigeon, to support this presumption. He was very likely ambitious to be "a reasonable theologian," as his father wished, and took his master's degree in 1732 with a view to pursuing further studies for the doctorate at the Sorbonne. The fact that he gave evidence in later years of no small professional competence in theology suggests that he may actually have carried on the studies which he contemplated at least for a few years and perhaps until the beginning of his legal apprenticeship with Clément de Ris in 1738 or 1739. He continued to receive pecuniary support from his father during this period, and he must have read voraciously in modern British philosophy and in natural science. He found time to learn English and Italian; whether he also learned some Hebrew is a question that must be left open.

If we consider, then, the sum total of Diderot's educational qualifications in the year 1747 and assume that the associated publishers Le Breton, Briasson, Durand, and David knew as much or more of his personal history than we now know, it should be apparent that they were making a relatively safe decision when they entrusted what was to be the most ambitious publishing enterprise of the century to his leadership. Despite his lack of practical editorial experience and despite his relative youth, he was a man who had received the best public education that France had to offer at that date; he had acquired not only a formidable stock of information and an excellent training in the specialized techniques of literary communication but also the skill that the best teachers (including Diderot himself [79]) have always tried to develop—the ability to make life itself a school and to begin in earnest the business of learning when the doors of the classroom close behind one for the last time. Diderot showed his truest scholastic aptitude when he began the task of finding out those things which the *Encyclopédie* was the first work of its kind to contain—most conspicuously the whole gamut of industrial arts, a field where he may truly be said to have done pioneering research. A brilliant student in and out of school, Diderot also managed to become a superb teacher, for his *Encyclopédie* not only educated the eighteenth century but has ever since remained an inexhaustible source of knowledge, humanity, and reasonableness.

1. "Livre des délibérations des sieurs Le Breton, David l'aîné, Durand et Briasson, libraires à Paris, intéressés dans l'impression du *Dictionnaire des arts et sciences de Chambers et Harris,* traduit en françois," Archives Nationales, U. 1051. The project which developed by successive stages into the *Encyclopédie* began in 1744 as a plan to translate Ephraim Chambers' *Cyclopedia;* it was subsequently decided to amalgamate with this work the similar English compilations of Harris and Dyche. Le Breton was at first planning to publish the work alone, and the original "staff" consisted of two translators. In 1745 and 1746, however, the plan was progressively enlarged, and to obtain additional capital a syndicate was formed, with Le Breton ceding a half interest to the other three "associated publishers."

2. Article "Encyclopédie," reprinted in *Oeuvres complètes de Diderot,* edited by J. Assézat and M. Tourneux, 20 vols. (Paris, 1875–1877), XIV, 463; hereafter cited as A.-T.

3. Franco Venturi, *Le Origine dell'Enciclopedia* (Rome, 1946), pp. 22–29. Mills, who appears never to have contemplated any extensive revision or amplification of Chambers' dictionary, had proposed the translation to Le Breton in 1744, but his competence as a translator evidently left much to be desired.

4. *Histoire de Grèce, traduite de l'anglois de Temple Stanyan,* 3 vols. (Paris, 1743); *Principes de la philosophie morale, ou Essai de M. S.°°° [Shaftesbury] sur le mérite et la vertu avec réflexions* (Amsterdam, 1745).

5. Jean-Jacques Rousseau, *The Confessions of Jean-Jacques Rousseau* (Modern Library edition), p. 289.

6. "Mémoires pour servir à l'histoire de la vie et des ouvrages de Diderot, par Madame de Vandeul, sa fille," in A.-T., I, xxiv–lxii.

7. J. A. Naigeon, *Mémoires historiques et philosophiques sur la vie et les ouvrages de Diderot* (Paris, 1821). Written, according to the editors' preface, between 1784 and 1795.

8. "Plan d'une université pour le gouvernement de la Russie" (written in 1775), A.-T., III, 534.

9. André Billy, *Vie de Diderot,* revised ed. (Paris, *ca.* 1932), gives most of the known details, some of them slightly romanticized (pp. 7–24). Some further information is presented by the Chanoine Louis Marcel, *Le Frère de Diderot: Didier-Pierre Diderot, chanoine de la cathédrale et grand archidiacre du diocèse, fondateur des écoles chrétiennes de Langres* (Paris, 1913), and "Diderot écolier: la légende et l'histoire," *Revue de l'histoire littéraire de la France,* XXXIV (1927), 377–402.

10. See in particular his "Entretien d'un père avec ses enfants," A.-T., V, 281–308, and his letter of August 3, 1759, from Langres just after his father's death: "What a task my father has imposed on me if I want ever to deserve the homage that they pay to his memory!" (*Lettres à Sophie Volland,* edited by André Babelon [Paris, 1938], I, 40).

11. Marcel, "Diderot écolier," *loc. cit.,* pp. 378–379.

12. *Ibid.*

13. *Ibid.,* p. 380.

14. See Note 9 above.

15. "Sur les exercices des cadets russes," A.-T., III, 545–546.

16. An extremely illuminating discussion of Jesuit theory and practice is contained in Emile Durkheim's *L'Evolution pédagogique en France* (Paris, 1938), II, pp. 69 ff., esp. pp. 111–114. See also Charles Daniel, *Les Jésuites Instituteurs de la jeunesse française au XVIIe. et au XVIIIe. siècle* (Paris, 1880).

17. A.-T., I, xxix–xxx. The same scene is described by Diderot himself in his letter of October 18, 1760, to Sophie Volland (*Lettres à Sophie Volland,* I, 148).

18. Marcel, "Diderot écolier," *loc. cit.*, pp. 388–389, points out some minor inconsistencies and improbabilities in the story, but these appear to be only dramatic exaggerations.

19. *Ibid.*, pp. 386–388.

20. Antoine Taillefer, *Tableau historique de l'esprit et du caractère des littérateurs françois, depuis la renaissance des lettres jusqu'en 1785: ou Recueil de traits d'esprit, de bons mots et d'anecdotes littéraires* (Versailles, 1785), IV, 217. Taillefer described himself as "avocat au Parlement, trésorier de la guerre, et subdélégué de l'Intendance de Champagne."

21. Billy, *op. cit.*, pp. 18–20.

22. A.-T., I, xxx. Marcel, "Diderot écolier," *loc. cit.*, p. 391, has pointed out that this episode appears almost down to the last detail in the third act, scene 5, of Sedaine's comedy, *Le Philosophe sans le savoir*. But Madame de Vandeul is not automatically convicted of plagiarism, and hence falsification, for Sedaine could perfectly well have based the incident on a real experience described to him by Diderot, who was his good friend.

23. Marcel, "Diderot écolier," *loc. cit.*, p. 391.

24. Taillefer, *op. cit.*, is silent on this point, though he states explicitly that Diderot began his studies in Paris with his year of "rhetoric," and Marcel accepts this assertion at face value. This is odd, because according to Marcel's own seemingly accurate calculations Diderot must have already completed those studies in Langres.

25. Gustave Dupont-Ferrier, *La Vie quotidienne d'un collège parisien pendant plus de trois cent cinquante ans (1563–1920). Du collège de Clermont au Lycée Louis-le-Grand* (Paris, 1921–1925), I, 56, 67, 79, 209–211, 224, 449; II, 32. See also Père J. de la Servière, *Un Professeur d'ancien régime. Le P. Charles Porée, S.J.* (Paris, 1899), p. 384 n.

26. Marcel, "Diderot écolier," *loc. cit.*

27. For Louis-le-Grand see Dupont-Ferrier, *op. cit.*, I, viii; for the colleges of the University, R. Salesses, "Diderot et l'université," *Revue universitaire*, XLIV (April, 1935), 324–325.

28. A.-T., I, 383–384.

29. *Ibid.*, p. 347.

30. *Ibid.*, p. 373.

31. *Ibid.*, p. 347.

32. *Ibid.*, p. 348.

33. *Ibid.*, p. xxxi.

34. Frédéric Masson, ed., *Mémoires et lettres de François-Joachim Cardinal de Bernis* (Paris, 1878), I, 16–21.

35. A.-T., I, xxxi.

36. "L'auteur de la lettre précédente à M. B[riasson], son libraire," A.-T., I, 398.

37. Masson, *op. cit.*

38. Salesses, *loc. cit.*, pp. 329 ff.

39. *Correspondance littéraire, philosophique et critique, par Grimm,*

Diderot, Raynal, Meister et al., edited by Maurice Tourneux in 16 vols. (Paris, 1877–1882), II, 504; III, 59; XV, 576. Hereafter cited as *Corr. litt.*

40. Rousseau, *Confessions*, p. 360. Rousseau speaks of the "treasurer of the Sainte-Chapelle," whom Salesses (*loc. cit.*, p. 329) identifies as the Abbé Le Monnier.

41. He received his M.A. from the University in 1733, according to Salesses, *loc. cit.*, p. 330.

42. Letter to General Betzky, dated "à la Haye, ce 15 juin 1774," A.-T., XX, 65.

43. "Plan d'une université," A.-T., III, 453.

44. A.-T., II, 399. My italics.

45. A.-T., III, 436.

46. Charles Rollin, *De la manière d'enseigner et d'étudier les belles lettres, par rapport à l'esprit et au coeur . . .*, 4 vols. (Paris, 1726–1728).

47. A.-T., III, 190, 431, 432.

48. Manuscrits latins, No. 8158, fo. 35.

49. Taillefer, *op. cit.*, IV, 217.

50. A.-T., I, xxxi–xxxii.

51. *Ibid.*

52. Archives de la Haute-Marne, Fonds Diderot-Vandeul, E4, No. 2.

53. This is the hypothesis originally suggested by R. Salesses, "Les Mystères de la jeunesse de Diderot," *Mercure de France*, CCLXXX (Dec. 15, 1937), 493–514. Salesses' argument would have been somewhat stronger if he had not accepted Madame de Vandeul's implication that 1732 was the beginning of Diderot's studies with Clément de Ris. Naigeon's account (*op. cit.*, pp. 11–16) allows for a considerable lapse of time between Diderot's exit from the Collège d'Harcourt and his legal apprenticeship and adds that this latter episode lasted "only a few months."

54. *Op. cit.*, p. 5.

55. A.-T., IX, 265. Marcel seems to have assumed that the expression "*prendre la fourrure*" referred simply to the taking of the master's degree, ignoring the words immediately following which indicate plainly that Diderot was speaking of the degree of doctor of theology. According to Diderot's own brief article "Fourrure" (*Encyclopédie*, VII, 262), "la *fourrure* est un habit particulier aux docteurs, licentiés [*sic*], bacheliers, professeurs, etc. de l'université." The Abbé Mallet, in his article "Docteur" (*Encyclopédie*, V, 4), indicates that at the Sorbonne the right to wear fur on academic costumes was enjoyed by doctors and professors and also by *bacheliers en license*—a degree that required at least three years of additional study after the M.A.—but he does not indicate that the *maître-ès-arts* had this distinction, and he describes the ceremony of conferring the doctor's degree in theology, during which the candidate was "revêtu de la fourrure de docteur."

56. A.-T., I, xxxii.

57. *Op. cit.*, pp. 5, 8.

58. This is the burden of his preface and notes to Shaftesbury's *Essay* (see Note 4 above), which he published in that year.

59. Dated November 21, 1765, by Babelon. *Lettres à Sophie Volland,* II, 92–93.

60. Chanoine Louis Marcel, *Le Mariage de Diderot* (Largentière, 1928), p. 197.

61. *Ibid.,* p. 27.

62. On occasion he was extremely harsh in denouncing "that science of the chimerical," which "has always produced and always will produce the same effect. . . . A country is prey to the greatest disasters if all its theology is not reduced to two pages" (Memorandum to the empress, cited in M. Tourneux, *Diderot et Catherine II* [Paris, 1899], p. 298). He also told Catherine that "Atheism may be the doctrine of a small coterie, but never that of a large number of citizens, and still less of those of a fairly civilized country. Belief in the existence of God, or the old trunk [of the tree of religion], will therefore always remain. And who knows what monstrosities this trunk might produce if it were abandoned and allowed to grow freely? Hence I would retain the priests, not as depositaries of truth, but as obstacles to errors that would possibly be even more monstrous; not as preceptors for sensible people, but as warders for those who are weak in the head" (A.-T., III, 517). Yet he may have been exaggerating for the benefit of the empress, whom he hoped to strengthen in her free-thinking tendencies. His more deliberate views, expressed in original articles which he contributed to the *Encyclopédie,* seem to be more in keeping with his life-long absorption in the preoccupations—if not the conclusions—of theology: "I know of no science that demands more penetration, more judgment, more delicacy or more subtlety of mind than does theology; its two branches (scholastic and moral theology) are immense, and they embrace the most important questions that exist" (article "Bible," A.-T., XIII, 435). Or his reply to those who thought theology should have been excluded from the *Encyclopédie:* "It is a science, . . . this science is very extensive and very curious; . . . it might have been made as interesting as mythology, and if we had omitted the latter they [the critics] would have regretted it" (article "Encyclopédie," A.-T., XIV, 488). Finally, there is his tribute to the University of Paris, to which, "in spite of its monstrous defects, . . . we owe the birth of every good thing that has been done from its origin to the present time" (A.-T., III, 435).

63. J. E. Barker, *Diderot's Treatment of the Christian Religion in the Encyclopédie* (New York, 1941), pp. 25–26.

64. *Ibid.,* p. 26.

65. Naigeon recalled that the thesis "was generally attributed to Diderot," who "advised the two authors [De Prades was assisted, according to Naigeon, by the Abbé Yvon, another member of the staff of the *Encyclopédie*] to 'get a little off the beaten path' and to speak sometimes the language of reason to the hardened ears of the doctors" and who "furnished them with the material

for five or six 'positions'" (*op. cit.,* pp. 160–161). The whole thesis only offered ten "positions" for defense. We know that Diderot wrote Part III of De Prades's subsequent *Apologie;* and Dieckmann's recent discovery of a manuscript copy of Part III, in which a section from Part II is incorporated, leads him to conclude that the rumor circulated in 1752 to the effect that Diderot had a hand also in Parts I and II may have been true, and that "we may attribute to Diderot the last chapter of the second part" (*Inventaire du Fonds Vandeul et inédits de Diderot, publiés par Herbert Dieckmann* [Genève, 1951], pp. 56–57). There is no proof, of course, that Naigeon was correct in implying that Diderot wrote a major part of the dissertation itself; and indeed De Prades might equally well have taken many of his unorthodox ideas from Jesuit defenses of natural religion which, as R. R. Palmer has shown, ran remarkably parallel with the ideas of the philosophes, *Catholics and Unbelievers in Eighteenth Century France* (Princeton, 1939).

66. A.-T., III, 510–518.

67. *Ibid.,* pp. 505–510; 497–505; 505.

68. *Ibid.,* p. 513.

69. *Ibid.,* p. 478.

70. A.-T., I, 376–380, with special reference to poetry, but the argument given seems to apply to any imaginative work containing figures of speech.

71. *Correspondance inédite de Diderot,* edited by André Babelon (Paris, 1931).

72. *Encyclopédie,* article "Collèges," III, 635.

73. A.-T., VI, 407.

74. A.-T., XVI, 274. Louis Marcel, "La Jeunesse de Diderot (1732–1743)," *Mercure de France,* CCXVI (1929), 62–64, has noted that there was another, more obscure, Randon who might have employed Diderot as a tutor, and who fits Mme. de Vandeul's description "financier" in that he was a *receveur des finances.* This was Elie Randon de Massanes d'Haneucourt, and it may be a misspelling of his name (as d'Harmoncourt) that occurs in Naigeon's *Mémoires.* He had two children, a boy and a girl—Mme. de Vandeul says her father was hired to teach two boys—and his daughter was probably born too late to have been Diderot's pupil in any event, since she was married in 1764. On the whole, it seems more likely that Randon de Boisset was Diderot's employer, and that the children involved were wards or relatives of the famous bibliophile.

75. *Mémoires et journal de J.-G. Wille, graveur du roi* (Paris, 1857), II, 90.

76. A.-T., IV, 337–339.

77. A.-T., VI, 401.

78. His article "Jansénisme" in the *Encyclopédie,* remarkable for its sympathetic tone, tends to bear out this interpretation. Again, in his four-page article "Langres" (A.-T., XV, 410–414), devoted almost exclusively to the geography and antiquities of the city, he went out of his way to include a long paragraph in tribute to the seventeenth-century Jansenist academician Barbier d'Aucourt, a native of Langres and a friend of the Port-Royal group. He

recommended to Catherine II (A.-T., III, 515–516) that her professor of theology, "while avoiding the ridiculous and dangerous subtleties of the casuists of the last century," should adopt the method of Sainte-Beuve, one of the Jansenist professors expelled from the Sorbonne in 1658.

79. "When we enter school we are ignorant, and when we leave we are students; we ourselves become teachers when we bring all our natural capacity to bear upon a particular object" (A.-T., III, 445).

[PAUL FARMER]

The Social Theory of

Frédéric Le Play

TOO few Americans of our generation appreciate the riches of French
social and political thought in the nineteenth century. Nowadays we
take interest in France as a factor in international politics, as a home of
art and literature, and as a pleasure resort, where both the taste for
elegance and an appreciation of the simple life linger on from a happier
previous age. But as a rule, we do not presume that we have much
to learn, which we can put to use in our own lives, from a nation so
different in its character. The American farmer, working a vast tract
of new land with an arsenal of machines, is much more than a matter
of miles removed from the French peasant, wresting his sustenance
from a minuscule holding in the same village as his forebears of centuries before. The worker in one of our immense factories cannot even
imagine the world of the French artisan, who fashions with his hands
wares of a matchless grace, which not even he can duplicate and no
one can imitate. The American businessman, statesman of an immense
industrial or commercial empire, cannot speak the same language as the
aristocratic French upper bourgeois. Even those Americans who most
warmly cherish France admire her mainly because her ways are not
our own, because she has withstood the drive of ambition, the pressure
of standardization, the worship of riches, and the other signs of mod-
ernism.

Those scholars who have paid tribute to France for her contribution to the intellectual heritage of the modern world have more often drawn attention to her achievements in the seventeenth and eighteenth centuries than in more recent times. Historians have been quick to recognize the French thinkers of the Enlightenment who did so much to define the postulates of rationalism, liberalism, naturalism, and progress, and to recognize the world-wide importance of the French Revolution of 1789. But even scholars have shown little interest in the debate on social and political issues which continued in France in the two or three generations after the Revolution. Bonald and De Maistre have been labeled theocrats and relegated to the encyclopedias; Saint-Simon and the other pioneer French socialists have been noticed mainly as predecessors of Marx and Engels; Comte, whose name was once better known in Britain and America than in France, has been forgotten; while Tocqueville has been remembered principally for his observations on America, as Sainte-Beuve and Taine for their literary criticism, and Proudhon has been dismissed as a madman. Few of the works of such men have been reappraised to discover what insight they offer into the problems of our age.

Yet within the period between the Bourbon Restoration in 1815 and the proclamation of the Third Republic in 1870, a succession of French writers carried on a continuous debate on the basic premises of social organization that was unequaled for the range of views expressed and the sharpness of analysis, and this debate laid bare most of the issues that have concerned the Western world ever since. Several circumstances combined to produce this efflorescence of ideas. One was the heritage of the Enlightenment, which had made speculation upon the bases of the social order a prime interest of men of intellect, and another was the heritage of the Revolution of 1789, which had made the issues of this learned discussion the crux of bitter practical dispute. Moreover, the experience of the Revolution had divided France into two antagonistic camps, one defending and the other attacking the "principles of '89," and in France these two camps were more sharply divided and more evenly matched in strength than in any other country. Hence the adversaries and the advocates of the new regime were alike under a relentless pressure to give convincing expression to their views and to make answer to their critics.

Nor was the opposition of the old regime and the new only a clash of ideas; it had its basis in social and economic experience. For France was one of the first countries to witness the encroachment of the new, urban world of the industrial revolution upon the older, stable world of the château and the village. We are apt to forget this, since it is a commonplace that, despite the upheaval of 1789, the old regime persisted in France well into the nineteenth century and that the industrial revolution never proceeded as fast or as far in France as in Britain, Germany, and the United States. In the first half of the nineteenth century, however, France well knew the problems associated with rapid urbanization. Nowhere, indeed, was the contrast between the old regime and the new sharper than between the rural provinces of France, where the peasant would doff his cap when talking to a *monsieur,* and the metropolis of Paris, where the rootless proletarian mob eased the pain of its wretched existence with memories of one uprising and dreams of the next. And no one could travel from the one world to the other, as any Frenchman of the educated classes would have occasion to do, without speculating on the meaning of the contrast.

The chronicle of the insurrections and revolutions of Paris is well known; historians have been beguiled by the heroism and the tragedy of these urban revolts and have made clear the impulses behind them. But the stolid, inarticulate, other world of rural France remains enigmatic. Few historians have undertaken to depict the village France of the nineteenth century, although the biography of nearly every Frenchman of note begins in the provinces; and scarcely any scholars have made a serious attempt to render intelligible the ideas and convictions of that substantial portion of the nation which steadfastly strove to preserve the France of the old regime against the inroads of the new world which Paris represented. Doubtless one reason why French conservatism thus remains *terra incognita* is that most French and American historians in our time, having been brought up in the liberal tradition, find it uncongenial to expound the ideas of men who championed the privileges of rank and inheritance and scorned progress. But another reason is that the slogans of French conservatism—monarchy, aristocracy, and an established religion—seem to have no relevance in the twentieth century. Certainly these catchwords seem anachronistic to the American mind, and probably none of those French conservatives who render lip-service to them seriously believes that a reconstruction of the institutions of the old regime would solve the problems of our age.

Even in the early nineteenth century, these slogans probably had less significance in the minds of the spokesmen of French conservatism as items in a program for institutional reform than as symbols representing a complex of attitudes and convictions concerning human nature, which define the characteristics of a viable social organization. It is because they subscribe to these basic principles that many Frenchmen of keen intellect still avow themselves partisans of the old regime, even though they realize that it is impossible, in the twentieth century, to restore monarchy and nobility and to re-establish a legal requirement of religious obedience. And the body of thought that underlies these slogans of traditional French conservatism affords an insight into the fundamental problems of social organization that merits the attention of anyone who is thoughtfully concerned about the crisis of liberalism in the modern world.

I

Among the spokesmen of French conservatism in the nineteenth century, Frédéric Le Play (1806–1882) is one who especially deserves a wider remembrance.[1] A mining engineer and metallurgist who became the founder of a school of social reform almost in spite of himself, Le Play was not a man of large influence in public affairs in his own time, and he was therefore never linked with decisive events. Nor is he remembered as a writer, for he expressed his ideas in a simple but unpolished style, devoid of special literary grace. Failing to command attention by reason either of practical influence or of rhetorical distinction, Le Play has suffered neglect also because his views were an unorthodox form of conservatism. While making a formal obeisance to the traditions of monarchy, aristocracy, and religion, Le Play never plunged into the political arena to do battle for the cause of throne and altar. Indeed, he became a personal associate and political servitor of Napoleon III, who was no less accursed by the doctrinaire conservatives of his time than by the zealots of republicanism. And though, like other conservatives, Le Play made Christian morality a cornerstone of his system of thought, he held aloof from the Catholic Church until late in his life, and he remained quite willing to endorse Protestant or even non-Christian religious morality.

Perhaps because his views were unorthodox, the ideas which Le Play expounded have a more accessible meaning for our time than those of most of his generation. He was exceptional, first, for the reason that his basic prescription was nonpolitical. Though he made clear his preference as among the possible forms of government, he did not believe that any particular scheme of political institutions, such as those of the old regime, was indispensable to social well-being. Unlike most of the conservatives of his age, moreover, he made a concern for the laboring classes one of the main features of his thought. Indeed, his doctrines implied a more severe restraint upon the rich, albeit self-imposed, than upon the poor, and in a social order based upon sound principles, he saw no need for the forcible repression of the masses. Nor is the relevance of his thought limited to France. To the degree that his argument is valid, it is applicable to any country of the Western world, perhaps even to any civilized people.

As is true of most conservatives, the circumstances of Le Play's life have considerable bearing upon the doctrines he was ultimately to espouse. Born in a little village near the coast of Normandy, Frédéric Le Play was a native of a region which had remained, throughout the upheaval that began in 1789, staunch in its loyalty to the proscribed old order. His mother was left a widow with only modest means, while her two children were still of a tender age, so that Frédéric and his sister grew up in humble circumstances, verging on poverty. He was the kind of child who found amusement out-of-doors and with his elders, rather than in children's games or reading, and he spent much time talking with the peasants and artisans of the village. From their reminiscences of the time before the outbreak of the Revolution, he gathered a nostalgic view of the peace and repose that had prevailed under the old regime. But with this favorable impression, he also garnered stories of the follies and derelictions of the privileged classes, which had earned them their chastisement.

As a boy, young Frédéric ingratiated himself with a local carpenter and builder, who offered to take him in as an apprentice and eventually to make him his heir. Both Frédéric and his mother were inclined to take advantage of the offer. But one of his schoolmates, who was planning to take the examinations for admittance into the Ecole polytechnique, urged Frédéric also to make application. With the thought of ascertaining whether the lad had an aptitude for technical studies, his mother took Frédéric to visit a friend of the family who was an engineer in the administration of public roads and bridges. The youth made such a favorable impression that the engineer, who was a bachelor, took him into his home and assumed charge of his studies in preparation for the examinations. The next year, 1824, Frédéric set off for Paris, where he passed successfully through the Ecole polytechnique and the Ecole des mines.

While a student in Paris, Frédéric applied himself assiduously to his studies. But no student in Paris in the 1820's could remain oblivious of the ferment of social and political ideas which was brewing in the capital. Le Play became exposed, in particular, to the ideas of the new Saint-Simonian school, since Jean Reynaud, the schoolmate who had first urged him to prepare for a technical profession, became a convert to this sect and labored to win Le Play over to the creed of progress through the application of science and technology to social problems. Even though Le Play refused to become a Saint-Simonian, his long arguments with his friend doubtless did much to make him more sensitive to the problem of social reform. He was also impelled to this concern by an incident of a personal nature. In the spring of 1830 he suffered a serious injury when an explosion occurred in the laboratory where he was at work. His hands were badly burned, and for months thereafter he was in excruciating pain. It was while he was recovering from this accident that the Revolution of 1830 broke out, Charles X was driven from the throne, and after the hopes of the republicans had been drowned in a welter of blood, Louis Philippe was installed upon the throne. The news of the insurrection, brought to Le Play by his friends as he suffered his anguished convalescence, made a deep impression on him, strengthening his determination to discover some path to social peace.

The answer which he sought was suggested to him by the experience he gained in extensive travels. Le Play began these excursions in the summer of 1829, before his accident, as part of the fieldwork required of students in the Ecole des mines, and he resumed them as soon as his health permitted. In the course of some twenty years, he thus visited, at various times, Spain and Italy, England, Scotland, Ireland, the Low Countries and Germany, Scandinavia, Russia, the Balkans, and Asia

Minor. Some of these journeys he undertook on his own initiative, giving over his summers to them, while others were occasioned by invitations to study or advise upon mining and metallurgical technics. His sojourn in Russia, for instance, was at the request of Prince Anatole Demidov, who asked him to survey the mining operations on the estates of the Demidov family in the Donetz basin. In all, Le Play traveled some two hundred thousand miles, much of this distance on foot.

Although Le Play made his trips mainly to inspect mines and forges, he became a serious observer of social conditions in the lands he visited. Wherever he went, he made it his practice to inquire as to which family in each locality, whether rich or poor, was widely regarded as an example of well-being and virtue, and he attempted a systematic study of such families. From these observations, eventually he began to discern what seemed to him empirical evidence of the conditions requisite to the good life.

But Le Play did not develop his ideas solely from observations abroad. He continued to make his home in Paris, remaining at the Ecole des mines, where he became a professor in 1840. While pursuing his technical studies of mining and metallurgy, which issued in a series of publications and soon won him renown, he read widely in history and the literature of social and political problems. He also developed a circle of acquaintance which included some of the principal spokesmen of conservative principles in public life, and he established a kind of salon, where such persons met and exchanged ideas. Among his acquaintances were Tocqueville, Thiers, Montalembert, and Augustin Cochin. From these discussions, doubtless, Le Play drew some of the ideas he was to incorporate into his own doctrine of social reform.

It was the Revolution of 1848, once more plunging the capital into a blood-bath, that determined Le Play at last to publish the conclusions of his thought as to the true path of peaceable social reform. This initial work took the shape of a folio volume, entitled *Les Ouvriers européens* and published at the expense of the government in 1855, comprising an introductory essay and detailed case studies of thirty-six families which Le Play had observed in the course of his travels. In the introduction, he set forth the outline of his thought. In brief, he argued that the ultimate unit in the consideration of social problems was not the individual, but the family, and that the key to human happiness was not the freedom of the individual to seek his own pleasure, but the well-being of the family, which alone could afford the individual a complete and secure happiness. The proper method of social reform, he further held, was not a speculative discussion of one or another series of principles dealing with the state and the citizen, but rather the scientific observation of particular families. Accordingly, he specified the procedure for the compilation of case studies, or family monographs, involving an examination of the background of the family, its sources of income, the conditions of its work, its habitation and diet, recreation, and moral and religious convictions and practices. As a means of rendering the observation more precise and objective, he urged a careful inventory of all its capital, including household furnishings and wardrobe, and a budget of its annual expenditures.

Thereafter Le Play devoted an ever larger share of his time to public affairs. He served as commissioner-general in charge of the international exposition held in Paris in 1855, later in charge of the French section of the similar exposition in London in 1862, and again as commissioner-general of the Paris exposition of 1867. Meantime he was appointed to the Conseil d'état, and subsequently was made a senator. However, his interest in the propagation of his doctrines of social reform did not diminish. In 1856 he organized a Société d'économie sociale, which drew his disciples together for the discussion of reform according to the principles he set forth. In 1864 Le Play brought out a new work, *La Réforme sociale en France,* in the hope of making his ideas more accessible to the public than in the formidable folio of *Les Ouvriers européens.* Early in 1870, he issued still another version, *L'Organisation du travail,* which included a more elaborate statement of his views on the proper relations between capital and labor. In the decade of the 1870's, after the downfall of the Second Empire and the emergence of the Third Republic, he redoubled his efforts to develop an organized following, setting up a number of local societies, called Unions of Social Peace, as dependencies of the Société d'économie sociale. In the same endeavor to broaden his circle of readers, he issued a number of other works, of which the more notable were *L'Organisation de la famille* (1872) and *La Réforme en Europe* (1876), but these added little or nothing to the ideas expounded in his earlier books. In 1881 the Société d'économie sociale began the publication of a series of volumes

entitled *Les Ouvriers des deux mondes,* by various contributors, including Le Play, on the model of the studies included in *Les Ouvriers
européens.*[2]

The Société d'économie sociale survived Le Play's death in 1882,
and it issued a periodical under the name of *La Science sociale* which
attracted some attention in the 1880's and 1890's. However, it placed
more emphasis upon the sociological elements in Le Play's thought, as
represented by his interest in the family monograph, than upon his concern for social reform. The latter interest was kept alive for a while in
the local Unions of Social Peace. But by the turn of the century the
emergence of the new authoritarian conservatism, to which the Action
Française gave voice, as well as the drift toward Marxian socialism
on the part of the popular classes, gave evidence of an atmosphere in
which Le Play's ideas could no longer evoke a wide response. The movement he founded soon lost vigor, and gradually the name of Le Play
passed into obscurity.

II

The ideas Le Play propounded are of more interest than his modest
career as a man of affairs and a reformer, which, as appears from the
foregoing résumé, was of minor dimensions. Let us examine these ideas
as a system rather than in the order of their presentation in Le Play's
writings, singling out those which are of present importance and passing over those which bear only upon the issues of his times.

The basic premise in Le Play's thought is his conviction that the
scientific student of society and the practical social reformer alike must
treat the family as the ultimate unit.[3] Men do not live as individuals,
each quite by himself, nor, manifestly, could mankind as a species
survive if they did. Hence we may not assume that the normal process
of human life involves the search of the individual for his own happiness
or that men either succeed or fail in such an endeavor, independently of
their fellows. Rather, men live only in a series of relationships with other
persons, and the happiness of each depends upon proper relations with
others. Much the most important of the personal associations in any
man's life are those of kinship with other members of his family. For
the family is the institution through which alone the basic human
wants, both material and psychological, can be satisfied. From an eco-

nomic point of view, the family is the means by which the burden of supporting the nonproductive elements of the population is placed upon the shoulders of those in the full vigor of maturity, who must inevitably provide for the needs of the aged, the infirm, and the immature young. By one means or another—by a kind of social insurance, if not the family—this burden must be put upon those in middle years, but it is made easier within the family, inasmuch as the mature are repaying a debt to their aged parents, who previously suffered the charge of their upbringing, and have the knowledge that their own children, for whom now they are making sacrifices, will, in due time, provide for their old age.

No less does the family provide for the subjective needs of men for respect and affection. Men do not live by food and shelter alone, Le Play emphasizes, but also demand a sense of dignity and a knowledge of their own importance in the sentiments of others. Only for a few, who are fortunately placed in society or who have exceptional gifts that permit them a role in public affairs, can this hunger be satisfied by the esteem of a wide circle of neighbors or fellow citizens. But for even the simplest and humblest of men and women, a closely knit family provides respect for the elders, affection for the children, and each kind of esteem, in the normal passage of time, for everyone.

The family as an institution takes on different forms in different times and places, Le Play pointed out. One of the principal patterns is the patriarchal family, characteristic of pastoral or nomadic peoples and surviving in Le Play's time among the peasants of Slavic Europe. In the patriarchal family, the eldest male is the master of the entire household, which includes, besides the patriarch and his wife, their married sons, daughters-in-law, and grandchildren. In such a family, there is no private property; all the wealth of the family is held in common, and the patriarch makes provision for the needs of all its members. The patriarchal family never dissolves. Its members pass from childhood to maturity, and eventually die within its fold; on the death of its head, his oldest son succeeds to the role of the patriarch, but otherwise the family continues undisturbed in its timeless course. Such a family had much to commend it, Le Play thought, but it was characteristic of a primitive stage of human life. It was not ideally suited to modern society, he believed, for the reason that it reduced all members of the family to an utter dependence upon the patriarch, providing for their needs but depriving them of personal responsibility and therefore of complete moral stature.

A second type is the unstable family. This was characteristic of western Europe in Le Play's time, as it is generally of Europe and America today. The unstable family comprises only the parents and their immature children; as soon as the children reach marriageable age, they leave the parental home to found new families of their own. Hence each family takes its start and reaches its terminus within the span of a single generation, and no family has any persisting tie with any other. Le Play acknowledged that such a family has the minimum virtue of providing for the care of the young and, in contrast to the patriarchal family of a more primitive age, the further merit of devolving upon each son, as he attains maturity and becomes the head of his own family, a full measure of personal independence and thus of moral responsibility.

From the deficiencies of the unstable family, however, arises most of the unhappiness of the modern world. First, the unstable family makes inadequate provision for the aged. A dutiful and generous son may make room in his home for his parents when they are no longer able to fend for themselves, but in such an event, the parents are at best honored guests and at worst unwelcome intruders. Furthermore, in a society where the unstable family is characteristic, there is no adequate provision for those who, for one reason or another, are unable to found families of their own. For example, there is no better than a bleak prospect for the spinster, the widow without children, the invalid, the cripple, the simple-minded, or those who, by reason of any other handicap of body or mind or temperament, may not assume the role of head of a family but could lead a happy and useful life as a member of a family. Because the unstable family must perish within a generation, moreover, it undermines the wholesome impulse of a man to build for the future. Even under the most favorable circumstances, the man in the full vigor of his years dares not look far ahead, because he must recognize that, within only a short time, his children will scatter from beneath his roof to seek their own fortunes, that at his death the home for which he labored will become the abode of strangers, and that the means he worked so hard to husband will be distributed among his several heirs.

The third type of family which Le Play distinguishes he calls the *famille-souche,* which can perhaps best be translated as the "root-and-branch" family. It combines features of the patriarchal and of the unstable family. Like the patriarchal family, it is a conglomerate, comprising, besides the husband and wife and their immature children, their aged grandparents, unmarried aunts or uncles, sisters and brothers, and perhaps a son-in-law as well as daughters-in-law, with their offspring. A domestic servant who has long served the family may earn the status of a member of the family, as also a hired man, in a peasant household, or the orphaned child of a friend of the family. Ordinarily, Le Play estimated, the *famille-souche* includes about fifteen persons. All of these form a single, communitarian association, pooling their resources and drawing upon the common store according to their needs. Normally the oldest male has final authority, as in the patriarchal family, but he may choose to hand down his authority to his heir as soon as the latter reaches full maturity. Usually, the eldest son becomes the heir to the head of the family, but the latter may designate another son or a son-in-law, if the eldest son lacks the temperament or ability to assume the role, or prefers to strike out for himself, or, being junior to numerous sisters, is too young for such a responsibility.

The *famille-souche,* retaining grown children within the household of their parents, shows a constant tendency to increase in size, and obviously, the family cannot accommodate such a growth forever. To relieve the pressure, the *famille-souche* sends forth its daughters to the families of their husbands, and its surplus sons to found new families of their own, as under the regime of the unstable family. However, the heir remains at home, so that the original, or root-family never dies. Nor is any member under a compulsion to leave unless he so desires, nor prevented from returning, if he chooses. Thus the *famille-souche* always makes room for its unmarried or unmarriageable children. Moreover, the root-family remains in touch with its off-shoots, that is, the families of those sons who set off for themselves. The head of the *famille-souche* sees to it that such a son learns a trade, and supplies him with the capital to buy a home and set up a farm or shop so as to support the new branch-family. And such a son recognizes his continuing tie with the root-family, returning home, should an emergency arise, to help meet the crisis. For example, a younger son would return at once, if his older brother, designated to succeed their father as head of the *famille-souche,* should die before his time. Unlike the patriarchal family, the *famille-souche,* constantly giving birth to new families, thus affords a regular avenue by which the more adventurous members may strike out for themselves and assume the moral burden of an independent life. But in contrast to the unstable family, the *famille-souche* lasts forever, eternally providing shelter for those of its members who lack the strength to make their own way or who are stricken by adversity.

The patriarchal family is well suited to the needs of primitive peoples, Le Play believed, but it is obsolete among civilized peoples. In our time, the *famille-souche* is the key to human happiness. Where it flourishes, society is well; where the unstable family is normal, society suffers pains and distress beyond cure by any other agency. Even if society could provide for the economic needs of all persons—as we now sometimes imagine might come to pass under an ideal regime of social planning, though Le Play would never have entertained such a dream—no other institution but the *famille-souche* can assure a position of respect for the aged, which is as necessary to their happiness as economic security, or provide the warmth of intimate association for the ill-favored daughter who does not achieve the vocation of marriage, or for the son who cannot measure up to the hazards and torments of an unfriendly world.

Only within the family, moreover, is there a favorable environment for the development of the moral sense. For the family defines the basic moral obligations of each of its members—the duties of husband to wife and of her to him, of the children to their elders, of the aged to the coming generation, of the well to the ill, of the strong to the weak—in terms so simple and precise that no one can mistake them. And to support the commands of duty, the family lends the impulse of affection, relieving the burden of virtue with the strength of blood-relationship.

As the role of each person in the family determines his duty, the interest of the family as a whole affords the ultimate guide in human relations. For if the well-being of the family is the key to the well-being of each of us, the aim of social endeavor must be the preservation and nurture of the family. Hence Le Play defines the essence of morality as *prévoyance,* or foresight, by which he means the intelligent dedication of one's energy to the long-range interest of the group. In simpler terms, this may be reduced to industry and thrift. Indeed, there is much in the outlook of Le Play which suggests that of the prosperous and ascetic Puritan. The path to virtue, he declared, lies through work, the fruit of work is wealth, and while riches are often the temptation to evil, their only worth is to support a life of virtue.[4]

At bottom, it is apparent, Le Play was a moralist, preaching the need of each man to subordinate the gratification of his own desires to his obligations toward his fellows. There are only two kinds of men, he once remarked, *ceux qui savent se dévouer*—those who know how to dedicate themselves—and those who lack this, the elemental virtue. Yet Le Play was not at all the caricature of the preacher who opposes virtue to happiness. On the contrary, he presented his system of thought as the answer to the question: How can men best attain happiness on earth? He did not think of devotion to one's fellows as something to be preferred to personal happiness. Rather, he argued that virtue, in this sense, is the only way to personal happiness, since this can be attained only within the circle of the family. It is impossible, according to the logic of his argument, for a man to be both vicious and happy, or to be happy without being morally upright, since the man who seeks his own pleasure by and for himself is doomed to defeat his own purpose, while the wiser man chooses service to others because he knows that he can never attain contentment save in a group. This, Le Play insisted, is an empirical truth, which can be verified by observation. But it is also the common doctrine of all great religions, expressed in the Ten Commandments—the Eternal Decalogue, to which Le Play made repeated allusion—and in the Christian Gospels, and equally evident in the teachings of Buddha, the Confucian classics, and the Koran.

Concern for the well-being of the family provided the touchstone in Le Play's appraisal of all other aspects of social life. He was well aware that the family must have a livelihood and that some kinds of livelihood are better suited than others to the needs of the family.[5] The source of its income must be such, he recognized, that the family may maintain a permanent home of its own, since the family is a timeless institution which will outlive its members. Moreover, he pointed out, its income should be derived from a vocation that is heritable, so that the children may take up its work as their parents grow old. The normal and optimum occupation, Le Play acknowledged, is agriculture, because a parcel of land, a herd of livestock, and a homestead form a store of wealth that can provide sustenance for an indefinite succession of generations, because labor on the land affords a variety of tasks, giving useful work to all members of the family, men and women, young and old, according to their strength, and because the skills needed in agriculture are simple enough to be handed down from father to son, even if the latter has only a modest endowment of intelligence. On the same grounds, Le Play admitted that artisan manufacture and small-scale commerce could also provide a suitable support for healthy family life.

However, he did not dissemble his view that wage-labor in large-scale industry affords only an unfavorable basis for the family. Urban life, such as industry commonly requires, seldom allows the family of the working class to own its home, nor does work in a factory give the family security of income, nor does it readily permit the father to raise his son to follow in his vocation. The apparent advantages of the factory system, Le Play frankly declared, are not sufficient to compensate for the detriment to the family, since, in his view, the increase of wealth, no matter how great, is of no value save insofar as it furthers the well-being of the family. Le Play was also dubious as to whether the learned professions of law and medicine are appropriate to the support of a *famille-souche*, since the father cannot be sure that his son will have the aptitude for such a career. Without question, he believed, the savant —the man who owes his livelihood to an unusual intellectual endowment—can never found a *famille-souche*. Certain other vocations, such as those of the priest and the schoolmaster, are best filled by unmarried men, so Le Play believed, but he was willing to give sanction to men who choose such a career, even though they must forego family life, because their work is socially indispensable.

Inevitably, Le Play recognized, some families must depend on wage-labor for their livelihood. This was regrettable, but he considered it utopian to envision a nation made up exclusively of property owners and the self-employed. Inevitably, too, he believed, the principal responsibility for the well-being of such families must rest upon the employer. To be sure, the family of the working class, like the family of another class, has the duty of *prévoyance;* so far as it can, it must provide for its own needs by hard work and frugal living. In the last analysis, however, such a family depends for its existence upon the hired labor of its members, and the conditions of such labor are not under its control, but subject rather to the dictates of the *patron*. This places a clear moral obligation upon the *patron*.[6] First, it lies upon him to see to it that his workingmen have steady employment, even when it is unprofitable for him to keep them at work. Second, it lies upon the employer to see to it that his workingmen receive a wage sufficient to permit them to support their families, even if the *patron* must sacrifice his own profit in order to pay an adequate wage. Finally, it lies upon him to set his workingmen a good example, by measuring up to the duties of his station and by maintaining a model family of his own. Unequivocally, Le Play denounced the idea of *laissez faire,* which would permit the property owner to use his riches simply to his own advantage. The sole purpose of wealth, Le Play reiterates, is to support virtue, and virtue requires the rich man to use his wealth in the service of the family. But no less is Le Play averse to what we would call "social legislation," that is, laws compelling the rich to provide for the poor. His reason is simple: it is vain to seek to coerce the rich, for never in history has a downtrodden class been relieved of its distress by forceful dictation to the rich; only by the voluntary action of the upper class, in response to the prodding of conscience, has the condition of the poor been bettered.

The reform of political institutions, it is obvious, had only a secondary interest for Le Play.[7] He was forthright, to be sure, in indicating his notion of the optimum constitution. He epitomized his view by declaring that government should be democratic at the level of the town or village, aristocratic in the province, and monarchical at the apex. The common people are competent to pass upon questions of local interest, because the peasant and the artisan have no less personal knowledge than their superiors of affairs in their own community. Matters of broader, regional importance are best entrusted to the care of the "social authorities" of the region, who will accept the responsibility for the management of public affairs, without compensation, as part of the duty of their fortunate station. As an example of what he meant, Le Play pointed with admiration to the English justices of the peace. For the nation as a whole, monarchy is the best form of government, because a ruling dynasty is in itself a *famille-souche,* which must view its realm with the same sense of attachment that a family of the peasantry feels for the land that is its patrimony.

While preferring such political arrangements, Le Play clearly did not think them indispensable to the welfare of the nation. Though most of his associates were royalists, who detested Bonapartism as both a usurpation and a new guise of democracy, Le Play was quite willing to serve

Napoleon III. And after the downfall of the Second Empire, while the royalists were making a desperate attempt to restore the monarchy, Le Play took little interest in the debates of the National Assembly at Versailles. The only political reforms which he urgently advocated were a revision of the French inheritance law, which required the distribution of an estate among all the children in equal portions and thus doomed the family to the partition of its patrimony, and legislation, intended to combat sexual irregularities, that would permit a woman who had been seduced to establish the paternity of her child and place financial responsibility upon the father.[8]

III

Such was the simple message of Le Play. Its limitations are manifest. We can scarcely help but note that Le Play presents an idyllic view of the family, quite without mention of the tension, antagonism, and bitterness that often develop within the close world of kinship. Doubtless Le Play would answer that such discord within the family is merely a sign of the want of virtue on the part of members of that family. But others would regard this answer as evidence of a want of psychological insight on the part of Le Play. Nor can we mistake that he sets his face against what seems to us the march of progress. Indeed, he denounced the very concept of progress, along with that of the natural goodness of man, as one of the cardinal errors of the modern age. He was quite willing to halt the advance of industrialism, no matter what increase of riches it might promise, for the reason that it was injurious to the family. He attached but little more value to science. Though he was himself a man of science, he placed no premium upon the increase of knowledge for its own sake, nor did he give evidence of a concern for aesthetic preoccupations. To be sure, he did not take a determined stand against such pursuits, as he did in respect to industrialism, and the logic of his argument would permit a man to cultivate intellectual or artistic impulses, provided that he first fulfilled his duties as a member of his family. But Le Play did not equivocate in his view that men have no other merit or duty that can excuse derelictions in their responsibility to the family.

Moreover, his teachings have the weakness, as well as the force, of any scheme for social improvement that is primarily moralistic. He attached supreme importance to the response of the individual to the dictates of duty; he never admitted that an adverse environment could excuse the moral failure of an individual or prevent him from perceiving and fulfilling his obligations. Le Play had no solution for such a problem as the business cycle, nor did he admit that such a problem was of crucial importance; he did not recognize that at times, economic circumstances might make it impossible for even a man of good will and prudence to provide for the needs of his family or to furnish uninterrupted employment at a living wage to all those who ordinarily depended on him for their work. Indeed, Le Play had no sympathy whatever for the argument that political action is necessary in order to create the conditions for a good life. And because we are now habituated to this postulate, we cannot help but feel that Le Play is a man of a by-gone age.

Yet, though we may thus dismiss Le Play, his simple message comes back to haunt the mind. Can we refuse his premise that our aim is *bonheur*—well-being and happiness? Can we deny his argument that *bonheur* requires the warmth of intimate human relations, which can be provided only within the family, or that a happy family life depends only in part upon riches, to the extent that the family requires a certain minimum of economic ease and security? Can we say otherwise than that riches are of no value in themselves, but only as a means to happiness, and that an increase of economic welfare is a human loss if it is had at the expense of the welfare of the family?

Perhaps it is because we have mistakenly placed too much emphasis upon the economic prerequisites of the good life, and not enough upon what Le Play meant by virtue, that we find something wanting in our life which the welfare state cannot provide, even though it may minister to our economic needs from the cradle to the grave. For it is remarkable that, although the mass of the people throughout the Western world now have a higher material standard of living than ever before, a nostalgia for an earlier age lingers on, even in those countries that have seen the most remarkable progress in social welfare. So common is this nostalgia, which withstands all the historian's evidence of the want, disease, and distress in earlier times, that nowadays we believe it a normal trick of the human mind to dream of a golden age in the past. But by no means has this always been the habit of mankind. Previous generations were as wont to pity their forebears as we to envy them. Perhaps we cannot lose our longing for the dimly remembered days of our youth or the days of our elders' memories because we recognize that, even though we may live in a neat, four-room apartment, provided at low cost with a public subsidy, there is something missing in our lives that will not fit into four rooms.

And it may also be evidence of an unconscious recognition of the simple truths which Le Play articulated, that everywhere in the Western world the family has been showing new vigor in our generation, despite all the terrors of world-wide upheaval. Thinking in terms of the traditional liberal point of view, we can only marvel at the rash daring of our contemporaries, and we must say, in the words of another French social critic, that fathers are "the great adventurers of modern times." We are nearly driven to a mystic conviction that somehow nature is making provision for the survival of our race, against the holocausts in store for us. But Le Play suggests another explanation. Perhaps we have unwittingly perceived that, in an age when the collective impulse for a better life seems to lead only to improvements on the atomic bomb, men can buttress themselves against the shock and strain of an adverse world only within the private association of the family.

We may also find meaning in Le Play's emphasis upon personal responsibility. In an age that indulges nearly any deficiency of character by putting the blame upon environment and makes an improvement in laws the main highroad to human happiness, we may do well to ponder an argument that men of high and low estate alike have moral responsibilities as individuals and that, however vicious they may wish to be, they can never attain happiness in defiance of their duties. We may even reflect to advantage upon Le Play's observation that through conscience, rather than legal compulsion, is the way the well-born recognize their obligation to the less fortunate, and that the common people, for their part, are in no wise exempt from the moral imperative of foresight.

If we agree with Le Play's argument that the family is the key to the good life, we must also agree that the ultimate social reform does not involve political action. There is little that can be done, as a matter of public policy, to supplant the unstable family with the *famille-souche*. The pattern of family life is a function of social custom more than legal prescription, and a change in its form such as Le Play advocated must depend primarily upon the personal decision of individuals.

Perhaps this points to the principal lesson we can draw from Le Play: that there is an area of human affairs beyond the competence of the state and that the final determination of human happiness lies in this zone of private life. Le Play well knew this, and because he asks little more of the state than to abstain from action that will impede *bonheur,* he seems to stand with the liberals of his time, despite his reputation as a conservative. Nevertheless, he was right in regarding himself as a critic of liberalism. For, as later generations were to discover, opposition to the state is not an unchanging characteristic of liberalism, and the sphere of political action was never to be broadened so far as it was in the twentieth century under the guidance of men who thought of themselves as liberals, or at least, as heirs to the older liberalism. It now seems clear that the crux of liberalism is its emphasis upon the individual as the human atom. From this definition, the logic follows that requires the equal treatment of all individuals and ultimately dictates action by the state to eliminate disparities among them due to the accidents of birth and inequalities of inheritance, under a regime of private property. In Le Play's thought, which defines the family, rather than the individual as the minimum human organism, there is no such compulsion toward equality. On the contrary, inequality is not only compatible with the well-being of all but inseparable from it, since the family as an institution inevitably implies distinctions of rank and places upon different persons the responsibility for decision and the duty of obedience.

In the twentieth century we cannot remain so negative in our attitude toward the state or as indifferent toward social inequality as was Le Play. Our world has become so complex that we must demand a more positive public management of social life than Le Play envisioned. Even if Le Play was right in believing that the presumed advantages of industrialism and urbanism, which now give rise to an all-pervasive *étatisme,* are not worth the price, probably our society cannot reverse its evolution and return to a simpler, poorer, and happier condition. Nevertheless, we can adapt some portions of Le Play's thought to the circumstances of our age, as part of our criteria of social improvement. We shall do well to bear in mind, as Le Play argued, that the desideratum is not a rising standard of living or equality of social condition, but *bonheur,* which can quite easily diminish even as we make progress toward a merely prosperous and democratic social order. And we may also benefit from Le Play's reiteration that the way to happiness is also the way to morality, and from his conviction that no man can attain inner peace who does not recognize his obligation not only to the remote world of mankind but also to those fewer fellow men whom every day he meets face to face.

1. There is no satisfactory biography of Le Play, or scholarly study of his ideas and influence. A number of his disciples published memoirs, most of which appeared at the time of his death or soon after, sketching his life and summarizing his teachings. Among these are: Edmond Demolins, *Le Play et son oeuvre de réforme sociale* (Paris, 1882); Jules Lacointa, *F. Le Play, étude sur sa vie et ses travaux* (Paris, 1882); A. Du Saussois, *P.-G.-F. Le Play* (Paris, 1884); Charles de Ribbe, *Le Play d'après sa correspondance* (Paris, 1884). An extensive exposition of his doctrines is included in J.-B.-Maurice Vignes, *La Science sociale d'après les principes de Le Play et de ses continuateurs*, 2 vols. (Paris, 1897); however, Le Play's ideas are merged with those of his disciples, with some change of emphasis. Other studies are: E. de Curzon, *Frédéric Le Play, sa méthode, son oeuvre, son esprit* (Paris, 1899); and Fernand Auburtin, *Frédéric Le Play d'après lui-même* (Paris, 1906). A more recent critique, together with selections from some of his writings, is Louis Baudin, *Frédéric Le Play* (Paris, 1947).

2. In addition to those mentioned above, which are the principal works of Le Play dealing with problems of social reform, he also published an admiring study of English social and political institutions, *La Constitution de l'Angleterre* (1875), and an ultimate epitome of his message, *La Constitution essentielle de l'humanité* (1882).

3. *La Réforme sociale en France*, 8th ed., 3 vols. (Paris, 1901), I, 383 ff.; *La Réforme en Europe et le salut en France* (Tours, n.d.), pp. 101 ff.; *La Constitution essentielle de l'humanité*, 2nd ed. (Tours, 1893), pp. 30 ff., 94 ff.; *L'Organisation du travail*, 7th ed. (Tours, 1906), pp. 36 ff.

4. *La Réforme sociale en France*, II, 7 ff., 412 ff.

5. *Ibid.*, II, Chapters 32–40.

6. *Ibid.*, II, 444–474; *La Réforme en Europe*, pp. 102–119; *L'Organisation du travail*, pp. 140–172.

7. *La Réforme sociale en France*, III, 281–628; *La Réforme en Europe*, pp. 197–240.

8. *La Réforme sociale en France*, I, 249–319; *L'Organisation du travail*, pp. 222–297.

[MELVIN KRANZBERG]

An Emperor Writes History:

Napoleon III's

Histoire de Jules César[1]

MANY history books are written *about* emperors, but very few history books are written *by* emperors. Hence, the rumor in 1860 that the Emperor Napoleon III of France was engaged in writing a book on history occasioned some surprise. When he had been merely the pretender Prince Louis Napoleon Bonaparte, Louis had written on various topics: economics, sociology, military science, and political philosophy. Once on the throne, however, he ceased writing, and there were mixed reactions to the sudden renewal of the Emperor's literary activity.

That original "old curmudgeon," Count Horace de Vielcastel, looked with disfavor upon the Emperor's venture. He believed that "people do not want kings to be learned men and writers of books; they want them to attend to the interests of their subjects." [2] But there were others who looked upon the Emperor's literary activities more favorably. Emile Ollivier thought that Napoleon III would never have turned away from affairs of state to pursue the literary life unless he intended to abdicate some of his dictatorial powers.[3] Ollivier welcomed the Emperor's writing of history as a harbinger of the liberal empire to come.

Perhaps the decision of the Emperor to write history portended nothing in the political sphere, yet it gave gossip-mongers the opportunity to speculate *why* Napoleon III had assumed the mantle of Clio. Various reasons were advanced, and many contained some degree of truth. Louis Napoleon could not be satisfied by killing two birds with one stone; each stone must be capable of killing at least three or more birds. So there were probably several reasons which motivated him to write history.

Napoleon III worked hard at being an emperor, and he may have viewed history as an appropriate relaxation for the imperial mind.[4] Unfriendly critics, however, could and did interpret this sedentary pursuit as a substitute for other relaxing and restorative treatments, involving females, in which a younger Louis Napoleon had perhaps been over-indulgent. The Emperor was getting older, and sickness was beginning to sap his strength.[5] The frivolous pastimes of the court during its early years began to slacken, and Napoleon III sought distractions of a more intellectual nature.[6] There is no doubt that Louis wanted to earn a scholarly reputation,[7] and "had a taste for historical researches." [8]

Besides, it was the fashion for French political figures of the nineteenth century to write history. Guizot, Louis Blanc, Lamartine, and Thiers had become historical authors. The Emperor should be able to write history as well as his political opponents. Furthermore, a serious historical work might gain the imperial author admission to the Académie Française, an honor which he coveted [9] but which the members of that august assemblage, a stronghold of the Orleanist faction, refused to grant.

Perhaps we have been seeking the Emperor's motivation in the wrong way when we have asked, Why did Napoleon III write history? The answer to the question of motivation might be simpler if we asked: Why did the Emperor Napoleon III write a history of Julius Caesar? There may be many reasons. One might say that an account of Caesar was the sort of thing that an emperor should do, if he intends to write history at all. Other rulers had been interested in Caesar, and perhaps Louis Napoleon, in his endless efforts to prove that he was one of the royal "brothers" of Europe, was simply adhering to the "union rules." Louis Napoleon even went to the trouble to list the others who had studied the subject.[10] These included Charles VIII of France, the Emperor Charles V, the Sultan Suleiman II, Henry IV (who translated the first two books of Caesar's *Commentaries*), Louis XIII (who translated the last two books), Louis XIV (who translated the first book of the *Commentaries*), and—of most overwhelming importance to Louis Bonaparte—the Emperor Napoleon I, who had written an *Outline of the Wars of Caesar* while at St. Helena.

It may be foolish to search for Napoleon III's motives in writing this history of Julius Caesar when he has stated them so clearly himself: "This aim is to prove that, when Providence raises up such men as Caesar, Charlemagne, and Napoleon, it is to trace out for peoples the path they ought to follow; to stamp with the seal of their genius a new era; and to accomplish in a few years the labour of many centuries." [11] In other words, the aim of Louis Napoleon's historical writing was to give added proof to a theory of hero-worship, the "great-man" interpretation of history. "What is more erroneous," asked Louis Napoleon, "than not to recognize the preeminence of those privileged beings who appear in history from time to time like luminous beacons, dissipating the darkness of their epoch, and throwing light into the future." [12]

The importance of this theory to Louis Napoleon should not be underestimated, for it would provide a justification for the First and Second Empires. His fondest hopes—like those of his uncle, who was always conscious of his parvenu status—were to "legitimize" the usurpations of power by Napoleon I on the eighteenth of Brumaire and by Napoleon III on December 2, 1851. The success of the coups d'état resulted from the application of force or the threat of it. But the Bonapartes attempted to mask this fact by appeals to that amorphous quantity, the will of the people, which they then proceeded to count by means of plebiscitary devices. Yet was the will of the people exercised in conformity with any law? This is where the "great-man" theory of history applied. It furnished a legitimation to the Bonapartist regimes, because it introduced a force which transcended any possible man-made laws. Providence raises up these great men, and who would defy fate by failing to recognize such heroes? "Happy the peoples who comprehend and follow them! woe to those who misunderstand and combat them!" [13]

"But by what sign are we to recognize a man's greatness?" asks Louis Napoleon. "By the empire of his ideas, when his principles and his system triumph in spite of his death or defeat. . . . Caesar disappeared and his influence predominates still more than during his life." [14] It is easy enough to recognize a Caesar's pre-eminence in antiquity. But how

do we recognize a Caesar in the nineteenth century? Louis Napoleon
implies an answer to that question: he will always be called Napoleon!

Both Napoleonic regimes were based upon the principles of "Caesarism." As interpreted by Louis Napoleon, "Caesarism" stands for "democracy incarnated in one man, a national leader above classes and
parties, ruling 'by the grace of God and the will of the people,' pledged
to the protection of order, but not of privilege." [15] Louis Napoleon had
imposed this pattern upon the acts and alleged opinions of Napoleon I
in a book which he published in 1839, *Les Idées napoléoniennes*. This
provided the political philosophy for his interpretation of the First Empire as well as justification for his own Second Empire. These same
principles were restated in the preface to the Julius Caesar, and it may
be said that the entire biography of the Roman leader is a parable of
the Napoleonic ideas.

The life of Caesar, however, could provide more than a philosophical
justification for the regime of the two Napoleons. It furnished many
parallels in situation and personalities between the time of Caesar and
the times of the two Napoleons. The parallels had been openly avowed
by the Bonapartists, and their enemies were quick to see them and to
use them. Inasmuch as the despotic regimes of the two Napoleons did
not allow open criticism, any attacks on them had to be oblique. What
could be more useful than criticizing similar regimes in the past, with
the hope that the audience would detect the thinly veiled allusions?
Turn-about may be considered fair play in such a battle of wits; if the
critics of the Empire could attack it by castigating certain Roman figures
and developments, why could not the proponents of the Empire defend
it by upholding these same Romans? The biography of Julius Caesar
provided Napoleon III with an admirable opportunity for an apologia.

The self-justification which Louis Napoleon was trying to accomplish
through the medium of the biography of Caesar was done by identifying himself and his uncle with the Roman dictator. The analogy of
Napoleon Bonaparte to Julius Caesar was apparent when the Consulate
and First Empire were in existence, and the early life of Louis Napoleon
was reminiscent of that of Octavius, Caesar's nephew.[16] But the parallel
with Augustus broke down at the point where Louis Napoleon became
president of the Second Republic; hence it seemed more suitable for
Louis Napoleon to stretch for a comparison with Caesar. Julius Caesar
had had an uncle too, Caius Marius, and Louis Napoleon's interpretation

of Marius makes him almost a prototype of Napoleon I. Marius, a great warrior, is presented as an early champion of the people, possessing all the proper Caesarian ideas,[17] which he could not bring to fulfillment because of the machinations and conspiracies of his aristocratic opponents. It was under his nephew, Caesar, that these principles could be brought to their fruition.[18] Yet the analogy between Marius and Napoleon I is not maintained throughout the book. By and large, it can be said that the Emperor equates both Napoleons with Julius Caesar.

It required no wide stretch of the imagination to make the careers of Caesar and Louis Napoleon seem alike. The prince-president had early emphasized the parallel when he used the code-word "Rubicon" on the folder containing the plans and decrees for his coup d'état of December 2, 1851. Furthermore, the situation in France after the 1848 Revolution was in many respects similar to the party strife prevailing in Rome when Caesar seized power, and there were other possible similarities.

Perhaps the revival of parliamentary opposition in the 1860's made it seem imperative to Louis Napoleon that a political tract be written. The lesson which the Emperor thought the career of Caesar might teach was that parliamentary disputes and factionalism lead to civil strife. A strong hand is needed at the helm to guard the interests of the people. In ancient Rome, the strong hand had been Caesar's; in modern France, the strong hand had been that of Napoleon I and now was that of Napoleon III. Thus the political motivation was extremely important, and the character and quality of the biography as written by Louis Napoleon were in large measure determined by it.

The content was also affected by the way in which it was compiled. It is in his gathering of materials and writing that Louis Napoleon differs most from the usual writer of history. After all, many people besides emperors have written historical works in order to prove a thesis, so that Louis Napoleon was not traveling new paths. But, being an emperor, he had many more resources than the professional historian. As Emperor, he could command the talents of the best minds in France; he could afford the services of experts and scholars in many fields who would be anxious to serve him for either glory or reward. The resources of libraries and learned societies came to him, instead of his having to ferret out materials. With such resources at his disposal, we could expect him to have written a historical work which might well deserve the trite description "definitive."

Teachers of History

We who live in an age of the professional ghost writer might suspect that the Emperor would simply delegate the onerous tasks of research and writing to the savants who were anxious to do his bidding and merely sign his name to the completed product. That was not the case, even though the research and writing represented collaborative work to some degree. Louis Napoleon did use the findings, criticism, and advice of his helpers, but the final work bore the unmistakable stamp of his thoughts and his writing. No one has ever seriously suggested that his book, or even any portion of it, was another's. The only "ghost" that stalks the pages of the history of Julius Caesar is the ghost of Napoleon I.

Since the *Histoire de Jules César* was essentially the work of Louis Napoleon himself, it may be well to look at his ability and learning. A thorough study of ancient history would seem to demand proficiency in the classical languages, but there is some question about Louis' linguistic competence. According to his close friend, Madame Cornu, he could read Latin fluently and was not too bad at Greek.[19] Ollivier, however, states that the Emperor "was not a good enough Latinist to read the texts without a translation opposite."[20] Since translations were usually available and since he had the help of eminent scholars, perhaps it was unnecessary for Louis Napoleon to possess the competence in Latin and Greek which we expect of professional scholars.

In archaeology and historiography, Louis Napoleon was extremely naïve. Quite early in his research, however, he learned the limitations of the source material available. In the spring of 1860 he sent for Micheland, the librarian of the Bibliothèque Impériale, and asked him for all the "documents inédits" on Julius Caesar and Roman military affairs. When Micheland replied that there were none, the Emperor stated, "That is to say, none that you know of. But I hear that you have rooms full of manuscripts of the time of Julius Caesar and earlier, which your indolent academicians have not examined. The lost books of Livy's *Tacitus* are probably among them." When Micheland assured him that the Bibliothèque Impériale possessed no such treasures, the Emperor, still undaunted, said, "At least you must have plans of Roman fortresses and specimens of Roman engines of war?" Micheland informed him that these could be found on ancient bas-reliefs and on coins but were not among the resources of his library. However, the Emperor was not to be put off so lightly in his earnest quest for knowledge: "But there must be some in your illuminated manuscripts." Imagine his disappointment when Micheland told him that such manuscripts all dated from the Middle Ages.[21]

But if the Emperor did not approach the subject with vast historiographical knowledge, he possessed an enthusiasm that made him exhaust all available sources. His two volumes are filled with references to the works of Livy, Strabo, Polybius, Plutarch, Cicero, Appian, Diodorus Siculus, Suetonius, Sallust, Dio Cassius, Asconius, and, of course, the works of Caesar himself.

Not being an archaeologist or classical scholar, Napoleon was also forced to rely a great deal upon secondary works. But here there were some curious gaps in his knowledge. For one thing, he remained almost unaware of the work of scholars outside of France. Although this was the era when Niebuhr and Mommsen were revolutionizing the scientific study of antiquity, Louis Napoleon rarely refers to their works or to those of Merivale, the foremost English classicist of the period. The Emperor was aware of Mommsen's existence, for he had corresponded with him, had opened the libraries of France to him, and had contributed money for publication of research by Mommsen's students. There was even a rumor that Mommsen had contributed in some way to Louis Napoleon's history of Caesar, and that he had received a pension of ten thousand francs for so doing, but this rumor was untrue.[22] Yet Mommsen got only a casual footnote in the first volume of the *Histoire de Jules César*, and in the second volume Louis Napoleon had no qualms about disagreeing with the great German scholar in a lengthy footnote. It must be admitted, however, that on this occasion he relied upon the work of another German scholar, Zumpt.[23] There was one German scholar, however, to whom Napoleon made constant reference. General von Göler had published portions of his work on the military aspects of Caesar's career,[24] and Napoleon used him as a "whipping boy," setting up Göler's ideas and then demolishing them.

How are we to account for Napoleon's ignorance or avoidance of English and German works? Language was no barrier, since he was extremely well-versed in both, having been brought up on German as a boy and having spent much time as Pretender in England. Perhaps national pride prevented Louis Napoleon from paying much attention to non-French works. But Napoleon III was so international in his outlook that such a judgment may be unfair. Perhaps the blame for this neglect of foreign scholarship should be placed at the door of the French savants who guided his research, and the charge of nationalism may best be leveled at them.

By neglecting the work of foreign scholars, Louis Napoleon did diminish somewhat the quality of his historical performance, but not as much as might be expected. Much good work in the field of antiquity was being done in France; hence the Emperor was not divorced from all the latest results of historical research. For example, in dealing with the state of Gaul in the time of Caesar and the political causes of the Gallic Wars,[25] Louis Napoleon leaned heavily on Amédée Thierry's *History of the Gauls*, without, however, giving any special credit to him. Nevertheless, Thierry's work was the best on that subject then available.

In the field of archaeology, Napoleon III made full use of the latest findings. Perhaps the question of nationalism did not enter here, for, after all, the Gallic Wars were in France, and here French scholars dominated. Napoleon, despite his unfamiliarity with the subject, patronized archaeology and archaeologists. He subsidized excavations at the points where Caesar's legions were said to have pitched camp and at ancient battlegrounds. The excavations of most interest to him were those at Puy d'Issole in 1865 to uncover the ancient site of Uxellodunum,[26] and those around Mont Auxois from 1862 to 1865 to describe with great exactitude the siege of Alesia.[27] This ability to utilize the resources of a great state for his private research allowed the Emperor to make discoveries and collect material in a way that no private person could.

His exalted position also gave Louis Napoleon the opportunity to call on the greatest authorities in France to assist him. He had a corps of what we in modern American university life would call "research assistants" to furnish him with information and documentation. These men were all professional scholars and occupied important positions. Napoleon III collected an amazing variety of specialists: epigraphers, military tacticians, naval architects, archaeologists, numismatists, astronomers, ballistic experts, cartographers, military engineers, as well as poets and novelists, plus some general secretarial and editorial helpers. He gave credit to his assistants, carefully noting their contributions in appropriate footnotes.

The Emperor was so anxious to get the best possible assistants that he did not care about their political opinions, and the scholars and specialists did not have to be supporters of the Empire. Albert Maury, for example, had voted for Cavaignac against Louis Napoleon in 1848 and had voted *no* in the plebiscite, but this did not keep the Emperor from making him his chief collaborator. Although he did acquire a personal liking for the Emperor, working with Napoleon did not make Maury change his political ideas.[28]

How did Napoleon choose his helpers? Some were already in the imperial service, as either officials of the University, state librarians, or members of the armed forces. Since he had merely to command, there was no difficulty about their service. Others, however, Louis Napoleon knew only by reputation, and intermediaries had to sound them out on the possibilities of giving assistance to the imperial historian. However, Napoleon III could not be expected to be familiar with specialists in all branches of knowledge, and these were called to his attention by others.

His chief intermediary, or "recruiting officer," was Madame Hortense Cornu, a childhood playmate and the daughter of one of the ladies-in-waiting to Queen Hortense. In appearance, she "resembled one of the witches from *Macbeth*," [29] but she had a first-class mind and was a devoted friend and advisor of Louis Napoleon. When he had been imprisoned at Ham, Madame Cornu had helped him with his writing, at the same time keeping him in touch with the leading members of the democratic party. The coup d'état of 1851 had destroyed her faith in Louis Napoleon, and she broke off all relations with him. However, the war against Austria in behalf of Italian nationalism removed her previous animosity toward the Empire, and when Napoleon III asked her to help him on his life of Caesar, she responded enthusiastically.[30] Not only did she herself assist in some of the research, but she suggested other collaborators for the Emperor. Chief among these was Albert Maury.

A member of the Académie des Inscriptions et Belles-Lettres, Albert Maury was a classical scholar already well known for his erudition and his writings. Although he was opposed to the Empire, Madame Cornu did not hesitate to recommend him to Louis. The Emperor showed Maury some of his material and asked for candid criticism. Maury said that it was well done, although incomplete, and frankly pointed out those parts which he thought required further attention.[31] Napoleon was pleased and appointed Maury librarian of the Tuileries, surely a sinecure, since there was no library there. Maury was simply to assist the Emperor. Maury's work on the history consisted of numerous details: he looked up dates, fixed geographical locations, rummaged through libraries for additional material, and helped in the editing by grammatical or literary criticism and by proofreading.[32]

Through Maury, Victor Duruy became involved in the project. Duruy had been an outstanding student and teacher of history, and his book, *Histoire des Romains*, had won him international acclaim. The Emperor had read his book, and Marshal Randon, a friend of Duruy's, had arranged an audience with Napoleon III in 1859.[33] Nothing came of this audience, but in February, 1862, probably at the suggestion of Maury, Napoleon III wrote to Duruy asking him for his opinion of an historical generalization which had caught the imperial fancy, namely, that the greatness of a man of genius can be measured by the duration of his influence on the world. Duruy was quick to rise to the bait. He dashed off a 2,500-word letter to the Emperor the next day in which he agreed completely with the Emperor's thesis and went into great detail to prove it. In November, 1862, the Emperor got in touch with Duruy again, and then the latter began several months of assisting Napoleon in writing his history. Duruy describes his work on the life of Caesar as one of "reading proof and making a few observations here and there."[34]

Not all these observations agreed with Louis Napoleon's opinions; Duruy objected to the theory of providential men and to the Emperor's treatment of Caesar's part in the Catilinian conspiracy as unhistorical and merely an attempt to justify the coup d'état of 1851, of which Duruy had disapproved.[35] This frankness did not harm him, for his reward was the post of minister of instruction. In this office he made a great contribution to French education, modernizing the whole educational system and restoring the University to a position of prestige.

Another of the more important assistants of Louis Napoleon was Commandant Baron Stoffel, an artillery officer in the Imperial Army. The Emperor sent him around the countryside to follow the itinerary of Caesar and his troops and to check on the campsites and battlegrounds.[36] Commandant Stoffel was well suited by his artillery experience for the task. Stoffel was rewarded by being made military attaché in Berlin, where he functioned from 1866 to 1870. He distinguished himself in that post by writing a series of reports in which he continually and correctly warned against the growing military might of the Prussians. It was Stoffel, incidentally, who continued Napoleon III's work by writing the military history of Caesar's civil wars.[37]

There were others whose services the Emperor used. Le Verrier, for example, determined the concordance between the ante-Julian calendar and the Julian calendar for the years of Rome 691–709, and the lengthy tables in which he established the concordance were appended to Napoleon's *History*.[38] The Emperor corresponded with a certain M. E. Celesia, who was preparing a work on ancient Italy, in order to determine the location of Ocelum.[39] Cessac's excavations at Puy d'Issolu were watched closely by Napoleon,[40] and he also sent Commandant Locquessye to explore the areas around Mount Falhize and Namur in order to find out where the *oppidum* of the Aduatuci was located.[41] Other staff officers found themselves locating the battlesites of the first century B.C. instead of preparing for those of 1870.[42] Napoleon even employed the services of a Prussian major, Von Cohausen, who shared his interest in the battlegrounds of antiquity,[43] and located the spots where Caesar had wintered his troops after their return from Britain.

This by no means exhausts the list of those who assisted the Emperor, to a greater or lesser degree. The epigrapher Renier did research at the Vatican, and Renan poked around in the Imperial Library for additional material.[44] Caignart de Saulcy and Prévost de Longerier did additional archaeological research, and Colonel Reyffye attempted to reconstitute the ballistics of the ancients.[45] These official assistants were aided by a host of unofficial and self-appointed experts and authorities who came forward to offer their services and pet theories as soon as it became known that the Emperor had embarked on historical researches.

The whole court reflected the Emperor's interest in Roman history. Chamberlains and ladies-in-waiting began studying ancient history and were soon talking about Caesar, Cicero, and Catiline with as much authority as they talked about Garibaldi or Cavour or Victor Emmanuel. Elaborate arguments were held, in which the Empress declared herself against Catiline, while the Emperor spoke for him.[46] In the park of Saint-Cloud, experiments were conducted on firing javelins by means of catapults;[47] Admiral Jurien de la Gravière directed the construction of a Roman trireme, which remained immobile at Asnières because no oarsmen could move it.[48] The autumn theatrical performance in 1865 at the imperial house party at Compiègne, written by the Marquis Philippe de Massa, was entitled *Les Commentaires de César,* and it was so successful that it was played at Compiègne on two successive evenings and was revived, with some additions, at the Paris Exhibition of 1867, before an audience of kings.[49]

The actual composition of the history was normally as follows: [50] Maury usually prepared a rough outline and classification of the Emperor's notes collected from the various specialists. The Emperor then dictated a first draft to his secretary Mocquard. Mocquard and Maury then checked and edited this draft, making grammatical corrections and polishing the style. Oftentimes Mérimée, the one literary figure of consequence who had been attached to the imperial cause from the beginning, wrote some preliminary notes or did some final polishing. Napoleon frequently tested the manuscript before he was satisfied. He would have Duruy read portions of it, for example, or he would read sections of it to members of the Institute whom he invited to dinner.[51] It is obvious, then, that from start to finish, from the initial research through the final readying of the manuscript for publication, Napoleon had capable assistance from specialists of the top rank.

With so much editing and polishing of phrases, it might be expected that the style of the book would either be cramped or laden with purple rhetoric. That is not the case. Despite some adverse criticism to the effect that the Emperor had "little ear for beauty of cadence, and little appreciation of neatness of diction," [52] the work is written in the style which Louis Napoleon employed in his previous literary endeavors. The Emperor did not stoop to rhetorical devices, and although there is an occasional striving for epigrams, these do not come off very well, and the style remains simple and concise—and nothing more. Certainly the style does not warrant the glowing praise poured on it by courtiers anxious to please or by admirers of the Emperor who saw in it "perfection of choice of words and simplicity." [53] Napoleon III could not turn a phrase like his uncle Napoleon I. The most that can be said for the style is that it is unnoticeable; it does not get in the way of the ideas. It is clear, straightforward—and dull.

Once the work had been edited and polished it was ready for the publisher. Despite a joking rumor that "though the Emperor could command some fifty legions, he could not command a publisher," [54] there was little difficulty. Not only did the Emperor find a French publisher, Henri Plon, but arrangements were made for translations and the publication of English, American, German, Italian, Portuguese, Russian, Danish, Norwegian, Swedish, and Hungarian editions. The translations sometimes did violence to the Emperor's prose; the English translation, for example, was stilted, perhaps because the translator endeavored to use a more imperial style than the author himself had employed. The first volume was published in 1865 and the second volume and atlas were published the following year. The atlas was a handsome job, containing thirty-two plates, showing the maps of Caesar's Gallic campaigns, plans of battles, and details of the Roman military works.

The outline of the history is interesting, for it is much more than a biography of Caesar. As a matter of fact, the book never reached the death of Caesar. Volume II ends with Caesar ready to cross the Rubicon; a third volume, including an index, was contemplated, but it remained for Colonel Stoffel to complete the work after the downfall and death of the Emperor. By stopping at the Rubicon, Napoleon III was, of course, able to avoid the embarrassing question of the assassination of Caesar, which might have suggested dangerous ideas to those who disapproved of the later Caesar.

Nor did the volumes begin with the birth of Caesar. The work was divided into four books, and Caesar did not appear on the scene until Book II, some three hundred pages after the beginning. The first volume was prefaced by a programmatic statement in which Napoleon enunciated his purpose and gave his version of the "great-man" theory of history. Book I is a general outline of Roman history until the appearance of Caesar, although it does not start with the legendary founding of Rome, but rather with the founding of the Roman institutions by the kings. In Book II Caesar makes his appearance but can hardly be said to be the main actor. More attention is paid to the political milieu than to Caesar himself, although he gradually becomes more prominent as he takes a more active role in the main events of the period. This book carries the story to the point where Caesar assumes the government of Gaul.

The entire second volume deals with the Gallic Wars and contains Books III and IV, although the arrangement is a curious one. Book III is an account of the Gallic Wars, closely following Caesar's *Commen-*

taries. The campaigns are described in detail, but no attention is paid to the contemporaneous political developments in Rome. Book IV starts the Gallic Wars all over again, but now an attempt is made to incorporate the political happenings in Rome and explain why Caesar was led to cross the Rubicon, the point at which Book IV ends. Volume II includes four appendixes: the lengthy concordance of dates of the ancient Roman calendar with the Julian calendar for the years of Rome 691–709; a concordance of Roman and modern hours for the year of Rome 699 (55 B.C.); a list of ancient coins found in the excavations at Alise; and a series of notes on Caesar's lieutenants.

Although the arrangement of Books III and IV is strange, it has the merit of separating the serious historical scholarship from the political propaganda which characterizes Books I, II, and IV. It was for Book III that the Emperor tore staff officers away from their desk jobs in Paris and sent them to dig in the tumuli of ancient Gaul. To fix the exact dates and times of Caesar's campaigns for this same book, the modern Caesar utilized astronomers, oceanographers, and other scientists. In other words, Book III contains the results of the work of many specialists, and is a real attempt to verify the historical data of the *Commentaries.*

Pursuing this method, the Emperor caused every place of note mentioned by Caesar to be explored by his military engineers and archaeological assistants, and in many cases they succeeded in identifying sites whose locations had been in doubt. For example, Louis Napoleon described in detail the entrenchments with which Caesar barred the Rhône passage to the Helvetii,[55] found the place on the Saône where Caesar defeated the Helvetii,[56] and fixed the location of Bibracte at Mont Beuvray, near Autun.[57] Another striking example of this collation of archaeological fieldwork with Caesar's text is shown in the excavations made at Puy d'Issolu in 1865 which "leave no further doubt as to the site of Uxellodunum." [58]

The results of this type of research are best stated by Louis Napoleon himself:

The investigation of the Battle-fields and siege operations has led to the discovery of visible and certain traces of the Roman entrenchments. The reader, by comparing the plans of the excavations (in the Atlas) with the text, will be convinced of the rigorous accuracy of Caesar in describing the countries he passed over, and the works he caused to be executed.[59]

Although Book III represents the serious historical contribution, this does not mean that the other three books are not scholarly. Throughout the Emperor employs all the apparatus of scholarship, including voluminous footnotes. Unfortunately, he does not list the editions of the works which he consulted, so that it is impossible to check all the footnotes. However, those footnotes which can be checked are absolutely correct, and it may be assumed that the remainder are. If there was one thing in which the Emperor had capable assistance, it was in the checking of his footnotes.

The close examination of the *Commentaries* in Book III did not lend itself to the editorializing which was so important an element in the other three books. Books I, II, and IV gave the author an opportunity to deliver himself of *obiter dicta* in regard to many of the problems which faced him. For example, the Emperor's discussion of the economic life and prosperity of the Mediterranean basin before the Punic Wars permitted him to express his desire for a peaceful solution of the Eastern Question in his own time.[60] Also, the Roman Question—the perplexing problem of papal temporal power in the nineteenth century—was a troublesome one for the diplomacy of the Second Empire, and Louis Napoleon could not let it pass unnoticed when dealing with Roman questions of two thousand years earlier. He noted that in antiquity the world "preferred the protecting sovereignty of Rome to independence itself," while in his own day "all nations execrate the power of Rome," and yet he recognized that "that power preserves them from still greater evils." [61] Similarly, Napoleon III's consideration of the War of the Allies allowed him to expound one of his pet ideas, namely, the principle of nationalities,[62] and Caesar's treatment of the Helvetii enabled the Emperor to remark how important it was for Switzerland in his own time to remain independent.[63]

But it is in discussing the political situation in Rome which eventually "forced" Caesar to seize power that the Emperor makes the case for himself, or rather, for Caesar. The situation in Rome when Caesar first makes his entrance on the political scene is described in dark colors of political corruption and party strife.[64] A strong man was needed to set things straight. "That man was Caesar." [65]

Caesar, acting as if he were guided by Louis Napoleon's interpretation of the Napoleonic legend, was not "the man of a party," but represented all citizens.[66] Luckily, the people recognized this.[67] This reliance upon the people, rather than parties or parliamentary institutions, was one of the foundations of Napoleonic doctrine, and provided the basis for the characteristic political device of the plebiscite. And the attack upon the aristocratic party which opposed Caesar [68] could also be interpreted as an attack upon the Bourbons who opposed Napoleon I and the Legitimists and Orleanists who opposed Napoleon III.

Discussion of the Senate's opposition to Caesar, Louis Napoleon hoped, would justify his own conduct vis-à-vis the Assembly of the Second Republic. In case the reader were unable to see the parallel implicit in the text,[69] the Emperor made it explicit in a footnote:

At all times the assemblies have been striving to shorten the duration of the powers given by the people to a man whose sympathies were not with them. Here is an example. The Constitution of 1848 decided that the President of the French Republic should be named for four years. The Prince Louis Napoleon was elected on the 10th of December, 1848, and proclaimed on the 20th of the same month. His powers ought to have ended on the 20th of December, 1852. Now, the Constituent Assembly, which foresaw the election of Prince Louis Napoleon, fixed the termination of the presidency to the second Sunday of the month of May, 1852, thus robbing him of seven months.[70]

The role of Caesar with respect to the Roman Republic is the same as the Bonapartist interpretation of the role of the two Napoleons during the First and Second French Republics, namely, to save the Republic from anarchy by substituting an energetic authority for parliamentary strife.[71] The aristocratic party had placed itself above the law, "and placed right on the side of Caesar." [72] In this "decisive conflict between two hostile causes, between the privileged classes and the people," Caesar, as the representative of the people, is driven to forceful measures.[73] Even though he must always undergo the calumny of his enemies,[74] he puts an end to anarchy and arises as "the indispensable pilot" to restore liberty and order.[75]

Garbing Caesar in Bonapartist dress is both the merit and the defect of Napoleon III's *History of Julius Caesar*. It has the merit of giving us a glimpse into the mind of the French Emperor; it has the defect of preventing us from taking a good look at the Roman dictator. The book was written to fit a thesis, and Louis Napoleon tended to disregard or to twist the facts which did not fit his theory. The effectiveness of the work as political propaganda for the Bonapartist regime rests on an identification of Caesar with the two Napoleons. Hence, the history necessarily represents a whitewash of Caesar.

Caesar can do no wrong. Napoleon III makes this obvious at the very beginning of the work when he deprecates those historians who have attempted to diminish the stature of his great man, accusing them of lacking "good sense" and of arriving at "erroneous" conclusions.[76] In Louis Napoleon's book, Caesar emerges from the Catilinian Conspiracy completely innocent.[77] He is always "animated by a single motive, the public interest."[78] His vices, as in the affair with King Nicomedes of Bithynia, are hidden. Napoleon III shows Caesar as "aspiring with a noble ambition to power and honours," but he is "not ignorant that historians in general give other motives for his conduct."[79] The Emperor belittles such historians and their "other motives," saying, "Let us not continually seek little passions in great souls."[80]

It is not enough that Caesar be whitewashed and elevated. His contemporaries must be blackened, and oftentimes Catiline, Cato, Cicero, Crassus, Pompey, and other important figures are presented as mere caricatures. Only when these men are performing an act which assists Caesar in his rise to power are they acting correctly; otherwise, their careers are represented as a series of grave and continued mistakes.

Yet even the hero, Caesar himself, can be criticized. Although Caesar can do no wrong, he is not above reproach—*if* the reproach has already been delivered by the Emperor Napoleon I. In his *Outline of the Wars of Caesar,* Napoleon I had presented a picture of Caesar not unlike that drawn by his nephew. But Napoleon Bonaparte had ventured to criticize Caesar for his massacre of the principal citizens of Morbihan, despite their submission to him. Louis Napoleon, the heir to the Napoleonic tradition, dutifully follows his uncle in criticizing Caesar for this action.[81]

Indeed as a devoted nephew should, Louis Napoleon follows Napoleon I on any statement which the latter made regarding Caesar. Napoleon I had called a "fable" the story that Catiline wanted to burn Rome and give it up to pillage in order to rule over the ruined city afterward. Napoleon III agrees.[82] Napoleon I had analyzed the principal cause of the weakness of Gaul "as the spirit of isolation and locality which characterized the population." Napoleon III agrees.[83] Napoleon I had said that on Caesar's first descent into Britain he embarked from Boulogne and landed at Deal. Napoleon III agrees and goes to great lengths to prove that it must be so.[84] This blind obedience to the *obiter dicta* of Napoleon I is indicative, of course, of the major flaw in Napoleon III's work as history. A great portion of it is propaganda disguised as serious and scholarly history. All the facts are interpreted, rightly or wrongly, to fulfill the author's purpose of building up a predetermined picture of Caesar. To the extent that historical data are perverted in order to cast the most favorable light upon Caesar's actions, it is poor history.

The reception given the two volumes is indicative of the fact that the book was dualistic in nature, representing both a study of ancient history and current political propaganda. Naturally, the publication aroused great interest, for it was not every day that an emperor attempted to write a serious historical work. Some political observers sought for hidden significance in the fact that the two volumes were published when they were, in March of 1865 and May of 1866. Was the Emperor trying to cover up his aggressive intentions by pretending that he had been too busy on his writing to concern himself with political plotting? Or, was he merely trying to establish in the eyes of the public that he was essentially a peaceful man and had no thought of war? Actually, no sinister political calculations were involved.[85] Louis Napoleon had been writing a *History of Julius Caesar* in two volumes; as he completed each volume he published it, and that is all there was to it. Indeed, if there is any significance to the appearance of the volumes at this time, it would appear that they were very ill timed, for the outcome of the impending duel between Austria and Prussia indicated that the Emperor of the French might well have applied his mind more fruitfully to matters other than writing.

If there were no political considerations involved in the time chosen for publication, there might be some significant political implications in the work itself. Hence, the politicians and diplomats studied the book carefully, thinking that it might give them some guide to the future actions of the Emperor. Strangely enough, Napoleon III, his motives, and his policy were regarded as enigmatic by his contemporaries, and it was hoped that this book would shed some light which might help resolve the enigma. Yet few rulers have been more articulate than Napoleon III in explaining their political philosophy. His *Histoire de Jules César* adds nothing new to his basic political ideas as expressed in the *Idées napoléoniennes*. It merely reinforces those notions and shows how they fit into his interpretation of the events of 1851. As an expression of the hidden political designs of the Emperor, the history of Julius Caesar offered nothing new; it was merely more of the same.

The volumes on Julius Caesar did, however, give the public an opportunity to praise or deride the Emperor. This praise or derision was, in large measure, independent of the merit of the Emperor's *History of Julius Caesar* and was a function of how the readers felt regarding Napoleon III himself. Their minds were made up before they read the volumes—if they bothered to read them at all.

As might be expected, the French journalists were extravagant in their praise. Phrases such as "nobility of thought," "beauty of form," "depth of view," and other clichés of the reviewer's trade were frequently used. Although the closely supervised press of the Second Empire did not allow a free expression of opinion, *La France,* a paper subsidized by the imperial government, had stated that "the utmost latitude" would be given for criticism. One critic took this seriously and found himself under arrest.[86] Most reviewers were careful to review the censorship situation before they reviewed the book; the result was a chorus of approval.

In addition to the writers for the journals, many private individuals— prominent French and foreign literary men and political figures—were honored with presentation copies by the Emperor. The Emperor also bestowed the book on especially favored persons who had performed some service for him. A deluge of flattering letters thereupon descended on the Emperor's private office.[87]

Some fulsome praise even came from scholarly circles, but as Guedalla points out, not all of it was motivated by a sincere interest in scholarly work:

All Germany, the international, scholarly Germany of 1866 whose arid ingenuity lies embalmed in the *apparatus criticus* of every classic, poured its gratitude into the Tuileries letter-bag, and from the Emperor's correspondence it almost seemed as though Europe from the Rhine to the Russian frontier was populated by an impecunious race of scholars animated by a single ambition to possess (without paying for it) a copy of his book.[88]

Praise from scholarly circles in France was also forthcoming. Only the most naïve would have been surprised at the compliments which

Victor Duruy lavished; [89] after all, Duruy had been one of the Emperor's assistants and a beneficiary of imperial rewards.

But some praise came from unexpected quarters. George Sand, although of strong republican sympathies and *ipso facto* expected to disapprove of any work bearing the name of Napoleon, nevertheless praised it highly, calling it: "without defect as a literary work . . . marvelously clear . . . eminent work . . . talented execution . . . filled with elevated sentiments . . . will tend to raise the level of ideas." When her republican friends were scandalized by this apparent defection, she reassured them that she had only been approving of the book, but that did not mean that she approved of Caesar. Furthermore, she predicted that the book would meet with little success.[90]

Yet, even in France, not everyone was enthusiastic, although the criticism did not find its way into print. A revealing incident in this connection occurred to Sainte-Beuve, the premier literary critic of France. It was highly desirable that Sainte-Beuve should bestow his accolade upon the Emperor's work. But Saint-Beuve refused to review the *Julius Caesar*. When Limayrac, editor of *Le Constitutionnel,* asked for a review of the book, saying that he had promised it to one of the Emperor's secretaries—an example of unsubtle pressure exercised by the imperial subordinates—Sainte-Beuve burst out:

> Do you want me to dishonor myself? . . . I am not free to speak of this book in *Le Constitutionnel* as I should like to: it is a book which has merit only in the documents furnished it by scholars. If you will let me argue against the theory of providential men, with which the author is enticed; if you will let me tell about . . . the vices of Caesar . . . I shall write the article.[91]

Professional historical scholars in France were circumspect in their criticisms. Writing in the *Revue des Questions Historiques,* C. Rossigneux ventured to disagree with the Emperor's location of Bibracte on Mont Beuvray. But Rossigneux first paid his respects to Napoleon III's history as possessing "real merit"; the misplaced location of Bibracte, Rossigneux said, was due to "faulty information" supplied the Emperor by one of his military assistants.[92] The work of the Emperor in fixing the location of many of the camps and battles of Caesar did not go unchallenged by some French scholars, however, and there was a small flurry of pamphlets in academic circles dealing with the location of Alesia and Uxellodunum. Some of these gave further proof of Louis

Napoleon's statements, and others ventured to disagree, but without directly quarreling with the Emperor's work.[93]

Criticism in foreign countries was not so easy to control as in France, although attempts were made. For example, Drouhyn de Lhuys, the foreign minister, asked all French representatives in the German states to try to prevent the circulation there of a libelous book published in Hamburg in 1865, *Les Propos de Labienus,* which had obviously been inspired by the Emperor's *Histoire de Jules César.*[94] In the case of a pamphlet published in Berlin entitled *La Vie du Nouveau César,* the foreign minister did succeed in getting the author prosecuted.[95]

In England we find the freest criticism of the book. By 1865 the salad days of Anglo-French co-operation were over, and many Englishmen had regained their suspicions of an Emperor bearing the name of Napoleon. Hence, the Emperor's work was treated rather roughly by many English reviewers. Since they did not sympathize with the doctrine of providential men as exemplified by Caesar and the two Napoleons, they quarreled with the author's basic philosophy of history. Nevertheless, most of them were willing to grant some merit to Napoleon III's investigations of an archaeological and military nature regarding Caesar's campaigns.[96]

The brief flurry in political and intellectual circles aroused by the Emperor's book was soon over. Most of the popular interest in the work had been caused by the Emperor's having written it, not because the public was avid for a new treatment of the life of Julius Caesar. The only portion of the work which created any excitement whatsoever was the Preface, in which Louis Napoleon had stated his philosophy of history and equated Caesar and Napoleon, speaking of both of them as messiahs who had been crucified by a public which did not appreciate them. The body of the work—and the solid historical scholarship that had gone into it—interested only a small group of specialists who were concerned with the minutiae of Roman history.

As a work of propaganda, then, Napoleon III's *Histoire de Jules César* was a failure. It convinced only those who were already confirmed Bonapartists or who wanted to be. Emile Ollivier, for example, wanted to be convinced of the Emperor's goodness and greatness, and he read into it indications that the Empire was turning to more liberal policies.[97]

If the work was intended to give the Emperor sufficient stature and prestige as an intellectual and scholar to earn him admission to the Academy, it also failed. As a matter of fact, the chair of J. J. Ampère, who had written on Roman history, was vacant at the time. The Emperor might well have hoped for election to this vacant chair. But the Academicians were almost impertinent, for they selected Prévost-Paradol, an opponent of the Empire and one who could be counted on to speak disparagingly of Caesar in the course of his remarks eulogizing his predecessor.

If the *History of Julius Caesar* was supposed to furnish some evidence of the way the Empire was going, it was a complete failure. In the 1860's the Second Empire was supposedly evolving in the direction of liberalism. A history of Julius Caesar, a man who destroyed a parliamentary body and instituted a dictatorship, can hardly be said to have been appropriate—if liberalization were really the aim of the Emperor. Indeed, it might lead one to have some doubts regarding the sincerity of Napoleon's restoration of parliamentary practices, especially when one reads his strictures against the factious strife of the Roman Senate.

In the final analysis, the work of Louis Napoleon was a history book, and should be judged on its merits as a work of history. As such, it was uneven. The parts dealing with political developments were slanted to fit the Emperor's thesis and provide justification for his own conduct. They present a better picture of Napoleon III than of Caesar. The commentaries on Caesar's military expeditions in Gaul, however, represented a tremendous quantity of scientific research done by specialists of various sorts, and this portion was a real contribution to history. Indeed, the best recent biographer of Caesar refers to Napoleon III's work as "the first serious study of Caesar to appear in France." [98] It might thus be said that the Emperor did make a real contribution to historical literature.

Yet, when all is said and done, the Emperor's contribution to ancient history was a type of scholarship which was important in the nineteenth century and which is now dead. Our insight into Roman history and the character of Julius Caesar is not affected one whit by all the work of the Emperor and his scholarly and famed assistants. All he did, historiographically speaking, was to help establish the times and places of Caesar's campaigns in Gaul. If this is all that remains of that vast expenditure of time, money, and effort, we are tempted to agree with the statement of the Count de Vielcastel regarding the Emperor's entrance into the field of historical writing: [99] "Reign, Sovereigns, that should be your trade!"

1. The research upon which this article is based was made possible by a grant-in-aid from the Social Science Research Council and a Sherman Pratt Faculty Fellowship from Amherst College.

2. *Memoirs of Count Horace de Vielcastel*, edited by Charles Bousfield (London, 1888), II, 289.

3. Emile Ollivier, *L'Empire libéral* (Paris, 1900), V, 77.

4. Philip Guedalla, *The Second Empire* (New York, 1922), p. 299; Ollivier, *op. cit.*, V, 68.

5. René Arnaud, *La Deuxième République et le Second Empire* (Paris, 1929), p. 280; Robert Sencourt, *Napoleon III, the Modern Emperor* (London, 1933), p. 254.

6. Charles Seignobos, *Le Déclin de l'Empire et l'établissement de la 3ᵉ République, 1859–1875* (Vol. VII of Ernest Lavisse, *Histoire de France contemporaine*) (Paris, 1921), p. 3.

7. Nassau William Senior, *Conversations with M. Thiers, M. Guizot, and Other Distinguished Persons during the Second Empire* (London, 1878), II, 316.

8. *Recollections and Letters of Ernest Renan* (New York, 1892), p. 225.

9. Edward Legge, *The Comedy and Tragedy of the Second Empire* (London, 1911), p. 58.

10. Emperor Napoleon III, *History of Julius Caesar* (New York, 1865–1866), II, iii–v. All references are to the American edition unless otherwise stated. This work will henceforth be referred to as *J. C.*

11. *Ibid.*, I, xiv.

12. *Ibid.*, I, xii.

13. *Ibid.*, I, xiv–xv.

14. *Ibid.*, I, xiv.

15. Albert Guérard, *Napoleon III* (Cambridge, Mass., 1943), p. xvii.

16. See *The Southern Quarterly Review*, XXVI (July, 1854), 1–37.

17. *J. C.*, I, Book I, Chapter 6.

18. *Ibid.*, I, 336–337.

19. Senior, *op. cit.*, II, 316.

20. Ollivier, *op. cit.*, V, 69.

21. Senior, *op. cit.*, II, 316–317.

22. Ollivier, *op. cit.*, V, 74 n.

23. *J. C.*, II, 542 n.

24. The complete work, *Caesars gallischer Krieg und Theile seines Bürgerkrieges nebst Anhängen über das römische Kriegswesen und über römische Daten*, was published in two volumes at Tübingen in 1880.

25. *J. C.*, II, Book III, Chapters 1, 2.

26. *Ibid.*, II, 390–395.

27. *Ibid.*, II, 339–366.

28. Ollivier, *op. cit.*, V, 71–72.

29. *Ibid.*, V, 69.

30. Ernest A. Vizetelly (Le Petit Homme Rouge), *The Court of the Tuileries, 1852–1870* (London, 1912), pp. 153–154.

31. Senior, *op. cit.*, p. 316.

32. Ollivier, *op. cit.*, V, 72.

33. Victor Duruy, *Notes et souvenirs, 1811–1894* (Paris, 1901), I, 108–110.

34. *Ibid.*, I, 183.

35. *Ibid.*, I, 183–184.

36. *J. C.*, II, 54 n–59 n; 305 n; 338 n.

37. Colonel Stoffel, *Histoire de Jules César, Guerre Civile* (Paris, 1887).

38. *J. C.*, II, Appendix A, pp. 595–637.

39. *Ibid.*, II, 61 n.

40. *Ibid.*, II, 392 n.

41. *Ibid.*, II, 129 n.

42. *Ibid.*, II, 285 n.

43. *Ibid.*, II, 155 n.

44. *Ibid.*, II, 225 n.

45. Jules Bertaut, *Napoléon III Secret* (Paris, 1939), p. 186.

46. Vizetelly, *op. cit.*, p. 48.

47. Ollivier, *op. cit.*, V, 68–69.

48. Maxime du Camp, *Souvenirs d'un demi-siècle, au temps de Louis-Philippe et de Napoléon III, 1830–1870*, 24th ed. (Paris, 1949), I, 139–140.

49. Comte de Maugny, *Souvenirs of the Second Empire* (London, n.d.), pp. 70–71, 75–84.

50. Du Camp, *op. cit.*, I, 139–140; Aubry, *op. cit.*, p. 318; Bertaut, *op. cit.*, p. 186; Ollivier, *op. cit.*, V, 72–73.

51. Vizetelly, *op. cit.*, p. 138.

52. *The Edinburgh Review*, CXXIV (October, 1866), 205.

53. Ollivier, *op. cit.*, VII, 311.

54. *British Quarterly Review*, XLI (April, 1865), 495.

55. *J. C.*, II, 53–59.

56. *Ibid.*, II, 65 n.

57. *Ibid.*, II, 72–76.

58. *Ibid.*, II, 390.

59. *Ibid.*, II, 13–14.

60. *Ibid.*, I, 154.

61. *Ibid.*, II, 405.

62. *Ibid.*, I, 256.

63. *Ibid.*, II, 405.

64. *Ibid.*, I, 314.

65. *Ibid.*, I, 278–280.

66. *Ibid.*, I, 305.
67. *Ibid.*, I, 332.
68. *Ibid.*, II, 535–536, 541.
69. For an example of this, see *J. C.*, I, 384.
70. *Ibid.*, II, 545 n.
71. *Ibid.*, I, 453; II, 487, 501.
72. *Ibid.*, II, 578.
73. *Ibid.*, II, 590–592.
74. *Ibid.*, I, 448.
75. *Ibid.*, II, 593–594.
76. *Ibid.*, I, xii.
77. *Ibid.*, I, 357–379.
78. *Ibid.*, I, 444.
79. *Ibid.*, II, 460.
80. *Ibid.*, I, 463.
81. *Ibid.*, II, 447.
82. *Ibid.*, I, 379 n.
83. *Ibid.*, II, 46–47.
84. *Ibid.*, II, 186–202.
85. Ollivier, *op. cit.*, VIII, 134.
86. *The Christian Observer*, Sept., 1865 (London), pp. 680–681.
87. Vizetelly, *op. cit.*, p. 146; Guedalla, *op. cit.*, p. 338; Frédéric Loliée, *Le Duc de Morny et la Société du Second Empire* (Paris, 1909), p. 324; De Maugny, *op. cit.*, pp. 83–84.
88. Guedalla, *op. cit.*, p. 339.
89. Ollivier, *op. cit.*, VIII, 128.
90. *Ibid.*, VII, 311–312.
91. When Sainte-Beuve reached home, after this outburst, he did dictate an article on Caesar and Napoleon which he never finished. Even had he completed it, he could not have published it because of its scathing character. C. A. Sainte-Beuve, *Nouveaux Lundis*, XIII (Paris, 1884), pp. 459–465.
92. C. Rossigneux, "Bibracte et le Mont Beuvray," *Revue des Questions Historiques*, I (1866), 426–446.
93. See reviews of Theodore Fivel, *L'Alesie de César près de Novalise*, and M. Bertrandy, *Première lettre sur Uxellodunum*, in *Revue des Questions Historiques*, I (1866), 627–629.
94. Letter from the Marquis de Lavalette, minister of the interior, to prefects of the Border Departments, April 18, 1865, Archives Nationales, F[18]300.
95. Letter from Drouhyn de Lhuys, foreign minister, to the Marquis de Lavalette, May 16, 1865, Archives Nationales, F[18]300.
96. *The Cornhill Magazine*, XI (1865), 495–503; *The Edinburgh Review*, CXXIV (Oct., 1866), 204–222; *The Dublin Review*, LIX (July, 1866), 1–32;

Fraser's Magazine, LXXI (May, 1865), 655–670; *The Contemporary Review*, II (1866), 457–468; III (1866), 118–129; *The British Quarterly Review*, XLI (April, 1865), 495–538.

97. See Ollivier, *op. cit.*, VII, 304–306. Through the courtesy of Emile Ollivier's family, I was able to see his personal copy of the *Histoire de Jules César*, in which Ollivier had made marginal markings. One of the most interesting of these markings, as perhaps revealing his hopes and ambitions, was a plus sign placed next to the following statement: "The best architect can build only with the materials at hand; but his [Caesar's] constant preoccupation was to associate the best men with him" (*J. C.*, I, 308, French edition).

98. Gérard Walter, *Caesar* (New York, 1952), p. 610.

99. Vielcastel, *op. cit.*, II, 289.

[ROBERT F. BYRNES]

Pobedonostsev as a Historian

KONSTANTINE Petrovich Pobedonostsev, who was the Over Procurator or the lay administrator of the Russian Orthodox Church from
April, 1880, through October, 1905, was as powerful in the 1880's in
determining the direction of Russian domestic policy as Bismarck
was for three decades in guiding the German state. Pobedonostsev is
known to history as the "evil genius" or the "Grand Inquisitor" of the
reigns of Alexander III and Nicholas II, when he was considered the
intellectual and political leader of the reactionary forces in Russia.
This essay will not attempt to discuss Pobedonostsev's career as a reactionary statesman or to determine to what degree Pobedonostsev's
reputation is deserved, but it will seek to cast some illumination upon
Pobedonostsev's earlier years, when he was a promising young historian and legal scholar.

Pobedonostsev's study of serfdom and his essays on the history of
Russian judicial procedure lifted him into prominence in Moscow in
the years just before serfdom was abolished and the entire Russian
judicial system was reorganized. When Pobedonostsev's writings and
his lectures in the School of Law of Moscow University attracted the
attention of those in charge of educating the sons of Alexander II,
Pobedonostsev became an imperial tutor. This position led to such
splendid promotions and prospects that Pobedonostsev in 1865 reluc-
tantly abandoned his historical research and went to St. Petersburg for
a career which led him ultimately to a post of unique importance in
the Russian government.

Nevertheless, Pobedonostsev never completely abandoned his interest in historical scholarship, and in the last two decades of his life he published materials he had discovered in the 1850's, letters and documents which friends had given him to edit and publish, and historical works by other scholars, obscure as well as prominent. In addition, during this period he published some of his own correspondence and other documents, and he prepared for publication after his death other letters and memoranda he had accumulated. As a consequence, even though some of the data Pobedonostsev left were lost or destroyed during and after the Russian Revolution, and even though some which survived have not yet been published or have been published only in part, the modern historian benefits greatly from Pobedonostsev's interest in historical scholarship and from his efforts to provide future scholars with information concerning his life and times.

Pobedonostsev's father, who had studied for the priesthood but who had been granted permission to leave that calling shortly after he graduated from the seminary, in 1814 became Professor of Russian Literature at Moscow University after a career as a secondary-school teacher, journalist, translator, and librarian. A very dull teacher, whose definition of literature was grammar, whose main interest was rhetoric, and who was reputed to have used the same lecture notes at his retirement in 1835 that he had used in 1814, Peter Pobedonostsev was hard working, pious, and patriotic. He had a very deep respect for the immortality conferred by the printed word, and throughout his career he was a prolific author and translator. He published a two-volume anthology before he graduated from the seminary, he edited five or six different literary journals at various points in his career, and he published a large number of translations, essays, and speeches.[2]

Peter Pobedonostsev educated all of his eleven children, and most of them grew up to become intellectuals and writers. One daughter, Varvara, translated highly moral English and French literature into Russian, and another daughter, Maria, translated French and German novels for Pogodin's *Moskvitianin.* One of his sons, Sergei, who died in 1850 at the age of thirty-four, was an authority on the Polish theater, an important collector of Russian chronicles and source materials, and the author of a large number of novels, essays, and historical studies published in a wide variety of Moscow journals.[3]

However, it was Konstantine, Peter Pobedonostsev's youngest son and the subject of this essay, who drew his father's closest attention as an educator. The future lay head of the Russian Orthodox Church was educated entirely by his father until he went to St. Petersburg in 1841 to attend the School of Jurisprudence. It is probably true that Pobedonostsev never fully recovered from the stamp his father impressed upon him. Even his literary style, which is clear but marked by eighteenth-century words and expressions, resembles that of Kheraskov and Lomonosov, whose works his father often read in class to Belinsky and other bored students.

Nevertheless, Pobedonostsev's father provided him with the training and many of the interests and qualities which helped him to become an able scholar and teacher. Pobedonostsev grew up in a family of intellectuals and in a close university circle, and he came as a boy to know and to respect scholars and writers, such as the Aksakovs, Lazhechnikov the historical novelist, and Pogodin the celebrated historian. He was brought up to assume that study, writing, and publishing were important achievements to which an educated man naturally devoted his life.

As a boy, Pobedonostsev acquired the ability to read and to speak Church Slavonic, Latin, Greek, English, French, German, and Polish. He acquired a deep knowledge and love for the Bible and for Russian and Western religious writings, he studied the Greek and Latin classics, and he read widely in the history and literature of Russia. He acquired an interest in western European literature of all varieties, which he retained throughout his life. In addition, he learned early in life to work, and he was trained to remember what he had read. As a consequence, his published works, particularly those which appeared before 1880, are distinguished by truly remarkable learning. Everyone who became acquainted with Pobedonostsev, from his closest colleagues to foreign visitors such as Senator Beveridge, was astonished at his capacity and love for intellectual work and at the depth and range of his knowledge.[4]

Pobedonostsev completed his studies in St. Petersburg in the spring of 1846 and returned to Moscow, where he entered the bureaucracy, to which he devoted almost sixty years of his life. He began his service as a law clerk in the Eighth Department of the Senate, a part of the Senate which was located in Moscow. In an age when it was simple and customary for government employees to combine their private researches with their official duties, Pobedonostsev accumulated and analyzed the materials for the flood of historical essays which he published in the years after 1858. Pobedonostsev often indicated that the two decades after 1846 were his happiest years, and it is evident that he truly enjoyed the lonely but blissful life of the dedicated scholar. His primary goal at that time was to publish a history of Russian judicial procedure since the middle of the seventeenth century, with particular emphasis upon the influence which the notaries and clerks of the courts had had in shaping the Russian judicial system. It is revealing that he did not abandon this aim until the late 1880's.[5]

Pobedonostsev was a prolific author, editor, and translator from 1858, when his first publication appeared, until his death in 1907. However, his most fruitful decade was that following 1858, when he was primarily a historian. Within the period from 1858 through 1863 alone, he published a translation of a German book,[6] one long volume of letters describing his tour of European Russia with the Tsarevich,[7] some poetry, and nineteen essays and reviews, which ranged from a few pages to two hundred pages in length.

In the 1850's, Pobedonostsev considered himself a student of the history of Russian institutions. He first attracted attention with his monograph on serfdom, and most of his early articles were those of a competent historian. However, Pobedonostsev was led by his training and his interest in serfdom, in the various kinds of landholding, and in property law into the study of Russian civil law. It is difficult, if not impossible, to draw a line between Pobedonostsev's historical studies and his work on Russian civil law, particularly since his civil-law studies were very much influenced by Savigny and the German historical school. However, it is possible to state that during the period from 1858 to 1868 Pobedonostsev's emphasis gradually and almost inevitably shifted from the history of institutions to the study and teaching of law.[8]

Pobedonostsev's master's thesis, "On Reforms in Civil Law Procedure," which he submitted to the School of Law of Moscow University in 1859, was considered so excellent that he was given a position on the law faculty. His lectures there led Count S. G. Stroganov, the rector of the University and one of those in charge of educating the sons of Alexander II, to invite Pobedonostsev to instruct these young men in the history of Russian institutions. Pobedonostsev's success as a tutor and companion for the Tsarevich on his tour of European Russia in 1863 brought him a promotion to Over Procurator of all the Senate departments in Moscow. In 1865, Pobedonostsev was invited to come to St.

Petersburg to continue his tutoring and to work in the Ministry of Justice. This invitation and the prospect of promotion to the very highest levels of the government led Pobedonostsev to abandon his beloved Moscow, the law school, and his historical research.[9]

Nevertheless, Pobedonostsev continued his study of Russian civil law, and between 1868 and 1880 he published his three-volume *Course in Civil Law*, which had developed from his university lectures and which won him high repute as a legal scholar. The first volume of this work, which appeared in 1868, dealt with patrimonial law; histories of various kinds of landholding in Russia and of Russian property law occupied about half of this volume. The second volume, which appeared in 1871, dealt with domestic relations, wills, and inheritance rights; about one-quarter of this volume consisted of historical material. The third volume, which was published in 1880, analyzed contracts and obligations and had very little historical data. The amount of historical material used in each of these three volumes was clearly influenced by the subject studied, but it is significant that as Pobedonostsev advanced, first to become a senator in 1868 and then to become a member of the Council of State in 1872, each successive volume of this massive study had less historical material. Indeed, the third volume relied very heavily on data derived from law cases which Pobedonostsev had reviewed as a member of the Senate.[10]

In any case, it is clear that most of Pobedonostsev's published work between 1858 and approximately 1865 was that of a historian, and his *Course in Civil Law* was heavily influenced by his historical studies and by his historical approach. The analysis in this essay, therefore, includes the *Course in Civil Law*, as well as the studies which Pobedonostsev published while his interest in historical research was primary.

Perhaps the most obvious characteristic of Pobedonostsev as a historian was his wide range of interests. One of his most interesting essays, for example, was a long review article on Near Eastern travel literature and on recent archaeological work in the Holy Land.[11] Another article published some new material Pobedonostsev had discovered on the establishment and early years of the Academy of Sciences,[12] and a third analyzed several books and articles on Russia and Russian history which had recently been published in England, France, and Germany.[13]

However, Pobedonostsev's most valuable historical studies were his two articles on the history of serfdom in Russia, his essays on the history of Russian judicial procedure, and his studies of various types of land-holding and property law which had developed in Russia. These last essays were incorporated in substance into the first volume of his *Course in Civil Law*. Pobedonostsev apparently considered his monograph on serfdom and several of his essays on notable court cases his most important historical works, because in 1875, in honor of his becoming a member of the Moscow Society of History and Russian Antiquities, he collected them in a book which he published the following year.[14]

Pobedonostsev was a firm believer in hard work in the sources and in careful study of the scholarly secondary works. He insisted that books should be studied, not read, and that "just reading" books was "dangerous and deceiving." In his lectures at Moscow University and in his writings, he emphasized that the best introduction for the scholar of Russian history and Russian legal institutions was to make careful and complete notes of the Full Collection of Russian Laws. "I assure everyone that such a reading of the law will at first require some strength, but it will gradually become interesting and for some even absorbing. With each volume, the reader will more deeply appreciate the power and value of this remarkable work."[15]

Pobedonostsev's historical works and his civil-law studies were distinguished by the vast amount of data which he had accumulated from the Full Collection of Russian Laws, the archives of the Senate and the Ministry of Justice, other state and private archives, and other previously published collections and studies of Russian institutions. Even those who criticized Pobedonostsev's *Course in Civil Law* most sharply were amazed by the amount of information it contained. It was primarily due to the store of well-organized information that several thousand copies of each volume were sold.[16]

Pobedonostsev's historical studies are cautious and limited in scope, for he believed that providing an "exact and conscientious account of the facts" was a very considerable achievement for a historian. In his monograph on serfdom he emphasized that a full and clear history of serfdom could be written only after serfdom had been abolished, more materials were available, and scholars were able to analyze more objectively its institutional and intellectual foundations.[17]

Pobedonostsev refused consistently even to suggest generalizations or conclusions which could not be supported. This reluctance to reach a conclusion, or to make a judgment, even on the basis of immense data, is demonstrated most clearly in his *Course in Civil Law*. Pobedonostsev proclaimed that these volumes were to provide a comparative study of various systems of civil law.[18] Accordingly, he began each section of the study by describing the history of the particular institution or practice as it had developed in Roman law and in the law of England, France, Germany, and Russia. Only very rarely, however, did he make any comparisons or comments on the similarities and contrasts, and the reader was left to make his own judgments from the information which Pobedonostsev had presented.

Pobedonostsev was particularly competent in writing review articles, which required little imagination but which did provide him an opportunity to use his immense fund of well-organized knowledge and his patience and skill in analyzing the use of sources and secondary works. His review articles were always clear, succinct, and objective, and on occasion they had devastating effects. For example, his review of Mikhailov's *Russian Civil Judicial Procedure in Its Historical Development* destroyed the reputation of that young scholar. In this long review, Pobedonostsev gave a page-by-page list of errors of fact, and carefully listed the errors Mikhailov had made in transcribing decrees.[19]

It is clear that Pobedonostsev's historical studies helped lead him to appreciate the serious failings of Russia's judicial system and to believe that reforms were overdue and vital. It is equally clear that his appreciation of the complexity of Russia's institutions, the backwardness of the people, and the slowness of change in Russian history led him to believe that radical change would be disastrous. In any case, Pobedonostsev's writings during the years from 1858 through 1865 indicate that he was a supporter of many kinds of reform, from revisions of the mortgage laws to new methods of collecting statistics.[20]

Above all, Pobedonostsev, who later became the symbol for reaction in Russia, was a prominent supporter of reform of Russia's judicial system. His master's thesis was a critique of the established system and an analysis of the principles upon which he believed the reformed institutions should be based. Pobedonostsev then denounced those who opposed change as "legal Old Believers" who did not see "history as a movement forward from dead ritualism to the soul of life." [21] Many of Pobedonostsev's articles in the years between 1859 and 1863 were published in the *Arkhiv istoricheskikh i prakticheskikh svedenii otnosiashchikhsia do Rossii*, which was founded and published by his friend

Nicholas Kalachov as a professional journal for historians of Russian history and Russian law and as an instrument through which the state could obtain the factual data necessary for sound reforms. In these and in other articles, Pobedonostsev ridiculed the overcentralized, complicated, ritualistic, and corrupt judicial system. His excellent series of individual cases demonstrated that some judicial decisions had been delayed from thirty to forty years by red tape and by political pressures, that innocent people had been tortured and sentenced, and that the wealthy and powerful when guilty usually went unpunished. Finally, Pobedonostsev was an important member of the committee which drafted the judicial reform of 1864, and some advisory members of the committee even considered him a radical. Later in life, of course, he not only denounced the new court system, but often declared that he had opposed it when he had been a member of its drafting committee.[22]

Even during the years when he was a supporter of reforms and when enthusiasm generally ran high in Moscow and St. Petersburg, Pobedonostsev remained objective and impersonal. His studies of celebrated court cases were factual and dry, although they could easily have been made effective emotional pieces. Pobedonostsev insisted that "the aim of historical research, and of legal research . . . is first of all the impartial search for the truth" and not the support of any political or moral position. He often repeated that the historian must always remember that customs and beliefs of historical ages differ and that he errs grievously who criticizes the acts of one age according to the views of another. He was a resolute critic of the moralistic interpretation of history.

The moral feeling is insulted by violence, but moral feeling alone cannot serve as a guide and instrument for the historian studying the political activity of an historical person; otherwise, the historian would judge and declare pernicious a government measure simply because it was accompanied by violence. This would be unjust. It is true that the greatest transformations in the soul of man have been effected by peaceful means, by people strong in soul but lowly and even base in social position. But these were exceptional occurrences. The rulers of the world usually act through material force, by external and not internal authority. It has always been so, and it will always be so, at least as long as moral force does not acquire decisive rule over material force in the rules of all society.[23]

The historical studies of Pobedonostsev are notable also for the lack of affection he demonstrated for Russia's past. He was sharply critical of those who believed that Russia had enjoyed a golden age before Peter. He was particularly critical of the Slavophils (although he never mentioned them as a group or criticized any individual Slavophil), because in their attacks on Peter the Great they were "carried away by their historical ideal, the features of which they find in the ancient history of Russia before Peter."

Pobedonostsev was also critical of the Westerners, whom he denounced for their practice of interpreting Peter's age and Peter's actions according to their own preconceived ideas. According to Pobedonostsev, Peter did not wish to give Russia new institutions and was not opposed to the old ones, even serfdom. He was a great man because he saw the needs of his age clearly and undertook nothing which was in sharp contradiction with the concepts then generally held. Peter simply acted in the interest of the state, using the established institutions when possible to increase the state's power and authority and revising the established institutions when necessary.[24]

In summary, for Pobedonostsev during the years when he was a historian and a legal scholar, the history of Russia was the history of the Russian state. Pobedonostsev saw all Russian institutions and leaders as the unconscious instruments or even weapons of the state. "History is explained not by chance alone, nor by personal arbitrary power alone, but by the whole course of history." No Russian ruler emerges from Pobedonostsev's early writings as a giant causing sharp breaks in the continuity of Russian history, which flows on eternally as the history of the state, its course determined by the "law of historical and political necessity." [25]

However, the flow of Russian history was not always forward, and it could be and often was influenced to some degree by particularly great individuals, such as Peter. Moreover, it was subject to outside influences, especially economic, and Pobedonostsev in all of his writings emphasized that the fundamental force causing change was economic. At the same time economic change developed slowly in a state as vast and unorganized as Russia, and the history of Russia in Pobedonostsev's eyes settled into a kind of slow, majestic, dignified, bargelike advance.

Pobedonostsev's interest in scholarship declined rapidly after 1865, when he married, moved to St. Petersburg, and began to acquire influence as an imperial tutor and as a high official in the Ministry of Justice.

Pobedonostsev never took a prominent part in St. Petersburg social activities, and he remained a voracious reader and continued to publish a great deal, though few of the items were scholarly. After he became lay head of the Russian Orthodox Church in 1880 and as he became more reactionary, his interests centered upon administering church affairs, improving primary-school education and establishing a parish school network, and tightening the censorship.

However, about 1885 Pobedonostsev's interest in historical scholarship began gradually to revive. In 1887 and 1890, he published some of the materials he had collected for his proposed history of the Russian judicial system in the hope that some young scholar might become interested in the subject and make use of the data. In 1895, he issued the notes he had taken in the 1850's on the Full Collection of Russian Laws with the intention of stimulating genuine legal scholarship.[26] He also published in these years other historical materials he had collected earlier, such as some of the correspondence of his predecessor as lay head of the Russian Orthodox Church, Count D. A. Tolstoy, and some letters illuminating the reign of Nicholas I.[27]

As Over Procurator of the Holy Synod, Pobedonostsev devoted great attention to the Holy Synod Press. By 1884 or 1885, he had reorganized and modernized the Holy Synod's publishing operation so that this press became one of the largest and most efficient in Russia. Pobedonostsev used the Holy Synod Press mainly to print and distribute enormous quantities of literature for the Orthodox Church and its new parish schools. However, he also used it to publish historical works. For example, under his direction the Synod Press in the 1880's and 1890's reprinted the works of Andrei N. Muraviev, who before his death in 1873 had written a large number of books about the history of the Russian Orthodox Church.[28] In addition, it was the Holy Synod Press which first published Kliuchevsky's famous *Course in Russian History*. Pobedonostsev, whose favorite historians had been Carlyle and Froude, became an enthusiastic admirer of Kliuchevsky. One of his principal pleasures in the last three years of his life was reading Kliuchevsky, and one of his dearest wishes was that the Holy Synod Press complete the publication of Kliuchevsky's volumes before he died so that he might read them all.[29]

As a historian, or at least as a former historian, Pobedonostsev was aware of the importance that source materials possessed for scholars. He assumed that future historians would be interested in his activities and ideas, and he apparently believed that they would treat him fairly, perhaps even generously. Pobedonostsev's principal contribution as a historian in the last twenty years of his life was the editing and publishing of materials left him by his friends and of letters and other documents of his own. For example, in 1893 he published the very lively and valuable correspondence of Baroness Edith Raden with the celebrated Slavophil historian of Russia's Baltic provinces, Iuri Samarin. He also helped Samarin's son publish a complete edition of his father's works, which involved persuading the censors not to interfere.[30]

Pobedonostsev was particularly helpful and generous in releasing correspondence he had received for publication in collections of the letters of his friends. Thus, all of the letters Nicholas Ilminskii had written to him between 1882 and 1891 were published in 1895. His letters from many leading churchmen and from some scholars were released so that complete editions of the correspondence of these men with Pobedonostsev could be printed.[31]

Above all, Pobedonostsev began to publish documents which cast illumination upon his own life. For example, in 1885 he published in a limited edition the diary which he had kept while a student at the School of Jurisprudence from 1841 until 1846. So far as I have been able to determine, no library in the West has a copy of this diary. However, Pobedonostsev obviously intended that it be made available for scholars, since he gave a copy of it to Peter Bartenev, editor of the *Russkii Arkhiv,* to whom he gave much other material for publication. Bartenev published part of this extremely interesting and valuable diary in *Russkii Arkhiv* immediately after Pobedonostsev's death in 1907.[32]

In 1894, Pobedonostsev published some extraordinarily sensitive religious poetry and meditations which he had written in Moscow between 1856 and 1864. In the 1890's he reprinted two translations he had done in the 1860's but which were out of print. In addition, he published a series of biographical essays concerning some of his closest friends during the period before 1880. Most of these he collected into a volume in 1896, and they are all precious sources concerning Pobedonostsev's life and times.[33]

Finally, in his last years Pobedonostsev began to organize all of the letters and documents he had accumulated. He scattered a great many of the letters which he had not already given to others for publication through various historical journals in a flood too large to enumerate here. He neatly bound into bundles, one for each year, the letters which he had received from Alexander III, Nicholas II, and some members of the imperial family. He also carefully arranged all of the other letters which he decided should not be published during his lifetime. In his will, he provided that these materials should be placed in the Rumiant-sev Museum (now the Lenin Library) for publication ten years after his death, which occurred in March, 1907. Most of these letters and documents have been published, but a great many still remain unpublished and some apparently have not even been examined by scholars.[34]

Pobedonostsev sought to provide future scholars with data on his life and times because of his continued interest in historical scholarship and because he had learned to appreciate the significance of historical records when he had been a promising young historian and legal scholar. His publications during the years when his primary concern was research and writing indicate that he possessed the interests and qualities required of a conscientious and objective historian: his works were marked by thorough and skilled research in the primary source materials; by careful study of all secondary works; by wide and deep knowledge of related fields and of historical developments in other countries; by penetrating analysis of all the data he had accumulated; and by cautious, accurate, and clear descriptions of his findings. Pobedonostsev's talents as a historian and his vast general learning made his historical studies valuable contributions to the study of Russia's past and reveal that he would almost certainly have had a distinguished career as a scholar. It was a misfortune for Russian historical scholarship that the qualities and accomplishments which Pobedonostsev possessed as a young scholar opened prospects to him in the state's service which led him to abandon his career as a historian.

1. This essay is a product of a Senior Fellowship of the Russian Institute of Columbia University awarded the author for two years of training in the Russian area and for research upon a forthcoming book: *Pobedonostsev: His Life and His Philosophy.*

2. Konstantine P. Pobedonostsev, *Pisma Pobedonostseva k Aleksandru III* (*Letters of Pobedonostsev to Alexander III*) (Moscow, 1925–1926), II, 330; Peter I. Bartenev, ed., "Iz dnevnika K. P. Pobedonostseva" (From the Diary of K. P. Pobedonostsev), *Russkii Arkhiv*, I (1907), 652; A. A. Polovtsov, ed., *Russkii Biograficheskii Slovar* (*Russian Biographical Dictionary*) (St. Peters-

Pobedonostsev as Historian

burg, 1896–1918), XIV, 141–143; Boris Glinskii, "Konstantin Petrovich Pobedonostsev. Materialy dlia biografii" (Konstantine Petrovich Pobedonostsev. Materials for His Biography), *Istoricheskii Vestnik,* CVIII (1907), 251; Raoul Labry, *Alexandre Ivanovich Herzen, 1812–1870* (Paris, 1928), p. 94; N. Benardaki and I. Bogushevicha, *Ukazatel statei sereznago soderzhaniia* (*Index of Articles of Serious Content*) (St. Petersburg, 1858), No. 4, p. 7; Grigori Gennadi, *Spravochnyi Slovar o russkikh pisateliakh* (*Reference Dictionary of Russian Writers*) (Moscow, 1875–1906), II, 149; V. S. Sopikov, *Opit Rossiiskoi Bibliografii* (*Experiment in Russian Bibliography*) (St. Petersburg, 1904–1905), Part iii, pp. 19, 31; Part iv, p. 302.

3. Nikolai N. Golitsyn, *Bibliograficheskii Slovar russkikh pisatelnits* (*A Bibliographical Dictionary of Russian Feminine Writers*) (St. Petersburg, 1888–1889), pp. 198–199; Nikolai Barsukov, *Zhizn i trudy M. P. Pogodina* (*The Life and Works of M. P. Pogodin*) (St. Petersburg, 1888–1910), VII, 79–80, 258–260; VIII, 166; X, 364; XII, 199–200; Konstantin P. Pobedonostsev, "Odin iz psevdonimov v russkoi zhurnalistike" (One of the Pseudonyms Used in Russian Journalism), *Bibliograficheskii Zapiski,* 1892, No. 8, p. 574; *Sbornik Imperatorskago Russkago Istoricheskago Obshchestva,* LXII (1888), 162; Polovtsov, *op. cit.,* XIV, 141–143.

4. Peter V. Pobedonostsev, "Liubov k otechestvu" (Love for the Native Land), *Trudy Obshchestva Liubitelei Rossiiskoi Slovesnosti pri Imperatorskom Moskovskom Universitete,* XV (1819), 5–13; Peter V. Pobedonostsev, *Slovo o sushchestvennikh obiazannostiakh vitii i o sposobakh k priobreteniiu uspekov v krasnorechii* (*Speech about the Essential Duties of Life and about the Means for Acquiring Eloquence*) (Moscow, 1831), pp. 27–33; Konstantine P. Pobedonostsev, ed., "Pisma I. I. Lazhechnikova k S. P. i K. P. Pobedonostsym" (Letters of I. I. Lazhechnikov to S. P. and K. P. Pobedonostsev), *Russkoe Obozrenie,* XXXII (1895), 881–886; Alexander N. Pynin, *Belinskii, ego zhizn i perepiska* (*Belinsky: His Life and Correspondence*), 2nd ed. (St. Petersburg, 1908), pp. 54–56; Claude G. Bowers, *Beveridge and the Progressive Era* (Cambridge, Mass., 1932), pp. 147–148; Hermann Dalton, *Lebenserinnerungen* (Berlin, 1906–1908), III, 98–99; Louise Creighton, *Life and Letters of Mandell Creighton* (London, 1904), II, 150–155; Evgenii M. Feoktistov, *Vospominaniia. Za Kulisami politiki i literatury, 1848–1896* (*Memoirs. Behind the Scenes of Politics and Literature, 1848–1896*) (Leningrad, 1929), pp. 219–221; S. Melgunov, ed., "K. P. Pobedonostsev v dni pervoi revoliutsii. Neizdannyia pisma k S. D. Voitu" (K. P. Pobedonostsev during the First Revolution. Unpublished Letters to S. D. Voit), *Na Chuzhoi Storone,* VIII (1924), 178; A. A. Polovtsov, "Dnevnik" (Diary), *Krasnyi Arkhiv,* III (1923), 94.

5. Konstantine P. Pobedonostsev, "Vospominaniia o Vasilem Petrovichom Zubkove" (Reminiscences about Vasilii Petrovich Zubkov), *Russkii Arkhiv,* I (1904), 302–303; Boris N. Chicherin, *Vospominaniia* (*Memoirs*) (Moscow, 1929–1934), IV, 102–103; Pobedonostsev, *Pisma,* I, 292.

6. Konstantine P. Pobedonostsev, tr., *Khristianskiia nachala semeinoi*

zhizni. *Perevod s nemetskago* (*Christian Principles of Family Life. Translation from the German*) (Moscow, 1861).

7. Konstantine P. Pobedonostsev, *Pisma o puteshestvii po Rossii ot S. Peterburga do Kryma* (*Letters from a Trip around Russia from St. Petersburg to the Crimea*) (Moscow, 1863).

8. Konstantine P. Pobedonostsev, *Kurs grazhdanskago prava* (*Course in Civil Law*), I, 3rd ed. (1883), pp. 713–714; Pobedonostsev, "Russkoe grazhdanskoe sudoproizvodstvo" (Russian Civil Law Procedure), *Arkhiv istoricheskikh i prakticheskikh svedenii otnosiashchikhsia do Rossii*, I (1859), Part i, *Kritika*, pp. 1–4; George P. Gooch, *History and Historians in the Nineteenth Century* (London, 1913), pp. 51–53; Nicholai M. Korkunov, *General Theory of Law* (Boston, 1909), pp. 149–150.

9. Konstantine P. Pobedonostsev, "O reformakh v grazhdanskom sudoproizvodstve" (On Reforms in Civil Law Procedure), *Russkii Vestnik*, XXI (1859), 541–580; XXII (1859), 5–34, 153–190; Iuri V. Gotie, "K. P. Pobedonostsev i naslednik Alexandr Alexandrovich, 1865–1881" (K. P. Pobedonostsev and the Heir, Alexander Alexandrovich, 1865–1881), *Publichnaia Biblioteka SSSR imeni V. I. Lenina. Sbornik*, II (1929), 110–112; Barsukov, *op. cit.*, XXI, 69; XXII, 1–3; *Sudebnaia Gazeta*, XV (1896), 10.

10. B. V. Nikolskii, "Literaturnaia deiatelnost K. P. Pobedonostseva" (The Literary Activity of K. P. Pobedonostsev), *Istoricheskii Vestnik*, LXV (1896), 724–725; A. E. Nolde, "Obzor nauchnoi iuridicheskoi deiatelnosti K. P. Pobedonostseva" (A Survey of the Scientific Juridical Activity of K. P. Pobedonostsev), *Zhurnal Ministerstva Narodnoi Prosveshchenniia*, VIII (1907), 95–98, 106–114; Gabriel F. Shershenevich, *Uchebnik russkago grazhdanskago prava* (*A Manual of Russian Civil Law*), 6th ed. (St. Petersburg, 1907), p. 18; Glinskii, *loc. cit.*, pp. 255–257. Several editions of each volume of the *Course in Civil Law* were published. The final complete edition was published in 1896, on the fiftieth anniversary of Pobedonostsev's entry into government service.

11. Konstantine P. Pobedonostsev, "Novyia puteshestvyia po vostoku" (New Travels through the East), *Russkii Vestnik*, XLIII (1863), 489–548.

12. Konstantine P. Pobedonostsev, "Materialy dlia istorii Akademii Nauk" (Materials for the History of the Academy of Sciences), *Letopis russkoi literatury i drevnostei*, V (1863), Part iii, 3–36.

13. Konstantine P. Pobedonostsev, "Knizhnyia zagranichnyia vesti o Rossii" (Information about Russia in Foreign Books), *Russkii Arkhiv*, IV (1866), 260–262.

14. Konstantine P. Pobedonostsev, "Zametki dlia istorii krepostnago prava v Rossii" (Notes on the History of Serfdom in Russia), *Russkii Vestnik*, XV (1858), 209–248, 459–498; XVI (1858), 537–582; Pobedonostsev, "Utverzhdenie krepostnago prava v Rossii v XVIII stoletii" (The Consolidation of Serfdom in Russia in the Eighteenth Century), *Russkii Vestnik*, XXXV (1861), 223–253; Pobedonostsev, "Anekdoty iz XVIII stoletiia: Moskovskaia Volokita. Ochistitelnaia Pytka" (Anecdotes from the Eighteenth Century:

Pobedonostsev as Historian

Moscow Red Tape. Purificatory Torture), *Arkhiv istoricheskikh i prakticheskikh svedenii otnosiashchikhsia do Rossii*, IV (1859), Book IV, Supplement, 1–22; Pobedonostsev, "Ubiistov Zhukovikh" (The Murder of the Zhukovs), *Russkii Vestnik*, XXX (1860), 462–501; Pobedonostsev, "Prichiny nepravosudiia i provolochki v prisutstvennikh mestakh" (The Reasons for Injustice and Delay in Courts), *Zhurnal Ministerstva Iustitsii*, XXVII (1866), 33–44; Pobedonostsev, *Istoricheskiia izsledovaniia i stati* (St. Petersburg, 1876), Preface; Pobedonostsev, "Odnodvorcheskiia zemli i nachalo spetsialnago mezhevaniia v Rossii" (Freeholding Lands and the Beginning of the Special Survey in Russia), *Zhurnal Ministerstva Iustitsii*, XV (1863), Part ii, 85–104; Pobedonostsev, "Priobretenie sobstvennosti i pozemelnyia knigi" (The Acquisition of Property and Land Books), *Russkii Vestnik*, XXVIII (1860), 5–39, 193–230; Pobedonostsev, "Imenie rodovoe i blagopriobretennoe" (Patrimonial and Acquired Property), *Zhurnal Ministerstva Iustitsii*, VIII (1861), Part ii, 3–75; Pobedonostsev, "O chrezpolosnom vladenii" (On the Strip System of Holding), *Iuridicheskii Vestnik*, Book III (1867), 3–18.

15. Konstantine P. Pobedonostsev, *Vechnaia Pamiat* (*In Memoriam*), (Moscow, 1896), pp. 57–58; Pobedonostsev, *Kurs*, I, 713–717; Pobedonostsev, "Russkoe grazhdanskoe sudoproizvodstvo," pp. 5–8.

16. A. Povorinski, *Sistematicheskii Ukazatel russkoi literatury po grazhdanskomu pravu* (*Systematic Guide to Russian Literature on Civil Law*) (St. Petersburg, 1886), pp. 80–81; I. Orshanskii, "Kurs grazhdanskago prava" (Course in Civil Law), *Zhurnal Grazhdanskago i Ugolovnago Prava*, Book II (1876), 260–262, 276–282; V. Spasovich, "Kurs grazhdanskago prava K. Pobedonostseva. Chast vtoraia" (Course in Civil Law, by K. Pobedonostsev. Part ii), *Zhurnal Grazhdanskago i Torgovago Prava*, Book I (1871), 134–157; A. Borzenko, "Pacta sunt servanda" *Russkoe Obozrenie*, VI (1890), 455–464; *Iuridicheskii Vestnik*, XXXIX (1890), 701–703.

17. Pobedonostsev, *Istoricheskiia izsledovaniia*, pp. 1–2; Pobedonostsev. "Russkoe grazhdanskoe sudoproizvodstvo," pp. 1–4.

18. Pobedonostsev, *Kurs*, I, 2nd ed. (1873), Preface.

19. Pobedonostsev, "Russkoe grazhdanskoe sudoproizvodstvo," pp. 1–62. See also, Pobedonostsev, "Obozrenie chastnikh trudov po sobraniiu zakonov i po sostavleniiu ukaznikh slovarei do izdaniia Polnago Sobraniia Zakonov Rossiiskoi Imperii" (A Survey of Private Works on the Collection of Laws and on the Composition of Indices before the Publication of the Full Collection of the Laws of the Russian Empire), *Arkhiv istoricheskikh i prakticheskikh svedenii otnosiashchikhsia do Rossii*, V (1863), 51–84, especially 68–73; Pobedonostsev, "Akty, otnosiashchiesia do iuridicheskago byta drevnei Rossii" (Legal Deeds concerning the Juridical Life of Ancient Russia), *Arkhiv istoricheskikh i prakticheskikh svedenii otnosiashchikhsia do Rossii*, IV (1859), Book IV, *Kritika*, 25–60; Pobedonostsev, "Mestnoe naselenie Rossii" (The Local Population of Russia), *Russkii Vestnik*, XL (1862), 5–34. Pobedonostsev's insistence on accurate scholarship in these years is especially

worthy of note because of the intellectual dishonesty he often displayed later in life. In his later publications, he frequently distorted the meaning of the books and articles he translated by omitting pages, paragraphs, sentences, and phrases, without any indication of this fact, and he was frequently guilty of plagiarism (Robert F. Byrnes, "Pobedonostsev's Conception of the Good Society," *Review of Politics*, XIII (1951), 173–174).

20. Konstantine P. Pobedonostsev, "Veshchnyi kredit i zakladnoe pravo" (Property Credit and Mortgage Law), *Russkii Vestnik*, XXXIII (1861), 409–451.

21. Pobedonostsev, "O reformakh," pp. 543–548.

22. *Arkhiv istoricheskikh i prakticheskikh svedenii otnosiashchikhsia do Rossii*, I (1858), iii–vii; Pobedonostsev, *Vechnaia Pamiat*, pp. 56–62; Pobedonostsev, *K. P. Pobedonostsev i ego Korrespondenty. Pisma i Zapiski. Novum Regnum* (*K. P. Pobedonostsev and His Correspondents. Letters and Memoranda. Novum Regnum*) (Moscow, 1923), I, 68–69; Pobedonostsev, "Statistiki angliiskikh grazhdanskikh sudov za 1858 god" (Statistics of the English Civil Courts for 1858), *Iuridicheskii Vestnik*, V (1860–1861), 46–54; Pobedonostsev, "Iuridicheskiia zametki i voprosy" (Juridical Notes and Questions), *Zhurnal Ministerstva Iustitsii*, XXVII (1866), 33–34; Pobedonostsev, *Istoricheskiia izsledovaniia*, pp. 236–325; A. F. Koni, *Na zhiznennom puti* (*On the Path of Life*) (Moscow, 1914–1929), III, 191–192; Grigorii A. Dzhanshiev, *Epokha velikikh reform*, 8th ed. (Moscow, 1900), pp. 365–367, 552.

23. Pobedonostsev, *Istoricheskiia izsledovaniia*, pp. 124–125, 175–180.

24. *Ibid.*, pp. 14–15, 47–55, 116–185, especially pp. 116–118, 156–159.

25. *Ibid.*, p. 146.

26. Konstantine P. Pobedonostsev, *Istoriko-iuridicheskie akty perekhodnoi epokhi XVII–XVIII vekov* (*Historical-Juridical Acts of the Age of Transition in the Seventeenth and Eighteenth Centuries*) (Moscow, 1887), Introduction, p. vi; Pobedonostsev, *Materialy dlia istorii prikaznago sudoproizvodstva v Rossii* (*Materials for the History of Chancellery Legal Procedure in Russia*) (Moscow, 1890), Introduction; Pobedonostsev, *Vypiski iz Polnago Sobraniia Zakonov* (*Extracts from the Full Collection of the Laws*) (St. Petersburg, 1895); Nolde, *loc. cit.*, pp. 102–103.

27. Konstantine P. Pobedonostsev, "Anekdot o Didro" (An Anecdote about Diderot), *Russkii Arkhiv*, III (1893), 101; Pobedonostsev, "K istorii snoshenii s inovertsami" (For the History of Relations with Other Religious Groups), *Russkii Arkhiv*, II (1894), 5–27; Pobedonostsev, "O vnutrennem sostoianii Rossii pri votsarenii imperatora Nikolaia Pavlovicha" (On Conditions within Russia at the Accession of Emperor Nicholas Pavlovich), *Russkii Arkhiv*, I (1895), 161–176; Pobedonostsev, "Iz pisem ego imperatorskago vysochestva velikago kniazia Konstantina Nikolaevicha k stats-sekretariu A. V. Golovninu" (From the Letters of His Imperial Highness, the Grand Prince Konstantine Nikolaevich, to Secretary of State A. V. Golovnin), *Russkii Arkhiv*, I (1895), 439–445; William J. Birkbeck, *Russia and the English Church in the Last Fifty Years* (London, 1895), p. 182.

Pobedonostsev as Historian

28. *Katalog knig prodaiushchikhsia v sinodaln kh knizhnikh lavkakh v S. Peterburge i Moskve (A Catalogue of Books on Sale in the Holy Synod Bookstores in St. Petersburg and Moscow)* (Moscow, 1896); Pobedonostsev, *Pisma*, II, 64–65.

29. Konstantine P. Pobedonostsev, *Moskovskii Sbornik (Moscow Collection)*, 3rd ed. (Moscow, 1896), pp. 111, 125, 188–189, 207–208; Vasilii O. Kliuchevsky, *Kurs russkoi istorii (Course in Russian History)*, 1st ed. (Moscow, 1904–1910); "Pisma K. P. Pobedonostseva k S. D. Voitu" (Letters of K. P. Pobedonostsev to S. D. Voit), *Russkii Arkhiv*, Book I (1917), 77; Melgunov, *loc. cit.*, pp. 183–184, 196; "Pisma K. P. Pobedonostseva k E. M. Feoktistovu" (Letters of K. P. Pobedonostsev to E. M. Feoktistov), *Literaturnoe Nasledstvo*, XXII–XXIV (1935), 530–531.

30. Konstantine P. Pobedonostsev, ed., *Perepiska Iuri F. Samarina s baronkoi E. F. Raden, 1861–1876 g. (The Correspondence of Iuri F. Samarin with Baroness E. F. Raden, 1861–1876)* (Moscow, 1893); Pobedonostsev, *Pisma*, II, 229; Pobedonostsev, *Novum Regnum*, II, 979.

31. Ivan Ianzhul, "Vospominaniia" (Memoirs), *Russkaia Starina*, CXLIV (1910), 10–11; *Pisma Nikolaia Ivanovicha Ilminskago k ober-prokuroru sviateishchago sinoda Konstantinu Petrovichu Pobedonostsevu (The Letters of Nicholas Ivanovich Ilminskii to the Over Procurator of the Holy Synod, Konstantine Petrovich Pobedonostsev)* (Kazan, 1895), pp. iii–iv; Sergei Petrovskii, ed., "Perepiska K. P. Pobedonostseva s Nikanorom episkopom Ufinskim" (The Correspondence of K. P. Pobedonostsev with Nikanor, Bishop of Ufa), *Russkii Arkhiv*, I (1915), 458; Sergei Petrovskii, "Pisma K. P. Pobedonostseva Illarionu, arkhiepiskomu Poltavskomu" (The Letters of K. P. Pobedonostsev to Illarion, Archbishop of Poltava), *Russkii Arkhiv*, LIV (1916), 129–171, 360–380; Vladimir S. Markov, *K istorii raskola-staroobriadchestva vtoroi poloviny XIX stoletiia. Perepiska Prof. N. I. Subbotina (Toward the History of the Sects and Old Believers in the Second Half of the Nineteenth Century. The Correspondence of Professor N. I. Subbotin)* (Moscow, 1915); Pobedonostsev, *Vechnaia Pamiat*, pp. 74–94.

32. Peter Bartenev, ed., "Iz dnevnika K. P. Pobedonostseva" (From the Diary of K. P. Pobedonostsev), *Russkii Arkhiv*, I (1907), 635.

33. Konstantine P. Pobedonostsev, *Prazdniki Gospodni (The Lord's Days)* (St. Petersburg, 1894); Pobedonostsev, tr., *Khristianskiia nachala semeinoi zhizni. Perevoi s nemetskago (Christian Principles of Family Life. Translation from the German)*, 2nd ed. (Moscow, 1901); Pobedonostsev, tr., *Fomy Kempiiskago s podrazhanii Khristu (Thomas à Kempis on the Imitation of Christ)*, 6th ed. (St. Petersburg, 1896).

34. Pobedonostsev, *Pisma*, II, 275–277; Gotie, *loc. cit.*, pp. 108–109; Alexander A. Kizevetter, "Pobedonostsev," *Na Chuzhoi Storone*, IV (1924), 257–258.

[EDWIN C. ROZWENC]

Henry Adams

and the Federalists

I

MANY readers of Henry Adams' *History of the United States in the Administrations of Thomas Jefferson and James Madison* have accepted it as a work in which the historical judgments are strongly influenced by a sympathy for Jeffersonian ideas. As early as 1890, a reviewer in the *Atlantic Monthly*, while cognizant of Adams' many strictures on Jefferson's actions, concluded that "Mr. Adams admires Jeffersonianism, and so depicts it that his readers will admire it likewise, at least as an abstraction." [1] Similarly, the English historian J. A. Doyle, at the time of publication of the nine-volume *History*, suggested that Henry Adams' historical judgment had been clouded by the attractive power of the Jeffersonian tradition. [2]

In more recent times, when further historical research has broadened so greatly the knowledge of Jefferson the philosopher as well as Jefferson the politician and, consequently, has brought Jefferson's reputation to its highest point in our history, Henry Adams has been repeatedly embraced as a kindred spirit by those historians who strongly admire Jefferson. These readers tend to discount or explain away the many stern judgments of the faults and failures of Jefferson and his associates which appear so often in the pages of Adams' *History*. Thus, in an introductory essay written in 1930 for a reissue of the famous *History*, Henry Steele Commager asserts that despite the "conflict in his mind

Henry Adams and the Federalists

. . . between the Jefferson of his ideal and the Jefferson of his facts,"
Henry Adams was "intellectually a Jeffersonian, an apostate from the
established order of things." [3] Similarly, Herbert Agar, who edited a two
volume condensation of the *History* in 1947, assures the readers of this
abridgement that they "will be surprised at the reverence and understanding with which [Adams] treats the democratic ideal" and even
suggests that Adams, while recognizing Jefferson's faults, looked upon
him as "a philosopher ruler on the Platonic model." [4]

In the most complete critical appraisal of Adams' historical writings
to appear so far, William Jordy has argued that the "failure" of Jefferson as presented in the *History* was only an earlier "version of the failure
that Adams later celebrated in his *Education*." The artistic intent of
Adams in constructing the narrative of the Jefferson administration was
to dramatize the plight of "the idealist crushed beneath reality." To develop this ironical purpose of the *History*, Adams was forced to establish Jefferson as a man of substantial worth—"as idealistic, public
spirited, friendly, sanguine, intellectual, essentially honest and honorable"—whose policies were overwhelmed by "disaster upon disaster,
mortification upon mortification." To Jordy, however, this manipulation
of Jefferson is not to be taken as evidence of Adams' successful artistic
detachment. The theme of "psychological paralysis, failure to arrive at
decisive conclusion, a sense of drift" was used so often by Adams in his
writings, and particularly in the *Education*, that we can assume a sympathetic identification with Jefferson at least at a deeper level.[5] To be
sure, Jordy also recognizes that, on another level, the *History* reveals a
strong intellectual preference for the northern Democrats in the Jeffersonian party, in opposition to the Virginian Republicans and New
England Federalists. Indeed, he goes so far as to state that "the *History*
was virulently anti-Federalist." [6]

Many readers of Henry Adams are confirmed in their acceptance of
him as a Jeffersonian by his own characterization of his historical bias.
Anyone who has read the letters of Henry Adams will recall his letter
to President Charles W. Eliot in 1877, in which he proposed that his
assistant, Henry Cabot Lodge, be allowed to set up a rival course in
American history coterminous with the one he was teaching at Harvard
for the reason that, "His views being federalist and conservative, have
as good a right to expression in the college as mine which tend to democracy and radicalism." [7]

Teachers of History

Unquestionably Henry Adams' relation to Jeffersonian democracy is a fascinating subject for American intellectual historians. Professor Commager was willing to say, several years ago, that "Henry Adams at Monticello is the most pregnant, the most profound problem in American history." [8] And in various ways many readers and critics have satisfied themselves that Henry Adams was able to achieve a sympathetic relation to the Jeffersonian tradition. Yet a re-examination of the *History* will show any careful reader that Henry Adams cannot be pigeonholed so conveniently. The time has come to determine more exactly the degree to which Adams was intellectually a Jeffersonian, what and how much he probably meant when he told President Eliot that his views in the teaching of American history tended to democracy and radicalism, and the nature and extent of his apostasy from the original Federalism of his own family tradition. Before we can deal successfully with the problem of Henry Adams at Monticello, we need to face the problem of Henry Adams' relation to Quincy.

II

Readers of the *Education* will recall that Henry Adams' treatment of his distinguished ancestors is both favorable and respectful. To be sure the ironic questions are present in these earlier chapters of the *Education* but the edges are blunted by his willingness to admit the greatness of his grandfather—overpowering as it was to a mere boy. To Adams, the family heritage was symbolized in the "law of Resistance; of Truth, of Duty, and of Freedom" and, if these represented an eighteenth-century system of order no longer applicable to the nineteenth and twentieth centuries, they had made for a distinguished family tradition of political responsibility. Evidence for this respect and regard for his family can be abundantly confirmed in the letters of Henry Adams. Family loyalty, whether Adams was willing to admit it or not, was a personal solution that he always clung to in the face of his "problem" of finding direction through space, of running order through chaos.

But family tradition was more than a mere legend for Adams; it was an intellectual experience as well. From his boyhood, he had lived under the spell of his grandfather's and great-grandfather's writings. As a boy, he had helped his father with the proofs of an edition of the work of John Adams. By constant use of the magnificent Adams family library he became familiar with the papers of John Quincy Adams. At one time, when trying to find some occupation for himself after graduation from Harvard, he toyed with the idea of editing the works of J. Q. Adams, but he abandoned the project because he thought "it is not in me to do them justice"—a judgment which betrays respect and reverence as well as his own insecurity and indecision at the time. Nevertheless, it is important to remember that Henry Adams' first significant publication in the field of American history, *Documents Relating to New England Federalism, 1800–1815*, was prepared in order to defend the reputation of his grandfather and to provide documentary evidence for the high motives of John Quincy Adams in his desertion of the Federalist party in 1807.[9] The publication of the *Documents* in 1877 began the painstaking spadework of investigation that was to result in the publication of the nine-volume *History* more than a decade later.

One does not have to read very far in the *History* to discover that Adams was definitely unsympathetic with the extremist Federalist leaders with whom J. Q. Adams had broken political relations in 1807. The disunionist conspiracy in 1804 of such Federalist leaders as Timothy Pickering of the Essex Junto and Roger Griswold of the Connecticut Federalists in league with the scheming Republican renegade, Aaron Burr, is described in language that is full of moral condemnation. Adams writes:

> The idea implied a bargain and intrigue in terms such as in the Middle Ages the Devil was believed to impose upon the ambitious and reckless. Pickering and Griswold could win their game only by bartering their souls; they must invoke the Mephistopheles of politics, Aaron Burr.[10]

Adams brings this chapter entitled "Conspiracy" to a dramatic climax with the duel between Burr, a leading conspirator, and Hamilton, who had opposed the conspiracy, and offers the observation:

> The death of Hamilton and the Vice-President's flight, with their accessories of summer-morning sunlight on rocky and wooded heights, tranquil river and distant city, and, behind all, their dark background of moral gloom, double treason, and political despair, still stand as the most dramatic moment in the early politics of the Union.[11]

This language of condemnation, however, is directed only at the extremist leaders of the Federalists. Henry Adams is careful to make clear that Pickering did not speak for all Federalists in Massachusetts by any means. The Federalist party in Massachusetts was divided: one portion followed the lead of the Essex Junto; the other and larger part was not willing to support rash men and reckless measures. In this regard Adams records pointedly that, in 1803, both Massachusetts seats in the Senate had become by chance vacant in the same year, and the moderate Federalists were strong enough to choose none other than John Quincy Adams for the long term and to allow Pickering, the other candidate, to enter the Senate for the short term. Nor does Henry Adams fail to remind the reader that John Quincy Adams received this honor though only thirty-six years old and twenty years younger than Timothy Pickering, who had been dismissed from his father's cabinet only three years before.[12] Even more important is the obvious satisfaction that Henry Adams takes in noticing his grandfather's opposition to the conspiracy of 1804. No sooner does he trace the outlines of the conspiracy than he informs his readers that "nothing could be more certain than that at the first suggestion of disunion Senator Adams and the moderate Federalists would attack the Essex Junto with the bitterness of long suppressed hatred."[13] The plans of the conspirators failed because the more moderate Federalists preferred to follow the lead of men like Adams, Rufus King, Oliver Wolcott, George Cabot, and Alexander Hamilton who, in various ways, worked against the disunionist scheme.

The conspiracy of 1804 was a foreshadowing of even more desperate intrigues in 1807–1808 provoked by the famous Embargo Act of Jefferson's second administration. This was the political crisis which led John Quincy Adams to break with the Federalist party, and Henry Adams leaves us in no doubt as to where his sympathies lie. The reader is abundantly prepared to yield a complete and sympathetic understanding for J. Q. Adams' political apostasy. We are led to feel the dire necessity of some kind of punitive action against the English and French, particularly the English for their degrading treatment of American trade and shipping. The story of the Chesapeake-Leopard affair is told in full detail to emphasize the humiliation which America had suffered at the hands of the British. Henry Adams whips the reader to a full pitch of indignation by writing:

For the first time in their history the people of the United States learned, in June, 1807, the feeling of a true national emotion. Hitherto every public passion had been more or less partial and one-sided; even the death of Washington had been ostentatiously mourned in the interests and to the profit of party; but the outrage committed on the "Chesapeake" stung through hidebound prejudices, and made democrat and aristocrat writhe alike. The brand seethed and hissed like the glowing olive stake of Ulysses in the Cyclops' eye, until the whole American people, like Cyclops, roared with pain and stood frantic on the shore, hurling abuse at their enemy who taunted them from his safe ships.[14]

When the Chesapeake-Leopard incident was followed with the obnoxious British orders-in-council of 1807, who would not be ready to stand with Senator John Quincy Adams, Federalist though he was, when he responded to Jefferson's request for an embargo law by exclaiming: "The President has recommended the measure on his responsibility. I would not consider, I would not deliberate, I would act!"[15]

The effect of the embargo on New England's commercial interests is more than a twice-told tale. The bitterness of Federalist opposition to the measure is well known to every American schoolboy. The political consequence was to strengthen the position of the extremists in the Federalist party. Pickering and the extremists now had their chance for revenge on John Quincy Adams. Taking advantage of the popular indignation in Massachusetts over the effects of the embargo, they maneuvered the Federalist majority in the legislature to reject his bid for another term in the Senate. The martyrdom of John Quincy Adams is described by Henry Adams with a full sense of the laws of Resistance, of Truth, and of Duty which he had come to know as the family tradition when only a ten-year-old boy:

John Quincy Adams . . . had been from his earliest recollection, through his father's experience or his own, closely connected with political interests. During forty years he had been the sport of public turbulence, and for forty years he was yet to undergo every vicissitude of political failure and success; but in the range of his chequered life he was subjected to no other trial so severe as that which Pickering forced him to meet. In the path of duty he might doubtless face social and political ostracism, even in a town such as Boston was, and defy it. Men as good as he had done as much, in many times and places; but to do this in support of a President whom he disliked and distrusted, for the sake of a policy in which he had no faith, was enough to shatter a character of iron. Fortunately for him, his temper was not one to seek relief in half-way measures. He had made a mistake in voting for an embargo without limit of time; but since no measure of resistance to Europe more vigorous than the embargo could gain support from either party, he accepted and defended it.[16]

And so, J. Q. Adams' political defection in supporting a policy which was anathema to New England Federalists, based as it was upon a faulty measure and following as it did the leadership of a President whom he distrusted, is presented by Henry Adams as an action based upon higher motives than those which ruled the Federalist leaders who had engineered his defeat. The account of his grandfather's defeat for re-election is followed by Henry Adams' scathing comment, "The Federalists of 1801 were the national party of America; the Federalists of 1808 were a British faction in secret league with George Canning." [17] To substantiate this denunciation, the vengeful Pickering who had accomplished the political defeat of John Quincy Adams is exposed as a man who was, at the same moment, engaged in treasonous correspondence with the British minister and one John Henry, a secret British agent sent to Boston from Montreal.

In the face of such factious leadership, John Quincy Adams crowned his acts of party desertion by accepting an appointment as minister to Russia from the hand of the new Republican President, James Madison. For the further edification of his readers, Henry Adams in the remaining volumes of the *History* keeps tabs on J. Q. Adams' services to the Republicans in St. Petersburg, in the peace mission at Ghent in 1814–1815, and finally his appointment as secretary of state by Madison's successor, James Monroe. This service of a one-time Federalist to Republican administrations is given no special justification by Henry Adams—it needs none, it is self-justifying in view of the continued course of Federalist party history in New England. To be sure, the repeal of the embargo at the end of Jefferson's administration had evaporated any treasonable schemes that might have resulted from the illicit liaison between extremist Federalists and the British Tories. Nevertheless, the further history of the Federalist party is presented as a sordid record of obstructive factiousness and narrowing particularistic interests which reaches its climax in the Hartford Convention of 1814.

III

While there can be no question of Adams' condemnation of the course of New England Federalism from 1808 to 1815, it would be a mistake to assume that he has thereby condemned Federalism *in toto*. It is fairly easy to establish that Henry Adams' disapproval of Hartford Convention Federalism is a partial and somewhat superficial aspect of his relation to the Federalist tradition. Only a careless historian would jump to the conclusion that his censure of the Federalist leadership of New England springs from a Jeffersonian bias—that the underlying presuppositions of the *History* are that Jeffersonian Republicanism was right in its ideas and policies and Federalism was wrong, or even that Jeffersonian Republicanism set in motion the currents that were to dominate the movement of American history, and that the Federalists were prisoners of anachronistic ideas and systems. Henry Adams' historical judgment is more complex than any such crude dualistic patterning of American history would suggest. We need to remember that there was sufficient basis for censure of New England Federalism after 1808 in the original principles of the Federalist party itself. That Adams was aware of this is abundantly clear and one cannot properly understand his historical judgment unless one reckons with the many evidences of Henry Adams' approval of certain basic and original Federalist principles.

The very sentence with which Adams justifies his grandfather's political apostasy suggests that his standard of criticism was Federalist and not Jeffersonian Republican in origin: "The Federalists of 1801 were the national party of America; the Federalists of 1808 were a British faction in secret league with George Canning." The Federalist party of 1801 was the Federalist party which great-grandfather John Adams had led but which had had to yield power to the Jeffersonian Republicans after the electoral battle of 1800. When Henry Adams speaks of the Federalist party as *the* national party in 1801, he does not mean only that the Federalists of that day would have scorned entangling intrigues with agents of a foreign power. He is referring also to the nationalistic political and constitutional principles which the Federalist party had accepted as basic party doctrine beginning with the adoption of the Constitution of 1787.

No one who reads carefully the nine volumes of the *History* can escape the knowledge that one of the persistent themes of that study is to show how the Jeffersonians were forced to yield to the process of centralization in American government which their opponents had set in motion and codified into one of their cardinal principles of politics. With almost wearisome regularity and thoroughness, Adams notes each departure of Jefferson and Madison from the decentralist principles which their party proclaimed so conspicuously in 1798 and used as slogans in the election of 1800 in order to accomplish the defeat of John Adams. Never does Adams miss the opportunity to remind his reader that each Jeffersonian surrender to the necessities of centralization was a return to the principles of Federalism. And so, with not too subtle irony, Adams sums up even the golden years of the first Jefferson administration as a triumph of Federalist principles:

Jefferson said with truth that the two old parties were almost wholly melted into one; but in this fusion his own party had shown even more willingness than its opponents to mix its principles in a useful, but not noble, amalgam. His own protests in regard to the Louisiana purchase and the branch bank at New Orleans were recorded. With such evidence on their side, the moderate Federalists who in the election of 1804 gave to Jefferson the nineteen electoral votes of Massachusetts and the seven of New Hampshire, could claim that they had altered no opinion they ever held; that the government had suffered no change in principle from what it had been under President Washington; that not a Federalist measure, not even the Alien and Sedition laws, had been expressly repudiated; that the national debt was larger than it had ever been before, the navy maintained and energetically employed, the national bank preserved and its operations extended; that the powers of the national government had been increased to a point that made blank paper of the Constitution as heretofore interpreted by Jefferson, while the national territory, vastly more than doubled in extent, was despotically enlarged and still more despotically ruled by the President and Congress, in the teeth of every political profession the Republican party had ever made. Had this been the work of Federalists, it would have been claimed as a splendid triumph of Federalist principles; and the good sense of New England was never better shown than when Massachusetts and New Hampshire flung aside their prejudices and told Jefferson that they accepted his inaugural pledge to be a Federalist as they were Republicans.[18]

The Embargo Act, of the second Jefferson administration, was an even more glaring resort to the principles of Federalist predecessors, carried to extreme results.

That President Jefferson should exercise "dangerous and odious" powers, carrying the extremest principles of his Federalist predecessors to their extremest results; that he should in doing so invite bloodshed, strain his military resources, quarrel with the State authorities of his own party and with judges whom he had himself made; that he should depend for constitutional law on

Henry Adams and the Federalists

Federalist judges whose doctrines he had hitherto believed fatal to liberty,—these were the first fruits of the embargo. After such an experience, if he or his party again raised the cry of States-rights, or of strict construction, the public might, with some foundation of reason, set such complaints aside as factious and frivolous, and even, in any other mouth than that of John Randolph, as treasonable.[19]

The tendency to centralization, already so evident in the Jefferson administration, was continued with few exceptions in the administration of Madison. By this time the Jeffersonian party had an infusion of new blood. The active leaders of the new Congress elected in 1810 were young men such as Henry Clay, John Caldwell Calhoun, William Lowndes, Langdon Cheves, Felix Grundy, Peter Porter, Richard M. Johnson.

None of these new leaders could remember the colonial epoch, or had taken a share in public life except under the Constitution of 1789, or had been old enough to feel and understand the lessons taught by opposition to the Federalist rule. . . . Of statesmanship, in the old sense, they took little thought. Bent on war with England, they were willing to face debt and probable bankruptcy on the chance of creating a nation, of conquering Canada, and carrying the American flag to Mobile and Key West.[20]

More than that, the new Republicans were no longer hampered by respect for old Republican traditions to which Jefferson and, indeed, Madison still paid lip service in the face of the centralizing tendencies which events had forced upon them. A revolution had taken place in the Twelfth Congress as radical as the "revolution of 1800" which had brought the Jeffersonians to power. The new Republicans resorted enthusiastically to measures which old Republicans had opposed in 1798. And Adams will not let even the most inattentive reader escape at this point, for he exploits the irony of this situation to the fullest extent.

That the party of Jefferson, Madison, Gallatin and Monroe should establish a standing army of thirty-five thousand troops in time of peace, when no foreign nation threatened attack, and should do this avowedly for purposes of conquest, passed the bounds of inconsistency and proclaimed a revolution. . . . These younger men were not responsible for what had been said or done ten or fifteen years before; they had been concerned in no conspiracy to nullify the laws, or to offer armed resistance to the government; they had never rested their character as statesmen on the chance of success in governing without armaments, and in coercing Napoleon and Pitt by peaceable means; they had no past to defend or excuse, and as yet no philosophical theories to preach—but they were obliged to remove from their path the system their party had established, and they worked at this task with more energy and more success than they showed in conducting foreign war. Even a return to Washington's system would not answer their purpose, for they were obliged to restore the extreme practices of 1798, and to re-enact laws which had then been denounced and discarded as the essence of monarchy.[21]

And these elements of "monarchy" were enumerated by Adams as "standing army of thirty-five thousand men, loans, protective duties, stamps, tax on distillation—nothing but a Sedition Law was wanting; and the previous question, as a means of suppressing discussion, was not an unfair equivalent for the Sedition Law."[22]

Already, Henry Adams was prepared to formulate a sequence of movement in American history in which he borrowed the idea of force from the field of physics and applied it to politics. At this point in his *History,* he detaches himself from the detailed analysis of the Twelfth Congress (but not from his own subjective enthusiasm) and observes:

After ten years devoted to weakening national energies, such freshness of youth and recklessness of fear had wonderful popular charm. The reaction from Jefferson's system threatened to be more violent than its adoption. Experience seemed to show that a period of about twelve years measured the beat of the pendulum. After the Declaration of Independence, twelve years had been needed to create an efficient Constitution; another twelve years of energy brought a reaction against a government then created; a third period of twelve years was ending in a sweep toward still greater energy; and already a child could calculate the results of a few more returns.[23]

This was not a momentary reflection tossed off as an idea in free flight. This idea of a pulsatory movement toward centralization in American life had already occurred to Henry Adams a decade before he wrote the *History.* In the famous centennial issue of the *North American Review* he had concluded a review of Von Holst's *Constitutional and Political History of the United States* with a perorating outburst which he called "my centennial oration." Some of these final sentences are worth quoting, for they foreshadow a major theme of his *History:*

We have no intention of deprecating foreign criticism or excusing inexcusable faults; but we have the right to claim and do claim that the Constitution has done its work. It has made a nation. . . . Above all the details of human weakness there will appear in more and more symmetry the real majesty and force of the national movement. If the historian will only consent to shut his eyes for a moment to the microscopic analysis of personal motives and idiosyncrasies, he cannot but become conscious of a silent pulsation that commands his respect, a steady movement that resembles in its mode of operation the mechanical action of Nature herself.[24]

No reader can escape Adams' sense of disgust and disappointment that these energies were frustrated and wasted by the failures of the Madison administration in the War of 1812. Indeed the movement toward national unity and centralization which had characterized the Twelfth Congress came perilously close to complete collapse by the time of the Hartford Convention. But the Treaty of Ghent and the return of peace restored the credit of the Madison administration in such a way that even Henry Adams forgets the hesitation in the beat of his pendulum and writes with obvious astonishment:

The effect of the news was so extraordinary as to shake faith in the seriousness of party politics. Although the peace affected in no way party doctrine and social distinctions, a new epoch for the Union began from the evening of February 13, when the messenger from Ghent arrived with the Treaty. No one stopped to ask why a government which was so discredited and falling to pieces at one moment, should appear as a successful and even glorious national representative a moment afterward.[25]

But Henry Adams' astonishment is not so great that he cannot appreciate the postwar measures of the Republican Congress occupied with creating a national bank, setting up a protective tariff, making appropriations for a large navy, moving to expand national funds to build a system of internal improvements. All of this signified a new burst of energy, and Adams, in a very revealing paragraph, is moved to give highest praise to the Fourteenth Congress:

The Fourteenth Congress, for ability, energy, and usefulness, never had a superior, and perhaps, since the First Congress, never an equal. Such abilities were uncommon in any legislative body, American or European. Since Federalist times, no Congress had felt such a sense of its own superiority; none had filled so fully the popular ideal of what the people's representatives should be.[26]

Consequently, we may assume that Henry Adams concluded with considerable satisfaction that when John Quincy Adams took office as secretary of state in the Monroe administration, he had remained truer to his original political principles than the Republicans who accepted him into their cabinet.

Old Republicans, like Macon and John Randolph, were at a loss to know whether James Monroe or J. Q. Adams had departed farthest from their original starting points. At times they charged one, at times the other, with desertion of principle, but on the whole their acts tended to betray a conviction that J. Q. Adams was still a Federalist in essentials, while Monroe had ceased to be an old Republican. In the political situation of 1817, if Jefferson and his contemporaries were right in their estimates, Federalist views of government were tending to prevail over the view of the Jeffersonian party.[27]

IV

One might rightly say at this point that this analysis of Henry Adams' examination of the tendency to centralization proves little more than that he evidently preferred the original centralist theories of the Federalists to the particularistic theories of the Jeffersonian Republicans. Herbert Agar confronts this problem of Jefferson's and Madison's retreat from their old Republican principles with the assertion that it merely adds to their glory, when he writes, "Yet, as Adams describes the process, we pity the two Presidents for the pain they suffered in the name of necessity, and we honor them for having the strength to subject theory to harsh truth." [28] Indeed many present-day historians sympathetic to Jefferson would grant quite readily that the original decentralist theories of the Jeffersonians were inadequate to cope with the realities of the nineteenth and twentieth centuries. They would make economic principles the primary test of a true Jeffersonian. They would assert that the keepers of the Jeffersonian conscience were those men who fought against the Federalistic economic system of national bank, tariffs, and government subsidies to private corporations in the promotion of schemes of internal improvement.[29] How does Henry Adams meet this test?

Anyone who has read the description of American society in the opening chapters of the *History* will recall immediately that Adams characterized the Jeffersonian hostility to all the machinery of capital as a "conservative habit of mind." More than that, Adams went so far as to assert that "this conservative habit of mind was more harmful in America than in other communities, because America needed more than older societies the activity which could alone partly compensate for the relative feebleness of their means compared with the magnitude of their task" in developing the material resources of a continent.[30]

But there is no better evidence of Henry Adams' conscious rejection of the economic theories of the Jeffersonian school than his devastating dismissal of the writings of John Taylor, who has been virtually canonized by historians with strong Jeffersonian sympathies. The following comment appears in the *History* concerning John Taylor's famous book, *An Inquiry into the Principles and Policy of the Government of the United States* published in 1814 as a reply to John Adams' equally famous *Defense of the Constitutions* published twenty-five years before:

In 1787, John Adams, like Jefferson, Hamilton, Madison, Jay, and other constitution makers, might without losing the interest of readers, indulge in speculations more or less visionary in regard to the future character of a nation yet in its cradle; but in 1814 the character of people and government was formed, the lines of their activity were fixed. A people which had in 1787 been indifferent or hostile to roads, banks, funded debt, and nationality, had become in 1815 habituated to ideas and machinery of the sort on a grand scale. Monarchy and aristocracy no longer entered into the public mind as factors in future development. Yet Taylor resumed the discussions of 1787 as though the interval were a blank; and his only conclusion from the experience of thirty years was that both parties were moving in a wrong direction. . . . Taylor's speculations ended only in an admission of their practical sterility, and his suggestions for restraining the growth of authority assumed the possibility of returning to the conditions of 1787.[31]

This acceptance of the machinery of capital is related to one of America's primary needs. "With half a continent to civilize," Americans need science and new technology. Adams, in the opening chapters of the *History*, deplores the popular apathy toward science and invention in the year 1800, and declares, "in order to make the Americans a successful people, they must be roused to feel the necessity of scientific training." But by the nature of their problems, Americans had to become a "speculating" as well as a scientific nation. "Hitherto their timidity in using money had been proportioned to the scantiness of their means. Henceforward they were under every inducement to risk great stakes and frequent losses in order to win occasionally a thousand fold." Only with the inducement of wealth and personal profit could Americans be roused to make full use of the force of science and invention. "Until they were satisfied that knowledge was money, they would not insist upon high education; until they saw with their own eyes stones turned into gold, and vapor into cattle and corn, they would not learn the meaning of science." [32]

Adams was not interested in science and invention as were the Greeks —simply for the love of mental speculation or for the diversion of playing with toy steam engines. He understood that technology must be accompanied by the machinery of credit and the organization of business and industry. Hence, another fundamental "sequence of human movement" that took place in the period under examination in the *History* was the development of "science" and the economic means to make it effective. In a concluding chapter, Adams notes that everywhere in 1816 there were signs of progress—banks and banking capital were multiplying, roads and canals were being built, steamboats were appearing on the western rivers of the country. Americans were roused from their earlier inertia.

The continent lay before them, like an uncovered ore-bed. They could see, and they could even calculate with reasonable accuracy, the wealth it could be made to yield. With almost the certainty of a mathematical formula, knowing the rate of increase of population and of wealth, they could read in advance their economical history for at least a hundred years. [33]

V

A historian of the Jeffersonian school might dismiss the foregoing examination of Adams' economic ideas, as Vernon Parrington does, by asserting that Adams was lacking in the necessary critical intelligence to deal with economic forces at the time that he wrote the *History*. [34] If so, this leaves the Jeffersonian historian with only one significant possibility of establishing the thesis that Henry Adams was intellectually a Jeffersonian. This approach would have to depend on an analysis of Henry Adams' appraisal of the intellectual characteristics of Jeffersonian democracy. In this connection, many historians interested in cultural history would emphasize the Jeffersonian struggle for personal freedom in all types of human endeavor and especially the freedom of inquiry as a turning point in the development of American democracy. For this reason, the Jefferson Memorial in Washington monumentalizes the famous sentence from Jefferson's letter to Dr. Rush in 1800—"I have sworn upon the altar of God, eternal hostility against every form of tyranny over the mind of man."

Adams was clearly aware of the existence of this ideal in the American popular mind. He not only included it in his summary of "American Ideals" in the first volume of the *History,* but he defended it against the sneers of European contemporaries:

> European travellers who passed through America noticed that everywhere, in the White House at Washington and in log-cabins beyond the Alleghanies, except for a few Federalists, every American from Jefferson and Gallatin down to the poorest squatter, seemed to nourish an idea that he was doing what he could to overthrow the tyranny which the past had fastened on the human mind. Nothing was easier than to laugh at the ludicrous expression of this simple-minded conviction, or to cry out against its coarseness, or grow angry with its prejudices; to see its nobler side, to feel the beatings of a heart underneath the sordid surface of a gross humanity, was not so easy. Europeans seemed seldom or never conscious that the sentiment could possess a noble side, but found only matter for complaint in the remark that every American democrat believed himself to be working for the overthrow of tyranny, aristocracy, hereditary privilege, and priesthood, wherever they existed. Even where the American did not openly proclaim this conviction in words, he carried so dense an atmosphere of the sentiment with him in his daily life as to give respectable Europeans an uneasy sense of remoteness.[35]

It was this popular belief which made democracy as powerful a force in American society as centralization, capital, or science. The power of this democratic force was expressed by Adams in his symbol of "the new order of man." The American, because his society had removed artificial barriers to human effort, stood in this world as a new order of man "stripped for the hardest work, every muscle firm and elastic, every ounce of brain ready for use, and not a trace of superfluous flesh on his nervous and supple body." Compared with this "lithe young figure," Europe was actually in decrepitude. Class distinctions, endless wars, huge debts, parasitic aristocracies, thought-stifling churches and governments, made of Europe a place where "common men could not struggle." [36]

Unquestionably, Adams is fascinated by the great pretensions of this democratic dream. He recognizes that of all the Americans of that earlier generation, Thomas Jefferson came "nearest" to expressing the "whole character" of this democratic tendency in American society. And so, in a significant passage of this early chapter in the *History*, Jefferson is made to define democratic progress as Adams "imagined" that he would:

> Progress is either physical or intellectual. If we can bring it about that men are on the average an inch taller in the next generation than in this; if they are an inch larger round the chest; if their brain is an ounce or two heavier, and their life a year or two longer,—that is progress. If fifty years hence the average man shall invariably argue from two ascertained premises where he now jumps to a conclusion from a single supposed revelation,—that is progress! I expect it to be made here, under our democratic stimulants, on a great scale, until every man is potentially an athlete in body and an Aristotle in mind.[37]

To this imaginary definition of democratic progress, Adams makes "the New Englander" reply immediately with the question, "What will you do for moral progress?" "Every possible answer to this question opened a chasm" because Jefferson "held the faith that men would improve morally with their physical and intellectual growth; but he had no idea of any moral improvement other than that which came by nature." To New Englanders, of course, this answer was not enough. "To their minds vice and virtue were not relative, but fixed terms." For an understanding of these fixed terms of morality, society needed the guidance of the Church, "a divine institution." In any case, "even should the new experiment succeed in a worldly sense," the New Englander would still ask, "What was a man profited if he gained the whole world, and lost his own soul?" Thus the struggle between New England conservatism and Jeffersonian democracy is depicted in its most fundamental divergence. "The two parties stood facing opposite ways, and could see no common ground of contact." [38]

Although previously in the world's history, the conservatives had always taken their stand with success, Adams speculates about the possible outcome of the Jeffersonian idea when he considers the native energy and inventiveness of Americans like Benjamin Franklin, John Fitch, Eli Terry, Robert Fulton, and Asa Whittemore. If "all of these men were the outcome of typical American society, and all their inventions transmuted the democratic instinct into a practical and tangible shape . . . who would undertake to say that there was a limit to the fecundity of this teeming source?" To be sure, the inventions of these men, as Adams had noted before, were not accepted until Americans understood that they brought wealth. But "who," Adams asks, "that saw only the narrow, practical, money-getting nature of these devices could venture to assert that as they wrought their end and raised the standard of millions, they would not also raise the creative power of these millions to a higher plane?" Indeed one might point to history to show that the Jeffersonian hope was not extravagant.

If the priests and barons who set their names to Magna Carta had been told that in a few centuries every swineherd and cobblers' apprentice would write and read with an ease such as few kings could then command, and reason with better logic than any university could then practise, the priest and baron would have been more incredulous than any man who was told in 1800 that within another five centuries the ploughboy would go a-field whistling a sonata of Beethoven, and figure out in quarternions the relation of his furrows.[39]

These "illusions" of the Jeffersonians, therefore, became the yardstick by which Adams proposed to measure "democratic progress" in America. This is the intent behind the questions with which Adams concludes the famous six opening chapters of the *History*.

Whether the illusions, so often affirmed and so often denied to the American people, took such forms or not, these were in effect the problems that lay before American society. Could it transmute its social power into the higher forms of thought? Could it provide for the moral and intellectual needs of mankind? Could it take permanent political shape? Could it give new life to religion and art? Could it create and maintain in the mass of mankind those habits of mind which had hitherto belonged to men of science alone? Could it physically develop the convolutions of the human brain? Could it produce, or was it compatible with, the differentiation of a higher variety of the human race? Nothing less than this was necessary for its complete success.[40]

Yet even though Adams accepted a Jeffersonian standard for measuring American social development, he was quick to deny that Jeffersonians alone were working toward higher forms of thought. The first volume of his *History* contains a significant defense of the contributions of New England intellectuals which should not be overlooked, the more so since it is aimed at Jefferson himself.

Jefferson prided himself on his services to free-thought even more than on those he had rendered to political freedom: in the political field he had many rivals, but in the scientific arena he stood, or thought he stood, alone. His relations with European philosophers afforded him deep enjoyment; and in his Virginian remoteness he imagined his own influence on thought, abroad and at home, to be greater than others supposed it. His knowledge of New England was so slight that he readily adopted a belief in the intolerance of Puritan society toward every form of learning; he loved to contrast himself with his predecessors in the encouragement of science, and he held that to break down the theory and practice of a state-church in New England was necessary not only to his own complete triumph, but to the introduction of scientific thought. Had he known the people of New England better, he would have let them alone; but believing that Massachusetts and Connecticut were ruled by an oligarchy like the old Virginia tobacco-planters, with no deep hold on the people, he was bent upon attacking and overthrowing it. At the moment when he was thus preparing to introduce science into New England by political methods, President Dwight, the head of New England Calvinism, was persuading Benjamin Silliman to devote his life to the teaching of chemistry in Yale College. Not long afterward, the Corporation of Harvard College scandalized the orthodox by electing as Professor of Theology, Henry Ware, whose Unitarian sympathies were notorious. All three authorities were working in their own way for the same result; but Jefferson preferred to work through political revolution,—a path which the people of New England chose only when they could annoy their rulers.[41]

Moreover, when Adams makes an examination in his final volume of "the movement of thought" which had taken place between 1800 and 1816, he gives considerable prominence to the growth and influence of Unitarianism in New England. This Unitarian tendency he characterizes as having a "high social and intellectual character" which would enable it to relax the severity of thought of orthodox Calvinism, replacing it with an optimistic humanitarianism. Adams is also at some pains to point out that while this movement in New England was contemporaneous with the sway of Jefferson's political ideas, the relationship was "remote and wholly intellectual." [42] Indeed, "the liberalism of Boston began in a protest against 'the foul spirit of innovation.'" [43] Of this intellectual movement "in all its new directions," Harvard College was the center. Yet "Harvard College," Adams insists, "seemed to entertain no feeling toward Jefferson but antipathy." [44] And it is with unconcealed pride that Adams records how the activity of "the College and church" in "the small society of Boston, numbering hardly forty thousand persons . . . produced a new era." Adams catalogues such names as John Quincy Adams, Edward Everett, George Ticknor, Henry Ware, William

Henry Adams and the Federalists

Hickling Prescott, J. G. Palfrey, George Bancroft, and Ralph Waldo Emerson as proof of the intellectual vigor of Harvard and Boston. Boston was a magnet which drew in the best from all of New England, for Adams maintains that Boston showed "no stronger proof of its vigor than when, in 1816, it attracted Daniel Webster from New Hampshire to identify himself with the intellect and interests of Massachusetts." [45] The structure of the chapter in Adams' final volume entitled "Religious and Political Thought" is all the more interesting because it begins with a sympathetic treatment of the non-Jeffersonian humanitarianism of the New England Unitarians, Henry Ware, Joseph Stevens Buckminster, and William Ellery Channing, and ends with a devastating dismissal of the sterile doctrines of John Taylor of Caroline, the leading philosopher of the Jeffersonian Republicans.

In Adams' view, then, two parallel developments contributed to the "movement of thought" in the American people between 1800 and 1817—Jeffersonian Democracy and New England Unitarianism. Both helped to form the traits of "intelligence, rapidity, and mildness" which "seemed fixed in the national character as early as 1817." [46] Yet Adams evades any definite judgments about the questions he has raised concerning the requirements of democratic social progress in the first volume of his *History*. Seventeen years is too short a time to provide answers to such questions, and he prefers to conclude with another series of questions:

They were intelligent, but what paths would their intelligence select? They were quick, but to what solution of insoluble problems would quickness hurry? They were scientific, and what control would their science exert over their destiny? They were mild, but what corruptions would their relaxation bring? They were peaceful, but by what machinery were their corruptions to be purged? What interests were to vivify a society so vast and uniform? What ideals were to ennoble it? What object, besides physical content, must a democratic continent aspire to attain? For the treatment of such questions, history required another century of experience. [47]

The ironic tone of these final questions will forever keep the reader of the *History* in doubt about Adams' judgment concerning the degree of success which the Jeffersonians achieved in bringing about democratic social progress.

VI

Thus, throughout the nine volumes of Adams' *History of the United States in the Administrations of Thomas Jefferson and James Madison,* the Jeffersonians are measured by Federalistic standards as well as their own. The Jeffersonians are given most approbation when they abandon their particularistic principles in favor of Federalistic centralization. The economic measures of the Fourteenth Congress, influenced as they were by Federalistic principles, are the work of a legislative body that "never had a superior." Jefferson himself had best expressed the aspirations of democratic progress, but Boston and Harvard had made important contributions to the moral and intellectual growth of the people, while John Taylor led the old Republicans down the sterile pathways of his impractical and outmoded system.

It is impossible to escape the impression from the pages of the *History* that the Jeffersonians were in no way the masters of their own destiny. The Jeffersonian leaders did not *lead* Americans to take a new direction in their development. Indeed, there were no heroes or heroic leaders in Adams' *History,* either Jeffersonian or Federalist. Adams pointedly reminds his reader of this fact in the concluding chapter of his *History.* There he stresses that the American historian must adopt different standards from those of Old World historians. Old World historians had developed a dramatic view of history with emphasis upon the hero in history. This was the result of the fierce struggles which characterized European society and gave it a character that must always be chiefly military. "The intensity of the struggle gave prominence to the individual, until the hero seemed all, society nothing." Against such a view of society, Old World historians "were among the last to protest and protested but faintly when they did so at all. They felt as strongly as their audiences that the highest achievements were alone worth remembering either in history or in art, and that a reiteration of commonplaces was commonplace." To the American historian, however, "War counted for little, the hero for less; in the people alone the eye could permanently rest." Hence a Jefferson and a Madison, and even a John Quincy Adams, were worth study as "types of character" in the make-up of the national character and "not as sources of power." [48]

Instead of dramatic or heroic treatments, American history required "scientific treatment." "The steady growth of a vast population without the social distinctions that confused other histories,—without kings, nobles or armies; without church, traditions, and prejudices—seemed a subject for a man of science rather than for dramatists or poets." [49] The study of the democratic evolution of a people was like the study of the ocean—"science alone could sound the depths of the ocean, measure its currents, foretell its storms, or fix its relations to the system of Nature." [50] In the "democratic ocean" of American history Jeffersonians and Federalists alike were carried along by more fundamental currents. This view of the relative powerlessness of American leaders was part of Adams' thinking as early as 1883, when he was still in the earlier stage of writing his *History*. At that time in a letter to a friend concerning Jefferson, Madison, and Monroe, Adams wrote, "I am at times sorry that I ever undertook to write their history, for they appear like mere grasshoppers kicking and gesticulating on the middle of the Mississippi River. . . . They were carried along on a stream which floated them, after a fashion, without much regard to themselves." [51]

So, in the period from 1800 to 1817, Adams saw such currents as centralization, science, capital, and democracy, in the "democratic ocean" of the United States. Or, in view of the dependence which all these forces have upon each other, an oceanographer might think of them as part of a single current system like the Gulf Stream which is complicated by the inflow and outflow of countercurrents, eddies, tributaries, and branches. At varying times, the Jeffersonians and the Federalists are either floating with the main current or have become countercurrents and eddies. When the Jeffersonians (or Federalists like John Quincy Adams) steer with the main current, then Adams' writing becomes loaded with his favorable adjectives—"energetic," "vigorous," "useful," "successful." On these conditions, and these conditions only, is Henry Adams ever a Jeffersonian.

1. *Atlantic Monthly*, LXV (February, 1890), 275.
2. *English Historical Review*, VIII (October, 1893), 805.
3. Henry Adams, *History of the United States in the Administrations of Thomas Jefferson and James Madison*, new ed. (New York, 1930), I, Introduction, xi; hereafter cited, from the first edition (New York, 1889–1891), as *History*.
4. Herbert Agar, ed., *The Formative Years* (Boston, 1947), I, ix–xii.
5. William H. Jordy, *Henry Adams, Scientific Historian* (New Haven,

1952). This examination of the artistry in the *History* is made in Chapter III.

6. *Ibid.*, pp. 73–74.

7. Harold Dean Cater, ed., *Henry Adams and His Friends* (Boston, 1947), p. 81.

8. Introduction to the 1930 edition of the *History*, I, x.

9. Ernest Samuels, *The Young Henry Adams* (Cambridge, Mass., 1948), pp. 273–274.

10. Henry Adams, *History*, II, 170–171.

11. *Ibid.*, II, 190–191.

12. *Ibid.*, II, 110.

13. *Ibid.*, II, 163.

14. *Ibid.*, IV, 27.

15. *Ibid.*, IV, 172–173.

16. *Ibid.*, IV, 239–240.

17. *Ibid.*, IV, 242–243.

18. *Ibid.*, II, 204–205.

19. *Ibid.*, IV, 271.

20. *Ibid.*, VI, 122–123.

21. *Ibid.*, VI, 154–155.

22. *Ibid.*, VI, 158. The House of Representatives had just adopted new rules to limit debate.

23. *Ibid.*, VI, 123.

24. Quoted in Samuels, *op. cit.*, p. 271.

25. *History*, IX, 80.

26. *Ibid.*, IX, 138.

27. *Ibid.*, IX, 140.

28. *The Formative Years*, I, xviii.

29. See Arthur M. Schlesinger Jr., *The Age of Jackson* (Boston, 1946), Chapter 3.

30. *History*, I, 65–66.

31. *Ibid.*, IX, 195–197.

32. *Ibid.*, I, 73–74.

33. *Ibid.*, IX, 173–174.

34. Vernon Louis Parrington, *Main Currents in American Thought* (New York, 1930), III, 218.

35. *History*, I, 175–176.

36. *Ibid.*, I, 159–161.

37. *Ibid.*, I, 179.

38. *Ibid.*, I, 179–180.

39. *Ibid.*, I, 183.

40. *Ibid.*, I, 184.

41. *Ibid.*, I, 310–311.

42. *Ibid.*, IX, 176.

43. *Ibid.*, IX, 205.

44. *Ibid.*, IX, 176.

45. *Ibid.*, IX, 206.

46. *Ibid.*, IX, 240–241.

47. *Ibid.*, IX, 241–242.

48. These historical ideas are summarized from pages 223–226 in last chapter of the *History*.

49. *Ibid.*, IX, 224.

50. *Ibid.*, IX, 225.

51. Cater, *op. cit.*, pp. 125–126.

[H. STUART HUGHES]

Gaetano Mosca and the

Political Lessons of History

AMONG American students of political science and history, Gaetano Mosca is usually considered as a kind of second-class Pareto. The leading ideas ascribed to the two thinkers are similar—the theory of elites, of the role of force and deception in history, in short, of a neo-Machiavellianism derived from a common Italian heritage. As sharp critics of parliamentary democracy and socialism, Pareto and Mosca appear to occupy similar places among the precursors of fascism— half-unconscious, perhaps, of what they were doing, but still in some ultimate sense responsible for the collapse of Italian democracy and the advent of Mussolini. From this standpoint, Pareto looms as the larger figure. His range is wider, his books are longer, his "scientific" apparatus is more impressive, and his criticism cuts deeper. Moreover, the Fascist chief himself honored Pareto and was happy to number him among his intellectual inspirers; apparently he never mentioned Mosca. Conversely, the latter's eventual opposition to Mussolini's regime was too quiet to attract much attention: the sweet notes of reasoned dissent reached the outside world through Croce alone, and other voices sounded muffled and ineffective. On all counts, then, Mosca has seemed a lesser figure; he wrote more gracefully than Pareto and his views were more moderate—but those were the only respects in which his work ranked higher.

The accidental circumstance that Pareto's *Trattato di sociologia ge-*

nerale appeared in English translation five years earlier than Mosca's *Elementi di scienza politica* partly explains the greater prestige the former work enjoys.[1] But even in Italy, where the two books were equally available to the reading public, Mosca's took second place. Although his theory of the "political class" quite obviously antedated Pareto's formulation of the "elite" concept, Mosca experienced the greatest difficulty in maintaining his claim to priority. The result was a polemic that went on for two decades to the eventual weariness of both the contestants and the other learned figures who were drawn in. There was no doubt that Mosca was the injured party. Pareto affected a lofty disdain for the whole controversy and simply "erased Mosca's name even from his footnotes." [2] But at the same time there must have been something profoundly irritating to the sage of Lausanne about the pertinacity with which a less-well-known scholar ten years his junior kept insisting on his title to an idea that was by no means totally original and that could plausibly be regarded as no more than the product of the general intellectual atmosphere in Western Europe just before the turn of the century.

It is not the purpose of the present essay to argue against the prevailing impression and to give Mosca his due. It is rather my intention to point out once again the obvious—if frequently overlooked—difference between the practical conclusions in which the two theories terminate, and in so doing to suggest that this contrast is due in great part to a different attitude toward history—an attitude that in Mosca's case was the product of a longer personal experience. Mosca's sense of history as an experienced reality, even against his expressed intention, worked gradual and subtle changes not only in his political ideas but even in the presuppositions behind them.

I

The difference between Pareto's and Mosca's practical conclusions is too well known to require elaboration. Pareto died, as he had lived, the sworn foe of parliamentary democracy. He had experienced only the first year of Mussolini's new government; he had expressed his reservations about it—but these were on matters of emphasis rather than principle. Mosca lived nearly two decades longer, virtually through the whole of the Fascist dictatorship. He had ample time to see what was happening, and he early came to a negative judgment, although once the regime was consolidated, he prudently kept his opinions to himself. This difference in age, however, was not decisive. Mosca had reached his new conclusions even before Pareto's death; the second edition of his *Elementi*, published a few weeks after Mussolini came to power, already shows his transformation from a critic of parliamentary democracy into its defender—a sceptical defender, indeed, but an extremely effective one. The difference lies, rather, in the divergent experience of the two writers during the quarter century preceding the March on Rome; while Pareto was living in scholarly seclusion and enjoying his self-imposed exile in Switzerland, Mosca was actively participating in Italian political life. The day-to-day contact with political reality was insensibly modifying his theoretical judgments and even the concept of history on which they were based.[3]

Mosca's original idea of history closely resembled Pareto's. It was a simple, straightforward view, reflecting both the heritage of the Enlightenment and the more recent teachings of French positivism. In its didactic emphasis, it recalled the Enlightenment. Like Voltaire or Gibbon, Mosca set out to ransack the records of past ages for instructive examples that would yield general truths on the political behavior of mankind. He had read widely and thoroughly both in the classics and in the published literature of European history. And he seemed able to remember nearly everything he read; as a young man of twenty-five, in the introduction to his first political work, he somewhat naïvely congratulated himself on the advantages he owed to his unusually retentive memory.[4]

Mosca was not only looking for examples. He was also seeking "laws." Here his debt to Taine was manifest and amply recognized. Like his French master, Mosca was radically dissatisfied with the methods and categories ordinarily employed by political writers. He found them imprecise, emotionally grounded, and generally unrelated to the recorded facts of political behavior. And the result had been that the study of politics and sociology had lagged far behind the other scholarly disciplines. It had not yet become a "science."[5] Mosca implied, although he refrained from making too flat-footed a claim, that his own works would rank as the founding documents of this new science.

This was positivist thinking with a vengeance. Mosca's scientific self-confidence, his cold disdain for sentimental ideologies, and his emphasis on force as the basis of human society were strictly in consonance with the prevailing temper of the post-Darwinian age. From this standpoint, he was by no means the innovator that he claimed to be—he was simply the typical bright scholar of his time. Yet he was too open-minded to allow himself to become imprisoned in his own formulas. He did not rest content with the materialist, mechanical explanations that to contemporary readers make the work of Taine so repellent. And he was careful to avoid the trap of historical determinism. The "political classes" whose role in history he was charting he subjected to no inexorable law of degeneration and fall from power. Their fate lay in their own hands. As Mosca's American editor has pointed out, it was simply "wrong political decisions that headed them toward decline instead of toward higher levels of civilization." [6] Hence Mosca's theory of society, as opposed to that of his leading predecessors and contemporaries, was "open" rather than "closed." It would have satisfied the rigorous requirements of the great living theorist of the "open society." Like Karl Popper, Mosca in effect argues that "we must learn to do things as well as we can, and to look out for our mistakes," and further, that "progress rests with us, with our watchfulness, with our efforts, with the clarity of our conception of our ends, and with the realism of their choice." [7]

Moreover, proud as Mosca was of his theory of the political class, and stoutly as he defended it from all competitors and detractors during more than half a century of catastrophic political changes, he never seems to have taken it with the deadly seriousness characteristic of most discoverers of new ideas. Mosca's mature work, despite the dogmatism of its major premise, is far from dogmatic in tone. It flows along pleasantly and easily in a style that combines the old-fashioned, piled-up periodic sentence with great simplicity and clarity of expression. It is full of sly asides, tantalizing hints of ideas that will never be developed, quiet jests—in short, of an ebullient Mediterranean good humor. The dominant tone is one of urbane scepticism. His own theory, Mosca implies, while it is doubtless the best produced to date, is, after all, only a theory. And all theories should be taken rather lightly. It is probable that Mosca never expected his ideas to have much effect—as indeed they did not—or to be taken to heart too literally by his contemporaries. It would be enough if he had planted in their minds the suspicion that the contrasting political ideologies they so vociferously supported were essentially fantasies—pious frauds of widely varying social useful-ness. Subsequently, when Mosca entered politics himself, his conduct was far from doctrinaire. Untroubled by apparent contradictions, he serenely permitted himself to be guided by his naturally pragmatic temper. Thus, although unconvinced of any practical advantage ac-cruing to Italy from the Tripolitan War, he declared himself a colonial-ist and even consented to serve as under-secretary of state for colonies during the First World War. "It is frequently better," he is reported to have remarked, "to make a bad deal than to cut a poor figure." [8]

The same good-humored disclaimer of infallibility cannot be found in Pareto. About many aspects of human behavior, Pareto was deeply sceptical—witness the conventional charge of cynicism brought against him. But about his own mental processes, his own conclusions, he per-mitted himself little doubt; in this respect he remained closer than Mosca to the original positivist faith. Pareto was content to respect the ultimate mystery of human motivation—but he was convinced that he had at least discovered enough about the laws of social mechanics to provide an adequate guide to mass manipulation. [9] Hence his writing has a rigidity of categorization and an asperity of tone that are found only in Mosca's earliest work. Moreover, Pareto's sociological writings are all of one piece. Only seventeen years elapsed between the pub-lication of the first volume of the *Systèmes socialistes* and that of the final volume of the great *Trattato*. And during this period the author's ideas underwent no significant alteration. He simply reworked them to give them a more "scientific" terminology and presentation. Once Pareto had retired to the shores of Lake Geneva, his attitude was fixed for all time; distinguished visitors came and conversed with the master, but the reverberation of the earth-shaking storms beyond the borders of Switzerland did not alter Pareto's fixed ideas any more than they upset the ordered, if rather eccentric, routine of his daily living. [10] Even the advent of Mussolini and the award of a seat in the Italian Senate could not induce him to return to Italy.

In Mosca's case the gap between the youthful moment of discovery and the ultimate retouches applied to his theory for the last edition of the *Elementi* published during his lifetime was a matter of fifty-seven years. In the interval the political configuration of Europe had changed utterly. For Mosca this was no particular source of dismay, either theo-retical or practical. Serene in his conviction that most political leaders were garrulous fools, he was not surprised by what had happened. On balance, he concluded, his theory had stood up well. There was little he wished to retract or alter. Even where he confessed that youthful intrepidity had led him to overstate his case, he noted "with a certain satisfaction" that the "fundamental principles" did not "need many corrections."[11] And "several of the most important predictions" that he had made had been "confirmed by events" either "in whole or in part."[12] Nevertheless the passage of time had left its mark. Under the stress of enlarged experience, the "open" element in Mosca's thinking began to predominate over what was merely positivist and doctrinaire.

To many of us today, Mosca's basic notion of history may seem profoundly unhistorical. The problem of historical knowledge never troubled him; he never questioned the credentials of his data. They were simply given "facts," transferable blocks for the political theorist to build with. To the end of his days the concept of history as a drama taking place in the mind of the historian never seems to have occurred to him—despite the fact that he was the contemporary, the countryman, and presumably (as a fellow senator) the acquaintance of Benedetto Croce. On the surface, Mosca retained his positivist allegiance. But somewhat deeper down, a more refined feeling for historical change gradually asserted itself. Despite his own professions, despite his denials of subjectivity, his essential historical-mindedness broke through. This is part of what Croce had in mind when he found a great deal of good sense in a book like the *Elementi* that rested on "philosophical presuppositions" so radically different from his own.[13]

II

This paradox is already apparent in Mosca's first published work. In a little treatise entitled *Teorica dei governi* (1884) that was intended to define the permanent truths of political behavior—derived from historical observation, it is true, but themselves timeless and unchanging—Mosca revealed how deeply his thought was anchored in his own historical situation. With a lordly scorn for his predecessors, Mosca dismissed their theories as based on faulty "historical preconceptions." He alone had discovered the "key to the great secrets of history."

Teachers of History

All the political history of mankind in all times, in all nations, and in all civilizations can ultimately be summarized under two major points of view: on the one hand, the degree of coordination of the various political classes, the number of resources that they are able to gather in their own hands, and the force of their collective action; on the other hand, the various elements that make up these classes, their different methods of imposing their rule, their rivalries, their struggles, their compromises and "combinations." [14]

And so he went on to elaborate in their first and most dogmatic form the basic theories associated with his name—the doctrine of the necessary predominance of an active minority in all times and under all forms of government, even those that call themselves the rule of one man or of all the citizens, and the parallel concept of the "political formula," the convenient myth that conceals the harsh realities of class rule under the respectable cloak of religious or ideological legitimacy.

This emphasis on class considerations in politics already begins to locate Mosca in a specific historical situation. As Karl Mannheim has pointed out:

It is almost possible to establish a sociological correlation between the type of thinking that appeals to organic or organized groups and a consistently systematic interpretation of history. . . . A class or similar organic group never sees history as made up of transitory disconnected incidents. [15]

Thus it appears to be no accident that during the past century the great integrated views of history have been associated with the aspirations and fortunes of fairly well-defined social classes. They have expressed the struggle of the urban working classes for economic improvement and social equality, as in the case of Marxism. Or, as with the theories of Pareto and Spengler, they have been phrased as last-ditch appeals to a tottering oligarchy to "shore up its fragments" of prestige and authority by infusing new life into the traditional aristocratic values. Finally—as in the case of Toynbee, or, in our own country, F. S. C. Northrop—they have been efforts to restore self-confidence to a great middle class, structurally unintegrated and unsure of its own political allegiance, by lifting to a higher plane of spiritual contemplation and extra-European validity, the somewhat shop-worn credo of liberalism inherited from the Enlightenment. In this schematic arrangement, Mosca's theories fall somewhere between the second and third categories. They began by more closely resembling the former and ended as a vigorous reaffirmation of liberal principles.

Mosca and Lessons of History

Thus Mosca, as a discerning and clear-headed anti-Marxist, confronts Marx with his own terminology. Unlike the conventional American refutation of Marxism, which denies the whole class interpretation of history, Mosca's theory accepts it but redefines it in such a way as to reverse its implications.

The existence of a political class does not conflict with the essential content of Marxism, considered not as an economic dogma but as a philosophy of history. . . . There is no essential contradiction between the doctrine that history is the record of a continued series of class struggles and the doctrine that class struggles invariably culminate in the creation of new oligarchies which undergo fusion with the old.[16]

But in Mosca's hands, the classes cease to be historical actors in their own right. They become simply a series of passive audiences, disciplined claques pathetically anxious to applaud the posturings of narrower groups drawn from their own ranks. History, Mosca assures us, cannot be the story of the political vicissitudes of classes conceived as entities—a moment's reflection shows this to be a technical impossibility. It can only be the record of the rise and fall of oligarchies. And if this is the case, then the whole apocalyptic vision of the new world of classless harmony simply vanishes into thin air. The new world will be very much like the old one. Mosca does not deny the possibility of human progress: the word occurs frequently in his writings, and the great ethical purpose behind his work is to confirm the progress that has already been made and to preserve the conditions essential to further advances. His own era—the last quarter of the nineteenth century—Mosca feels to be superior in nearly all respects to its predecessors. But this superior level of civilization is precarious and desperately threatened. A new political class is striving by methods of fraud and violence to displace the old oligarchy whose leadership has brought the European world to its current position of eminence. Under these circumstances, a revolution—the displacement of one oligarchy by another—far from opening up glittering vistas of further progress, would imperil and perhaps destroy the progress that has already been made.

Redefined in this fashion, the class interpretation of history is transformed from a revolutionary into a conservative doctrine. It becomes a vehicle for restoring the self-confidence of the European ruling classes, whose will to govern has been sapped by the Rousseauist dogmas of democracy and social equality. In effect, Mosca's teaching gives back to them a good conscience about their privileges. If history is simply a succession of oligarchies, it tells them, and political equality a mirage, then it is foolish to worry about one's own position as an oligarch. The democratic gestures inspired by such scruples will be worse than futile; they will pave the way to power for a new oligarchy—far inferior in talent, in ethical standards, and in respect for individual rights to the political class that is currently governing the European parliamentary states. Rather than pursuing the will o' the wisp of democracy, it would be better to take thought for the strengthening and improvement of the existing class regime.

Such was the final lesson of Mosca's neoconservative theory. In the 1880's, after a century of ideological debate, it brought a refreshing breath of realism and practical sense into a political atmosphere stale from the passionate repetition of conflicting slogans and credos. It is only in this context that Mosca's thought can properly be understood. As with the work of so many other political writers, it must be read as an answer to something that has been said earlier. It is neoconservatism—or, to use a contemporary term, sophisticated conservatism —in the sense that it is both postdemocratic and postsocialist. Like the majority of nineteenth-century conservatives, like Tocqueville or Burckhardt or Metternich himself, Mosca considered democracy no more than a brief halt on the way to socialism; the latter was already implicit in the Rousseauist "political formula." But unlike De Maistre and the original theorists of the counterrevolution, in repudiating democracy Mosca did not simultaneously reject the whole liberal tradition of the Enlightenment. On the contrary, he accepted the Enlightenment in its broadest emphasis on rationalized procedures, personal freedom, and limited government. At the same time he sought to free this tradition from the democratic accretions that had drastically altered its original outlines and that threatened eventually to destroy it. In the light of the experience of two generations of parliamentary government, he argued, one could at last locate precisely where liberalism had gone astray.

It was as a young but already self-conscious member of the liberal upper middle class, then, that Mosca composed his first treatise on politics. This class, which had figured in recent history both as the bearer and as the beneficiary of the liberal tradition, was in the 1880's the dominant group in the economic and political life of the three great parliamentary states of Western Europe. In all of them, it was true, the upper-middle-class oligarchy shared power with the old aristocracy—but with each year that passed the balance seemed to incline more heavily in favor of the former. When Mosca wrote his *Teorica,* this happy state of affairs was still of recent origin. In England it had existed at the most for half a century, in France and Italy for perhaps a decade. And yet it was already threatened with disruption. It was threatened not merely by the assaults of democracy and socialism. It was also being undermined by the malfunctioning of the very parliamentary institutions that had served as the vehicles of upper-middle-class supremacy.

In this historical situation, it was not surprising that Mosca should have devoted the whole second half of his little book to a critique of parliamentarism. After defining the eternal laws of political behavior, the intrepid young theorist quite logically turned his attention to the specific institutions through which these laws manifested themselves in his own time. One might study them, he noted, in England or in France, in the United States, in Austria, in Germany, in Spain, or in Italy. The reasons he gave for using his own country as his test case were not particularly convincing.[17] Presumably he chose it simply because he knew it best.

This choice of Italy, however, and the fact that Mosca was an Italian, were not merely incidental to what he had to say. They profoundly affected the character of his judgments on parliamentary institutions. For Italy in the 1880's was by no means the typical parliamentary country that Mosca claimed. On the contrary, it was an extreme and somewhat eccentric example of the general phenomenon. Still more, Mosca was a southerner, a Sicilian, and it was from southern Italian experience that he drew his most damaging instances of parliamentary malfunctioning. It was already enough that Mosca was writing from an Italian vantage point; the fact that he was a Sicilian compounded the distortion.

In fact if one were deliberately to choose a time and a place that would display parliamentary institutions to their maximum discredit, it would be hard to find a more telling example than southern Italy in the 1880's. Ever since the fall of the "old Right" in 1876—an event which liberal conservatives of Mosca's type regarded as an unmitigated calamity—Italy had been ruled by a "Left" that was leftist only in name and that in practice represented little more than the replacement of the oligarchy of birth and talent that had founded the new Italian kingdom with a less respectable "political class" of professional parliamentarians and officeholders. The franchise has just been extended to include a million and a half new voters—but still only about one out of every three adult male Italians was even theoretically entitled to participate in elections. And as a practical matter merely a fraction of those enfranchised actually exercised their privilege. Devout Catholics scrupulously refrained from participation in public life; thousands of other citizens shunned the polls through political apathy or distaste for the upstart regime that had overthrown their traditional allegiance. In Rome the parliamentary chambers had become the scene of an unabashed trading of votes against local favors. Under the supple manipulation of Agostino Depretis—prime minister for nearly a decade —party lines had dissolved and old oppositionists had been lured into the governmental majority. The word *trasformismo* had been added to the Italian language to epitomize all that was wrong with the country's parliamentary life.

It was quite obvious, then—and it took no great discernment on the young Mosca's part to detect it—that Italy was being ruled by a fairly narrow governing class. This was particularly the case in the South and Sicily, where quasi-feudal class relations persisted, where the bulk of the population was still illiterate, and where one or two "great electors" —a large landholder or other local potentate—could sometimes swing the vote of an entire constituency. Tightly knit cliques controlled the nomination of candidates and not infrequently called on the local *mafia* or *camorra* to enforce their will. What wonder that Mosca concluded—to cite his most celebrated thrust at the parliamentary system —that "it is not the electors who elect the deputy, but ordinarily it is the deputy who has himself elected by the electors." [18]

Presumably this was necessarily the case; under what Mosca's admirer Robert Michels has called "the iron law of oligarchy" no elective system could function otherwise. But in Mosca's early work the distinction between what is merely the normal condition of any political activity and what an abuse is not always made clear. The spirited polemical tone of the young author's writing frequently carries him beyond his expressed intention. At times he keeps rigorously to his professed position of detachment. As opposed to most other political commentators of the period, he is not shocked by the interference of the prefects in elections; indeed, he argues that in a majority of cases this may actually be a good thing, since it produces better candidates than those ordinarily chosen by the local political cliques.[19] At other times, however, Mosca gives way to his natural polemical bent and makes statements that sound like an unqualified condemnation of the whole parliamentary system. At such times he betrays what is obviously a deep personal annoyance.

One source of this annoyance is theoretical. Mosca is exasperated by what he regards as the hypocrisy of political rhetoric, and he is out to expose how shamelessly the "democratic" politicians violate the principles they profess. At all costs, he wishes to set the record straight. Beyond this, however, the careful reader can detect a class grievance. As a member of the educated upper middle class, Mosca understandably regards himself as belonging to the natural elite of the new Italian kingdom. Properly this class should be managing the affairs of the state. And to a large extent such is still the case. But through a cynical manipulation of the parliamentary system, the natural elite of the country is being displaced by a new and unsavory class of politicians and profiteers. Mosca protests against this state of affairs and looks around for a way to change it. An Italian Henry Adams, he resents being defrauded of his birthright.

It comes as no surprise, then, when at the end of his *Teorica* he predicts the end of the parliamentary system. Even the apparent stability of Britain, he notes, rests less on its parliamentary institutions than on the continuity of its governing class.[20] But here Mosca's theoretical difficulties begin. It is one thing to expose the deficiencies of parliamentary government. It is something far more difficult to devise a new system to replace it. Mosca is too acute a political observer to imagine that a return to a frankly aristocratic regime is possible. The idea of representative government—however fallacious the reasoning behind it—is far too deeply rooted to permit that. And so when he comes to outline his remedies, he appears somewhat at a loss. After all the vigor of his condemnation, he has few concrete changes to offer. A return to the letter of the Italian constitution, with executive authority again in the hands of the King, and a new method of appointing senators so as to make them truly independent of political considerations—this is virtually all he proposes. And he advances it somewhat lamely and diffidently, as though conscious that it is actually a reactionary proposal, unrealistic and impossible of attainment. He seems already to suspect that this is not a practicable way to attain his highest goal—"a true renewal of the whole political class . . . on the basis of personal merit and technical capacity."

Such is the direction in which Mosca's theory is actually heading. And his second great desideratum is even more revealing—a "reciprocal control among all the members [of the political class] so as to avoid, so far as is humanly possible, the arbitrary and irresponsible action of a single individual or group of individuals." [21] In this statement Mosca leaves open the way for his eventual reconciliation with the parliamentary regime itself.

III

In its original form the *Elementi*—published in 1896, twelve years after the *Teorica*—did not depart very far from the main principles embodied in the earlier work. It was longer, more detailed, more systematic in organization, and more moderate in tone. The theories of the political class and the political formula, however, were still its central features. And the windy abstractions of democracy and socialism remained the chief targets of Mosca's quiet scorn.

Nevertheless the emphasis had changed. Partly this change reflected the author's altered circumstances of life. In 1885, after the publication of the *Teorica*, Mosca became an unpaid lecturer on constitutional law at the University of Palermo. He was still at the bottom of the academic ladder and still confined to a Sicilian horizon. In the following decade he virtually severed his connections with Sicily. Although remaining a junior lecturer, he transferred to the University of Rome, where he could study national political life at the center rather than on its eccentric periphery. And, in addition to his university work, he had found a paying position that gave unequaled opportunities for observing politics at close hand. As editor of the journal of the Chamber of Deputies, Mosca occupied a unique vantage point for acquiring an education in the realities of parliamentarism.

The day-to-day view of a parliament in action, as opposed to merely observing electoral abuses in the local constituencies, seems to have mollified the uncompromising critic of representative institutions. In 1896 Mosca was not prepared to retract anything that he had said earlier; he still regarded the conventional justifications of parliamentary rule as largely fictitious. But from the practical standpoint he was more prepared to see the advantages of representative government and less eager to point out its failings. Parliamentarism—in the sense of a regime that concentrates in the parliament "all prestige and all power"— he still considered "one of the worst types of political organization"; it was simply the "irresponsible and anonymous tyranny of the elements that prevail in the elections and speak in the name of the people." But properly controlled and limited in their powers, representative bodies offered at least two great advantages. They permitted public opinion— or, as Mosca more sceptically phrased it, "certain sentiments and certain passions of the crowd"—to find an echo "in the highest spheres of government." And they guaranteed the "participation of a certain number of socially valuable elements in the rule of the state." In this fashion, representative institutions could help in attaining what Mosca still regarded as the prime desiderata of good government—a system that would permit "all the elements that have political value in a given society to be used and specialized to the best advantage, and to be subjected to reciprocal control and the principle of individual responsibility for what they do in their respective spheres of action."

All this was familiar to readers of the *Teorica*. At the same time the original version of the *Elementi* shows Mosca already beginning to shift his emphasis from the first to the second of his requirements for good government. He still speaks of the importance of recruiting and maintaining the best possible political class. He is still the technician striving to lay the theoretical foundations for a more competent oligarchy. But now he emphasizes more frequently than he did before the necessity of checking the oligarchs in the exercise of their functions. The danger of "arbitrary and irresponsible action" looms larger in his thought. "The true moral guarantee of representative governments," he finds, "is the public discussion that takes place in the assemblies." [22]

Necessarily, then, Mosca is led to re-examine his theory of the political formula. He reiterates his contention that all such formulas are equally mythical, but he is now more ready to distinguish between those of them that are socially useful and those that are dangerous. Specifically, he separates the two main "intellectual currents" that have produced the parliamentary formula. The democratic doctrine of Rousseau he finds almost wholly noxious. But the theory of limited government associated with the name of Montesquieu he considers "not fundamentally mistaken." [23] Actually Mosca might have gone much farther. Had he been less anxious to assert his own originality as a political writer, he might have been more generous in recognizing his debt to the great French theorist. He might have granted that on all essential points he and Montesquieu are in agreement. For, like Montesquieu, the Mosca of the *Elementi* draws "a sharp dividing line between despotism and all other forms of government." And, though an uncompromising foe of despotism in all its guises, he is too sceptical to "elaborate any radical solution" as a substitute for it. He lacks faith "in the capacity of men to effect and maintain a radically new society. . . . His awareness of the ambiguous character of progress, his insistence on slowness and caution in legislative changes—all this makes for a conservative but not necessarily reactionary attitude toward life." [24] These conclusions of a contemporary writer on Montesquieu describe with amazing accuracy the position that Mosca had reached midway in his career as a political theorist.

IV

The two decades following the publication of the first edition of the *Elementi* completely altered Mosca's circumstances of life. In 1896, just after the *Elementi* appeared, he had been made a professor at the University of Turin. This event established him as a man who had arrived in life—just as it shifted his orientation from Sicily to the northern part of the country. By 1908 he had attained a position of sufficient eminence so that he could "have himself elected" a deputy. And from that point on the highest public honors followed in regular succession. From 1914 to 1916 he served as an under-secretary in the government, and in 1919 he was appointed a senator of the realm. Mosca's ambition evidently reached no higher. His elevation to the Senate automatically made him an elder statesman, and it was in that capacity that in 1923, the year following Mussolini's accession to power, he accepted a chair at the University of Rome.

Such substantial success in the realm of public life is almost unique in the biographies of political thinkers. In itself it may have had something to do with the increasing mellowness of Mosca's writing and the more favorable attitude he came to adopt toward the parliamentary system. But his experience as a deputy and senator also entered in; he was participating in the activity of the chambers during a period when talent and devotion to the public service were perhaps more conspicuous in those quarters than they had been during the last decades of the previous century. He was experiencing as a historical reality the advent of universal suffrage and the shaky beginnings of Italian electoral democracy. And he did not condemn the new developments in the unrestrained terms that he might have used in the past. This was the more noteworthy since the period immediately following his appointment to the Senate witnessed a further historical change that might well have destroyed his whole new-found tolerance toward the parliamentary system—the virtual breakdown of that system during the three years preceding the March on Rome.

It would have shown a superhuman restraint on Mosca's part if he had refrained from reminding his fellow countrymen that they were now experiencing what he had predicted nearly forty years earlier. This is doubtless what he had in mind when in 1924 he congratulated himself on the accuracy of his foresight. In an essay on the "crisis in parliamentarism" published four years later, he stressed the gravity of the current breakdown in representative institutions. It had come about, he argued, largely through the "mistake" of conceding universal suffrage—a mistake, however, "which had become more or less necessary through the mentality of the times in which it was conceded." Once again he had little to offer in the way of a remedy. He simply gave his implied endorsement to a system of weighted suffrage "in which the vote of the poor and ignorant" would not count "exactly the same . . . as that of the educated person and of the person who has had the ability to acquire honestly a certain well-being." [25]

Yet at the same time he remained faithful to the basic principles of limited, representative government. He surprised a number of his intellectual disciples by refusing to rally to the new Fascist regime.[26] More than that, the very advent of the dictatorship reinforced his tendency to take a more charitable view of parliamentary institutions. In the first edition of the *Elementi*, he had stated that "the only practical criterion for judging . . . political regimes is . . . by comparing them . . . with those that have preceded them and, when possible, with those that have followed them." [27] The coming to power of Mussolini gave him a chance to apply this criterion—to judge the parliamentary system in the light of what had succeeded to it. Mosca's verdict was unqualified. In December 1925, during the debate on the bill that in effect ended the responsibility of the prime minister to the Parliament, Mosca rose from his seat in the Senate to make the following declaration:

> I who have always sharply criticized parliamentary government must now almost lament over its downfall. . . . Certainly representative parliamentary government must not and can not be immutable. As the conditions of society change political organizations are changed. But should the change have been rapid and radical, or should it have been slow and wary? This is the very grave question which vexes my soul. As an old adversary of the parliamentary regime, I believe that this problem must be solved in the most moderate and prudent manner.[28]

Beneath the cautious phraseology, the implication was unmistakable. Mosca rejected Mussolini's brutal solution of the parliamentary crisis. In the showdown, his loyalty to personal freedom and limited government took precedence over his elitist yearnings, which the Fascists had actually gone far to satisfy. Moreover, the tone of his retrospective judgment on the parliamentary system indicated a revised attitude toward history. The elderly senator, now in his late sixties, was far less confident than he had been as an intrepid young theoretician of twenty-five. He was now less sure that his "key" to history had unlocked all its secrets. Nearly half a century before, he had discovered the theoretical formulas that seemed to explain both the political systems of past ages and the course that would be followed by the representative institutions of his own day. And the formulas had worked. They had indicated the crisis in the parliamentary system that in fact had come to pass. But still something had been lacking. The positivist-minded syllogisms in which Mosca had tried to imprison the variety of human political experience had failed to embrace all contingencies. The elusive stuff of history itself had slipped through the theoretician's deftly shaping fingers.

In four decades of lived history, all the elements of his problem had altered. The institutions had changed, but the change had not merely been one of degeneration, as Mosca had earlier predicted. Electoral democracy had come to Italy, but its coming had not been quite the unmitigated catastrophe that he had expected. The virtual universal suffrage extended to the Italian people in 1912 had not destroyed the country's representative institutions. In some ways it had actually strengthened them, by bringing a number of "socially valuable elements" into the Parliament and by adding to it new deputies of unquestioned talent. After all, Mosca himself had been re-elected to the Chamber under the new extended suffrage. It was true that the postwar years had seen the collapse of Italian parliamentary government. But its overthrow had come not from the forces of socialism and syndicalism, as Mosca had long predicted, but from a new and unexpected radicalism of the Right. As late as 1925 it was difficult to determine the precise nature of the Fascist regime. But the old political theorist understood it well enough to know that it was even less to his taste than the system of government that had preceded it. An elitist reaction against democracy had come—but not in the form he had hoped for. Or was it perhaps that his theories themselves had changed? Was it perhaps the shift from emphasizing the mythical character of all "political formulas" to an insistence on their qualitative differences that caused him to render a negative judgment on the new Fascist regime? If something similar had come in the 1880's, might he have been willing to accept it? Or was it the theoretician himself who had gradually accommodated himself in practice to the characteristic institutions of his time? It was impossible to say—there were too many variables. In place of the old clear-cut lessons of history, the flux of human experience itself had taken over.

This new feeling for historical change is apparent in the second edition of his *Elementi,* published early in 1923. For this revision of a work that had already become a political classic, Mosca adopted an unusual and extremely honest approach. Aside from adding a few explanatory notes, he simply left the original text exactly as it stood. His later ideas and reflections he appended to it as a somewhat shorter second volume. While this arrangement makes for rather curious reading, it has the advantage of displaying the young and the old Mosca side by side. The leading ideas are the same—again it is simply the emphasis that has altered.

Although this second volume must have been written almost in its entirety before the March on Rome—since its publication followed so soon thereafter—it already reveals Mosca's new attitude toward parliamentary institutions that we have seen embodied in his statements of 1925 and 1928. And in some respects this new version of the

Elementi goes even farther. It praises representative government as the form of rule that "has succeeded in coordinating a maximum sum of energies and of individual activities for the benefit of the collective interest." And it includes a qualified endorsement of "the democratic tendency" as "in a certain way indispensable to . . . the progress of human societies." Mosca adds a characteristic justification for this rather surprising change of front:

> The democratic tendency, so long as its action does not tend to become excessive and exclusive, represents what in vulgar language would be called a conservative force. For it permits a continual addition of new blood to the governing classes through the admission of new elements that have innately and spontaneously within them the attitude of command and the will to command, and so prevents that exhaustion of the aristocracies of birth that is wont to bring on the great social cataclysms.[29]

This, then, is the message of the *Elementi* in their final form—a tentative recourse to "the democratic tendency" to revive the European elites that have so signally failed in their task of holding off the forces of despotism. And it is the youth that must accomplish the fusion of the old and the new elements in the political class. Mosca's second volume closes on a note of warm supplication—an appeal for political "vision" to the "noblest part of the youth" of his country, in the hope that they will rise to the responsibilities that the new age imposes upon them.[30]

V

The second volume of the *Elementi* represents the completion of Mosca's work as a political thinker. In the last two decades of his life, he felt himself too old to do much further writing. The period between 1923 and his death in 1941 saw the publication of two relatively minor studies and of the few notes he added to his *Elementi* for the third edition, which appeared in 1938. It is on the final version of this work that Mosca's reputation rests and that the contemporary relevance of his ideas may best be judged.

To a sceptical age that has seen the destruction of so many hopes and the blasting of so many illusions, Mosca's theory of society may well have a peculiar appeal. For it seeks in one formulation both to explain the revival of despotism that has characterized the past half century of Western history and to establish on a more solid basis the permanent validity of free government. The theory of the political class and the political formula cuts both ways: it exposes what is abstract and unrealistic in the doctrine of popular sovereignty at the same time as it insists on the supreme importance of preserving a liberal, constitutional regime. In drawing a sharp distinction between the liberal and the democratic traditions, it clarifies much that is imprecise and sentimental in contemporary historical writing and the contemporary discussion of political issues. And in establishing the priority of the former, both in time and in importance, it seeks a way out of a dilemma as old as Aristotle—the dilemma of a democracy that freely chooses to abdicate to tyranny. This ancient problem has reappeared with renewed force in our own time. The collapse of Italian, German, and French democracy in the period from 1922 to 1940 and the present precarious situation of the restored parliamentary regimes in those countries, have brought home to men's minds once again the age-old danger that democracy may degenerate into despotism.

Mosca's answer to this question was aristocratic, conservative, and largely ineffective. To check the excesses of democracy, he had nothing more promising to offer than a weighting of the suffrage in favor of education and property and a strengthening of the powers of non-elective officials. The very hesitation with which he advanced these remedies suggests that he half suspected how unrealistic they were; democracy, he admitted, "had become more or less necessary through the mentality of the times." Hence his specific proposals have little relevance for the contemporary world. It is rather his insight into the functioning of representative government that is useful to us—that and his insistence that the talent and ethical level of the political class can alone guarantee the preservation and progress of a free society. This teaching is only superficially inapplicable to a modern democracy. It is "undemocratic" only under a definition of democracy that seeks to add to an equality of rights an equality of attainments and ideas. The latter definition is widely held today, particularly in the United States. But it is coming under increasingly heavy attack from those who see the dangers to a free society that such a leveling of talents implies. For them Mosca's warnings carry a note of particular urgency. In a democracy—subject as it is to gusts of popular prejudice and passion— the systematic cultivation of talent, the persistent fostering of the higher-than-average individual, are indispensable to the proper functioning of free institutions.

We have seen how under the influence of a long experience of history itself, Mosca's concept of the political lessons of history gradually altered. We have seen how as an old man he was willing to grant what in his youth he would never have admitted, that under proper circumstances "the democratic principle" could actually function as a stabilizing force in society. Had Mosca lived a decade longer, he might have seen that a new turn of history had necessitated still a further revision in his theories. He might have recognized that in a country like the United States, with a standard of living unparalleled in history and the majority of its population assimilated in habits and attitudes to a vast middle class, his theory of a "political class" is no longer strictly applicable. It is too rigid to embrace the realities of our current society. In a situation in which the locus of political influence is almost impossible to establish, in which authority is diffused among a wide variety of mutually interacting pressure and "veto" groups, it is idle to speak of a clearly defined political class. In practice the rule of minorities still obtains; but their influence is exerted in so shifting and amorphous a fashion that it cannot be described any longer in terms of a specific ruling group.[31] Once more a loosening and reinterpretation of Mosca's categories is in order.

Nevertheless, even in such a society, the problem of the recruitment of political and administrative talent remains. It is perhaps the crucial problem that faces the United States today. Here the historical lessons taught by Mosca—for all their quaint conservatism—can still be studied with profit.

1. Introduction by Arthur Livingston to Gaetano Mosca, *The Ruling Class* (*Elementi di Scienza Politica*), translated by Hannah D. Kahn (New York, 1939), p. xxxvi. Mr. Livingston, who was responsible for the American editions of both Pareto's and Mosca's work, explains that the latter was originally intended to appear first. In the succeeding footnotes I shall refer to the fourth (and final) Italian edition rather than to the translation, since Mr. Livingston has somewhat rearranged the original order of Mosca's presentation.

2. Renzo Sereno, "The Anti-Aristotelianism of Gaetano Mosca and Its Fate," *Ethics*, XLVIII (July, 1938), 512. For an exhaustive summary of the question of priority, see Alfonso de Pietri-Tonelli, "Mosca e Pareto," *Rivista internazionale di scienze sociali*, VI (July, 1935), 468–493.

3. The only detailed biographical and critical study of Mosca that has ap-

peared to date is by Mario Delle Piane, *Gaetano Mosca. Classe politica e liberalismo* (Naples, 1952).

4. Gaetano Mosca, *Teorica dei governi e governo parlamentare,* 2nd ed. (Milan, 1925), pp. 5–7.

5. *Teorica,* pp. 11–18; Gaetano Mosca, *Elementi di scienza politica,* 4th ed. (Bari, 1947), I, Chapter 1.

6. Livingston Introduction to *The Ruling Class,* p. xxi.

7. Karl R. Popper, *The Open Society and Its Enemies,* revised ed. (Princeton, 1950), p. 463.

8. Robert Michels, *Italien von Heute: 1860–1930* (Leipzig and Zürich, 1930), p. 181.

9. This is essentially the view of Karl Mannheim in *Ideology and Utopia* (New York and London, 1949), p. 123.

10. For Pareto's domestic arrangements, see Manon Michels Einaudi, "Pareto as I Knew Him," *The Atlantic Monthly,* CLVI (September, 1935), 336–346.

11. Preface to second edition (1925) of *Teorica,* p. iv.

12. Preface to third edition (1938) of *Elementi,* pp. 5–6.

13. Benedetto Croce, review of the second edition of Mosca's *Elementi, La Critica,* XXI (November 20, 1923), 374–378; see also Delle Piane, *op. cit.,* p. 52.

14. *Teorica,* pp. v, 17, 35.

15. Mannheim, *op. cit.,* p. 126.

16. Robert Michels, *Political Parties,* new ed. (Glencoe, Ill., 1949), pp. 390–391.

17. *Teorica,* p. 148.

18. *Ibid.,* p. 250.

19. *Ibid.,* pp. 196–197.

20. *Ibid.,* pp. 266–267, 299.

21. *Ibid.,* pp. 263–264, 300.

22. *Elementi,* I, 207, 209, 212.

23. *Ibid.,* I, 272–273.

24. Franz Neumann, Introduction to *The Spirit of the Laws* by Baron de Montesquieu (New York, 1949), pp. xix, xliii.

25. Gaetano Mosca, "The Crisis in Parliamentarism and How It May Be Overcome," in *The Development of the Representative System in Our Times,* five answers to an inquiry instituted by the Inter-Parliamentary Union (Lausanne, 1928), p. 84.

26. Michels, *Italien von Heute,* p. 219.

27. *Elementi,* I, 375.

28. Quoted in Gaetano Salvemini's introductory essay to A. William Salomone, *Italian Democracy in the Making* (Philadelphia, 1945), pp. xv–xvi.

29. *Elementi,* II, 126–127.

30. *Ibid.,* II, 242.

31. David Riesman, *The Lonely Crowd* (New Haven, 1950), p. 252.

[PAUL L. WARD]

Huizinga's Approach to the Middle Ages

JOHAN Huizinga's *The Waning of the Middle Ages*,[1] from the time that I was first directed to it, has seemed to me at once fascinating and confusing. It offers a comprehensive view of the character of life in northeast France and the Burgundian Netherlands in the fourteenth and fifteenth centuries—a period of history that students have commonly found discouraging for its lack of fresh developments, or else of developments singled out by historians as important for succeeding centuries. Huizinga's sympathetic rendering of significant detail and his attention to central complexities seem to bring within grasp a more adequate historical understanding of the period. But when first I studied the book, I did not in fact end up with any clarifying propositions that proved of particular value. In various later attempts to teach the history of the period, I have not found any of its conclusions fitting into a more illuminating account of the sequence of major events. I do not doubt that the book has value as an impressionistic background study. The question that has troubled me is whether the same material could not be treated less confusingly and be made to contribute more directly to historical understanding and to the historical reconstruction of this difficult period.

Perhaps this question has a more general interest than the personal experience behind it would suggest. Since its publication three decades ago, Huizinga's book has secured a place in the select bibliographies of most American college textbooks on the history of the Middle Ages. It is often recommended to students as an illuminating study of the state of society that ended the Middle Ages and preceded the Renaissance.[2] Its chief value for general study seems, in fact, to lie in the analysis it gives of the particular psychological conditions that followed the breakdown of the medieval synthesis around A.D. 1300. To judge from their textbooks, American historians are increasingly accepting, as the best basic outline for organizing medieval history as a whole, the gradual development, climax, and collapse of medieval confidence and integration. This approach to the Middle Ages, this attention to matters of tone and confidence, presumably has a relevance to our present-day concerns. The twentieth century is indeed confronted by complexities and by a sense of declining confidence in many quarters that may in some features resemble the conditions at the end of the Middle Ages. Students of history deserve as perceptive an account as their teachers can give of those conditions, for the period seems the only one of its kind in our history for which we have such full evidence. It is fortunate that this scholarly and interesting book by Huizinga deals so directly with the subject.

And yet it is hard to see that Huizinga's book has had much influence in this country beyond the addition—now and then—of a separate section of background description to treatments of late medieval history. Historians have not been influenced to any recasting of the standard accounts of events and motives. Perhaps this is simply an example of the common failure of historical research to contribute to the central structure of what is taught. Scholars nowadays concede, perhaps too easily, that the work of historians does not yield a cumulative advance in knowledge. The contrast implied is obviously with the advance of the natural sciences. But it is quite possible that the massive accumulation of scientific findings in our day obscures from us the essential character of that advance. In the history of science we can find many confirmations of Whitehead's judgment that a body of thought can enjoy only a limited period of progress unless it proves able to burst through its current abstractions.[3] Historical work today may be similarly, at several points, up against limits set by convenient assemblages of past conclusions and current prejudices. Is it any such inflexibility of conventional history that has kept Huizinga's findings from entering more directly into the content of history courses? Since Huizinga's work itself bears ample evidence of thoroughness in research, we are the more free to focus our attention on his method of approach, to see how it differs from conventional historical work.

This method of approach can from one angle be easily characterized. Throughout his career Huizinga showed strong admiration for Jacob Burckhardt and for the historical method displayed in *The Civilization of the Renaissance*. To be sure, as a native of the Low Countries and specialist in their early history he could not accept Burckhardt's ready assumption that the developments in the North around 1400 were only a northern extension of the Renaissance, similar to the developments in Italy and simply less vigorous and slower to develop.[4] In *The Waning of the Middle Ages* Huizinga argues forcefully that the Van Eycks and their fellows belonged rather to the Middle Ages. He shows that in a number of ways Burckhardt, unfamiliar with the details of medieval civilization, "exaggerated the distance separating Italy from the Western countries and the Renaissance from the Middle Ages."[5] This particular contention Huizinga developed more fully in a monograph on "The Problem of the Renaissance," almost immediately after bringing out his main work.[6] In these respects Huizinga's work is to be associated with the reaction among historians against Burckhardt's impressionistic conception of the Renaissance, a reaction that took form at least as early as 1907 and that has continued to receive vigorous support from medieval historians in this country.[7] But Huizinga shows himself in many other significant respects to be a follower of Burckhardt. His *The Waning of the Middle Ages* seems plainly shaped to be complementary to *The Civilization of the Renaissance*. His method of approach, with its emphasis on the evidence of art, is much like Burckhardt's, and his whole book works up toward the advent of the Renaissance as its climax.

But the questions before us are not ones to be satisfactorily answered by quotations from the current debate over the scholarly value of Burckhardt's treatment of the Renaissance. Huizinga's approach to his subject is not identical with Burckhardt's; as we have just now seen, Huizinga is quite capable of improving in important ways upon the work of his predecessor. We are asking in what ways Huizinga's approach departs from the conventional canons of historical work, how it operates to expose the peculiar conditions of mind and life in the late Middle Ages, and whether, all in all, it may not be unnecessarily confusing. What Huizinga offers is an analytical picture of a difficult period of our history, treated not as transitional but as significant in its own right.[8] His approach can be most fairly judged in terms of that subject itself.

It will be convenient to begin by considering the aspect of Huizinga's work most open to criticism by historians. *The Waning of the Middle Ages*, like Burckhardt's famous work, treats a distinct field, and does so in topical rather than chronological style. Surprisingly, it is open to much the same criticism that Huizinga himself levels at Burckhardt. Even though his material is in fact rather strictly limited to the century or two centering on A.D. 1400, Huizinga notably fails to distinguish his period from the earlier centuries of the Middle Ages. The dividing line between his period and the succeeding Renaissance, which he recognizes as fluctuating rather like the water's edge on a tidal flat, is full of significance for him. But he uses the terms "late Middle Ages" and "Middle Ages" interchangeably, almost never noticing any change from conditions of the thirteenth century and earlier.[9] Students who do not already know well the period before A.D. 1300 can hardly rely on the book as a guide to the social conditions that followed the breakup of the medieval synthesis.

This is, however, only one illustration of the extent to which Huizinga fails to keep before his readers the chronology of change and the relevant geographical and social locations. Within his field itself, he points out no movement except the centuries-long decline of symbolism and the rise of naturalism in art [10]—until at last in his concluding chapter the approach from Italy of the Renaissance breathes more life into his colorful tableau. The geographical limits of his attention are hardly acknowledged after the title page, and he makes no effort to relate his findings to developments in any area of northern Europe outside the Netherlands and northeast France. The host of particular figures and writings introduced in evidence are only rarely provided with enough indication of date, place, and specific setting to place them clearly. It is therefore unfortunate that Huizinga's order of presentation also makes no concession whatever to these concrete relationships which ordinarily help so much to discipline our understanding. We find him only once, indeed, acknowledging that the Burgundian court had a central place in the activities he is describing.[11] The one incident he mentions in which its style was tellingly introduced elsewhere—Philip of Burgundy's creation of a splendid court of love at Paris in 1401—

171

tantalizingly suggests that all his material might have come more to life if he had consistently kept the relevant social groupings clear in the background.[12] Many of his observations seem insubstantial simply for lack of attention to the immediate situations—like Philip of Burgundy's sharp contest for influence over his miserable nephew the French king—which suggest the motives accompanying the intellectual and aesthetic events described.

A partial answer to this criticism is that Huizinga was writing for a European audience quite unlike average history students in this country, an audience already familiar to some extent with the chronology, the historical figures, and the writings. But consistent failure to give the historian's normal emphasis to chronology and circumstances seems in a few cases to involve Huizinga's analysis in inconsistencies. An example of this is found at the end of a chapter of comment on the splendid fictions of late medieval chivalry in his two pages devoted to the biographical romance called *Le Jouvencel.*[13] Quite unlike the other works discussed, the first part of this romance is described as realistic, fresh, and virtually modern. Huizinga does mention that the subject and instigator of this romance, Jean de Bueil, had fought under Joan of Arc, but he passes quickly on to conclude that this bit of writing was "an expression of true French sentiment," and an expression of sentiments dateless in their spontaneous humanity. Thereafter he cites *Le Jouvencel* several times quite as if it were typical evidence of the chivalry of the time.[14] Logical analysis would surely require treating this romance as significantly different and would suggest a search for specific analogues; historical analysis would be equally interested in further evidence on the possibility that this was a reflection of the particular encouragement transmitted by Joan to her associates. After singling it out for attention, Huizinga seems here to have glossed over an interesting discrepancy in his picture of the age.

At one point in the book, when he comes to consider the painting of Jan van Eyck, Huizinga does argue with care from the evidence of the specific setting. Here is the kernel of his argument:

The intellectual and moral life of the fifteenth century seems to us to be divided into two clearly separated spheres. On the one hand, the civilization of the court, and the nobility and the rich middle classes: ambitious, proud and grasping, passionate and luxurious. On the other hand, the tranquil sphere of the "devotio moderna," of the *Imitation of Christ,* of Ruysbroeck and of

Huizinga and the Middle Ages

Saint Colette. One would like to place the peaceful and mystic art of the brothers Van Eyck in the second of these spheres, but it belongs rather to the other. Devout circles were hardly in touch with the great art that flourished at this time.[15]

What follows is a valuable corrective to the easy assumption in textbooks that Flemish painting was a product simply of bourgeois life. But what is of interest to us now is that in this one case Huizinga is plainly invoking the evidence of concrete relationships—and at considerable length—to prevent his topical analysis from grouping together the confident painters and the confident mystics of that unconfident age. This exceptional treatment may well be due to his special interest in the Van Eycks. But his inclusion in the "tranquil sphere of the 'devotio moderna' " of St. Colette, whom he has previously described as a saint of extreme supersensibility, with a "horror of all that relates to sex," suggests to us that he is resisting the tendency to oversimplification through topical analysis.[16]

More attention to chronology and concrete circumstances throughout the book would presumably be, in the eyes of conventional historians, the proper safeguard against the dangers of such oversimplification. Huizinga seems to have deliberately chosen to hold to topical analysis alone—we may remind ourselves that this was Burckhardt's method of uncovering the central features of a period, and that Huizinga thought highly of Burckhardt's success. It is quite arguable that this method allows the pervasive peculiarities of late medieval thought and behavior to stand forth more plainly. Huizinga's evidence rests in a multitude of minor details that might lose cogency if accounted for one by one in terms of their particular settings. The general characteristics of an age have perhaps, of all historical phenomena, the least clear limits in time and space. All the same, there is much in the experience of historians to show that it is quite possible to accent the precise historical significance of evidence without losing the values of topical analysis.

Huizinga's choice of a method that departs from the normal ways of historical work evidently accounts for much of the difficulty of assimilating his conclusions into conventional treatments of the late Middle Ages. Does his work also show what is commonly the penalty for such disregard, an uncertain and often brilliant mixture of sound conclusions with others not so sound? Huizinga's distinguished record as an academic historian, the thoroughness of his scholarship in the field that he covers, warn us that he knew well the disciplines that his book so largely fails to show. The question may, however, remain in our minds as we look at other features of his approach to his field.

The Waning of the Middle Ages, as the title indicates, concerns itself with the period around A.D. 1400 as a time of decline and decay, rather than as seedbed of the Renaissance. In his special preface to the English edition, Huizinga explains his approach in these words:

"It occasionally happens that a period in which one had, hitherto, been mainly looking for the coming to birth of new things, suddenly reveals itself as an epoch of fading and decay." He found, he says, that the significance of the historical figures in his period "could be best appreciated by considering them, not as the harbingers of a coming culture, but as perfecting and concluding the old." [17]

Now we notice that Huizinga's disproportionate emphasis and attention is not being excused as appropriate for a monographic examination of simply a neglected phase; it is intended to redress a balance and clarify the whole of the picture. After all, the late Middle Ages is peculiarly difficult for us to understand as a whole. With the loss of confidence and the weakening of faith, the civilization of Western Europe seems to have undergone fragmentation into many less-related lines of activity and into scattered centers of initiative. It is all too easy for the student to fasten attention on those dramatic entities that claim his sympathies, the heroes and the lonely moderns, and so forfeit the chance of grasping the special characteristics of the whole. It may be advisable, in study or in exposition, to pass rather lightly over the familiar bright spots in the picture and to emphasize their associations with duller items. It is this procedure that we find Huizinga following throughout the book. As a basis for selection and emphasis of material it gives his approach to his subject a special character.

A second point evident in Huizinga's prefatory remarks is worthy of attention only if, as seems likely, it foreshadows a related characteristic of his treatment throughout the book. Huizinga promises to explore in the shadows not simply the fading and decay but also the "perfecting and concluding" of the old. To balance carefully the many imperfections with some things perfected is obviously a further aid to balanced judgment and the maintenance of sympathetic attention. In the treatments of *Le Jouvencel* and the brothers Van Eyck, we have already seen Huizinga setting light against dark in a way that surely may help to maintain sympathetic attention—but that also disturbs the course of his analysis. How characteristic is this of his procedure?

There are certainly other minor points at which Huizinga's interpretation runs into inconsistency, as if out of attempts to arouse sympathetic understanding. The book opens with the suggestion that the age was childlike and primitive, a suggestion often repeated. But we finally read that this very view is "egregiously mistaken": the spirit of late medieval art and religious life was a "spirit rather decadent than primitive, a spirit involving the utmost elaboration, and even decomposition, of religious thought through the imagination." [18] Huizinga, moreover, begins his discussion of late medieval chivalry by declaring that the chivalric ideal remained over the centuries "a source of energy, and at the same time a cloak for a whole world of violence and self-interest." [19] He then amply documents the second half of this statement but for the first half manages to say only that King John's creation of a quasi-independent Burgundy and the management of the crusade that met disaster at Nicopolis were tragic errors with chivalrous reasons as their avowed motives.[20] Some pages later, indeed, we find him saying forthrightly of the chivalric illusion that "reality perpetually gives the lie to it, and obliges it to take refuge in the domains of literature and of conversation." [21] But he chooses to close his discussion of chivalry with a quotation from Taine, that of all human sentiments aristocratic pride is the most "apt to be transformed into probity, patriotism and conscience"—which he supports simply by referring to *Le Jouvencel* and the patriotic poems of Eustache Deschamps.[22] Noticing how this bit of argument is qualified in the final paragraph, we can admit that it does not obscure his underlying judgment on late medieval chivalry. It may help retain the average reader's sympathetic respect for the subject, but its presentation is such as may cloud, for most readers, his rendering of the psychology of the time.[23]

At the opening of the second chapter the Renaissance receives its first mention: "We look in vain . . . for the vigorous optimism which will spring up at the Renaissance—though, by the way, the optimist tendency of the Renaissance is sometimes exaggerated." [24] It is this latter qualification that characteristically is amplified in the sentences following, even though these testify strongly, all the same, to the great change of tone that Renaissance would bring. Thereafter Huizinga is careful to point out that the impulse to art, the quest of personal glory, the aspiration to antique splendor, the boldness of irreverence, the use of mythology, all were evidenced in the late medieval world very much as in the Italian Renaissance.[25] Then, when he finally comes to discuss the aesthetic sentiment, he aptly quotes Michelangelo's reported criticism of Flemish painting. This quotation is strikingly effective, for the whole book up to this point is in part a preparation for it. And Huizinga is wholly in agreement: "Michelangelo here truly represents the Renaissance as opposed to the Middle Ages. What he condemns in Flemish art are exactly the essential traits of the declining Middle Ages: the violent sentimentality, the tendency to see each thing as an independent entity, to get lost in the multiplicity of concepts." [26] But at the beginning of the following chapter he speaks as if no such firm contrast can be made with the Renaissance; the difference between the two epochs is, he now says cautiously, hard to define and almost impossible to express, even though we feel it to be essential.[27] He denies himself any further mention of the Renaissance until he comes to his final chapter, on "The Advent of the New Form." Even here he devotes his efforts to underlining the medieval and even ridiculous quality of the Northerners' early efforts to imitate the Italians, until at the last—these are his last few sentences—the "incomparable simpleness and purity" of the new styles, the new spirit, began to take hold of men's minds.[28] Huizinga's fundamental enthusiasm for the Renaissance is plain enough from this recapitulation; but the impression left with the hasty or imperceptive reader is more likely to be confusing.

There surely are grounds here for supposing that Huizinga exercises such restraint in order to make possible a clearer view of late medieval conditions. His treatment of Jan van Eyck seems understandable in this light. Huizinga has told us, in his English preface, that the whole book sprang out of an effort "at a genuine understanding of the art of the brothers Van Eyck and their contemporaries." When he comes, late in the book, to his discussion of art, he ventures the judgments that the period knew only applied art and that men of the fifteenth century hardly had an aesthetic sense, properly speaking. Then suddenly he shakes off the force of this argument, by an artifice that we must notice later, and expresses strong admiration for the portraits by Jan van Eyck: "In each of these physiognomies the personality was probed to the last inch. It is the profoundest character-drawing possible." [29] From this he immediately recalls our attention to the environment and proceeds to argue at length that Van Eyck's art, as illustrated in the "Madonna of the Chancellor Rolin" and the "Annunciation," shows the same overloading with detail that seems so characteristic of the period and that Michelangelo had criticized.[30]

This is not consistent argument. These last paintings were done for the powerful Chancellor and the Church, and Huizinga has already emphasized the degree to which the artists of the day, in serving such personages as the dukes, were fettered by obligation to conform to the current ideas of what was splendid.[31] These are not the same paintings—it was the few portraits of wife and friends that were singled out earlier as most worthy of admiration, persuading us that Jan van Eyck was not typical of his age in Huizinga's and Michelangelo's terms.[32] Those few portraits receive no further attention after that one short emphatic paragraph on them.

A juster view of these inconsistencies is perhaps that Huizinga is presenting a double argument throughout his book. One argument is more on the surface and is the subject of most of the writing, calling respectful attention to the general characteristics of the age, the characteristics seen to be present in work of all degrees of quality. The other argument is largely suppressed but is carried forward effectively in asides and scattered strong paragraphs, conveying Huizinga's more forthright aesthetic judgments. This second argument is responsible for much of the vitality of the book, for it flickers up all the more dramatically from the gray to which the picture has been reduced by Huizinga's restraint. The attentive student may be better able to see the general characteristics of the whole because Huizinga plays down so carefully the whites and blacks on which it would be so easy for him to dwell, and yet the reader is provided with emphatic reminders of these same whites and blacks, so that they give sharpness to the picture. If, as seems safe to say, the central purpose of *The Waning of the Middle Ages* is to describe the tone of the late medieval period—his final chapter is a careful argument that the essence of the Renaissance lay in the new tone it brought to life—then the sharp juxtaposition of opposite judgments, in a picture predominantly gray, may be a proper way to represent the peculiar quality of the period.

But does this manner of handling the material do full justice to the evidence that is relevant? There seems warrant for saying that only Huizinga's particular enthusiasms—*Le Jouvencel* seems one—come through clearly, out of all the bright spots that he plays down or half takes for granted. His one paragraph of clear testimony to the virtues of the mystics is not much more than polite, and other references to such men as Ruysbroeck show no particularly impressive detail.[33] A quick reading of the book may well leave a student with the impression that St. Joan has not been mentioned, and even with more careful reading we find nothing to bring sharply to mind the excellence of the musicians of the day.[34] The brighter items in his period, and the darker ones too, are thus not given full value in his picture, and these are inevitably the key items for conventional historical presentation. The book as it stands is therefore properly a book for supplementary reading by students, and its method of double argument helps to make its findings difficult to incorporate directly into straightforward historical accounts.

But admitting these difficulties, what does Huizinga gain by his topical analysis and his dramatic balancing of arguments? It is not enough to say that he achieves a lively description of the period's tone or spirit, for as he himself shows in his reluctance to use such words, tone and spirit are terms too uncertain to mean much apart from specific illustrative details.[35] One value of his method is that it frees him to give great attention to more or less empty formalities, the fashions of social life that help make life an art and yet for the most part leave no monuments behind. His whole book is a demonstration of what can be accomplished by renouncing the widely accepted view that "to understand the spirit of an age, it sufficed to know its real and hidden forces and not its illusions, its fancies and its errors." [36] His method of topical analysis allows bringing together a great deal of such evidence that would otherwise remain scattered and insubstantial. And his half-suppression of the blacks and whites of our conventional interests allows the common features of the less-substantial fashions to show better their pervasive relations with the monuments of art and politics and religion. The outlines of the peculiar mentality of the period begin to take shape, even though Huizinga prefers simply to suggest these outlines in a variety of scattered comments.

Huizinga opens his discussion of fashions by asserting that man's quest for the ideal life has at all times seemed to have before it a choice of three different paths: aescetism, practical reform, and the conforming of life to the dream. This last, "the easiest and also the most fallacious of all," is what he finds characteristic of the late Middle Ages.[37] He has to admit that this framing of social life in an apparatus of dramatic and sublime formalities can be seen also in Byzantinism and the court of Louis XIV.[38] But he has here a point of departure which allows him to treat the elaborations of etiquette, vows, princely duels (never actually held), courtly love, bucolic fantasies, the images of death's horror, all as matters of sober human import. He frequently points out how closely related all these were to political forms, and in the rest of the book he gives an analysis of religious and artistic sensibilities that assimilates these also to the formal and more-or-less-empty fashions first discussed. His review of the extravagant vows in chivalric circles, from the fantastic Vows of the Pheasant to the merest mocking pleasantries, emphasizes therefore not merely the prevalent insincerity but the touches of seriousness; and his later discussion of the successive stages of extreme imagery among the mystics stresses not only the sincere struggle of the devout spirit for celestial joys but also its common sequel of sterile negations.[39] This balancing of judgments helps to show from many angles how generally and with what uniformity the men of about 1400 in France and Flanders tended to live by illusionary dreams and at the same time hardened actualities.

Now several points of interest seem to emerge from this organization of the evidence. One is that the recourse to formalities and fictions characterized a substantial part of what men thought and did, and absorbed much of their attention, time, and energy. Huizinga at times is inclined to call this "a passionate anxiety about formalities," but the few instances he gives of a troublesome anxiety seem better explained as deferences at moments of very practical diplomatic crisis.[40] As we have noticed earlier in looking at his interpretation of chivalry, his evidence seems to indicate that any troublesome intrusion of concern for fictions or formalities took the form less of passion than of simple mental inertia—the inability to shift quickly from habitual fiction to pressing fact. It is in this sense that Huizinga uses the words "mental inertia" to describe the remarkable blindness of fifteenth-century authors to the social importance of the common people.[41] He emphasizes how much wealth and attention the dukes of Burgundy poured into the splendor of their etiquette and of their Order of the Golden Fleece.[42] And he seems particularly illuminating when he points out how the prosaic burgher of Paris, in his personal diary, was obliged by his own sense of tragedy to record in high-flown allegory the horrible events of the Burgundian murders in Paris in 1418.[43] Men of the time seem to have felt that it was proper and necessary to cast solemn matters of many sorts in the forms of conventional fictions and formalities.

Huizinga does at one point resort to a commonplace metaphor by describing such formalities as "a thin veneer." [44] But his examples show otherwise, and he is forced to suggest that we "should rather picture to ourselves two layers of civilization superimposed, coexisting though contradictory." [45] Elsewhere he admits more directly that what we find is contradictory elements mixed up together "with a sort of ingenuous shamelessness." [46] It is one of the merits of his analysis that it leads him to recognize that in this period the ideals of men, although apparently seen and handled as if in a separate layer or layers of life, were in daily life mixed in with the contradictory actualities, often within single in-dividuals, as though the opposing emphases in life actually had to bal-ance each other in close juxtaposition. Since we know all too little about the various ways in which men can handle sharp contradictions between their proper activities and their simply practical behavior, Huizinga's evidence has definite value. It is not inappropriate that he acknowledges his own inability to solve this problem by speaking in the end of "the riddle presented by the religious personality of so many other men" of the day,[47] for the essence of a child's riddle is, after all, that it presents two incompatible meanings in one and the same word or phrase.

Huizinga shows us not only how much human energy was habitually devoted to illusionary formalities and how closely intermixed these were in life's actualities but also the degree to which they seem to have been maintained as a collection of cultural treasures. This may be in part an impression created by his topical method and by his emphasis on common features in his material. But one of the major works with which he deals is the thirteenth-century *Roman de la rose,* and he quite properly recognizes that we need some explanation for its profound and enduring influence on the two centuries of his period.[48] No one acquainted with history at large will be impressed by his first sugges-tion that love had to be formalized simply because life was becoming more ferocious. But a more helpful observation comes as if by accident later: the *genre gaulois,* though equally a fiction, was unfit to become an influential body of doctrine like the *Roman* because it did not have, as the latter had, a richness of aesthetic and ethical values. Huizinga makes virtually the same comment subsequently on the macabre vision of death's horror.[49] These observations put in a new light his hardly novel comment on the *Roman* itself: "By reason of its encyclopedic range it became the treasure-house whence lay society drew the better part of its erudition." [50] This may well indicate what he means when he finally says of chivalry, after all his criticism of its superficialities, "Its strength lay in the very exaggeration of its generous and fantastic views." [51] So we may have a right to interpret efforts to dress up other formalities with rich arrays of values as efforts to give them, also, a secure place amid the uncertainties of an age of pessimism.

This would explain, indeed, the remarkable way in which the fashions of late medieval life, as rehearsed in Huizinga's pages, seem to have taken on the trappings of pompous doctrines. But it hardly justifies what remains for readers a troubling feature of Huizinga's presentation, his treatment of even the most apparent frivolities, such as the princely challenges to duel, as quite on a par with the more secure and compelling formulations of religion and art. His distinction between the *genre gaulois* or macabre vision and the *Roman* would apply with even more force to distinguish fashion and play from religion and art, even in such an age. But without this virtual equating of all formalities and dreams his analysis might not have given us such clues for an understanding of the habits of the age as these that we have been noticing: the widespread role played by splendid formalities, their close intermixture with contradictory actualities, and the tendency to fit out all of them with a full range of aesthetic and ethical values.

We have not yet taken into account Huizinga's prime emphasis on the violence of the age and its tendency to go to extremes. He opens the book with a chapter of colorful examples of this, calling it "The Violent Tenor of Life." His analysis begins with the second chapter, and here we find the suggestion that the very prevalence of pessimism in the literature of the age made for the strength of the aspiration, in literature and in life, for the sublime or splendid.[52] This raises the interesting possibility that the period's tendency to pessimism should itself be regarded as an attitude, a form of life, going toward its extreme, like the opposite tendency to the dream and splendor of the ideal. But Huizinga seems to assume elsewhere—less perceptively—that any formulation of the facts of life is just the inescapable "hard facts," and no more. So he suggests, as we have seen, that love was formalized into courtly love simply because life was then more ferocious.[53] And when he points out that the lofty transports of the mystics were necessarily followed by a return to the "wise and economic system" of the Church, he seems to be regarding the latter as simply the essence of practicality, rather than the distressing extreme of late medieval decline which even freshman students are taught to recognize as the actual condition of the Church around A.D. 1400.[54] So too, at the end of the book, we find him simply expressing astonishment that the highly inquisitorial Church did not check the dissemination of the *Roman de la rose,* which with its flagrantly impious passages was, he notes, a very breviary of the aristocracy.[55]

But with his special interest in instances of extreme behavior, Huizinga does make suggestions that might bear on this last case. On chivalry he comments that "from the very beginning, reality gives the lie to the ideal, and accordingly the ideal will soar more and more towards the regions of fantasy."[56] "Without the brake of empirical observation," he remarks at another point, "the habit of always subordinating and subdividing becomes automatic and sterile, mere numbering, and nothing else."[57] Was the *Roman de la rose* perhaps sufficiently extreme in its formulations of love's doctrines, and sufficiently elaborate in its encyclopedic commentary, for churchmen to feel that it bore little relation to actual behavior? We find Huizinga giving us evidence, in an interesting account of the problem of common swearing, that to put a norm in extreme form at that time might simply rob it of practical effect. We are told that the two famous scholars Jean Gerson and Pierre d'Ailly urged the French authorities to renew the regulations against swearing but to be sure to lighten the penalties, so that these might really be exacted. Yet the subsequent decree of 1397 reissued the regulations with the traditionally extreme penalties, so that, according to evidence of 1411, there was no enforcement at all.[58] It almost seems that minds of the time preferred to put norms in extreme form so that—a comfortable state of affairs—they would have no practical effect.

This same Gerson, who was chancellor of the University of Paris, did regard the *Roman de la rose* as a dangerous pest and wrote the strongest of his statements against it in 1402.[59] He seems to have been unaffected by an immediately preceding incident. In 1399 Christine de Pisan had written her *Epistre au Dieu d'Amours,* voicing the serious complaints of womankind against the *Roman's* glorification of seduction and defending the earlier and less cynical tradition of courtly love. Her *Epistre* stirred up a strenuous literary debate at Paris between critics and adherents of the *Roman.* In the midst of this, in 1401, Duke Philip of Burgundy intervened—as we have noticed—by setting up a most elaborate new court of love, with numberless officials, rules, and forms of business. What is remarkable, from Huizinga's summary of the incident, is that among the prominent members of this new club formed to protect Christine's cause were those very persons who had just been attacking it. Huizinga concludes that it was all "merely a society amusement." [60] But this is the one case in Huizinga's book in which we can judge what it meant to introduce the extreme elaborateness of the Burgundian style; and the function of such elaborateness here seems clearly to have been to remove the subject of controversy from contact with the actual feelings that Christine's directness had aroused. This seems further evidence that the similar elaborateness of the *Roman de la rose,* as well as its encyclopedic array of values, customarily set it apart and beyond immediate relevance for churchmen other than such a clear-sighted thinker as Gerson.

Does *The Waning of the Middle Ages* give any more clues as to the character of this peculiar lack of connection between ideals, or elaborated fictions, and other parts of the life of the period? Huizinga uses one metaphor that we have not yet mentioned, in addition to those of the veneer, the two layers, and the riddle. The writer Chastellain, he remarks, "does his best to see his times through the tinted glasses" of his aristocratic conceptions; the fine forms of etiquette performed the function of "veiling cruel reality under apparent harmony." [61] There is nothing unusual about this metaphor, but it seems strikingly apt for the evidence. The great duke of Burgundy, Philip the Good, is near the head of the list when Huizinga comes to illustrate the remarkable "coexistence in one person of devotion and worldliness," and the paragraph describing the devotional practices of this duke leaves the impression that these practices were not only extreme but also logically correct according to the standards of the day.[62] In quite another connection, one of the most memorable quotations in the book is Chastellain's account of Philip's almost Homeric anger with his son, which with convincing realism exhibits the Duke in his impulsive life as thoroughly himself, insisting upon the full illogic of self-assertion.[63] May it not be that Duke Philip found it easier to support the double role of impressively pious chivalry and extreme self-indulgence because these two elements of his total behavior seemed to him so differently organized? We can remind ourselves that, in our own experience, it is normally hard to see any connection between pursuits such as movie-going and advanced mathematics without reducing one to terms comparable to the other's.

This at least may help us understand more readily a surprising passage in Huizinga's discussion of the forms of thought:

> The mentality of the declining Middle Ages often seems to us to display an incredible superficiality and feebleness. The complexity of things is ignored by it in a truly astounding manner. . . . Thus the presentment of a fact, in the minds of the epoch, is always like a primitive woodcut, with strong and simple lines and very clearly marked contours.[64]

These statements may well surprise us because in the preceding chapters Huizinga has provided impressive glimpses of the profundity of the period's thought; the complexity of it all is one of our strongest impressions. But this particular paragraph is commentary on a simple and direct account by a chronicler of the honorable burial of a man hanged by mistake in 1478. The chapter, in fact, is devoted to the propensity of the time in practical life "to take every idea by itself, to give it its formula, to treat it as an entity"; and the illustrative material has been such as the giving of names to inanimate objects, political speeches, proverbs.[65] This is not at all, therefore, the stuff of intellectualized ideals or fictions; it is instead the working of minds of the time on subjects more or less out of touch with such refinements. Is it not allowable to suppose that there was prevalent at the time a drastic contrast, even a lack of intercommunication, between the forms of thought and life in the one style and in the other? Most of us have a vivid impression of how baffling it was for Joan of Arc's mind, operating very much "like a primitive woodcut, with strong and simple lines," to try to communicate with her accusers and judges at Rouen.

If this interpretation has any validity, Huizinga's book gives us a pleasing illustration of this defect of vision from one style to the other, in a series of quotations from the book made up by the prosaic Chevalier de la Tour Landry for the instruction of his daughters in the fashions of romance.[66] The chevalier recalls the details of a neatly courteous conversation he had in his young manhood with a possible bride, but he does so simply in order to bring out the special forwardness of that young lady's manner that had repelled him then and that he wanted his daughters to avoid. The politely erotic imagery in that conversation was sheer formality, it seems. So also he tells his daughters unhesitatingly about an amorous order of noblemen and noblewomen in Poitou who were obligated to share wives—as though his daughters obviously should have a stock of such things to talk about.

It is out of such illustrations, as well as his commentary, that Huizinga allows us to form our own impression of the way in which, in the minds of the late Middle Ages, the brake of empirical observation so often failed to function, allowing for contrary extremes of pessimism or self-assertion and idealism or elaboration. It may not be necessary to suppose that any of the ideals of the day had within themselves the impulse to soar to fantasy; any idealization or elaboration may have served an immediate protective purpose of insulating the cherished modes of behavior, much as the court of love in 1401 seems at least in part to have quieted discord by imposing irrelevance. The extremes of sentimental emotion, the rushes of vindictiveness and of piety, that Huizinga describes in his first chapter may have arisen in part because the minds of the time were in this respect out of joint.[67] But these broad reflections must be taken simply as evidence of the possible value of Huizinga's cautious analysis. His findings on the violence and extremes of the age remain so imbedded in particular comment and apt illustration that the average reader may consider them simply amusing sidelights.[68]

Yet when Huizinga comes at last to deal with the art of the early fifteenth century in the Flemish area, he does have things to say that tie together many of his preceding comments. He has from the first treated fashions of the time as expressions of an overflowing aesthetic craving and insisted that art formed in that age an integral part of social life.[69] Now it is to an artist, Michelangelo, that he turns for the most trenchant comment on the declining Middle Ages, in the quotation already mentioned:

Flemish painting pleases all the devout better than Italian. . . . In Flanders they paint, before all things, to render exactly and deceptively the outward appearance of things. The painters choose, by preference, subjects provoking transports of piety, like the figures of saints or of prophets. But most of the time they paint what are called landscapes with plenty of figures. Though the eye is agreeably impressed, these pictures have neither art nor reason; neither symmetry nor proportion; neither choice of values nor grandeur. In short, this art is without power and without distinction; it aims at rendering minutely many things at the same time, of which a single one would have sufficed to call forth a man's whole application.[70]

This criticism by Michelangelo catches up a surprising number of Huizinga's preceding judgments, as if it had itself been in the back of his mind as he formed them. So it does not surprise us that Huizinga agrees wholeheartedly with this criticism and applies it to all aspects of the period; what Michelangelo singles out in Flemish painting are, he says, "exactly the essential traits of the declining Middle Ages." It is worth noting how, in completing this same sentence, Huizinga paraphrases the above quotation: the traits are "the violent sentimentality, the tendency to see each thing as an independent entity, to get lost in the multiplicity of concepts." These are items that have appeared often earlier in Huizinga's particular comments. The tendency to see each thing as an independent entity he has found characteristic not only of practical life but also of religious thought crystallizing into images, and even the images of death in the macabre vision.[71] The tendency to sterile multiplicity has been illustrated in the declining symbolism and philosophy and, very similarly, in chivalric elaborations.[72] The three traits named now, including the violent sentimentality, all recall to our minds specific cases of extremes of emphasis or elaboration. Huizinga's grouping of the three traits together seems at last to provide us with a single underlying characteristic of his period, a unifying conclusion emerging from his detailed analysis. What Michelangelo was talking about was plainly much less than all this, and probably somewhat different from it. But there seems warrant enough in the artist's words for Huizinga to rest a unifying conclusion partly on this testimony by a near-contemporary unusually qualified to pass judgment on the late Middle Ages. It is appropriate that Huizinga should arrive at a final conclusion through the perspective of art, and employing such evidence.

But Huizinga almost immediately discards this conclusion. When at the beginning of the next chapter he comes to speak judiciously of the problem of distinguishing between the Middle Ages and the Renaissance, we find him saying rather that "scrupulous realism, this aspiration to render exactly all natural details, is the characteristic feature of the spirit of the expiring Middle Ages." [73] He is on this page preparing to face directly at last the problem of explaining the greatness of Jan van Eyck and his fellows. Why, he now asks, when we find the writers of that day so insipid and tiresome, do the painters strike us as not only great but arrestingly fresh? "The explanation is that words and images have a totally different aesthetic function"; in painting, unlike writing, an exact rendering of external aspects will always of itself add "something inexpressible" which, so the next paragraphs insist, is enough to make the painting eternally fresh and profound in its insight. [74]

This is a startling opinion to find in this modern age of photography, especially from an experienced student of art like Huizinga. And yet it is the aesthetic judgment around which the remaining chapters of the book are organized and which they attempt to demonstrate. The literature of the period, Huizinga tells us, has merit whenever it works by means of direct observation, for then it approaches painting. [75] To be sure, literary efforts in fields like the comic were superior to their parallels in pictorial art—in this further chapter Huizinga seems once again to be carefully toning down his favorable judgments. His examples of admirable direct observation remind us disturbingly of what he has said earlier about the common tendency to see things with the simplicity of a woodcut, but he says nothing now to help us make more than superficial connections with his earlier analysis. [76] There is no unifying conclusion, although on his last page Huizinga describes the full value of the Renaissance in words that echo Michelangelo's. [77]

Is there any explanation for Huizinga's abandonment of the conclusion so firmly drawn from Michelangelo's words? Let us reassemble in order the steps of his presentation, starting with the first of his chapters on art. In this chapter, on "Art and Life," Huizinga mentions for the first time the brothers Van Eyck, and it is here that he feels obliged to argue that they belonged strictly with the circles of court and nobility already made familiar to us. In the next chapter, on "The Aesthetic Sentiment," he introduces the quotation from Michelangelo and shows how fully the strictures were justified. He is then ready to consider the relative excellence of the Flemish painters, but he has perhaps run into a difficulty. For no reason that is explicit, he opens the following chapter cautiously with his one formal statement on the problem of differentiating Middle Ages and Renaissance, and then asserts that the work of the artists like the Van Eycks is both in form and in idea "a product of the waning Middle Ages." [78] This is so much what we should expect that it is only surprising that it is said so formally. But it is now in this same paragraph that he singles out scrupulous realism as "the characteristic feature of the spirit of the expiring Middle Ages." And it is later on the same page that he advances suddenly the proposition that, in painting, literal reproduction inevitably brings with it the inexpressible addition of greatness.

The explanation would seem to be that Huizinga's method of double argument has at last created a serious embarrassment for him. His secondary argument, carried on in asides and scattered forceful opinions, has apparently represented his own strong judgments on the relative falseness or integrity of the forms that he reviews, even though his primary argument tries to assimilate all as parts of the pervading grays. Just before this point, his quotation from Michelangelo has provoked him to sum up sharply a considerable part of this secondary argument in words dictated in fact by his previous illustrations and judgments. Yet this unifying conclusion picks out the violent sentimentality, the tendency to see each thing as an independent entity, the tendency to get lost in multiplicity, as the essentials of his period. If he holds to this he cannot, evidently, show the Van Eycks to be great—as he plainly feels them to be—or else he must abandon his contention that they belonged to their times. His secondary argument, which calls for recognition of the high quality of these painters' work, is in danger of destroying his primary argument, simply because it has evolved, out of scattered *dicta* and sharp observation, into a cogency and definiteness of its own. And so Huizinga chooses to abandon his secondary argument and hold to his primary one. He shifts to a formula that allows him to judge Jan van Eyck to be wholly late medieval and at the same time fresh, even great.

Unless memory is untrustworthy, when as a student I first read *The Waning of the Middle Ages* my experience was that the book seemed to go forward with a sense of increasing understanding up to this break in the basic argument; thereafter it seemed confusing and confused. Any interpretation of a chain of thought like Huizinga's is bound to remain partly subjective. But if the evidence now assembled justifies my interpretation, it is clear that Huizinga's commentary for the first five-sixths of his book deserves attention apart from what follows in the last sixth. It provides a cumulative and cautious analysis of the peculiar psychological condition of life in the Franco-Flemish area around A.D. 1400. This analysis at its clearest is seriously obscured for the reader by an abrupt break in the argument, evidently provoked by Huizinga's failure to see how the great painters could rise above what he judges to be the limitations of their times. Of the several weaknesses of Huizinga's book, this may be the least easy to recognize. Given his method of presentation, and his use of double argument, it may still have contributed significantly to the evident difficulty of using the book for more than interesting background reading.

The question may be raised whether *Kulturgeschichte*, the "history of civilization" to which Huizinga's book was a deliberate contribution, is not a distinct subject of study, entitled to its own methods and liberties. This may call for debate at the level of university teaching and research, but in the college teaching of history in this country an answer seems dictated by current practice. If recent textbooks are any indication, the history of civilization is not a separate subject but a combination of the findings of historical workers in the various fields of research. A course which alternates unrelieved stretches of political narrative with unrelated tableaux of the life of one period after another is obviously unsatisfactory, but attempts are made to give even this type of outline integration by a similarity of disciplined treatment in the successive sections, with cross references—just as political narratives preserve the interrelations of the histories of separate countries. The story of the Romanesque and Gothic cathedrals has often been told in its own separate style, since many historians have seen in this development simply the aspirations of the age and the technical advances of anonymous local craftsmen. Now we learn that a central thread is the rise of master craftsmen whom we can follow in their ideas and careers very much as we follow Abelard and St. Thomas Aquinas.[79] Again, the outlines of the century-long depression following the Black Death of 1348 are emerging more clearly from research, so that the relations between the economic and other movements of the late Middle Ages have a claim to more precise treatment.[80] The advance of research, in short, itself indicates that the effort in this country to produce an intelligible history of civilization for college students need not stop short of applying the usual standards to whatever material seems directly relevant.

Teachers of History

Huizinga's commentary on Franco-Flemish life and thought around A.D. 1400 has an obvious bearing on the events and personalities already given a place in conventional history courses, and it should be helpful in relating these to the developments in religion and literature and art that equally claim attention. This is a more difficult task than simply to draw upon his book for transitional paragraphs of general comment and for enrichment of descriptive paragraphs. It raises the problem of whether his specific analysis of the psychological condition of the time is constructed solidly enough to bear the weight of emphasis in explaining the course of events. We can hope that research will in time illuminate the whole topic. Even now there is the chance that attempts to make more intelligible the transition from Middle Ages to modern times will find warrant for adjustments of organization and emphasis that will bring out more clearly such features as Huizinga calls to our attention.[81]

To present more firmly the character of late medieval decline would not be simply to round out the account now given of the rise and fall of the medieval form of society. It would also bring into better focus the character of the opening Renaissance. This has been obscured in past decades by the increasing concentration of light on medieval achievements and their relevance to later times. The dramatic quality of the Renaissance, felt by many of its participants and relished by countless students since then, is worth recapturing if it can be done by a more accurate rendering of the conditions of mind and life at the time when the Renaissance came into flower in Italy. This is no sound excuse for perpetuating the nineteenth century's gratifying identification of itself with those "first moderns" who restored to Europe a sense of fruitful creativity. Neither can we safely identify our present day's sense of uncertainty with the *malaise* that spread across Europe around A.D. 1400. But a more careful investigation of those developments is surely warranted. Huizinga's method, in spite of various confusions to which it evidently has led him, has yielded a series of precise suggestions worth exploring if historical study is to contribute more adequately to the understanding of actual human behavior.

1. J. Huizinga, *The Waning of the Middle Ages: A Study of the Forms of Life, Thought and Art in France and the Netherlands in the XIVth and XVth Centuries* (London: Edward Arnold, Ltd., 1924). First published as *De*

Huizinga and the Middle Ages

Herfsttij der Middeleeuwen (Haarlem, 1919); the 5th edition (1941) is reprinted in Huizinga's *Verzamelde Werken* (Haarlem, 1948–1951), III, 3–435. The English translation, according to its preface, is "the result of a work of adaptation, reduction and consolidation under the author's directions" (p. vi). There has therefore seemed no need in this paper to refer back to the Dutch editions, which are hardly used by American students. A convenient summary of the historical work of Johan Huizinga (1872–1945) is found in B. H. Slicher van Bath, "Guide to the Work of Dutch Mediaevalists 1919–1947," *Speculum*, XXIII (1948), 247–248.

2. For example, R. R. Palmer, *A History of the Modern World* (New York, 1950), p. 852 (bibliography by Frederick Aandahl, Jr.); *Readings in Medieval History*, edited by J. F. Scott, Albert Hyma, and A. H. Noyes (New York, 1933), pp. 550–554.

3. A. N. Whitehead, *Science and the Modern World* (New York, 1925), p. 86.

4. Werner Kaegi, *Das Historische Werk Johan Huizingas* (Leiden, 1947), pp. 15–17. Professor Kaegi of the University of Basel, where Burckhardt taught betweeen 1845 and 1893, has been since 1928 the translator and interpreter of Huizinga in the German language.

5. *Waning*, pp. 58–59; also pp. 22, 30, 60, 143, 193; summed up p. 252.

6. First published in Dutch in *De Gids*, IV (1920); conveniently available now in J. Huizinga, *Wege der Kulturgeschichte*, translated by W. Kaegi (Munich, 1930), pp. 89–139.

7. W. K. Ferguson, *The Renaissance in Historical Thought* (Boston, 1948), pp. 226–227, 290 *et seq.*; G. C. Sellery, *The Renaissance: Its Nature and Origins* (Madison, 1950).

8. This is stressed by Kaegi, *op. cit.*, p. 21.

9. The exceptions are three set pieces of narrow scope on the rise of party struggles (*Waning*, p. 13), on the replacement of the sin of pride by the sin of cupidity (p. 18), and on the revival of chivalry (p. 59). The irritability of men in his period, he mentions in passing, was like that shown in "the *chansons de gestes* of some centuries back" (p. 7).

10. *Ibid.*, pp. 188, 241.

11. *Ibid.*, p. 31. We find the Netherlands contrasted with France in respect of the *devotio moderna* (pp. 160, 174), but there is no further recognition of distinctions between places or groups.

12. *Ibid.*, p. 103.

13. *Ibid.*, pp. 63–65.

14. *Ibid.*, pp. 87, 93, 212.

15. *Ibid.*, p. 238.

16. *Ibid.*, p. v; pp. 173, 176; cf. p. 205.

17. *Ibid.*, p. v. The English word "waning" is hardly adequate to translate Huizinga's original title; the "autumn" would imply also the harvest season.

18. *Ibid.*, pp. 1, 29, 38, 140, 214, and then 241.

19. *Ibid.*, p. 66.

20. *Ibid.*, pp. 82–84.

21. *Ibid.*, p. 89.

22. *Ibid.*, pp. 93–94. It has been suggested that Deschamps' patriotism was aroused by Charles V's vigor (R. L. Kilgour, *The Decline of Chivalry* [Cambridge, Mass., 1937], pp. 85–86).

23. We similarly find one paragraph attributing some solid worth to the bucolic fiction: "The pastoral genre was the school where a keener perception and a stronger affection towards nature were learned" (*Waning*, p. 121 [cf. p. 269]). And the recital of the ridiculous refinements of court etiquette is offset by citations of Goethe and Emerson to the effect that no outward sign of politeness is without profound moral foundation (p. 36).

24. *Ibid.*, p. 22.

25. *Ibid.*, pp. 30, 58, 60, 143, 193.

26. *Ibid.*, p. 244.

27. *Ibid.*, p. 252. His final word in this passage seems, however, a cautious equivalent to Michelangelo's comment: "The triumph of the Renaissance was to consist in replacing this meticulous realism by breadth and simplicity" (p. 253).

28. *Ibid.*, p. 307.

29. *Ibid.*, p. 254; cf. pp. v, 224, 243.

30. *Ibid.*, pp. 256, 257; cf. p. 244.

31. *Ibid.*, p. 233. The greatness of Philip the Bold's Chancellor has also been emphasized (p. 240). We find Huizinga admitting all this in a parenthesis near the close of his discussion of Van Eyck's art: "he [Van Eyck] can give the rein to his craving for endless elaboration of details (perhaps one ought to say, that he can comply with the most impossible demands of an ignorant donor) . . ." (p. 258).

32. Cf. *ibid.*, p. 237.

33. *Ibid.*, p. 205, cf. pp. 179–180, 203.

34. *Ibid.*, pp. 141, 222, 238, 247; cf. Index under Arc.

35. Cf. *ibid.*, pp. 23, 222, 307. Thus he feels that the difference between Middle Ages and Renaissance, though essential, is as impossible to express as "the difference of taste between a strawberry and an apple" (p. 252).

36. *Ibid.*, p. 47, cf. p. 44.

37. *Ibid.*, pp. 28–29.

38. *Ibid.*, p. 31.

39. *Ibid.*, pp. 77–81, 201–205.

40. *Ibid.*, pp. 35–36.

41. *Ibid.*, p. 49.

42. *Ibid.*, pp. 31, 76.

43. *Ibid.*, p. 192.

44. *Ibid.*, p. 38.

45. *Ibid.*, p. 97.

46. *Ibid.*, pp. 84, 111. Huizinga makes this point more firmly when he comes to consider the types of religious life (p. 160).

47. *Ibid.,* p. 240.

48. *Ibid.,* p. 96.

49. *Ibid.,* pp. 99–100, 134.

50. *Ibid.,* p. 96.

51. *Ibid.,* p. 94.

52. *Ibid.,* p. 28.

53. *Ibid.,* p. 96. In another place Huizinga permits himself to say that "The more crushing the misery of daily life, the stronger the stimulants that will be needed to produce that intoxication with beauty and delight without which life would be unbearable" (pp. 229–230, cf. also p. 199); such language runs the risk of simply persuading the reader that the age was out of its head and so beyond understanding. Huizinga has already given a helpful warning against mistaking the hearty *esprit gaulois* for realism; this was, like courtly love, an artificial substitute for reality, a dream selecting the animal side of things (p. 99).

54. *Ibid.,* p. 204.

55. *Ibid.,* p. 307. Huizinga's touch is possibly not as sure on religious subjects; we find him saying positively, "The excesses and abuses resulting from an extreme familiarity with things holy, as well as the insolent mingling of pleasure with religion, are generally characteristic of periods of unshaken faith and of a deeply religious culture" (pp. 145–146). Surely such abuses and insolence were not characteristic of the *devotio moderna,* which displayed the "collective habit of earnestness and fervour" (p. 205). Perhaps here again Huizinga is taking the grays for the whole of his picture.

56. *Ibid.,* p. 66.

57. *Ibid.,* p. 197.

58. *Ibid.,* pp. 146–147. Huizinga seems not to have seen the force of this episode for his general problem, for we find him saying earlier (p. 94): "The soul of the Middle Ages, ferocious and passionate, could only be led by placing far too high the ideal towards which its aspirations should tend. Thus acted the Church, thus also feudal thought." It is doubtful whether analysis is furthered by such references to "the passionate and violent soul of the age" (p. 40).

59. *Ibid.,* pp. 104–105.

60. *Ibid.,* pp. 102–104.

61. *Ibid.,* pp. 44, 49. Chastellain, despite firsthand acquaintance with the wealth of the Flemish towns, was dazzled by court magnificence into believing that "the power of the house of Burgundy was especially due to the heroism and the devotion of knighthood" (p. 48).

62. *Ibid.,* p. 163. Huizinga elsewhere emphasizes the logical character of the princely duel, which Duke Philip loved to prepare and never carried through (p. 84).

63. *Ibid.,* pp. 263–266. For a fuller account see J. Huizinga, "La physionomie morale de Philippe le Bon," *Annales de Bourgogne,* IV (1932), fasc. 2, 101–129 (*Verzamelde Werken,* II, 216–237).

64. *Waning*, p. 214. The few sentences that I have omitted contain no transition.

65. *Ibid.*, pp. 206 *et seq.*

66. *Ibid.*, pp. 78, 112–113. The Chevalier was certainly viewing everything from a secure footing in the practical world; on the marriage of the Virgin Mary, he explained that "God wished that she should marry that saintly man Joseph, who was old and upright, for God wished to be born in wedlock, to comply with the current legal requirements, to avoid gossip" (p. 153; cf. p. 145).

67. Huizinga says of the religious life that we must recognize "a general lack of balance in the religious temper, rendering both individuals and masses liable to violent contradictions and to sudden changes" (*Ibid.*, p. 160).

68. It is worth noting that Huizinga's comments show no signs of being influenced by any standing presuppositions as to the nature of social decline in general. His analysis of the deterioration of European culture in our day, in his *In the Shadow of Tomorrow* (New York, 1936), is quite different in terms and character and suggests no comparison with the late Middle Ages.

69. *Waning*, p. 44.

70. *Ibid.*, p. 244.

71. *Ibid.*, pp. 206, 136, 124. The simile of the woodcut (p. 214), which we have quoted, invites comparison with the emphasis Huizinga lays on the woodcuts vividly picturing death (p. 124).

72. *Ibid.*, pp. 188–189, 197; p. 61.

73. *Ibid.*, p. 253. This seizes upon a single element in Michelangelo's comment but—as the next sentences show—does violence to the meaning of that comment as a whole.

74. *Ibid.*, pp. 253–254; cf. p. 271.

75. *Ibid.*, p. 269.

76. A comment (*Waning*, pp. 290–291) recalls no more than one of Michelangelo's points. Compare Huizinga's sharp comment earlier (pp. 241–242), *before* the introduction of his new interpretation. An art historian has recently judged that the apparently irreconcilable ways of looking at things "could variously interpenetrate in the fourteenth century and ultimately merge, for one glorious moment, in the painting of the great Flemings" (Erwin Panofsky, *Gothic Architecture and Scholasticism* [Latrobe, Pa., 1951], pp. 19–20). This interpretation seems much more adequate for the evidence carefully presented by Huizinga.

77. *Waning*, p. 307.

78. *Ibid.*, p. 252.

79. John Harvey, *The Gothic World 1100–1600* (London, 1950).

80. *Cambridge Economic History of Europe*, Vol. II, edited by M. Postan and E. E. Rich (Cambridge, 1952), pp. 191, 338, 456. It is interesting that the abundant evidence for this depression seems contradicted—in the fashion characteristic of the times?—by the large amount of luxury building in addi-

tions to churches and the like (*Times Literary Supplement,* January 2, 1953, p. 2).

81. Panofsky has summarized the developments in philosophy and art from the ninth to the fifteenth centuries in an analysis that opens up similar possibilities (*Gothic Architecture,* pp. 3–20).

» II «

HISTORIOGRAPHIC

TRADITIONS

[BURR C. BRUNDAGE]

The Birth of Clio: A Résumé and Interpretation of Ancient Near Eastern Historiography[1]

JOSEPHUS, writing for a vast Near Eastern audience, once advanced the claim that Oriental historians were superior to the Greek, in the fact that their ancient civilizations had kept full public records and thus they always had source material at hand to incite them to the expert compilation of sober and trustworthy history.[2] Perhaps enough attention has not been paid to this passage in Josephus. If Herodotus was the father of history, there still may have been some godfathers.

Temple walls, palace murals, freestanding stelae, and carved rock inscriptions in abundance from the preclassical period enlighten us regarding the ancient Near East. These are open records meant to proclaim power to the public gaze. One has the impression that, as compared with Hellenic and Roman custom, the ancient Near East did lay enormous stress on public documentation, and that Josephus was therefore probably correct.

The abundance of public source material may have been one of the significant factors encouraging the development of historiography in the ancient Near East, but it certainly does not explain the reasons why written history should have appeared in this area at all.

Teachers of History

This paper is an explication of the hypothesis that the forms antecedent to the earliest true written history are of courtly origin, that they belonged from their very inception to the king, surrounded as he was with divine or magical sanctions.[3] True written history, however, could not and did not arise in the Near East until kingship was viewed as something less than holy. In other words, only when history was written *about* kings, and not *by* kings, could the requisite detachment be secured. The case of Israel proves this point. Israel probably wrote the first true history; it was also the first nation to create a popularly based constitutional monarchy *not sustained magically*.

Eduard Meyer notes that it is immediate need that forces men to speculate on history and finally to create the art of written history itself.[4] This in principle allows our contention that written history in the ancient Near East was first an instrument of rule and appeared prominently when there was a specific need to strengthen or celebrate kingship. Only after it had been well launched under such auspices was it captured by the ecclesiastic and made to blossom into the finer flowers of the spirit, both moral and speculative.

Written history and its prototypes in the Near East are enshrined in three primary literary forms: lists (date lists and king lists), chronicles, and annals.[5] The list is the most primitive. The chronicle is an outgrowth of the king list and appears in the middle of the period under review. Annals are an entirely separate form and are limited to strictly imperial ages; they therefore tend to cluster in the later part of the period.[6]

Considered as written history, the pertinent books of the Old Testament, the Apocrypha, and Pseudoepigrapha do not fit any of these categories exactly, but, while partaking of the nature of all, reveal a structure of ever-surprising novelty. With some justification, therefore, our survey omits these, though properly they are Near Eastern. To have obtruded the complex questions of Hebrew historiography into this short essay would have simply confused the line we attempt to establish in regard to the more general development of the art.

I

Epic is of the highest importance in the understanding of the historical arts and, because of its undoubted influence on written history in the cuneiform area, brief mention of it must be made here.[7]

One clue to the literary dynamics which produced the Mesopotamian chronicle out of the jejune king list lies in the fact of the antecedence in this area of the Sumerian epic and the near-epic narratives of Sargon and Naram-Sin.[8] We note that in the land of the Nile the epic did not exist; correspondingly, as far as we know, the list did not there develop into the chronicle. Even if the archaeologist's spade should bring to light a true Egyptian chronicle—perhaps one of Manetho's sources— it would probably still be a correct statement that that historical form was a feeble growth in the body of Egyptian literature.

Epic recounts, generally in meter, the deeds of heroic leaders of the near past who are faced with supreme obstacles. The hero is tested and his end is not always happy. Epic posits a partially uncontrolled or hostile universe, and it is the hero's challenge to this hostility that produces the noble pathos so prominent in the epic ambient. In Egypt pharaoh was a god, and the dogma that Maat (the true or just order) was established by his mere presence precluded any overt preoccupation with danger or strife. His towering figure dwarfed all mortals under him; none could be heroes where theologically there was room for only one hero.[9] Epic starved in the Nile valley for lack of provender.

In the land of Sumer and Akkad, from the very beginning, the wretchedness of men and the narrowness of their limitations was thoroughly and explicitly acknowledged. Their universe was an uneasy equilibrium between order and chaos, and one would have been rash indeed to have wagered on the permanence of either. Godland was itself the scene of conflict and hard annual decisions. As a pale reflection, therefore, the clashing of human wills on earth could be fully understood. In literary art the Sumerian epic first enshrined this tension.

There are three major extant groups of epic and epiclike material which exerted influences upon the beginning of the historical arts in the Tigris-Euphrates valley and the Anatolian plateau: the earliest Sumerian epics, clustering around such figures as Gilgamesh,[10] Enmerkar, etc.; the widespread group of texts concerning the two great figures of the Akkadian dynasty, Sargon and Naram-Sin (near the end of the Sumerian period); and, finally, indigenous Hittite material of which we possess fragments.[11] When and if Washshukkani, the glittering capital of Mitanni, is uncovered, we shall no doubt recover evidences of Hurrian epics.

As will become apparent in the following sections, the first two groups were important catalysts in the development of the historical arts in Mesopotamia. For the king list the early Sumerian epic is important. For the later expansion of the king list into the chronicle, the Sargonic material (mingled with romance and legend) is basic. Sargon particularly is one of the truly heroic figures in literature, his figure exerting a powerfully fertilizing effect upon Near Eastern thought in general.[12] As an epic figure he may well have provided just that focus of historical interest necessary to tip the king list over into literary channels—in this case, the chronicle.

Almost surely the epic and date list do not stand alone as the only seedbeds of later Sumerian and Babylonian historiography; the richness of written history as an art precludes any such simple deduction. Nevertheless the fragmentary state of our knowledge at present forbids any more extended statement. Kramer draws our attention to a Sumerian "sense of historical detail" already apparent about 2400 B.C. (short chronology) in tablets from the city state of Lagash—roughly three hundred years before the redaction of the Sumerian King List, to be mentioned below.[13] That this already-well-developed historical aptitude may have flowered in documents of a type other than those we now possess is always a possibility. Kramer points out further, in connection with the Entemena text, the complete and harmonious interweaving of divine and human action in the events recorded in the historical introduction, recalling most vividly the type of action which we see in the *Iliad*.

II

Epic is in a sense folk history. As such it satisfied the Sumerian craving for an integration with and an understanding of the parts of his past which were most meaningful for him. Now along with the earliest written epics there existed (somewhat later in time?) the earliest lists already mentioned—two totally different genres. At first the list was simply a roster of royal names and numbers of years ruled, with some indication of the city-state referred to. With the passage of time the scribe—who compiled, let us say, the famous Sumerian King List—

added, for the purposes of mere academic display, to the names of legendary kings short references to their activities as known from the current epics. Thus, for example, from the dynasty of Uruk, Enmerkar is *the one who built Uruk;* Gilgamesh is qualified as follows, *his father was a lillu-demon, a high priest of Kullab;* Sargon of Akkad, *his . . . was a date-grower—cupbearer of Ur-Zababa,* etc. These and others are abbreviated references from a large body of epics which were well known to the scribe. There are also undoubted references from myth, legend, and folklore, but with these we are not concerned. In any case recollections from epic in the Sumerian King List served to stretch the medium.

These epic reminiscences filling out the bare skeleton of the king list certainly revealed to the scribe later on the possibilities of a new literary form, the chronicle.

Let us now go back and consider the lists in more detail, inasmuch as they are first in point of time and lowliest in the scale of sophistication. We have arbitrarily produced a twofold division into date lists and king lists simply to distinguish the simple from the semiliterary or fuller form. The first group is strictly utilitarian and therefore appears in all periods of ancient Near Eastern history; they were designed as scribal aids in the divinatory and historical arts and in legal and commercial transactions where the use of past data was indicated. In this group fall such pieces as the Egyptian Turin list,[14] the Assyrian Eponymous lists, the Synchronistic Chronicle (not a chronicle at all according to our terminology), and the Babylonian king lists. Essentially they are bald listings of reigns, years of reigns, and such minimal material as may conveniently locate some desired point in time. Dynastic divisions are sometimes present.

In Egypt there must have been early date lists, but those which we have cluster in the New Kingdom, the imperial period *par excellence,* with peculiar relevance to the nineteenth dynasty, a new house of northern pharaohs which followed the Amarna collapse.[15] The dream of the two great pharaohs of this dynasty, Seti I and his son Ramses II, was to restore the vanished glories of the empire in Asia. Taking the form of a true political and military renaissance, this period in consequence looked backward for its sanctions.[16] A chapel dedicated to the ancient kings was erected on the holy site of Abydos and a list of all former rulers engraved on the walls. The list itself is negative and was simply copied from some such mnemonic aid as the Turin Papyrus. The motive for the public presentation of this Abydos list, however, is obvious; it was designed to add the strength of legitimacy (and therefore the odor of sanctity) to the militarily enforced power of the new dynasty. In the motive prompting the publication of the Abydos list of Seti I we have then a counterpart to the motive leading to the publication of the Sumerian King List of Utuhegal (to be mentioned fully below), for both rulers followed crucial periods when kingship had been under a cloud.

Little need be said of the Babylonian and Assyrian lists except to stress again their utilitarian, nonstructural character.[17] They reveal no special pleading.

The group of king lists is represented by the Palermo Stone from Egypt and the Sumerian King List from Mesopotamia. These two compositions are still basically tables or lists, but they are no longer in the source material or utilitarian class. They stand as documents with a purpose of their own, designed to support a specific policy.

The Palermo Stone was called into being as an instrument of royal power in a revolutionary period—the Re crisis of the fifth dynasty.[18] Up to this time, throughout the Protodynastic and the early Old Kingdom period, the king had been advancing his claims to be the sole great god in whom, as in a pure monolithic institution, all power centered. We know little of the rise of the Heliopolitan cult of Re, but we can see that it implicitly disputed the divine primacy of pharaoh, and that in the end it won a partial victory. The pharaohs became in titulary the bodily sons of this powerful god. The redaction of the Palermo Stone, which for its day must have been a formidable literary undertaking, attests to this momentous change in Egyptian history. The following excerpts will illustrate parts of this document; three consecutive years are selected from the reign of a second-dynasty king, and one from the reign of the fourth-dynasty pharaoh Snefru (the numbers at the end of each year entry are supposed to be the height of the Nile in that year). No selections are taken from the years of the fifth-dynasty Re kings inasmuch as they simply refer at length to cult additions and pious foundations.

year 12: Worship of Horus. Sixth occurrence of the numbering (census). 4 cubits, 3 fingers.

year 13: First occurrence of the feast "Worship of Horus of Heaven."

Hacking up of the city Shem-Re. Hacking up of the city "Horus-of-the-North." 4 cubits, 3 fingers.

year 14: Worship of Horus. Seventh occurrence of the numbering. 1 cubit.

.   .   .   .   .

year X + 2: Building of a 100-cubit "Praise-of-the-Two-Lands" ship of cedarwood, and of 60 sixteen-barges of the king. Hacking up the land of the Negro and bringing back 7,000 living prisoners and 200,000 large and small cattle. Building of the wall of the Southland and Northland called "Houses-of-Snefru." Bringing 40 ships filled with cedar logs. 2 cubits, 2 fingers.[19]

The Palermo Stone is basically a record of the piety of these Re kings of the fifth dynasty, and is thus a proclamation of their exemplary correctness. The scribes who compiled the material made their selections from a strong sacerdotal bias, and while secular events in the lives of past kings are recorded,[20] they are subordinate to a desire to prove the salient fact of piety in the long tradition of kingship. This reconstruction of the purpose of the Palermo Stone is hypothetical. The stone is exceedingly fragmentary; we possess neither beginning nor end. It is probable that the text began with the earliest days when Re himself was king of Egypt. If true, this would of course support our thesis.

The Sumerian King List, like the Palermo Stone, is a crisis document, appearing as it does at the beginning of the Sumerian renaissance.[21] It was designed to illustrate how, in the ages before Utuhegal, Sumerian kingship was the stable factor which alone gave continuity and meaning to history.[22] Needless to say, the feeling in it for history as process is very weak, it being a simple noncausal chronology, a mere accumulation of unembellished data. Its subject is political kingship, but it is not narrowly confined to the parochial interest of any specific city. Its purview is cast over the entire valley and it traces the wandering of kingship, following it from city to city. In a sense it is esoteric writing and could have touched few people. We are led to conclude that it was thoroughly courtly in origin. The following is a typical excerpt showing how the kingship passed from the city of Akshak to Kish and thence to Uruk.

Akshak was smitten with weapons; its kingship to Kish was carried. In Kish Puzur-Sin, son of Ku-Baba, became king and reigned 25 years; Ur-Zababa, son of Puzur-Sin, reigned 400 years; Simu-dar reigned 30 years; Usiwatar, son of Simu-dar, reigned 7 years; Eshtar-muti reigned 11 years; Ishme-Shamash reigned 11 years; Nannia, a stonecutter, reigned 7 years—7 kings reigned its 491 years. Kish was smitten with weapons; its kingship to Uruk was carried.[23]

The Sumerian King List uses the legendary Flood as its chronological pivot, history being thus either antediluvian or postdiluvian. It is of great interest to note that the antediluvian section was added later, showing us the scribe actually constructing history backward. This introductory section is taken from a mytho-legendary text from Eridu, which Jacobsen has assigned to what he calls the epic-historical genre.[24] For its day this addendum was a notable stretching of the historical imagination. The opening lines of this section reveal a desire to investigate beginnings, for they state the provenience of rule, "When kingship was lowered from heaven, the kingship was [first] in Eridu."

This particular scribe was not led to carry his story back to the creation, however, because of the limited nature of his motivation; he is not interested in the past of mankind for any interest of its own, but only insofar as it proves the purity and antiquity of kingship over the Sumerian city states. Another piece of evidence of the strong secularism in the Sumerian King List is the honesty with which the scribe approached his sources. Concerning a period of political turmoil he simply writes, "Who was king, who was not king?" or with a broken or illegible tablet before him he notes, "Destroyed! To the heavenly Nidaba [goddess of writing] is it clear!" He is thus no mere romancer but a writer of great singleness of purpose. It does not affect our conclusions that at the same time the scribe was guilty of "an effort to force correct evidence into a mold shaped by an erroneous theory of Babylonian history." [25]

III

The chronicle advances out of the class of lists by virtue of being attracted into literary form. In this group we should of course place the late Hellenistic histories of the Egyptian Manetho and the chronicles of the Babylonian priest Berossus and the somewhat later Philo of Byblos, whose work is based on the earlier Phoenician cosmogonist and historian Sanchuniathon. Of these writers we have only extracts and résumés in later Greek and Christian writers; we do not possess the original texts. For lack of space we here omit consideration of these, though they undeniably form the last chapter in the development of the Near Eastern chronicle, heavily touched though they are by Greek influences. The most notable examples of the chronicle which deserve our attention here are the Narim-Sin Text, the Weidner Chronicle, and lastly the great Neo-Babylonian Chronicle. In this genre the basic chronological scheme is used, but certain royal figures from the past are now singled out and their deeds and fates are particularly noted.

The fragmentary state of the Narim-Sin Text, as reconstructed by Güterbock,[26] forbids extended discussion; it would seem, however, that we have here a literary form not motivated by considerations of legitimacy. In point of time it is later than the Sumerian King List, and we are therefore not surprised to find a fuller and richer treatment of events, but we *are* surprised to find that a pronounced shift in emphasis has taken place away from considerations of the origins of rule in order to show an ecclesiastical interpretation of history. The text begins (freely translated from Güterbock):

After Enlil's storm had destroyed Kish like the Bull of Heaven and had ground the dwellings of the land of Uruk like the great Bull into the dust— while at that moment Enlil had turned over to Sargon in its entirety the sovereignty and the kingship, then did the holy Innanna designate Akkad as her august quarters, setting up her throne in Ulmaš. . . .

The text goes on to develop the prosperity and joy of Akkad under this dispensation of the goddess Innanna down at least through the reign of Naram-Sin, and then apparently relates how this prosperity was destroyed by invaders at the command of Innanna herself. The faint possibility exists that this text is part of an old Sumerian historical work of much grander proportions than what we have today. The most notable aspect of this text is its purely literary quality. Aided by this new fullness, it is now beginning to present certain personalities (Naram-Sin, for instance) as tragic figures in history, though as yet history is not itself tragically conceived.

The Weidner Chronicle is also later and fuller than the Sumerian King List. Composed apparently in the period of the first Babylonian dynasty, like the Naram-Sin Text, it is national in scope and ecclesiastical in tone. It pivots on the founding of Marduk's cult and his temple of Esagila. Our interest is heightened when we consider the fact that now for the first time, to our knowledge, a cosmogony serves as a prelude to history, for the text opens upon a scene in heaven with the high gods Anu and Enlil. Kingship here passes on from city to city only as the kings of these cities are favorably or unfavorably disposed to Marduk and his Babylonian cult. In fact it reads Marduk well back into the Enlil period. It is definitely special pleading of a priestly kind, though still utilizing the passage of royalty as the theme of its history. In the latter respect it obviously owes much to the Sumerian King List. I have considered the Weidner Chronicle so important a milestone in the origins of historiography as to include a translation of Güterbock's rendering of the best-preserved portion of it as an appendix to this paper.

The first Babylonian dynasty, of which Hammurabi was the most distinguished member, marks thus a milestone in the development of the art of history; the new and vigorous cult of Marduk the national god greatly stimulated that development. Royalty and its problems had earlier touched off the first attempts in this direction, and royalty in this later period is still impressively the subject of written history as well as its promoter, but the authors are now patently priests; the result is a literary genre more heavily charged with speculation and more copious in content. History has become moral (narrowly interpreted by the Marduk priesthood of course) and has thus acquired a *point d'appui*.

The Neo-Babylonian Chronicle is a great series of tablets written in the Neo-Babylonian and Persian periods.[27] It relates events beginning with the inescapable Sargon of Akkad, and carries the reader down into the Persian era. It was composed in the temple libraries of Marduk in the city of Babylon.[28]

With the exception of the Old Testament, the Neo-Babylonian Chronicle is the first world history of any length; it reveals a professional ability on the part of its authors to stand above the scene and survey it without noticeable passion or prejudice—as witness the account of the capture of the city of Asshur. But while this incipient universalism freed the Babylonian historian so that he was enabled to write true history, he did not utilize any consistent criterion of judgment by which he could make a meaningful selection of facts from his data. At times the result is a welter of disparate facts adding up to no particular theme or thesis about history as such—except when the scribe is pressing his theme of Marduk's sovereignty over history (which he never does as rigorously as did the author of the Weidner Chronicle). Sophistication, with some of its secular implications, has weakened the scribe's religiosity, and to that extent has confused his formerly clear principle of interpretation. To this Babylonian, history was not as purely whimsical as it was to his Sumerian predecessors, to whom it had been a mere bundle of childlike vagaries of gods and men, but when it did not relate to the sacred it became simply disjointed and curious, as witness this account from the fourth year of Mushezib-Marduk:

In the month of Nisanu, the 15th day, Menanu, king of Elam, suffered a stroke, his mouth was paralyzed, he was unable to speak. In the month of Kislimu, the 1st day, the city of Babylon was seized, Mushezib-Marduk was made a prisoner and brought to Assyria. Four years was Mushezib-Marduk king in Babylon. In the month of Addaru, the 7th day, Menanu, king of Elam, died. Four years was Menanu king in Elam. Hummahaldashu sat himself on the throne in Elam.[29]

Between the Old Babylonian attempts at historiography and the Neo-Babylonian Chronicle, the secular or nonsacred has made heavy inroads. Events such as the resounding fall of Nineveh in 612 B.C. are recorded in the Neo-Babylonian Chronicle as mundane events; the gods are now not wholly necessary to explain the configurations in the historical scene, and the niceness of dating (day, month, year) in the text is convincing evidence of a new history for its own sake. Written history has at length freed itself to become a literary discipline *sui generis,* humanistic at its center though still leaving wide peripheral areas for divine or providential intervention. Nevertheless this history is still neither artistically conceived as in Herodotus, dramatic as in Thucydides, nor interpretative as in Eusebius.

In the early tablets of the series the scribes carry on unchanged and without further development the depiction of stock tragic figures, but as the series approaches a culmination in the magnificent entry of Cyrus into Babylon (539 B.C.), we note a new subdued suspense leading up to it, carried in part by the bitter and contumacious refrain "and Nabonidus stayed in Tema," and we are further aware of an undertone of dread at the consequent nonobservance of the great religious festivals so necessary to the well-being of the state. An ominous mood is well developed in the last tablet, which deepens our appreciation of Nabonidus as a fated and god-abandoned creature. The entire scene is very skillfully contrived and bears witness that written history was almost of age. The account of the actual entry, quoted later in this paper, is a sustained statement of joy in the unfolding of the climacteric event.

We have thus seen that from the Naram-Sin Text to the Neo-Babylonian Chronicle it was the priests of Marduk who developed the art of history. To the city of Babylon therefore our profession owes its first serious debt.

IV

The campaign annals are in a class apart. True written history, as we would judge it today, does not begin until the author or authors collate two or more source texts, with the resultant a new, indirect, and therefore interpretative account. First person accounts of contemporary events are therefore not properly historiographic. Such are the annals of the kings. They are nevertheless peripheral types of history and as such concern us here.

They appear in the Near East shortly after 1500 B.C. and are to be linked with the phenomenon of imperialism. All of them, Egyptian, Hittite, and Assyrian, are relatively independent in origin as far as we can see; all except the Hittite are monumental. The public character of the campaign annals contrasts with the chronicles, which primarily were not intended for the public gaze.

Though autobiographical in form, the annals explicate some of the most distinctive prerogatives of the crown; they assume therefore a larger-than-autobiographical status, for always in the Near East the crown was the state. They were worked up from actual campaign records or army logs—which have of course disappeared. In the case of the Hittite annals material was also garnered from the state archives. Literary convention and striving for effect are prominent characteristics of this form, and it may well be said that they are the most self-conscious and possibly the most inaccurate of the historiographical genres we have considered.

The pharaonic annals may owe their inspiration to the royal stelae of the late seventeenth dynasty, though there is ground for the strong suspicion that the overriding originality of one particular pharaoh, Thutmose III, popularized them as an instrument of royal self-glorification. His Karnak annals are an unequal selection from his campaign journals.

At least one of these journals was in part the work of an exceptional young Egyptian courtier, Tjaneni by name, who accompanied the army in the capacity of recorder.[30] It is clear that the full text of his leather book was ruthlessly pruned for use on the inner walls of the temple of Amon at Karnak; thus we have these annals only in an ecclesiastical edition. A priestly bias was certainly not present in the original scroll.

The camaraderie of the seventeenth- and eighteenth-dynasty war camps and the common use of the council of war could not but have humanized and secularized to some extent the dogma of the pharaoh's unapproachability.[31] In the annals of Thutmose III this new humanization of the royal dogma is evident, particularly where we find citations to the exact day and even hour. Never before had pharaoh been this specific. A new secular time sense is allowed to appear before the public view, in decided contrast to the timelessness of the god's time. A more factual and intimate style results, almost modern. The scene of the tough generalissimo Thutmose in his staff meeting at Aruna is worthy of a Villehardouin.

Campaign annals were carefully kept throughout the early and middle period of the eighteenth dynasty by the more vigorous pharaohs.[32] This period, beginning with Kamose (last king of the seventeenth dynasty) and ending with Amenhotep III, is therefore the most flourishing era of Egyptian annals writing. With the second period the old dogma of the full sanctity of the pharaoh has returned to overlay our recovered records with a thick mass of adulation and hyperbole. That Seti I had full annals composed can be inferred; that Ramses II and Ramses III did so is obvious, though the effusions on their temple walls have warped them considerably from the originals. Our last Egyptian annals, those of Ramses III, are scattered in form, overblown with rhetoric, and both incoherent and turgid to the modern taste. Unlike the Assyrian annals, which continued to develop steadily and surely as a literary form, the *published* Egyptian annals deteriorated rapidly under the influence of state dogma and priestly eulogy. The ancient doctrine that flux was insignificant and without meaning returned, and a promising lead toward an understanding of the unique event was extinguished.

The first Hittite annals known to us fully are from the reign of Mursilis II, a monarch of the Hittite New Kingdom (roughly contemporary with the late eighteenth dynasty of Egypt and with Arik-den-ilu of Assyria, see below). There are three sets: the annals of his father

Suppiluliumas, the compilation of which he personally ordered,[33] and, from his own reign, both the Decennial and the Complete Annals.[34] There are also fragments of the annals of Hattusilis III and Tudhaliyas IV, whose reigns just preceded the rapid decline of Hatti.

Little can be stated regarding the literary evolution of these remarkable documents except that, while the actual published form which we have may well have been first used by Mursilis, there seems to be reason to look for prototypes in the Hittite Old Kingdom. From the Old Kingdom we possess fragments of texts which lie in a kind of twilight zone between epic and legend on the one hand and true written history on the other,[35] and we are also aware of the importance of Akkadian translations in Hittite literary life.[36] No definite statement can be made connecting these forms with the annals. Gurney claims on the other hand that the Hittite annals spring naturally out of the old undifferentiated royal proclamation (which could be a treaty, a decree, or a simple pronouncement) with its ever-present historical introduction,[37] but this is impossible for the simple reason that the annals are not historical; they are always contemporary in intent.

We fail furthermore to understand Gurney's statement that the Hittite annals generally have a religious theme.[38] That the king be pious was undoubtedly insisted upon, but the actual account is too thoroughly narrative in essence to lead one to suspect a *strong* ulterior interest. It is true that we can suspect that the Annals of Mursilis were put together in the first instance as a "thank-offering" of the king to his well-disposed deity, the Sun Goddess of Arinna, but the document itself bespeaks a historical skill and a delight simply in the telling of the story which are impressively secular.

The Hittite annals are different in texture from either the Egyptian or Assyrian documents. The Assyrian annals are aggressively egotistical almost to the point of monomania; the Egyptian annals rapidly move from the naïve narrative style of Thutmose back into that ancient and unpleasing literary smugness known from earliest times in Egypt. The king in the Hittite annals, on the other hand, is neither on the defensive nor does he make himself ridiculous by overconfidence. He presents himself rather as a hard-working, battle-begrimed feudal king in a political atmosphere far less sophisticated than that prevailing among his greater neighbors to the south. His annals are sober, direct, and stereotyped. The incidents of the campaigns tend stylistically to a primitive repetitiousness—the challenge by messenger, the formal defiance, the march, the siege, the hasty submission by the overawed enemy, the parceling of the booty, and the triumphal return. Different events are compressed into a somewhat unimaginative sameness. The Assyrian annals do the same, but the events are more boldly styled and superficially more impressive. That the Hittites made a definite literary effort is evident, for the Complete Annals are purposely more varied and vivid than the Decennial Annals. That some of the motifs in these annals, such as the written or spoken challenge and response, were influenced by as-yet-undiscovered epic forerunners is very likely. In the Egyptian and Assyrian annals no epic reminiscences can be distinguished.

When all this is said, the Hittite annals are by far the most superior historiography in this class of documents. The sobriety of statement, the willingness to ascribe portions of the glory to others, and the *comparative* lack of vainglory all contribute to this conclusion. There is even an occasional flash of human drama. In the introduction to the Annals of Mursilis,[39] we see him as a youth just come to the throne only to find himself pelted from all sides by the jeers and insults of his enemies, powerful feudal princes on his borders; and we are told of the resolution of his cruel predicament by his solitary appeal to the great Sun Goddess and of her first epiphany before his eyes—an episode very like the disparagement of Telemachus by the suitors and the comforting friendship of Athena for that unlucky youth.

About the Assyrian annals we are most fully informed, for here we can behold the various stages in the development of this form over a space of about six hundred years. They spring out of the old dedicatory or building inscription, itself ultimately of Sumerian origin. The actual campaign annals are the outgrowth of that part of the inscription which serves to identify the king who erects or reconstructs such and such a temple or public edifice; and we are thus certain that the Assyrian annals is a truly indigenous form. With Arik-den-ilu (*ca.* 1300 B.C.) we see this process already fairly well developed. With Ashur-nasir-pal (885–860) the annals finally separate entirely from their dedicatory matrix to become a literary form *sui generis*.[40] Under Esarhaddon (681–668) the strict chronological order of campaigns can be replaced by the more literary, though less exact, topical order—all the Urartian campaigns together, all the Egyptian campaigns together, etc. The great series culminates logically in the annals of the last great Assyrian prince, Asshurbanipal (668–626), a dual culmination in both excellence of style and sheer revolting gruesomeness. The description of the salting and the insulting of the corpse of Nabu-bel-shumate is almost without parallel in any literature.[41]

The style of the Assyrian annals is bold and stereotyped; the early annals, which set the phraseology, do not sound like transcriptions from army campaign journals,[42] such as we know was true of the annals of Thutmose III. They more closely resemble true literary efforts,[43] self-conscious, boastful, and abounding in hard and brilliant hyperbole. The swelling chorus of self-glorification develops easily into the psychopathic. However repellent this may be, the unlimited use of it certainly adds to the homogeneity of this group of documents. The phraseology being standardized, the refrain, repeated down from king to king, strikes one with a peculiar and deadly repulsion, "I destroyed, I devastated, I burned with fire."

For all their brilliance of style, however, the Assyrian annals fail to achieve dramatic suspense. By the time of Sennacherib the beginnings of a sense of drama appears; the description of his eighth campaign is terrifyingly concrete and vivid. Esarhaddon's annals are introduced by the thrilling story of his efforts to gain the royal power, and there is a real sense of resolution in the favorable omens that are divulged as he finally takes the throne. This new autobiographical intimacy reaches a climax in the annals of his son Ashurbanipal, wherein we find interesting revelations of the character of the king, an account of his youth, his education, the condition of the kingdom at his accession, the gathering of the gods in Babylon, etc.[44] These—the last Assyrian annals—tremble on the verge of true autobiography.

Throughout the Assyrian annals remarkable success is achieved in portraying the king as swift violence and sheer power, omnipresent, utterly skilled, gigantic ("like a fish I caught him up out of the sea and cut off his head"). They far surpass even the later Egyptian annals in this regard.

We should mention in this place a remarkable document that is annalistic in sense but not in genre, for it is couched in the form of a letter from Sargon of Assyria to his national god Ashur.[45] It purports to give an account of Sargon's eighth campaign, but in full narrative style. Here are the faint beginnings of characterization, as witness the delineation of the figure of Ursa the Vannic king.[46] The battle itself is related in lively dramatic style, and there is a definite foreshadowing of Herodotus in colorful details of the horse-loving Urartians, of the destruction of Ulhu orchards, and of the attack on the city of Urzana, and finally of the almost Rousseauesque description of the swift, dark cascades in those far and distant mountains. It is not a strictly historiographical document, but its lucky recovery makes the later rise of written history in Anatolian Greece easier to understand.[47]

V

It is not enough to survey the literary canons in which Near Eastern historiography was enshrined. Attention must also be drawn to the *sense of history* which informs them. It is obvious to the student that throughout the period under consideration the sense of history was considerably augmented, if not actually changed, just as were the written vehicles of that sense of history. In the brief space of this essay we cannot follow the chronological development of these concepts, and so must content ourselves with a more simple and artificial analysis of the *tendency* or *intent* of these cultures in their understanding of men's past careers on earth.

The most important criterion by which we attempt to test a people's sense of history is the degree to which they see history as mastered from outside itself, and their identification of that personality or force which stands over it. Some few groups, such as the dialectical materialists of recent times, have assumed (though not without inner contradictions) that history has no master but is simply a function of itself. A larger group has been confused and uncertain upon the question. Others—perhaps the majority of peoples—have with no hesitation whatsoever bowed before a mysterious personality or personalities, good or evil as the understanding might be, sovereign over man and history. Among these latter are to be found all the peoples of the ancient Near East.

Perhaps the best way to understand the significant achievement of the Near Eastern mind in this field is to set it beside the more familiar Greek example for purposes of comparison. That the Greeks produced written history immeasurably superior in form and artistry to the Near Eastern records is incontestable. That the Greek sense of history, however, is more subtle or richer may well be questioned. The dress is more splendid; the form no more ethereal.

From its beginnings, Hellenic historiography was highly professional. As a group its practitioners were individualistic and exceedingly various in their professional objectives, but they were all united in one basic confusion: they were unable to solve satisfactorily that most knotty of all historical problems, the problem of whether history has a master, and if so in what sense that mastery is exercised. This confusion gave Greek historical thought a peculiar poignancy, a savor of tension in the midst of moral obtuseness. Herodotus, for example, alternates swiftly between belief in the suzerainty of a major malignant personality in history, on the one hand, and, on the other, a monotonous and relentless mechanism informing history, depersonalized and neutral.[48] These of course are mutually exclusive concepts. The fact is that the Greek historian makes an attempt to picture a supernal personality overruling history, but he is at the same time unwilling to accept evil in history as chargeable against himself. He must therefore charge it against deity; this picture, because it cannot long be supported by thoughtful men, collapses to give way to that of a bleak and masterless world of history—a conclusion which must in turn disintegrate, being unconformable to the facts of men's inner experience. Thus originates the basic "Weltschmerz" in all Greek historiography which has been often adverted to. Diodorus of Agyrium typically says, "God in his Providence has related in a single system the evolutions of the stars of heaven and the characters of men, and maintains them in perpetual motion to all eternity, imparting to each the lot which destiny assigns." [49] In this statement, positing two mutually contradictory things at once, he implies that history is meaningless (rule by destiny) and that it is meaningful (rule by god). The Greek historian Polybius seems about to break out of the vicious circle when he says, referring to Hellas and the catastrophe of the middle of the second century B.C., "In the light of the facts as seen in detail, they [the Greeks] must be held responsible for a disaster on account of their deliberate actions. . . . She committed acts so monstrous as to disgrace her name." [50] Here our eminent historian comes to grips with the sense of sin in history. Immediately, however, as if amazed and hurt by so un-Greek an admission, he destroys the conclusion by retracting the implication, "Personally I should say that the majority had strayed from the true path *in ignorance* [my italics], and that the sin lies with the politicians by whom an ignorance of such profundity has been fostered." [51] Greek historical thought was not unaware of the freedom of men in history, nor of the corollary that sin emerged in part at least from their own voluntary choice of evil. But the Greek finally and in almost every case repudiated this aspect of history, admitting it only in lapses or in implications he could not avoid. No one ever put this necessary human predicament as lucidly as did the English novelist Meredith when, in *The Egoist,* he said, "We must have a couple of powers to account for discomfort when Egoism is the kernel of our religion."

Near Eastern historiography, whether Egyptian, Mesopotamian, or Hittite, as we have outlined it, took a relatively clear stand on the complete subordination of history to a personal controlling will or wills. One can surely make out evidence for a sense of fate or impersonality in the Near Eastern picture, but it plays no very basic role. The Near Eastern historiographer had thus a simpler task outlined for him than did his Hellenic congener, which is why his product does not reveal as clearly as do the Greek histories the tensions and strains that interpenetrate history, though the Neo-Babylonian chronicler seems to have been on the threshold of some such development. But let us take up the Near Eastern cultures individually in their interpretation of history.

The Egyptian understanding is difficult to interpret satisfactorily to the twentieth-century mind.[52] The pharaoh when living was an avatar of Horus and when dead was Osiris; he was also the earthly son of the sun god Re, and it was he who maintained Maat, the divine order, as it had been originally established by the gods. Thus in the matter of full divinity, the pharaoh competed with the great gods. One claim alone was not advanced in his favor—he was not Atum-re the creator god.

The Egyptian mind was certain that divine power englobed the world of men, though it never settled upon a solution of how far removed from men the divine seat was. If full power to alter the destiny of men lay with Atum-re, king of the gods, then pharaoh was only a subordinate deity who merely policed the divine order. This may have been the usual dogma, particularly after the fifth dynasty. From the Protodynastic period and early Old Kingdom comes the previous and more powerful insistence that pharaoh was no mere godling, but a compeer of the great gods themselves and a foe worthy of respect. This aspect of Egyptian kingship cannot be easily documented following the Old Kingdom, but it survives as a *feel* throughout Egyptian history, thus confusing any discussion of the ultimate locus of divine power in the Egyptian's world. But the larger fact of the Egyptian's acceptance of divine sovereignty cannot be questioned.

The Egyptian world divides from the common understanding of the rest of the Near East. The dogma of the pharaoh's divinity, coupled with the amazing development of the Egyptian funerary apparatus, absorbed so much of this people's speculation that the presence of misery and evil in the world failed for centuries to stimulate historical thinking. With a god among them upholding Maat (which really was all that was essential), vicissitude and evil perforce had to be relegated to unorthodox areas of speculation. Maat being pre-eminently just, pharaoh's divinity which maintained it was therefore nomistic and his ways predictable. Evil in theory thus was always overcome by the mere fact of the majestic presence. We can see now why a sense of national sin and wrong-doing was peculiarly absent from Egyptian thought.[53] By refusing to grapple with the problem of evil in the affairs of men, the Egyptian of necessity evaded the sense of sin, which is the one most effective catalyst precipitating a sense of history. In Egyptian thought wrong-doers were always more foolish than sinful.

The Mesopotamian picture is clear. Sumerian, Akkadian, Babylonian, and Assyrian were united in the utter certainty of the subordination of the course of human events to the divine will expressed in the annual fixing of destinies by the gods assembled in heaven.[54] The effect of this powerful and unconditional Sumero-Semitic statement of faith is second only to the superior statement by Israel to the same effect—minus the role of destiny, of course.

It contrasts signally with the Egyptian smugness, this harrowing sense of insecurity and wretchedness which informs the understanding of the cuneiform areas of the Near East. Religious and intellectual speculation was probably somewhat keener in Mesopotamia than in Egypt. Myths of origin are certainly richer in content and more numerous by far there than in Egypt. A more important difference is the Sumerian view of deity as essentially anomistic and whimsical—witness this description of the compelling figure of Enlil, a mighty deity whose ways are incomprehensible and whose turnings are sudden like those of an insane person:

The Birth of Clio

What has he planned . . . ?
What is in my father's heart?
What is in Enlil's holy mind?
What has he planned against me in his holy mind?

O father Enlil, whose eyes are glaring wildly,
how long till they will be at peace again?

. . . . .

O thou who closed thy heart like an earthen box, how long?
O mighty one who with thy fingers sealed thine ears, how long? [55]

This then partially accounts, in the case of the Sumerian, for the incidence—overlaying all his thought—of an admission of human inability to control the processes of history.

Another fertile source of human misery is recognized in the righteous wrath of the gods because of sacrilege or sins of ceremonial omission or commission done by their human serfs (for according to Sumero-Semitic doctrine men and women were created for the sole purpose of ministering to divine needs and comforts). In the Old Babylonian period our texts, playing on this theme, now begin to abstract the tragic element of "sad stories of the death of kings." The Akkadian conqueror Sargon committed sacrilege and therefore, "On account of the sacrilege he thus committed, the great lord Marduk became enraged and destroyed his people by hunger. From the east to the west he alienated them from him and inflicted upon him as punishment that he could not rest in his grave." This willingness of the ancient historiographer to see tragedy in a heroic and much revered figure from the past evinces a novel detachment. The Babylonian scribe thereby moved closer to an understanding of the encompassing power of history, even as it was able to engulf the most untouchable figures out of his past.

The Hittite conception was in general agreement with the views of its parent culture. It too is explicit in its sense of the subjugation of the affairs of men to the mysterious norms of divinity—in this instance not an assembly of gods under a president, but two powerful and unrelated deities, the Storm God and the Sun Goddess of Arinna. One of the prime mechanics of history in the Hittite belief is delayed chastisement by the gods for sacrilege. In the moving and pathetic Plague Prayer of Mursilis [56] the sins of the father are visited upon the son in true Biblical fashion. Here, because of an outrageous deed perpetrated by a pre-

219

vious king, the gods reserve a great plague for the years of Mursilis. The reactions of the Hittite king are of great interest. He notes with despair that history destroys the good indiscriminately with the wicked, and he accepts this fateful mystery, though in regard to himself, like Oedipus, he insists on the unfairness of the punishment, inasmuch as he is guiltless personally. Men's sins in the Hittite world picture thus have effects on a national level; history comes to crisis because of sin.

For the Egyptian, then, history was a single state of being, harmonious in the logic of its whole divine inner structure. For the Sumerian, the Babylonian, and the Hittite, history was a hectic play of divine forces, oftentimes incongruous in its parts and almost always replete with the powerful tensions which existed between men and gods, a truce at best between the divine and human, and sometimes indeed a smothered rebellion. It is obvious from these generalizations that a true sense of history—which can ultimately only be a sense of tension and consequent struggle—would appear more easily in the cuneiform cultures than in the valley of the Nile, which is exactly the case as we find it. The materials of history, full yearly records methodically arranged, were, it seems, even more available to the Egyptian scribe than to his Sumerian counterpart. No list which we have from the Near East is so complete, informative, and early as the Palermo Stone, and records from the first dynasty on were publicly engraved. But this rich crop was never adequately harvested (except into the arid date lists, which as published are late). By the end of Egyptian history—the Saitic period, perhaps a bit earlier—there is, however, evident a slow, half-suffocated movement toward a fuller grasp of history as conflict, though this was no doubt partly stimulated by the Greek world outside.[57]

VI

Beginning in the late eighth century B.C. the nations of the Near East seem to have grown very old—by their own admission. A strong archaizing tendency appeared in language, art forms, literary genres, and religious observances.[58] There is undoubtedly a decadent aspect to this phenomenon, such as the maundering of Nabonidus and the schizophrenia of the Saitic nobles, but it also produced the library of Asshurbanipal, one of the cultural milestones in history, and accelerated the development of the art of written history, notably in Babylonia. This period, during which the scribes and peoples of the ancient Near East turned back to survey their long and glorious past, lasted until it fused with academic Hellenistic learning and antiquarianism. The names of Berossus, Manetho, and Philo of Byblus mark the end of the period. After them native Near Eastern historiography is dead.

This period produced the cosmogonic and historical work of the Phoenician Sanchuniathon,[59] whose writings we do not possess, and the great Neo-Babylonian Chronicle already considered. This latter represents the apogee of ancient Near Eastern historiography (exclusive of the Old Testament) and deserves to rank in importance with such milestones as the histories of Thucydides, Orosius, and Ranke. Secular history as we know it today here first appeared, though in juvenile form; it was a history that had begun to believe that virtue was not as simple as implied in the earlier lists and annals, a history in short that had begun to indulge the luxury of comparative impartiality, curiosity for its own sake, and the power of savoring the uniqueness of each and every event.

Impartiality and curiosity are obvious derivations from a sense of secular history. The sense of the unique event, however, carries implications of the greatest possible significance, for without it the feeling for history is nullified. We do not contend here that we necessarily owe our traditions of written history to these earliest practitioners of the art, via the Greeks,[60] but we can make the assertion that by the beginning of the Achaemenian period the Babylonian historiographers had achieved this all-important recognition—even as they were about to pass into oblivion. A process beginning with the simple date lists and king lists, influenced no doubt by the writing of the annals, had come to fruition. We can illustrate the full realization of the unique event by the following quotation from the Neo-Babylonian Chronicle:

> Nabonidus fled. The 16th day Gobryas, the governor of Gutium, and the army of Cyrus entered Babylon without battle. Afterwards Nabonidus was arrested in Babylon when he returned. Till the end of the month the shield-carrying Gutians were staying within Esagila, but nobody carried arms in Esagila and its buildings; the correct time for a ceremony was not missed. In the month of Arahshamnu, the 3rd day, Cyrus entered Babylon, and green branches were spread in front of him. The state of "peace" was imposed upon the city, and Cyrus sent greetings to all Babylon.[61]

The never-to-be-forgotten entry of Cyrus into the hoary city of Babylon is here outlined, not as the entry of any foreign conqueror, of whom

Babylon in her chequered past had known many, but as an event which had no past replicas, as witness the preternatural calm reigning within the precincts of Marduk's temple Esagila, so well described by the chronicler. Instead of bloodshed and tumult, the usual accompaniment of conquest, peace and good-will reigned. Though this fitted none of the scribe's previous patterns, he was able to describe it forcefully and competently with all the flavor of the unique event. In the Sumerian King List the great flood is mentioned, an event which in our eyes would have been memorable because of its uniqueness and magnitude had we been writing of it. The Sumerian scribe simply assumed that it was an integral part of a divinely ordered past and that nothing more could be learned from it; he asked it no further questions. With the royal annals the events connected with the yearly campaigns begin to stand out in slightly bolder colors, but the events themselves are the usual foregone conclusions, the expected victories of the crown. Only when we arrive at the period of the Neo-Babylonian Chronicle do we note that the historian's eyes can now take in and imaginatively estimate the unexpected event in history. Only at such a point can written history as we understand it begin.

The new Persian order which superseded the older Babylonian modes can be accurately sensed in Xerxes' exalted declaration of faith,[62] where moral concepts are now for the first time introduced into the imperial scene (exclusive again of the case of Israel), and where history will now be made by all men and women everywhere, by their choice or rejection of Ahuramazda, and not just by the king and the gods. This new strain of thought flowing into the rapidly developing Hebrew tradition introduces us ultimately to universal history.

Even as Near Eastern historiography began, it ceased. It had attained one priceless insight into the nature of individual events. It had won a certain degree of transcendence over its national and religious prejudices so that it could record with candor the reverses of its kings and honorably mention the deeds of the foreigner. But it had no spindle upon which to wind these lengthening threads. The old idea of the yearly assembly of the gods to decree the events of the forthcoming year was palpably insufficient to explain the new complexity of things, and no new understanding took its place at the crucial time. Zoroastrianism, Manichaeism, and Gnosticism as patterns of creation came too late to serve as guideposts of history. Having thus no internal supports, Babylonian historiography collapsed.

As we stated above, we have refrained from including Hebrew historiography in our discussion. How much it owed in its outward structure to Egyptian, Hittite, or Babylonian models we do not know, though we must bear in mind a possible debt. Out of the contrapuntal harmonies of Egyptian and Mesopotamian thought it was called into life. The Hebrew experienced providence in history in a new sense, but we can still guess that it was partially factored out of the dogmatic certainties of one valley and the keen anxieties of the other.

For the sense of the unique event was with Israel from the first finding of Yahweh in Midian. All other Near Eastern cultures of note had been monarchies from time immemorial. Israel was a tribal amphictyony and so felt sundered from her larger and more antique monarchic neighbors. Her whole history was therefore out of pattern and itself was unique. More than this, the Covenant had been a voluntary and unprecedented act and had initiated the story of Israel as a nation in a *historical* and not a *cosmogonic* context. Whatever forms of history therefore the Hebrews may have borrowed in later times from the general corpus of Near Eastern literature, her uses of these forms were from the beginning, in dramatic intensity and profundity, far and away beyond that of the Neo-Babylonian Chronicle. From the first the Hebrew historian appreciated the uniqueness of historic events, and in terms of the transcendence of Yahweh and the ethical and legal implications of the Covenant he possessed the key to the interpretation of the whole of the past and the future.

VII

The emergence of true written history and its prototypes is, we have seen, a by-product of the institution of kingship; it is *royal* history and all events are at first viewed as ancillary to this supreme focus. In this sense the first historiography can be considered an instrument of the crown. Only when the writing of history was taken up by peoples lacking the living reality of sacred kingship (Hebrews, Greeks, and Romans for instance) was historiography freed to realize the fruits inherent in it. The books of the Old Testament and the histories of

Herodotus and Thucydides display that catholic shifting of foci of interest which bespeaks the emergence of the spiritually centered individual, where previously he had been subordinated to an order of events that multiplied only the glories of kingship.

As an instrument of royal rule in the Near East, historiography appeared under the royal aegis during those periods when a challenge existed for some particular king or kingly house. Later on empire appeared, enlarging the horizons of men and stimulating and professionalizing an intellectual and learned class. These were the priestly votaries of Marduk in Babylon, and it was their care to impose upon their historical data an ecclesiastical interpretation. They were therefore no longer simply panegyrists for the king, but incipient observers of the historical scene through their own eyes. The subject of historiography was still royalty, but the crown was now viewed as being implicated *in* history rather than being itself the essence *of* it. This is not yet the critical sense, but it is certainly a necessary precursor. The advent of the Achaemenian Cyrus upon the scene brought the development of the Babylonian chronicle to a climax, for a radically new basis of kingship had been established. Written history, which began as an instrument of rule, had by the sixth century B.C. broken out of its rigid mold and was becoming available for the uses of priests as well as kings. The Greeks would make it available for the uses of men.

The separation of history from nature was first achieved in the Near East, men turning from the endless pantheistic rhythms of nature to the beginnings of the realization that no two events are ever the same. In the process of refining their historical insights, the scribes caught the first faint glimmerings of the truth that a portion of every act is *sui generis*. The way was open for the perception that men are free agents and that by consequence whatever is undertaken by them in history is in its very essence unique.

APPENDIX: *The Weidner Chronicle*

The best preserved portion is here translated from Güterbock's rendering (*GHT*, first part, pp. 54 ff.).

In the reign of King Puzur-Sin (?) of Akšak, the fishermen of Esagila took
. . . they caught fish for Bel's service. The king's overseers took the fish away

(from them); the fishermen [had to renew their fishing]. After eight (?) days had passed the fishermen caught a fish (again) . . . house of Ku-Bau . . . Ku-Bau gave bread to the fishermen and gave them water. . . . Because of this the mighty lord Marduk looked upon them with satisfaction and spoke as follows: *and so on.* He gave to Ku-Bau kingship over all the lands.

Urzababa [commanded (?)] [Sargon his cupbearer] . . . the drink-offering to exchange. Sargon did not exchange, he showed himself pious and brought . . . hastily(?) to Esagila. Marduk, Son of the Abyss, beheld him with joy and gave him the kingship over the four quarters of the world. The charge of Esagila . . . Babylon . . . of Bel . . . of his mouth he tore out, and over against (?) Akkad (?) he built a city; Babylon he called it by name. Because of the impious thing which he had committed Bel renounced him. From the sunrise to the going down of the sun they rose against him and he (Bel) inflicted him with sleeplessness.

Naram-Sin destroyed all the living creatures of Babylon . . . the second time he (Marduk) raised the hordes of Gutium against him and gave his kingship to the Guti hordes. Gutium, a seditious people who know not godly piety, who are ignorant of the proper manner of the ritual and its ordinances, (acted as follows): At the head of the great sea, Utuhegal the fisherman had caught a fish "of the gift." This fish, before it could be offered to the great lord Marduk, should have been presented to no other god. The Guti took from him the fish (already) cooked but not yet offered out of his hand . . . took the kingship of the lands from the hordes of the Guti and gave it to Utuhegal. The fisherman Utuhegal lifted his hand evilly against his city, and the river carried his body away. To Shulgi, son of Ur-Nammu, he (Marduk) gave the kingship over all the lands. His statutes he did not keep; his purification rites he sullied, his sin. . . .

1. The following abbreviations are used in this paper: *ANET* for James B. Pritchard, ed., *Ancient Near Eastern Texts Relating to the Old Testament* (Princeton, 1950); *BAR* for James H. Breasted, *Ancient Records of Egypt*, I–IV (Chicago, 1906); *GAM* for A. Götze, *Die Annalen des Mursilis* (Leipzig, 1933); *GHT* for H. G. Güterbock, "Die Historische Tradition und ihre literarische Gestaltung bei Babyloniern und Hethitern bis 1200," first part in *Zeitschrift für Assyriologie*, XLII (1934); second part in *Zeitschrift für Assyriologie*, XLIV (1938); *LAR* for D. D. Luckenbill, *Ancient Records of Assyria and Babylonia*, I, II (Chicago, 1926, 1927); *SKL* for T. Jacobsen, *The Sumerian King List* (Chicago, 1939).

2. *Against Apion,* Introduction.

3. The reader interested in checking this hypothesis against some former

surveys should consult, among others: Mowinckel, "Die vorderasiatischen Königs- und Fürsteninschriften," in *Forsch. zur Religion und Literatur der A. und N. Testaments*, N.F. XIX (1923); Täubler, "Die Anfänge der Geschichtsschreibung," in *Tyche* (Leipzig-Berlin, 1926).

4. Eduard Meyer, *Geschichte des Altertums* (Berlin, 1887), I, Erste Hälfte, paragraphs 130–135.

5. As working definitions of terms employed in this paper, we have understood the following: *autobiography* concerns one person and is generally a statement of virtue (rarely of sin) irrespective of the historical scene; *biography* also concerns one person only, though an integration of the personality with the historical process is always either implied or stated; *epic* interrelates many people on a single generation level; *written history* alone concerns many people on many generation levels. Written history is centered in the affairs of men whereas *myth* relates the activities of the gods; epic often bridges the two. By *campaign annals* we mean the listing in literary form of the king's military deeds and the exaltation of his powers. The term *chronicle* is reserved to refer to a third person account of times that began previously to those of the author and in which data is accumulated in simple chronological form and generally without any strong principle of selection. The chronicle is thus a type of written history.

6. The following approximate dates b.c. will assist the reader in the discussion which follows: *For Egypt* (fifth dynasty—2500–2350, eighteenth dynasty—1570–1320, Thutmose III—1490–1436, nineteenth dynasty—1320–1205). *For Mesopotamia* (classical Sumerian period—2600–2400; dynasty of Akkad [includes Sargon and Naram-Sin]—2400–2200; the Guti—2255–2130; first dynasty of Babylon—1890–1590, Hammurabi—1790–1750; Assyrian empire—1100–612; Neo-Babylonian empire—612–539). *For Hatti* (Hittite Old Kingdom—1680–1460; Hittite New Kingdom—1460–1190, Mursilis II—1334–1306).

7. Interesting material touching this relatively unexplored field can be found in *American Journal of Archaeology*, LII (1948), two articles specifically, Albert B. Lord, "Homer, Parry, and Huso," and Samuel N. Kramer, "New Light on the Early History of the Ancient Near East." For an example of a true Sumerian epic see S. N. Kramer, *Enmerkar and the Land of Aratta: A Sumerian Epic Tale of Iraq and Iran* (Philadelphia, 1952). See also footnote 60 *infra*.

8. The earliest Sumerian catalogues of literary works (*ca.* 2000 b.c.), in the few instances where the titles can be identified, list epic tales among other forms but no recognizable king lists or chronicles (*Bulletin of the American Schools of Oriental Research*, No. 88, pp. 10–19). This, however, is only an argument from silence, for the date list and the king list very possibly were not considered as literature in that period, and thus would have escaped classification.

9. "The Egyptians differ from the Greeks also in paying no divine honors to heroes" (Herodotus, II, 50).

10. The so-called Gilgamesh Epic is too weighted with powerful speculative and intellectual impulses to be considered as a typical epic. While the subject matter is purely epic, the intent of the author was not simply to glorify his hero but to be heard on the problem of immortality. For the latest translation see *ANET*, pp. 72–99.

11. For an English translation of parts of one of these epic or near-epic texts, see O. R. Gurney, *The Hittites* (Penguin Books, 1952), p. 178 f.

12. E. A. Speiser, "Some Factors in the Collapse of Akkad," *Journal of the American Oriental Society*, LXXII (1952), 97.

13. S. N. Kramer, "Sumerian Historiography," in *Memorial Volume for Professor Cassuto*, to appear under the auspices of the Israel Exploration Society. Kramer's translation of the Entemena Boundary Cylinder reveals the competence of the Lagashite scribe in handling historical material from several documentary sources (mainly former boundary stelae) reaching as far as two centuries backward into the past. The document itself, however, is in no sense to be included in any category of historiographical genres; it is simply a boundary text ending in a curse upon any future violators of the frontier between Umma and Lagash.

14. Farina, *Il Papiro di Re Restaurato* (Rome, 1938). Herodotus is no doubt referring to just such a date list in Book II, 100.

15. For a concise bibiography of these Egyptian king lists see E. Drioton and J. Vandier, *Les Peuples de l'orient mediterranéen, II. L'Egypte,* 3rd ed. (Paris, 1952), p. 159.

16. John Wilson, *The Burden of Egypt* (Chicago, 1951), p. 240.

17. For the most recent translations of the Babylonian King Lists A and B, the Synchronistic Chronicle (which is a list, not a chronicle), and excerpts from an Assyrian Eponymous list, see *ANET*, pp. 271–274.

18. For bibliography on the Palermo Stone see Drioton and Vandier, *op. cit.,* p. 156; *ANET*, p. 227.

19. *BAR*, I, 62 f., 65 f.

20. Destruction of cities, a royal hunt, shipbuilding, foreign expeditions, palace construction, selections of pyramid sites, and the biennial census, *BAR*, I, 57–72.

21. The analogous publication of the Roman *Fasti Capitolini* (18/17 B.C.) is instructive. The *Fasti* appeared at a similar juncture in Roman history.

22. Utuhegal was the Sumerian warrior king who finally delivered the city states in the valley from the yoke of the barbarian Guti. After his victory he naturally assumed the kingship over the whole land, or at least claimed it. Thus he may have ordered the redaction of the document to sanction his action by historically binding it to those of past legitimate rulers, see *SKL*, p. 140 f.

23. *SKL*, pp. 107–111.

24. *SKL*, p. 144; see also footnote 113, p. 59.

25. *SKL*, p. 164.

26. *GHT* (first part), pp. 25–36.

Teachers of History

27. C. J. Gadd, *The Fall of Nineveh: The Newly Discovered Babylonian Chronicle* (London, 1923), p. 1. B. Landsberger and Th. Bauer ("Zu neuveröffentlichten Geschichtsquellen der Zeit von Asarhaddon bis Nabonid," *Zeitschrift für Assyriologie*, XXXVII [1929], 61 f.) agree with Gadd as to the essential unity of the whole series of tablets; they believe there was one official edition of the corpus of Babylonian history carrying the story from Sargon to Cyrus; they base their reasoning on the "canonical" character of all learned Babylonian literature.

28. The main tablets in this series are as listed below (catalogue numbers refer to British Museum); future discoveries may of course add to this. For complete list see Landsberger and Bauer, *op. cit.*, pp. 63–66.

Tab. 26,472   From Sargon of Akkad to Irra-imitti.

Tab. 96,152   Continuation down to beginning of Kassite period.

Tab. 27,859   From eleventh to seventh centuries.

Tabs. 84-211,356 and 92,502   From accession of Belibni to accession of Shamashshumukin.

Tab. 21,901   From tenth year to seventeenth year of Nabopolassar.

Tab. 35,382   From first year of Nabonidus to fall of Babylon.

29. *ANET*, p. 302.

30. *BAR*, II, 164 f.

31. This is adumbrated in the stele of Kamose, last king of the seventeenth dynasty, who initiated the thrust against the Hyksos (see Carnarvon Tablet, *ANET*, p. 232 f.). This record is the first of its kind in Egyptian history, it being undoubtedly an abbreviated statement from a now vanished protoannals of this king. As it stands there is nothing ecclesiastical about it; on the contrary it is a strongly secular picture of a heroic, energetic, and hard-hitting king.

32. See *ANET*, pp. 234–241, for selections, recently translated, of the annals of Thutmose III. The Memphis and Karnak stelae of Amenhotep II attest to the existence of annals behind them (*ANET*, pp. 245–247). Amenhotep III most probably ordered the inscription of excerpts from his now lost Nubian annals on the walls of a Delta temple (*BAR*, II, 337–340).

33. E. Cavaignac, *Les Annales de Subbiluliuma* (Strasbourg, 1931).

34. *GAM*.

35. *GHT* (second part), p. 111 f.; see also footnote 11.

36. *GHT* (second part), pp. 49 ff. *et passim;* A. Götze, *Kleinasien* (Munich, 1933), pp. 161 ff.

37. Gurney, *op. cit.*, p. 173.

38. *Ibid.*

39. *GAM*, pp. 15–23.

40. The Kurkh Monolith is the first annalistic Assyrian text completely divorced from any parent building inscription (*LAR*, I, 177–182).

41. *LAR*, II, 312.

42. In a few instances we do see the bare bones of the army itinerary with little or no literary garnishing, see *LAR*, I, 115, 128 ff., 161.

43. This may explain the decided unreliability of the Assyrian annals as far as the actual facts go. They become even more unreliable as they develop, see A. T. Olmstead, *Assyrian Historiography* (Columbia, Miss., 1916), pp. 6, 7, 40, 41, 53.

44. *LAR*, II, 378 ff.

45. *LAR*, II, 73–99.

46. This is roughly the period when the Vannic rulers on the Armenian plateau to the north were writing down their own scanty annals. These annals need not concern us in this survey, but the interested reader may most conveniently consult Nicolas Adontz, *Histoire d'Arménie* (Paris, 1946), pp. 161–167, 171–176, for the most recent translation.

47. Lionel Pearson, *Early Ionian Historians* (Oxford, 1939).

48. The following passages from Herodotus are pertinent: I, 90–91, 131, 207; III, 16, 40–43; VII, 10, 17, 45–47.

49. Quoted in A. J. Toynbee, *Greek Historical Thought* (Mentor edition, 1952), p. 48.

50. *Ibid.,* pp. 199, 201.

51. *Ibid.,* p. 201.

52. One is particularly indebted to John Wilson's excellent analysis of the Egyptian ethos as set forth in his essay "Egypt" in H. Frankfort et al., *The Intellectual Adventure of Ancient Man* (Chicago, 1946), and in his interpretative history, *The Burden of Egypt* (Chicago, 1951).

53. Not cynicism, however. The official dogma never completely blinded the Egyptian to reality. In the Harper Songs, the Suicide Song, and in scattered references to the creation of men from the tears of the gods (see *ANET*, pp. 6, 8, 11, 366) we are aware of this constant current. This frame of mind would have allowed and even encouraged historiographical enterprise if it had been able to compete on even terms with the pharaonic dogma.

54. Güterbock (*GHT*, first part, pp. 13 ff.) posits a Sumerian feeling for history, beginning at least with the Naram-Sin Text, in which *"Fluchzeit"* alternates with *"Segenszeit,"* a kind of Mesopotamian Yin and Yang. If he implies a primitive cyclical sense of history we must disagree with him. The Sumerian world was in no sense mechanistic or endlessly repetitive, as sometimes conceived by the Greeks. The gods had no grand plan for men but simply improvised according to their moods.

55. T. Jacobsen's translation quoted from H. Frankfort et al., *op. cit.,* p. 144.

56. For translation, see *ANET*, pp. 394–396.

57. W. G. Waddel, *Manetho* (London, 1948).

58. For a short résumé of this backward-looking tendency, see W. F. Albright, *From the Stone Age to Christianity* (Baltimore, 1940), pp. 241 ff., and also Drioton and Vandier, *op. cit.,* pp. 588–591. As late as the reign of Darius, king lists and chronicles were being copied and edited by Babylonian scribes, see L. W. King, *Chronicles Concerning Early Babylonian Kings* (London, 1907), I, 2.

59. Floruit *ca.*700–500 B.C. (?), see W. F. Albright, *Archaeology and the Religion of Israel* (Baltimore, 1946), p. 70.

60. It becomes increasingly clear that a cultural channel of great magnitude existed between Hurrian, Hittite, and Phoenician on the one hand and early Greek on the other. Note particularly in this respect the new texts which reveal the heavy mythological indebtedness of Greeks to Hurrians: H. G. Güterbock, "The Hittite Version of the Hurrian Kumarbi Myths: Oriental Forerunners of Hesiod," *American Journal of Archaeology*, LII (1948). In the realm of epic similarly it is possible that the Ugaritic *Keret* indirectly influenced the Homeric epics, though Cyrus Gordon suggests we might go so far as to interpose a *Caphtorian* (i.e., Cretan) epic tradition from which both the Iliad and Keret are ultimately derived (*Journal of Near Eastern Studies*, XI [1952], 212 f.).

61. *ANET*, p. 306.

62. *ANET*, p. 316 f.

[ROBERT SIDNEY SMITH]

Spanish Population Thought before Malthus

I

SPANIARDS have recognized the importance of demography at least since the Middle Ages. In Barcelona the demand for accurate information on the loss of population from recurrent epidemics led to the elaboration of "bills of mortality" two centuries before John Graunt prepared his statistics of plague deaths in London.[1] Interest in population questions increased when Spain, in order to safeguard religious conformity, expelled the Jews and the Moors. Involuntary emigration, combined with voluntary migration overseas, frequent wars, pestilential mortality, and economic distress, raised the specter of depopulation. Hardly less significant, in the minds of most writers, was the growing number of mendicants, vagabonds, and idle clergy. Cures for the related maladies of depopulation and idleness predominate in Spanish population literature for three centuries prior to the appearance of the *Essay on the Principle of Population*.[2]

Generally, the depopulationists had meager quantitative data on which to ground their fears. An enumeration conducted by ecclesiastical authorities in 1587 indicated a population of 6,631,929 for Castile, while an official count of households for tax purposes in 1594 produced an estimate of 6,701,600 persons for approximately the same area. As these were independent surveys, the consistency of the results inspires greater confidence than can be placed in earlier and, indeed, many later records. Contemporaneous estimates for the Basque provinces, Aragon, Catalonia, and Valencia are lacking or incomplete; but Edge supposes that a conservative allowance for unenumerated regions and for exempted classes would push the 1594 population of peninsular Spain to 8,206,-791.[3] Whether Spain was more, or less, populous at the end of the sixteenth century than on the eve of the discovery of America is a question hopelessly obscured by contradictory testimony and the lack of trustworthy data. Estimates exceeding 20,000,000 have been given for 1492, whereas a tax list for 1541 puts the Castilian population at only 4,257,270. One result is as improbable as the other, and attempts to adjust the figures seem to compound the confusion. Professor Hamilton, who has shown that conditions in the sixteenth century favored capital accumulation and employment, estimates that Spain gained 15 per cent in population, "in spite of emigration to the New World, the garrisoning of fortresses in Italy, Flanders, and Africa, and heavy losses in continuous wars." [4] Seven million inhabitants may somewhat overstate Spanish populousness at the commencement of New World colonization.

Guesswork is the principal ingredient of all seventeenth-century estimates of Spanish population. So certain were writers of the drastic decline that they accepted the virtually impossible figure of 3,000,000 inhabitants for 1650. In view of the persistent deterioration of the economy under Charles II, the decline could not have been arrested before the end of the century. Perhaps at the nadir Spain numbered fewer than 6,000,000 people,[5] though this estimate seems low in relation to the fairly dependable census return of 9,307,804 in 1768. The census of 1799 enumerated 10,351,000, a bare 12-per-cent increase over 1768. To put the population at 6,000,000 in 1700 presupposes a 55-per-cent increase in the first sixty-eight years of the century, which is equivalent to an annual rate of growth much higher than during the last three decades of the century. It would be easier to believe that the rate of increase rose during the latter part of the eighteenth century and that, therefore, the 1768 estimate is too high or the 1700 figure, too low. Even in the nineteenth century population grew at the rate of only .6 per cent yearly.

Spanish Population Thought

II

No one was in a position to write with assurance on the amount or rate of change in Spain's population during any period prior to the second half of the eighteenth century. But statistical ignorance never stood in the way of patriots possessed of panaceas for the perennial ills of the nation: a declining population, a decrease in the proportion of the population productively engaged, or, if the population seemed to be rising, the failure of population to grow rapidly enough. Few of the scores of authors who wrote on economic and social problems in 1500–1800 failed to dwell on the size and the quality of the country's population.[6]

The expulsion of the Jews in 1492 climaxed a decade of persecution at the hands of the Inquisition, which had already uprooted, despoiled, tortured, incarcerated, and burned at the stake uncounted thousands of heretics. Writing in 1863, Colmeiro collected more than a dozen estimates, ranging from 90,000 to 800,000, of the number ultimately driven off the Peninsula. Anticipating the results of more exhaustive research, Colmeiro accepted 160,000 as the most likely figure.[7] Those who believed that absolutely the number of émigrés was not large emphasized the indirect loss to the nation from the removal of people notoriously industrious and successful in accumulating capital. Furthermore, Spain's loss was accentuated by the contribution of Spanish Jews to the industry and commerce of the countries to which they emigrated.[8]

Many of the Moors remaining in Spain after the fall of Granada were compelled to emigrate during the sixteenth century; and, finally, in 1609 Philip III decided to rid the country of the Moriscos—Moors who had nominally embraced Christianity. Contemporary estimates of the number affected by the expulsion orders ran into the millions, but modern revisions push the calculations downward to a probable maximum of 150,000.[9] As in the case of the Jews, criticism of this violent uprooting of inhabitants, almost universally defended on religious grounds, shifted from lament over the absolute loss in numbers to alarm over the withdrawal from the economy of hard-working and technically skillful producers. González de Cellorigo described the Moriscos as "people of great benefit [to the nation] by reason of their dedication to work, whereas we Christians loaf." In 1597 he expressed the hope that these people, reinforced in their Christian faith and assimilated into the population, would be spared the fate of the Jews.[10]

Some writers minimized the significance of the Moorish expulsions. Moncada, a contemporary of Philip III, thought immigration made up for their loss within a few years; [11] and an eighteenth-century economist said the "bleeding" of Spain by the exodus of Moors (and Jews) was stopped by the immigration of "good Catholics" from all parts of Europe.[12] Lately, Professor Hamilton has shown that prices and wages in the regions from which the Moors were expelled showed none of the consequences to be expected from the loss of laborers and the decline in productive efficiency. Either great numbers of Moors did not leave the country or their going did not matter much economically. "If the Moors were strikingly superior and if great numbers were expelled, why did they not develop the geographically similar Barbary States into which most of them passed?" [13]

Depopulationists repeatedly lamented Spain's loss of people through voluntary emigration, not only to the Indies but to Flanders, Italy, and Africa; and some regarded this phenomenon as the most important cause of depopulation.[14] Peñalosa, an early seventeenth-century writer, believed that those who had left the country since the days of Ferdinand and Isabella "would not fit into ten Spains"; but he found it a source of pride that Spaniards, through emigration, had gained souls to populate heaven.[15] In the eighteenth century, Macanaz urged the crown to curb the flow of emigrants to the New World, so that the mother country "at the end of a certain time would achieve the desired population"; [16] and Campillo, an otherwise well-informed minister of Philip V, accepted 10,000 emigrants annually as the correct basis for estimating how much more populous Spain would have been without colonies.[17] But Uztáriz, writing a widely read mercantilist treatise in 1724, dismissed emigration to the Indies as an insignificant cause of depopulation. Most of the colonists were destitute and "perhaps would not have married, even if they had remained [in Spain]; and if they had, they would have exposed themselves to perish in misery, with their wives and children, so that their lives would have been snuffed out, leaving little or no posterity." In the Indies they were able to marry, and even send money home to help support their parents, thus indirectly helping to increase Spain's population.[18] Ward, too, thought that the Spaniards who went to America were "in large part an idle lot of people, with some gentlemen and officials, and soldiers who, if they had not gone, would have died in the same fashion in Italy and Flanders." They were more productive in the colonies than they would have been at home.[19]

As Spanish trade and colonization drew people away from the interior of the country to towns along the coast, many writers mistook the decline of inland population centers for general depopulation. But Larruga, citing the case of Toledo province, found depopulation severe in regions that had furnished few colonists; and Capmany noted that Aragon had suffered population losses during the two centuries that the Aragonese were barred from emigrating to the New World.[20] Uztáriz thought the northern provinces were the most densely populated, although they had provided the greatest number of emigrants.[21] The maritime provinces, too, tended to receive a major share of immigrants, which some observers recognized as a more-or-less-adequate remedy for depopulation caused by emigration. Demographic statistics were lacking in Uztáriz' day, and not much has been done since to improve the estimates of Spanish migration overseas in the colonial period.[22]

The population drain resulting from war and national defense, which kept Spanish armed forces abroad year after year, was calculated in various ways. Fernández Navarrete, writing in 1626, considered it "a certainty that more than 40,000 persons trained for all the services of sea and land leave Spain every year." Few returned to their homes and "very few are those who through matrimony propagate and increase the population."[23] Suspicious of earlier accounts of the size of armies and battle mortality rates, Capmany believed that war directly had had little to do with Spanish depopulation. "The Swiss, a nation of reduced area, have for many centuries supplied troops to all nations, and instead of having its body weakened by these bleedings, its population always grows."[24] The truth of the matter was left for Colmeiro to discern: "more people die of epidemic in a single day than in a whole campaign . . . and pestilence is not the greatest impediment to the propagation of the human species."[25] But indirectly, several writers thought, war and compulsory military service were depopulating. Army life engendered "a species of aversion to matrimony." Most recruits did not marry; or they married late in life merely to have legal mates eligible for widows' military pensions.[26]

Fear of the depopulating effects of clerical celibacy, not anticlericalism, inspired the repeated complaints of the inordinate growth of religious establishments in Spain. Fernández Navarrete, an official of the Inquisition, recalled protests "many years ago" that priests, monks, and nuns were too numerous; in the meantime their numbers had tripled. He strongly supported the proposal of the Royal Council that the Pope be requested to deny Spaniards the privilege of organizing new religious foundations and monasteries.[27] The census of 1768 put the number of regular and secular clergy at 209,988, or about 2.3 per cent of the population; but there is nothing except the bold assertion of several writers to show that this represented double the number in the seventeenth century.[28]

What would Spain have gained without a celibate clergy? Campillo noted that if all those celibate for religious reasons were to marry, they could "in a few years people a new world." [29] Macanaz believed that population would increase "in the highest degree" with ten or twelve thousand marriages (annually?) among those who took religious vows from indefensible motives.[30] Those who spread the alarm over the depopulating effect of clerical celibacy took it for granted that the churches and monastic orders embraced people who, but for their religious vows, would have married and procreated. Other writers, however, found a high propensity to celibacy in nonclerical ranks.

Because men were shunning marriage, González de Cellorigo wanted to make it easier for girls to acquire dowries and thus "fertilize our nation" by more numerous marriages.[31] In 1622 Philip III sent to the Cortes the findings of his Reform Commission, established to study depopulation and related problems, which included various proposals for raising marriage and birth rates. Believing that "the greatest danger of all, and the one that has placed this Monarchy in the greatest peril, is the lack of people," the commission sought to liberalize the laws on consanguineous marriage, subsidize the marriages of poor and orphaned girls, grant life-long tax exemptions to the fathers of large families, and encourage young men to marry by exempting them from public office-holding in their communities.[32] Jerónimo Zevallos proposed that the heirs of bachelors should be compelled to invest a third of the decedent's estate in government annuities, "inasmuch as (unmarried individuals) gave no children to the state." [33] Sempere y Guarinos (and others) thought lay celibacy had increased since the sixteenth century. For reasons far from obvious Sempere took the number of married persons in Madrid—58,588 out of an adult population of 113,282—as proof of the growing aversion to connubiality.[34] Actually, the ratio of the married to the total Spanish population seems to have remained remarkably constant: 37.5 per cent in 1768; 37.9 per cent in 1787; 37.6 per cent in 1797; and 36.0 per cent in 1857.[35]

III

Depopulationists, who accepted expulsions, emigration, war, and celibacy as satisfactory explanations of Spain's loss of people, generally supposed that curbs on emigration, the reduction of the armed forces, checks on clerical celibacy, and similar direct measures would lead to repopulation. The greater part of the repopulationist writings, however, views these factors as symptoms of underlying weaknesses of the state and the economy. Repopulation depended upon political and economic reforms.

In the seventeenth century economists joined legislators in blaming the crushing burden of taxation, falling most heavily on the poor, for the inability and unwillingness of Spaniards to find jobs, establish families, and bring up children. The Royal Council, finding "depopulation and the lack of people . . . the greatest . . . since your Majesty's progenitors commenced to reign," told the crown that heavy taxes compelled men to desert their children, wives, and homes, "in order not to die of hunger, and to go off to regions where they hope to be able to support themselves." [36] Centani, whose work on agriculture anticipated the Physiocrats, believed Spain could support a population of thirty million. The greatest obstacle to reaching this goal was the burden of taxes, aspirated from "incisions made in the arteries of the poor, so that for every ten ducats which are collected for His Majesty, a vassal is lost; and the greatest wealth consists in increasing families." [37] Uztáriz considered taxes on the necessities of life especially inimical to population growth. The high cost of living discouraged marriage; or, if a tax-burdened worker did marry, his wife, subsisting on bread and water, could not feed her children properly. Taxes reduced consumption so drastically that premature death overtook the ill fed, ill clothed, and ill housed. The revival of commerce, Uztáriz reasoned, would increase the revenues of the state and at the same time lighten the burden of taxes.[38]

Zavala, a contemporary of Uztáriz, also condemned the regressive character of Spanish taxation. The poor, who paid sales and other taxes which raised the price of food, clothing, and shelter, were driven into idleness, vagabondage, and prostitution. "For this reason, an infinite number stay in the villages without marrying, because, being unable to support themselves and pay taxes while single, they will be less able to maintain a wife and children, whose upkeep doubles the taxes; and this is one of the principal reasons why Spain is so depopulated." Increasing the opportunities for employment in agriculture would augment population, because vagabonds, of whom Spain had more than any other country, would be encouraged to establish permanent homes and marry.[39]

Confusing cause and effect, the leading mercantilists pleaded for commercial policies which would restore to Spaniards the employment of which they had been deprived by imports of foreign goods and exports of precious metals. Martínez de la Mata, who "proved" that high taxes had not caused depopulation, understood clearly the interdependence of industry and agriculture. Repeated subdivision of farmlands among successively more numerous families reduced the average acreage per family. Thus, agriculture furnished "a limited means for the increase and preservation of the population." Industry arose to absorb the surplus of rural population, giving employment as apprentices to the children of poor farmers. But when Spain allowed foreign manufactures to enter the country, domestic industry languished; and this was "the only cause of the depopulation, poverty, and sterility of Spain." He commended the laws of 1623 which offered inducements to young people to marry but doubted their efficacy in the absence of other remedial measures. "Privileges are good to facilitate matrimony, if there are ways of obtaining work in order to eat; and if they are lacking, there are no exemptions which can make up for the need which the abuse of foreign trade has introduced." Repopulation was principally a question of re-employment in industry, induced by the prohibition of imports of manufactures.[40] Many other writers dealt in the same coin. "Spain's whole remedy," Moncado said, "is to produce her manufactures. . . . Prohibiting foreign goods, Spain becomes populated." [41] Zevallos, also, was confident that imports destroyed jobs in native industries, causing poverty and idleness, "which is entirely against [the interests of] Your Majesty, since greatness consists in the multitude of vassals." [42] In 1686 Alvárez Osorio came up with an esoteric calculation showing that Spanish agricultural resources were adequate to support a population of seventy-eight million. The secrets of re-population—his goal was to double the population in four years—were found in preventing money from leaving the country, reviving the demand for domestic manufactures, and furnishing jobs for the idle and the poor, especially for the "multitude" of marriageable girls who "perish from destitution in the corners of their houses." [43]

A good share of eighteenth-century thought followed the same mercantilist track, although there was a growing realization that the encouragement of domestic industry involved more radical changes than the mere expedient of prohibiting the use of foreign goods. It was clear to Uztáriz, whose work was acclaimed by two generations of Spanish economists, that population growth depended upon the expansion of industry and trade; these were "the most effective and almost the only means" to increase population. Amsterdam, which could not support a fifth of its population on the agriculture of its hinterland, subsisted as it were on the fruits of its manufacturing, trade, and navigation. "To establish industries in a place, or encourage navigation and commerce in a country, is the same as furnishing the seed to perpetuate the increase of the population, wealth, and power of a state." [44] Ulloa, too, realized that depopulation was not the cause of economic distress but that poor economic conditions arrested population growth. Unable to develop his idea logically, he adopted the extreme position that "all the diminution in people which we observe in Spain and America results from clothing ourselves by foreign labor, because to the extent that the inhabitants of the North [of Europe] increase, working to supply our needs, it is inevitable that our inhabitants become fewer." An "infallible rule" could be deduced: "Spain has the key to depopulate other nations and to populate herself," i.e., by ceasing to use foreign-made goods. [45] Writing on "the importance and necessity of asylums, foundling homes, and hospitals," in 1798 Pedro de Murcia reiterated the argument that the lack of factories, "whereby we so greatly enrich the foreigner, perhaps our enemy," was the cause of depopulation. Population

emerges from two principles: the first being that by reason of the lack of industry, through which people can support themselves, innumerable marriages fail to be consummated, since . . . whenever two people can maintain themselves, a marriage is contracted; and the other [principle] being that if two destitute persons marry, most of their children die of want, because under-nourished mothers cannot give them the necessary food.[46]

A tract on craft gilds, written in 1778, vigorously defended restrictions on apprenticeship and employment as conducive to population growth. "The population of a country," declared Palacio, "is one of the simplest and easiest rules for judging the goodness of its constitution. When depopulation increases, the state marches toward its ruin; and the country that increases its population, though it may be the poorest, is certainly the best governed." Parts of Spain, "spit out men as the sea spews sand," because these regions—Galicia, Catalonia, Asturias, and Vizcaya—"have in their customs and constitution certain active and constant principles of reproduction." The "principles" were assured jobs in farming and industry, which provided subsistence and encouraged matrimony. These were better protected by the association of workers and masters along craft lines than by the "anarchy" of a free labor market. Liberty, "the soul of commerce," might increase the total amount of labor demanded; but it was more important to stabilize the trades and crafts and distribute employment among settled families, "who are fecund and perpetual beehives of population." [47]

Immigration, many believed, would transplant and diffuse among the Spaniards mechanical proficiency and good work habits and thus afford a quick means of stimulating industrial and agricultural production. As early as 1599 Mariana proposed heavy taxation of certain foreign wares in the belief that "many artisans of these products, in hope of profit, will flow into Spain, by which the population will be increased; nothing is better for augmenting the wealth of both the Prince and the province." [48] Saavedra feared the corrupting influence of religious and cultural differences which foreigners brought in but conceded that this drawback was "not very significant" in the case of immigrants destined to till the soil or work at trades.[49]

In order to encourage industry and "gain time in [restoring] the population of Spain," Uztáriz wanted to encourage 200,000 foreign artisans to immigrate.[50] Marqués de Santa Cruz in 1732 proposed several inducements to spur immigration and repopulation: any foreigner who invested ten thousand ducats in a landed estate should have the same privileges as a native-born Spaniard to engage in commerce and industry; and citizenship would be extended to married immigrants at the end of five years. He also recommended relaxing the navigation acts to permit the employment of foreign seamen to the extent of half of a ship's crew.[51] Marqués de la Ensenada, Philip V's able navy minister, considered the immigration of foreign craftsmen, preferably Englishmen, the only remedy for reviving the shipbuilding trades and increasing the efficiency of the dockyards. "In matters of mechanical knowledge," he wrote, "we are most ignorant and, what is worse, without realizing it." [52] In 1747 Ensenada promised traveling expenses to Catholic families who wished to emigrate to Spain and approved of agreements with foreign agents to recruit German and Dutch immigrants.[53]

Ward agreed with Uztáriz and Ensenada that immigration necessitated state encouragement. Spain had less than "a third of the people which it would maintain if the land were well cultivated"; but there was "not the slightest probability" of reaching this goal in five centuries unless economic conditions improved. Immigrants were needed to stimulate agricultural and industrial improvement, and it was not enough merely to permit foreigners to enter. "The way to attract many useful people is by arranging for them to find greater profit here than in their country; this is the only secret, since no one leaves his country in order to be worse off." Immigration had to be planned and propaganda organized in European capitals to combat the common notion that Spain was backward, insalubrious, and priest-ridden. In order to bring foreign capital into the country, titles of nobility should be offered to wealthy foreigners who settled, without cost to the government, as many as two hundred families of artisans and farmers. Hoping to attract English capital to Spain, Ward wanted to train Catholics to manage Spanish firms financed by Protestant foreigners, who would be unwelcome as immigrants.[54]

Apparently, no state-encouraged immigration materialized until 1767. Under a contract with a Prussian army officer, Spain admitted and colonized about six thousand German and Flemish nationals at Sierra Morena (in Andalucia). The government provided the settlers land, livestock, and tools and granted them tax exemption for ten years. The elaborate instructions for the administration of the colony included provisions for facilitating their intermarriage with Spaniards; but the immigrants were permitted to have only elementary schools, lest too much learning turn them away from "agriculture, grazing, and the mechanical arts." [55]

Remedies for mendicancy and vagabondage, repeatedly deplored as depopulating factors, abound in the repopulationist literature. An endless flow of moral, political, and historical writing carried on the search for solutions to poverty, vagrancy, and idleness, while through innumerable laws the government struggled, usually in vain, to cope with the problems. As Sempere remarked: "One will scarcely find any other legislation more severe against robust mendicants than that of Spain. But, for a very strange and deplorable misfortune, neither will there be found any nation in which voluntary and criminal mendicancy meets with greater inducements and support." [56] It is impossible, within the limits of this paper, to deal adequately with the development of either the legislation or the literature of poor relief and vagrancy. The following paragraphs do no more than suggest some of the landmarks, emphasizing proposals inspired by the hope of correcting the evil of depopulation.

Moral philosophers and legislators agreed on one point: the nonproductive population should be divided into two groups, the "truly" poor who were unable to work for a living and the able-bodied idle who lacked the will, the incentive, or the opportunity to work. The former should, and could, be taken care of by public and private charities, for, as the learned Vives had counseled in 1526, "no one must die of hunger." [57] To deal with the able-bodied idle—malingering beggars, vagrants, and the unemployed—required vigorous state action; as Ward pointed out, putting the idle to work was practically the same as adding two or three million to the population. "This is the greatest undertaking and the most profitable conquest which the Monarchy of the Spains can make—making useful [citizens] of those who are not." [58]

Disagreement over the proper way to "exile idleness" began with the recognition of the complex origins of the phenomenon. Were Spaniards naturally indolent, as many Spaniards and, perhaps, the majority of foreigners believed? González de Cellorigo, early in the seventeenth century, was alarmed by the universal disregard for "natural laws which teach us to work." Idleness, "the mother of all vices," had increased with the influx of precious metals from the New World; it was the abundance of wealth in this form which led Spaniards "to flee from that which naturally sustains us"—work.[59] Asso, an able historian imbued with many Physiocratic ideas, regretted that in Aragon custom and law had done away with the medieval practice of working in the fields from sun-up to sun-down. By the end of the sixteenth century, eight hours, "portal to portal," was the customary work day, and even this included much time lost in taking refreshment and resting. Asso saw little hope of teaching the younger generation to be more diligent "as long as they had before their eyes the pernicious example of their parents and those like them." [60] Some Spaniards took a less dim view of their compatriots. Although Macanaz advised, "let those who eat, work," he thought voluntary idleness could be attributed to the "lack of rewards" for honest effort—low wages and high taxes left too little incentive.[61] Beggars flourished, in the opinion of Marín y Borda, in consequence of the "lack of other activities more lucrative to which to devote themselves." Idleness and want were the results, not the cause, of a diseased body politic. If jobs were available, men would be ashamed to loaf; "idleness would be exiled, marriages would be made easier, and the population would be increased." [62]

Bernardo Ward's Pious Foundation (*Obra Pía*), a plan published in 1750,[63] called for the co-operation of public authorities and private organizations to eradicate destitution and idleness in all their forms. Caring for the unemployable poor, supposed to number only 50,000, would not greatly burden the state or private charities; but the deserving poor had to be carefully distinguished from the other groups of idle. Many of the 200,000 able-bodied vagrants would go to work as soon as the government commenced to enforce "the many and good laws" on vagrancy; about fifty public workhouses would be required to shelter and employ those who would never work except under compulsion. The most serious problem was that of re-employing an estimated 2,000,-000 involuntary idle. (This was a conservative estimate, for in another place Ward said 1,500,000 women at home were idle practically all of the time.) The *Obra Pía*, financed by a lottery, would make small loans to farmers idled by the loss of a mule, the lack of seed, or any other misfortune; it would find jobs for others in a well-planned program of public works, such as roads, canals, and irrigation projects; and it would disseminate mechanical knowledge, promote inventions, import improved machinery, and in numerous ways help to resurrect and modernize Spanish industry. The reduction of idleness through industrialization would allow the population to rise to 20,000,000, the number Ward considered Spanish agriculture capable of supporting.[64]

Demographic as well as moral considerations justified state intervention for the protection of orphans and foundlings. In the seventeenth century institutions for the care of homeless boys were looked upon as good sources of supply of seamen, gunners, and pilots.[65] But the number of orphan asylums and foundling homes always seemed to be incommensurate with the need. Many writers deplored the inexcusable loss of population because so many foundlings died of exposure or starvation before they could receive institutional care, while malnutrition and inadequate nursing raised mortality rates inordinately within the homes and asylums. Gil de Jaz, the historian of the Oviedo hospital for orphans and foundlings, claimed that ninety out of every one hundred foundlings died (in infancy?). Correct care and Christian education in a well-administered children's home would preserve many lives; the number of marriages among young men and women would grow "to infinity"; and "it will come to be realized that this is the only device for the repopulation of Spain." [66] Similarly, Arriquibar thought that institutions for homeless youth would help increase the population, because farmers would not hesitate to marry their sons to girls who had acquired skills and good habits in such homes.[67]

In the first year of the nineteenth century Joaquín Xavier de Uriz, a prelate and member of the governing body of the Pamplona General Hospital, published an exhaustive treatise on foundling homes, condemning their almost universal mismanagement and decrying the high mortality among the inmates. In support of numerous humane and practical recommendations for reform, he tried to calculate the country's gain in population from prolonging their lives by improved diet and proper medical care. Everyone, he thought, accepted the "solid principle" that populousness combined with industriousness constituted the foundations of a nation's happiness, wealth, and power to resist invasion. Twelve thousand infants seemed to be a reasonable estimate of the number of foundlings institutionalized every year. He doubted that children's homes could lower mortality to the level obtaining in the general population (about 50 per cent between birth and age seven); but proper care would "save" 200,000 foundlings over a period of fifty years. Uriz wanted to show by geometrical progression what Spain would gain in population from a similar saving in the course of a century, but the mathematics struck him as an "incomprehensible snare." He realized that the foundlings would need vocational training and that industry and agriculture would have to be improved to absorb them, but he never doubted that resources would be adequate to care for the nation's "supply" of abandoned children.[68]

To make Spain more populous was one of the motives underlying numerous proposals for curbing luxury, abolishing latifundia, limiting mortmain, extending enclosure, and reforming other social and political institutions. The Court, Saavedra declared in 1640, was "the principal causes of depopulation." [69] Absentee landlords, squandering their time and rents in Madrid, deprived workers of jobs which would have been available if the owners personally supervised their estates. In 1623 the crown had enjoined landowners to stay on the land, so that vassals who "were supported and gained their livelihood under their protection" would not be idle; but neither legislation nor moral suasion greatly reduced the penchant of the *caballero* to live in the shadow of the royal family. Late in the eighteenth century, Larruga found in Madrid a "multitude of nobles—some opulent, others rich, and in great part poor—who contribute not a little to the decadence of its population, agriculture, commerce, and manufactures." False pride kept them from accepting useful employment. "In Spain," Larruga explained, "every descendant of a person of noble origin, however poor or vagrant he may be, is noble; as, on the contrary, the laborer and artisan, however great wealth he may have gained by his trade and industry, in benefit and advantage to the state, never will be noble unless he was born noble, or unless such a privilege is granted to him by the king." Spanish law had long since permitted the nobility to engage in industry and trade, without prejudice to their status, but legislation had not sufficed to erase the traditional preference for the "nobility of idleness" over the "nobility of work." [70]

The leading economists of the eighteenth century were unanimous in decrying the depressing and depopulating effects of primogeniture, entail, and mortmain. By the middle of the century one-fifth of all real property in the twenty-two provinces of Castile had passed into the inalienable possession of religious and eleemosynary organizations; the rest, so many believed, consisted of estates entailed in primogeniture (*mayorazgo*). Sempere, who was far from anticlerical or socialistic, said that "the most essential evil of the entail of real estate" had been the diminution of production. "If it were possible that lands accumulated and entailed in few hands, ecclesiastic or lay, should be better cultivated than those divided among many proprietors, entail, far from being harmful, could perhaps be useful, since the result of greater cultivation would be a greater output and greater population, which increases naturally with subsistence." But experience had demonstrated that "without a multitude of proprietors a vigorous agriculture cannot exist, and without this industry and commerce will never prosper." The maladministration of estates controlled by the Church subtracted 500,-000,000 pesos annually from national income. Disentailment would transfer property from "dead hands" to "live hands" and thereby increase national output, tax receipts, and population.[71]

Two other outstanding political economists shared or anticipated Sempere's views on entail. "It is an assured principle," Conde de Campomanes wrote, "that the happiness of a state consists in not having individuals very rich, because the rest are reduced to being their wage-earners, they beg, they do not marry, and the state is diminished; while the rich become enervated by dissipation, gluttony, and other vices." Entailed estates, concentrating landed property in few hands, included much uncultivated land; agricultural production dropped and the country lost a part of its "most precious wealth, which consists in the multitude of inhabitants." [72] Similarly, the illustrious Jovellanos concluded that "large entailed estates, since they foment excessive luxury and the corruption inseparable from luxury, are as pernicious to the state as the very small ones, which maintain in idleness and haughtiness a great number of poor noblemen, who are just as much lost for the useful professions, which they disdain, as for the distinguished careers, which they are not able to pursue." Jovellanos, who pleaded eloquently for many sound reforms in Spanish agriculture, believed that "the greatest of all stimuli which can be offered to agriculture" would be changes in land tenure to "reunite" the interests of those who tilled the soil and those who owned the land.[73]

Before the century ended the reformers won a partial victory. In September 1798, the government established the Royal Amortization Fund and required all *lay* hospitals, asylums, foundling homes, and benevolent associations to surrender their real property to the fund in exchange for 3 per cent annuities. Religious foundations were urged to follow suit. The major purpose of the legislation, however, was not to curtail mortmain but to enable the treasury, in an emergency, to borrow money at a relatively low rate of interest.[74]

IV

Spanish predecessors of Malthus include a small group of writers who, although they sometimes embraced dubious proposals for rapid repopulation, clung to the principle that subsistence limits population. Distinguishing them from the depopulationists and repopulationists previously discussed is admittedly a highly arbitrary procedure. None of the men considered in this section recognized the law of diminishing returns. They gave erroneous or incomplete answers to the question, What limits food supply? Their generally fragmentary writings on population were not set in the framework of principles of production and distribution.

Surprisingly, one of the best explanations of the checks to population comes from an anonymous seventeenth-century tract which remained unnoticed until 1871.[75] In an essay entitled "Secrets of Domination," the author noted the propensity of man, after the original sin, to procreate without restraint. Nature provided the check to overpopulousness:

As abundance springs from the small number of individuals who consume the foodstuff, barrenness likewise proceeds from the great number of these. The earth, which, needing rest from time to time, diminishes rather than increases the annual crop, cannot keep up with human propagation, which goes on multiplying continuously. As a result, these two productions being naturally contrary, despite the fact that one depends upon the other, it is evident that the former and the latter seek the solution in vain, remaining subjected to the untoward accidents which happen every day. And to throw more light on this truth, it is fitting to know what is the area of the land, granted that whenever the number of persons living exceeds its capacity and the quantity of the food which it can produce, beyond doubt the cure for its ill will be violent, as it cannot be resolved except by means of hunger, pestilence, or war.

Ignorance of the laws of returns led him into confusion. He assumed an absolute limit to the land capable of producing food (about one-quarter of the earth's surface) and calculated that this would support an ultimate population of 4,123,800,000. Obviously, he did not believe that the world's population even approximated this total; yet he found war already operating as a check to population growth and accused rulers of provoking war to get rid of excess people. Measures to keep the birth rate in check were to be preferred. "The sovereign remedy would be to think continuously of death, since by tempering our unbridled passions in this way, we would come to belittle temporal suffering and give all our attention to deserving and realizing eternal bliss." Although he could hardly have been unaware of the century-old complaint that the clergy had increased inordinately, our seventeenth-century reformer wanted to build more monasteries and increase relatively the number of people, in religious institutions and out, bound by vows of celibacy. Finally, he thought the state should limit marriages: the right of matrimony should be denied whenever it appeared that the land could support no more children. Women who became mothers without benefit of clergy should be severely punished.

Mirabeau's *L'Ami des hommes,* a work "probably more responsible than any other for the attention given to population questions in the third quarter of the eighteenth century," [76] inspired the *Recreación política* of Nicolás de Arriquibar. An admirer of Davenant, Arriquibar clung to the notion that imports hurt population growth. Home production of the manufactures Spain imported could double population; and "population, or depopulation, is the only measure of the power or weakness of the realm, because only people enrich it and defend it." [77] The fundamental cause of depopulation was the lack of employment: "The jobless man is a dead man, so far as the state is concerned; the employed man is a live plant who not only produces but propagates." Arriquibar accepted Mirabeau's dictum that "the measure of subsistence is the measure of population," but he thought the French economist misunderstood the principles governing food supply. Demand, primarily that originating in the purchasing power of nonagricultural workers, constituted the chief limitation on agricultural output. "The whole remedy [for depopulation] is reduced to two propositions contrary to those of the Friend of Men: encouragement of industry and extension of agriculture, or, better said, the first, because the second is a consequence of it." Industrialization, which included internal improvements, could stimulate those engaged in agriculture and grazing to provide subsistence for a tripled population. [78]

Other writers, not recognizing the factors restricting productivity, were inclined to share Arriquibar's optimism. Lecturing on population at the Royal Seminary for Nobles (in Madrid), Professor Danvila y Villagrasa said everyone agreed that Europe should, and could, be more populous. The limited supply of food checked population growth, whether of men or of fish. But the relationship was reciprocal:

> As the lands produce more, the more they are cultivated, and the more they produce, the greater number of people they maintain, it being impossible to determine the limits to the production of the land, since it is not possible to fix the limit of improvement in the cultivation of the fields, neither can it be determined what point the means of subsistence can reach.

One thing seemed sure: "The more men there are, the easier it is to maintain them." This law of increasing returns—not Danvila's expression, of course—he said he had learned from Baron Bielfeld.[79] Bernardo Ward, as we observed, did not share the naïve depopulationist and repopulationist views of his contemporaries. "In every country," he wrote in 1762, "the population will always be proportional to the subsistence and comforts which are found in it." It was correct to say that "the wealth of the sovereign consists in the number of his subjects,"[80] but only useful inhabitants should be counted. A million loafers, vagabonds, and mendicants, far from contributing to the nation's wealth, constituted an impoverishing burden. The beneficial effects of a population increase would be realized when the idle had become productive; population would increase naturally whenever economic conditions favored early marriage. If subsistence were scarce, young men and women would go into religious institutions, give themselves up to vice, or "perish miserably in the flower of their age from a thousand misfortunes." The prudent would postpone marriage, but when a woman waited until age thirty-five to marry, "the state loses two parts [in three?] of her fecundity."[81]

Refuting foreign allegations that inhumane treatment had decimated the Indians in the Spanish colonies, Juan Nuix asserted: "Without the least doubt . . . the mines of Mexico and Peru, and not the other most inept and ridiculous causes which foreigners allege," brought about depopulation. The enlarged supply of precious metals raised prices; imports of foreign goods destroyed Spanish manufactures, and, because of rising costs, Spain lost its export markets. Thus: "The excess of the precious metals ruined agriculture and manufacturing in Spain. With the downfall of these two, there was introduced, of inevitable necessity, a general misery in the midst of the opulence of a few, and with it, depopulation." Reason and experience both taught that people who turn to mining "always become poor, and the decline of population necessarily follows the dearth of food and comforts. . . . To the extent that the fecundity of the metals increases, the sterility of the women rises."

Further reflection on some of the alleged inferiorities of the Spaniards led Nuix to make extravagant statements concerning the standard of living. Spain's poverty was not the sort, found in many countries, which allowed people to die of hunger; rather, the Spaniard had to endure a stringency of means which prevented him from "taking a wife, in keeping with his station in life, or being able to support a numerous family." This was the depopulating factor, "since men multiply in proportion to abundance and conveniences." Both Spain and Spanish America had relatively small populations, but their numbers

must be considered commensurate with their present condition; and, circumstances remaining unchanged, it is not desirable for them to be larger. Dispel the clouds of error which obscure this point about population, and the truth of what we are saying will be seen clearly. What more crass error can be made than to shout continuously, as do certain political writers, population, population, without limit? Natural reason ought to suppress these words, since it clearly dictates that a country ought not to crave a larger population than can be supported.

Thus, in searching for means to combat foreign ridicule of a depopulated or sparsely-populated Spain, Nuix hit upon the idea, inconceivable to his contemporaries, that populousness is not the measure of the wealth of nations.[82]

"Until the end of the eighteenth century," Colmeiro observed, "political writers generally believed, as an axiom of government, that the power of states consisted in a numerous population, and they harbored no fears that there might occur a real exuberance of inhabitants burdensome and even oppressive for the country, whose means of existence might not suffice to feed them. It was considered certain that, doubling the hands, the national income would also double." [83] Colmeiro did not cite Nuix; but he found few political economists, even in the first half of the nineteenth century, who did not concern themselves with ways to make Spain more populous. While Alvaro Florez Estrada,[84] as well as Colmeiro, accepted Malthusianism [85] many years before the appearance of the first Spanish edition of the *Essay*,[86] the fear of depopulation lived on. Instead of recognizing the ameliorating effect of emigration, in the middle of the nineteenth century Pascual Madoz declared that emigrants weakened the country and disgraced themselves.[87] Alarmed at the falling birth rate in the twentieth century, Spanish demographers have suspected a growing disregard for the mandates of religion and the interests of the nation. Family limitation tends to impoverish the state, whereas "the first duty of every Spaniard is to make Spain great." [88]

1. R. S. Smith, "Barcelona 'Bills of Mortality' and Population, 1457–1590," *The Journal of Political Economy*, XLIV (1936), 84–93.

2. Writings on pre-Malthusian population theory are numerous. The first substantial work was that of C. E. Stangeland, *Pre-Malthusian Doctrines of Population* (New York, 1904), which contains a few references to Spanish writers. The French materials have been exhaustively treated in J. J. Spengler, *French Predecessors of Malthus* (Durham, N.C., 1942), while James Bonar, *Theories of Population from Raleigh to Arthur Young* (London, 1931), deals mainly with English ideas. References to Spanish population thought appear mainly as by-products of broader studies of economic history and theory. See, for instance, E. J. Hamilton, "Spanish Mercantilism before 1700," in *Facts and Factors in Economic History* (Cambridge, Mass., 1932), pp. 214–239, and "The Mercantilism of Gerónimo de Uztáriz," in *Economics, Sociology, and the Modern World* (Cambridge, Mass., 1935), pp. 111–129.

3. Tomás González, *Censo de población de las provincias y partidos de la Corona de Castilla en el siglo xvi* (Madrid, 1829); P. G. Edge, "Early Population Records in Spain," *Metron*, IX (1932), 229–249. Early "census" records are in terms of households (*vecinos*), and the usual assumption of five persons per household is not above suspicion.

4. E. J. Hamilton, "The Decline of Spain," *Economic History Review*, VIII (1938), 169; *American Treasure and the Price Revolution in Spain, 1501–1650* (Cambridge, Mass., 1934), pp. 298–299.

5. Hamilton, "The Decline of Spain," p. 176.

6. Manuel Colmeiro's *Biblioteca de los economistas españoles de los siglos xvi, xvii y xviii* (Madrid, 1880) is still the best introduction to the literature of the period. Although remedies for monetary problems occupied the attention of a large proportion of the writers, a treatise on depopulation, idleness, or poor relief may be found on nearly every page of this 172-page bibliography.

7. Manuel Colmeiro, *Historia de la economía política en España*, II (Madrid, 1863), 57–58.

8. José Amador de los Rios, *Historia social, política y religiosa de los Judíos de España y Portugal*, III (Madrid, 1876), pp. 387–432; A. Rodríguez Villa, "Los Judíos españoles y portugueses en el siglo xvii," *Boletín de la Real Academia de la Historia*, XLIX (1906), 87–103.

9. José García Barzanallana, *La población de España* (Madrid, 1872), pp. 19–20.

10. Martín González de Cellorigo, *Memorial de la política necesaria y útil restauración a la República de España* (Valladolid, 1600), including two papers "sobre los moriscos," one of which is dated March 1, 1597.

11. Sancho de Moncada, *Restauración política de España* (Madrid, 1746), p. 72. These essays were first published in 1619.

12. Bernardo Ward, *Proyecto económico*, 4th ed. (Madrid, 1787), pp. 61–62. But it was hard to scotch the idea that the effects of the Inquisition were depopulating in the extreme. "To calculate the number of victims of the Inquisition," a nineteenth-century historian exclaimed, "is the same practically as to show one of the most powerful and effective causes of Spain's depopulation. For, if to the millions of persons which the inquisitorial system took away from it, by inducing the total expulsion of Jews, subjugated Moors, and baptized Moriscos, we add close to half a million families ruined by the punishments of the Holy Office, it will clearly appear that but for the existence of this Tribunal and its rules Spain today would have twelve million more persons in addition to the eleven million it is supposed to have" (Juan Antonio Llorente, *Historia crítica de la Inquisición de España*, VIII [Barcelona, 1836], 85–86).

13. Hamilton, "The Decline of Spain," pp. 171–173.

14. Colmeiro, *Historia*, II, 46–47.

15. Benito de Peñalosa y Mondragón, *Libro de las cinco excelencias del español que despueblan a España para su mayor potencia y dilación* (Pamplona, 1629), pp. 33–37, 155.

16. Melchor Rafael de Macanaz, "Representación . . . expresando los notorios males que causa la despoblación de España," in Antonio Valladares, *Semanario erudito*, VII (Madrid, 1788), 201.

17. Colmeiro, *Historia*, II, 48, citing a 1741 manuscript of José Campillo y Cossío. Surprisingly uncritical on this point, Colmeiro agreed that "the greater part of the people who went to the Indies caused the mother country a loss, without rendering her overseas provinces a proportional gain."

18. Gerónymo de Uztáriz, *Theórica y práctica de comercio y de marina*, 3rd ed. (Madrid, 1757), pp. 19–20.

19. Ward, *Proyecto económico*, p. 60.

20. Eugenio Larruga y Boneta, *Memorias políticas y económicas sobre los frutos, comercio, fábricas y minas de España*, VII (Madrid, 1790); Antonio de Capmany y de Montpalau, *Qüestiones críticas sobre varios puntos de historia económica, política, y militar* (Madrid, 1807) pp. 70–71.

21. *Theórica y práctica de comercio*, p. 21.

22. Richard Konetzke has fully outlined the nature of the task and pointed out the documents available in Spanish and American archives ("Las fuentes para la historia demográfica de Hispano-américa durante la época colonial," in *Anuario de estudios americanos*, V [Sevilla, 1948], 267–324). Partial lists of "pasajeros a Indias" are being published by C. Bermúdez Plata (*Catálogo*

de pasajeros a Indias, I—[Sevilla, 1940—]). Ramón Carande cited fragmentary data giving the names of 20,047 emigrants to America in 1509–1558 (*Carlos V y sus banqueros,* I [Madrid, 1943], 45–46), but he had no data for several years and did not regard the statistics for twenty-nine years as necessarily representative for the three centuries of emigration.

23. Pedro Fernández Navarrete, *Conservación de monarquías y discursos políticos,* 4th ed. (Madrid, 1792), p. 81.

24. *Qüestiones críticas,* p. 71.

25. Colmeiro, *Historia,* II, 46.

26. Larruga, *Memorias,* I, 12.

27. *Conservación de monarquías,* pp. 378–384; Academia de Estudios Histórico-sociales de Valladolid, *Archivo Histórico Español,* V (Madrid, 1932), 27–38. The Cortes of 1619 complained that too many "ordinary people," sons of farmers and artisans, were entering the orders and asked for a papal agreement on limiting the endowments of religious institutions, "since today most of them have sufficient funds to support an adequate number of *religiosos"* (*Actas de las Cortes de Castilla,* XXXIII [Madrid, 1911], 27).

28. Pascual Madoz, in *Anuario estadístico de España correspondiente a 1859 y 1860* (Madrid, 1860), pp. xxxiii–xxxiv, 234–235.

29. According to Colmeiro, *Historia,* II, 52.

30. Melchor Rafael de Macanaz, "Avisos politicos" (1747), in Antonio Valladares, *Semanario erudito,* VIII (Madrid, 1788), 232. Macanaz asserted that only one out of four persons took vows for reasons of piety; the rest were coerced by parents or led on by the promise of an easy living. As early as 1619 the Royal Council took the stand that "many persons" entered convents and monasteries "fleeing from need" and "in search of the pleasure and ease of idleness." The Council thought no one should be allowed to take his final vows before the age of twenty (*Archivo Histórico Español,* V, 27–28).

31. *Memorial de la política necesaria,* fol. 17.

32. *Archivo Histórico Español,* V, 391. By the law of Nov. 18, 1625, the crown established a Population Commission (*Junta de Población*), "taking into consideration that one of the felicities of the realms consists in the abundance of people with which they are populated." The accomplishments of the Junta appear not to have been noteworthy (Biblioteca del Ministerio de Hacienda, Madrid, "Historia de la Real y General Junta de Comercio," V, fol. 1).

33. *Arte real para el buen gobierno de los reyes* (Toledo, 1623), pp. 31–32.

34. Juan Sempere y Guarinos, *Historia del luxo,* II (Madrid, 1788), 186.

35. *Anuario estadístico de España, 1859–1860,* pp. 234–235, 239, 240–242, 250.

36. *Archivo Histórico Español,* V (1619), 13. Two years later the council repeated the observation that the principal cause of depopulation was the burdensome tax system, but it also found "not the least cause of depopulation" in "the large number of people whom enemies capture at sea, because of the little defense . . . in it" for Spaniards (*ibid.,* pp. 65–71).

37. Francisco Centani, *Tierras* (Madrid, 1671). Centani favored shifting taxes to land, "the physical and true [source of wealth], and the veins which contain the blood of the body of the Kingdoms."

38. *Theórica y práctica de comercio,* pp. 22–23.

39. Miguel de Zavala y Auñón, *Representación al Rey N. Señor D. Phelipe V* (Madrid, 1732), pp. 8–11, 76–77. Zavala had some sensible notions about agriculture. He recommended abolition of price-fixing, freedom to export grain, reorganization of public granaries, and measures to bring idle land under cultivation.

40. Francisco Martínez de la Mata, "Memoriales," in *Apéndice a la educación popular,* IV (Madrid, 1777). First published by Campomanes, the "Memoriales" date from the middle of the seventeenth century.

41. *Restauración política de España,* pp. 7–8, 18–19, 36, 50.

42. *Arte real,* p. 150.

43. Miguel Alvárez Osorio y Redín, "Memoriales," in *Apéndice a la educación popular,* I (Madrid, 1775), 11–22.

44. *Theórica y práctica de comercio,* pp. 18–20.

45. Bernardo de Ulloa, *Restablecimiento de las fábricas y comercio Español,* II (Madrid, 1740), 223–224.

46. Pedro Joachín de Murcia, *Discurso político sobre la importancia y necesidad de los hospicios, casas de expósitos, y hospitales* (Madrid, 1798), p. 14.

47. Ramón Miguel Palacio, *Discurso económico-político en defensa del trabajo mecánico de los menestrales* (Madrid, 1778), pp. 35–40.

48. Juan de Mariana, *The King and the Education of the King,* translated by G. A. Moore (Washington, 1948), p. 305.

49. Diego de Saavedra Fajardo, *Idea de un príncipe político cristiano,* III (Madrid, 1819), 17–18. The first of numerous editions dates from 1640.

50. *Theórica y práctica de comercio,* pp. 26–28.

51. *Comercio suelto y en compañías generales y particulares* (Madrid, 1732), pp. 86–93.

52. C. Fernández Duro, *Armada española,* VI (Madrid, 1900), 357.

53. A. Rodríguez Villa, *Don Cenón de Somodevilla, Marqués de la Ensenada* (Madrid, 1878), pp. 143–144, 163.

54. *Proyecto económico,* pp. 58–70. Ward also wanted to encourage wealthy colonists to return to Spain, where their money and influence would do more good than in Lima or Mexico. Otherwise questionable, Ward's argument may be judged in the light of his feeling that "the day can come when the Indies no longer belong to Spain."

55. *Novísima recopilación de las leyes de España,* libro 7, título 22, ley 3. Under the law of May 1, 1768, the Spanish government arranged to settle a Greek colony migrating from Corsica.

56. Juan Sempere y Guarinos, *Biblioteca española económico-política,* I (Madrid, 1801), 47–48.

57. Juan Luis Vives, a Valencian by birth, set a precedent for much of the

subsequent discussion of poor relief. Addressing the Senate of his adopted city of Bruges, he proposed the complete registration of all those receiving alms for any reason. Able-bodied foreign vagrants were to be returned, at public expense, to their native land. The rest of the vagrants were to be rounded up and given vocational training, if they were unfit for the available employment. Home relief or institutional care, depending upon the circumstances, was to be provided the needy poor, the infirm, and homeless children. No one, he thought, was so lacking in mental or physical skill as not to be able to produce a part of his upkeep. Whatever else was needed for the support of the poor would always fall within the means of public and private giving (*De subventione pauperum sive de humanis necessitatibus* [Bruges, 1526]. The essay was not translated into Spanish until 1781. There is an English translation: M. M. Sherwood, "Concerning the Relief of the Poor or Concerning Human Need," *Studies in Social Work*, No. 11 [New York, 1917]).

Two priests, writing in 1545, took opposite positions on poor relief. Father De Soto vigorously attacked public measures for aiding the poor on the grounds that government intervention would weaken the motives for private giving and destroy the Christian virtue of charity. Father Medina, asserting that vagrants and idlers far outnumbered the "truly poor," wanted to separate those unfortunately destitute from malingerers. Public authorities should find work for the latter group. "Although beggars may be lacking, the poor will never be absent"; therefore, no one should fear the loss of opportunities to practice discreet charity (Domingo de Soto, *Deliberación en la causa de los pobres* [Salamanca, 1545]; Juan de Medina, *La caridad discreta practicada con los méndigos* [Salamanca, 1545; also Valladolid, 1757]). Miguel Giginta's *Tractado de remedio de pobres* (Coimbra, 1579) also attacked those who maintained that it was inhuman and uncharitable to round up the poor and put the able-bodied to work.

58. *Proyecto económico*, p. 58.

59. *Memorial de la política necesaria*, fols. 1–5.

60. Ignacio de Asso, *Historia de la economía política de Aragón* (Zaragoza, 1798), pp. 210–211.

61. In *Semanario erudito*, VII, 168; VIII, 226–227.

62. Manuel Josef Marín y Borda, *Memoria . . . para desterrar la costumbre que hay en muchos pueblos de acudir en tropas . . . a pedir limosnas a los forasteros* (Madrid, 1784), pp. 415–454 (a separate from a volume of essays on this topic, published by the Royal Economic Society of Madrid).

63. First published separately, *Obra Pía* was republished as an appendix to the *Proyecto económico*.

64. Among many other schemes to deal with poverty and idleness was Anzano's plan for a general asylum. A director of the Royal Asylum of San Fernando in Madrid, Anzano proposed to bring into the institution the poor and aged, orphans, vagrants, and prostitutes. One of the benefits of the institution would be the increase of population, "the most worthy objective of

the government of a civilized nation." While a "natural" right required society to provide subsistence to those incapacitated for work, a general asylum would educate and rehabilitate a large proportion of its inmates and release them to private employment. Young people especially would be trained for jobs and encouraged to marry, so that "the population may not suffer the diminution attributed to this part of the people, which is not small" (Tomás Anzano, *Elementos preliminares para poder formar un sistema de gobierno de hospicio general* [Madrid, 1778], p. 71).

65. In 1623, the crown ordered the directors of orphan asylums to provide instruction in useful arts, particularly navigation, "because of the lack of pilots in this realm" (*Novísima recopilación de las leyes de España*, libro 7, título 37, ley 1); in 1677 plans were announced for a foundling home and orphanage in Cádiz for the express purpose of training seamen (*ibid.*, libro 7, título 37, ley 2); in 1681 the government established the Colegio Seminario de San Telmo in Sevilla to raise and educate orphaned boys for service in the navy and merchant marine (British Museum, 501. g. 4 (3), *Copia de las cédulas reales, que su Magestad mandó expedir para la fundación del Colegio y Seminario que mandó hazer para la educación de niños en la ciudad de Sevilla*).

66. Isadoro Gil de Jaz, *Ordenanzas aprobadas por S. M. para el régimen y govierno del hospicio y hospital real de huérfanos, expósitos, y desamparados . . . en la ciudad de Oviedo* (n.p., n.d., probably 1752), pp. 9–15.

67. *Recreación política*, I, 55.

68. *Causas prácticas de la muerte de los niños expósitos en sus primeros años* (Pamplona, 1801), I, iv–v, 6–7, 79–85; II, 475–512. Marqués de Santa Cruz (*Comercio suelto*, pp. 237–256) argued that by useful employment in foundling homes and asylums the homeless children and vagrants would produce more than the cost of their maintenance.

69. *Idea de un príncipe político cristiano*, III, 19. This was not a novel idea. In 1621 the king's advisers complained that "almost the entire kingdom" had converged on Madrid, leaving the rest of the country depopulated. If the nobility and other landlords, and widows who had inherited large estates, were compelled to leave the Court, many idlers would go with them "to work and cultivate the land, which is the principal occupation of which the strength of the state consists" (*Archivo Histórico Español*, V, 75–87).

70. Larruga, *Memorias*, I, 9–13.

71. Juan Sempere y Guarinos, *Historia de los vínculos y mayorazgos* (Madrid, 1805), pp. 328–329, 348–350, 416–438. Sempere thought Spain could support more than fifty million inhabitants.

72. Pedro Rodríguez Campomanes, *Tratado de la regalía de amortización* (Gerona, 1821), pp. 413–414, 431–438. (The *Tratado* was first published in 1765).

73. Gaspar Melchor de Jovellanos, *Informe de la Sociedad Económica de esta Corte . . . en el expediente de ley agraria* (Madrid, 1795), pp. 56–74.

74. *Real cédula . . . en que se manda cumplir el decreto inserto, por el*

qual se dispone que se enagenen tódos los bienes raices pertenecientes a hospitales, hospicios, casas de misericordia, de reclusión y de expósitos, cofradías, memorias, obras pías y patronatos de legos (Madrid, 1798).

75. A. Cánovas del Castillo, "Otro precursor de Malthus," in *Problemas contemporáneos*, I (Madrid, 1884), 331–360. Cánovas places the writing between 1650 and 1700. Excerpts from the manuscript were first published in *La Ilustración de Madrid* in 1871.

76. Spengler, *French Predecessors of Malthus*, p. 129.

77. *Recreación política: reflexiones sobre el amigo de los hombres en su tratado de población*, I (Vitoria, 1779), xiii–xiv. The publication was posthumous, the work having been composed in 1764–1771.

78. *Recreación política*, I, 43–59, 104–106.

79. Bernardo Joaquín Danvila y Villagrasa, *Lecciones de economía civil o del comercio* (Zaragoza, 1800), pp. 111–122. (The first edition appeared in 1779.) "The most powerful means to increase population," Danvila said, "is monogamy, together with the indissolubility of marriage."

80. Apparently, a gloss on Saavedra, who said: "The might of kingdoms consists in the number of vassals. He who has more is the greater prince" (*Idea de un príncipe político cristiano*, III, 15).

81. *Proyecto económico*, pp. 58–59. Like Ward, a Catalan writer, Francisco Romá y Rosell, believed that "naturally" population increases up to the limit imposed by the means of subsistence and "when population reaches the level which is proportional to the production and industry of a country, it neither increases nor decreases." When war, pestilence, hunger, and other calamities diminish population, "as soon as the cause ceases, nature redoubles her efforts, in proportion to the support which agriculture, industry, and commerce give her to replace the past losses" (*Las señales de la felicidad de España* [Madrid, 1768], quoted by J. Carrera Pujal, *Historia de la economía española*, III [Barcelona, 1945], p. 485).

82. *Reflexiones imparciales sobre la humanidad de los españoles en las Indias* (Madrid, 1782), pp. 60–64, 113–120.

83. Manuel Colmeiro, *Tratado elemental de economía política ecléctica*, I (Madrid, 1845), 303.

84. *Curso de economía política* (London, 1828).

85. *Malthusianismo* does not appear in the tenth edition of the Spanish Academy's *Diccionario de la lengua castellana* (Madrid, 1852) or in the *Nuevo diccionario de la lengua castellana* (Madrid, 1888).

86. *Ensayo sobre el principio de la población*, translated by José María Noguera and Joaquín Miquel (Madrid, 1846).

87. *Anuario estadístico de España, 1859–60*, p. xxxii.

88. José Ros Jimeno, "El decrecimiento de la natalidad y sus causas," *Estudios Demográficos* (Madrid, 1945), pp. 79–81.

[JAMES F. CLARKE]

Father Paisi and
Bulgarian History

THAT historians often exert decisive influence on nationalism is amply recognized. Conversely, historians frequently reflect the temper of their times and write in accordance with nationalistic rather than historical principles. The Athos monk Paisi is commonly credited with fathering the Bulgarian revival as well as Bulgarian historiography. The "Slaveno-bulgarian History" Paisi wrote in 1762 may not have exerted all the influence attributed to it a century later, but it was the first Bulgarian history by a Bulgarian and was a striking manifestation of nationalism at a time when Bulgarian national consciousness seemed about to expire. The purpose here is to consider Paisi as a historian and to examine his role and that of Bulgarian historiography in the national awakening.[1]

In preliberation Bulgarian historiography three Bulgarians stand out: Paisi, the first to attempt a history of the Bulgarians; Rakovski, his greatest Bulgarian disciple; and Drinov, his rediscoverer and rehabilitator. Three foreigners also made important contributions: Rajich, a Serb, author of the first published Bulgarian history; Venelin, a Russian, who "discovered" the Bulgarians and their history; and the Czech Jireček, who wrote the first complete, scholarly history of the Bulgarians. From Paisi and Rajich to Drinov and Jireček about a century elapsed, in the course of which the Bulgarian Slavs emerged from the general mass of Greek Orthodox *rayah* and their vague sense of kinship with the Serbs into fully conscious Bulgarians on the verge of national independence, with strongly developed antagonisms toward their neighbors on all sides.

To a great extent Bulgarians had lost contact with their own past and with the free world, and for geographic and other reasons were more completely subordinated within the loosely organized Ottoman state than their Christian neighbors. The Rumanian principalities, enjoying a peculiar autonomy within the Ottoman Empire, were periodically involved in the dynastic and military adventures of Poland and the Hapsburgs and later in the imperialist schemes of the Muscovites. Transylvania served as a Rumanian bridge to the West, a fact not always appreciated by Rumanians to the east. Greek connections with Venice originated long before the arrival of the Turks and lasted as long as Venice itself; the classical and religious interests of Europe in Greece and Greek Orthodoxy, the widespread and flourishing Greek mercantile activities and the privileged position of the Fanariotes in the Ottoman system helped preserve Greek continuity. Greek hopes as well as Greek waters were stirred by the Russian navy before Russian soldiers trod Bulgarian soil. Although in many ways the Orthodox Serbs shared the lot of the Bulgarians, they were more directly involved in Western efforts to push back the Turks, and for a short period some of them even "enjoyed" Hapsburg annexation. Even more important were their South-Slav kinship with the western-oriented Croats and contacts with their refugee brothers in liberated Hungary. Thus national consciousness survived better and revived earlier among the Serbs, the Greeks, and even the Rumanians, threatened though they were with Slavic as well as Greek cultural denationalization.

The increasing national "unconsciousness" of the Bulgarian people was accompanied by individual denationalization in all directions. The occasional diaries and travelogues of Europeans going to and from Constantinople (to whom we owe much of the little that is known about Bulgaria under the Turks until the nineteenth century) report progressive decline, demoralization, and ignorance as seen from the main travel routes. Nevertheless, there existed a vestige of intellectual and political activity, which is obscured for the historian and was lost to the Bulgarian cause because it frequently lacked a Bulgarian label. The disguise of Bulgarian elements was fostered in particular by the peculiar confusion between religion and nationality under the *millet* system prevailing in the Ottoman Empire, which for administrative convenience placed all "Greek" Orthodox under the Greek *millet,* or nation, and patriarch. Thus the eventual upsurge of Greek nationalism swept along many Bulgarians who were conscious only of their Greek Orthodox label.

A few examples may illustrate the dissipation and dispersal of Bulgarian effort. The Counter Reformation undertook to conquer new territory in the Balkans, where there had been relatively few losses to the Reformation. In addition to the notable gains made in eastern Europe through the Uniate formula, Rome, aided by Catholic Ragusan traders and Croat and Bosnian missionaries, succeeded in the seventeenth century in stirring up considerable political as well as religious activity among Bulgarians. Although a number of Bulgarian converts achieved prominence in this movement, its essentially alien nature and the preponderance of non-Bulgarian elements deprived the Catholic Reformation in Bulgaria of lasting significance. For example, the energetic Bulgarian Peter Bogdan (Deodatus) Bakshish wrote edifying works in "Illyrian" and Latin and ended up as archbishop of Antivari in Montenegro; another Bulgarian, Archbishop Peter Parchevich, preached Romanism and revolt to converted Bulgarians in behalf of Catholic Austria, but Turkish retribution led to mass emigration and the discrediting of the Catholic cause. There was also a Jesuit abbot of Czanad in Hungary who signed himself "Christophorus Peichich Bulgarus," and devoted his literary efforts to proving, mostly in Latin, to "Illyrians" the superiority of the Western over the Eastern Church.[2] Filip Stanislavov, Catholic Bishop of Bulgarian Nicopolis, might have been the author of the first printed Bulgarian book, the *Abagar,* published in Rome in 1651, a collection of prayers for Bulgarian Catholics, had it not been more Croatian than Bulgarian.

The constant seepage of refugees across the Danube, beginning with the Turkish conquest and continuing intermittently until independence was achieved, might have been more debilitating to Bulgarian national resources but for the ultimate advantages which accrued. At one time much of the left bank of the Danube was more Bulgarian than Rumanian, and Wallachia came to be looked on as an extension of Bulgaria, a situation which lasted almost to the liberation. In addition to seeking asylum—which reached the proportions of an exodus following the recurrent Turkish wars with Austria and later with Russia, often accompanied by native revolts—Bulgarians were drawn by the freer economic and political climate north of the Danube, by the richly endowed Moldavian monasteries, and by the less definable attraction of Moscow as the "Third Rome," made more tangible in the eighteenth century by Catherine's efforts to colonize south Russia. But in the long run this emigration served the same function performed by Serbs in liberated Hungary and by the other South Slavs in Hapsburg territory. For it was the Bulgarians in Transylvania, the Principalities, Bessarabia, and Odessa who ultimately were the chief agents of Bulgaria's cultural and political liberation.

In another direction also there were both losses and gains for the Bulgarian patrimony. Had the Hapsburgs been more farsighted and less involved in dynastic affairs, the problem of the Balkans and Bulgaria might have received a less "Orthodox" and more "Austro-Slav" solution. Until well into the nineteenth century the differentiation between Orthodox Serbs and Bulgarians was less than between Catholic Croats and Orthodox Serbs. Some of the earliest indications of national revival, including Paisi's "History," are found in Macedonia and western rather than eastern Bulgaria and have much in common with similar developments among the Serbs. A more vigorous and enlightened Austrian policy might have reduced Russian Orthodox inroads and had Bulgarians as well as Serbs looking to Vienna instead of Moscow.[3]

But the element which above others siphoned off Bulgarian spiritual forces and which came closest to being fatal was Hellenism. It was not only the Moslem Turks and European Christians who confused Greek Orthodoxy and nationality; it was also the Greeks and even the Bulgarians themselves. The fact that the Greek neoclassical revival, sparked by Evgenios Vulgaris, came during the second half of the eighteenth century, when Bulgarian national consciousness was at its lowest, and found sympathetic reception in both classicist and Romantic Europe made it easier for Bulgarians to succumb to its undeniably strong appeal. It is not surprising, then, to find Bulgarians participating in the Greek revolutionary *Hetairia Philike* and suffering "for the Faith" (*Zavera*), as the Greek Revolution and, in fact, any revolt or plot against the Turks was called. Young Ypsilanti might have had more success had he raised the flag of Greek Orthodoxy in Bulgaria instead of in Rumania. But the Greeks were eventually hoist by their own Hellenism. The encroachments of the Fanariotes in church and school, coupled with Europe's growing Romantic interest in the Slavs, helped remove the Greek scales from Bulgarian eyes.[4]

Yet until the establishment of an independent Greek state and the resulting stimulus to Greek chauvinism, Bulgarian intellectuals educated in Greek schools were accustomed to write and to correspond with each other in Greek. Before abandoning this practice and their foreign cultural allegiance, many Bulgarian "Hellenists" underwent a searching of heart. Others in spite of seeming awareness of their Bulgarian nationality never quite forsook their first love. The most notable example, Dr. Nicolas Piccolos, professor of philosophy at Lord Guilford's Greek University of Corfu, became an associate of Adamantios Korais in Paris and acquired a European reputation as a classical scholar. In 1821 Piccolos was one of the four signers of Korais' appeal to Americans for aid in the Greek cause. A cosigner was another Bulgarian expatriate in Paris, Dr. Atanas Bogoridi, grandson of the famous Bulgarian patriot Sofroni, Bishop of Vratsa, who was Paisi's first copyist. Until the second quarter of the nineteenth century it was common for Bulgarians in Europe to pass themselves off as Greeks.[5] After 1830 Piccolos, disillusioned about modern Greece, devoted himself to classical studies until his death in Paris in 1865. He is an extreme example of the lack of national convictions among Bulgarian intellectuals of his time, serving as he did, successively or simultaneously, the interests of classical and modern Greece, the Bulgarian and Rumanian causes, and finally French scholarship and letters.[6]

In addition to the blandishments of Greek society and culture, Bulgarians found solid advantage in association with Greek merchant circles at home and abroad, in Vienna, for example, and in Moscow, where they joined the so-called "Nezhin" Greek colony which enjoyed special privileges even before the development of Russo-Turkish trade relations after the Treaty of Kuchuk-Kainardji in 1774. There were also those Bulgarians who personally profited from participation in the Greek Fanariote system. A unique case was that of Stefan Bogoridi (1775–1859), another grandson of Bishop Sofroni, for half a century the most important "Fanariote" in the sultan's service, privileged to have twelve rowers for his Bosphorus *caique*, when ordinary pashas had only three. Successively "kaimakam" of Wallachia and "prince" of Samos, he is credited along with Stratford Canning (and the Russian army), with persuading Mahmud to yield independence to Greece.[7]

Paisi and Bulgarian History

In time, however, the unabashed greed of the Greek Church and the nationalism of Greeks in general, flushed with their victory over the Turks, made enlightened Bulgarians realize that what was sauce for the Greek gander could also be sauce for the Bulgarian goose. The reluctance of the Fanar to give up its golden eggs brought about the head-on clash between the Greek Church (and hence the Greeks) and nascent Bulgarian nationalism so that the Bulgarian Church Question merely became the first phase in the battle for Bulgarian independence.

Yet as early as the middle of the eighteenth century there was already at least one Bulgarian who was acutely worried by the encroachments of the Greeks and by the growing decline of national consciousness among his fellow countrymen. In 1745 a twenty-two-year-old Bulgarian came to Mount Athos from Bansko in Macedonia and entered the monastery of Hilendar as Paisi. In 1798 he died and was buried in Samokov in western Bulgaria. Little else is known of Paisi except that he occasionally solicited Bulgarian pilgrims and alms for his monastery, that he made a pilgrimage to Jerusalem, and that in 1762 he compiled a "Slavenobulgarian History of the Bulgarian People and Kings and Saints and of all the Bulgarian Acts and Events," which was an extraordinarily eloquent warning to Bulgarians of the threat of national extinction.[8] By supplying them with a glorious past he hoped to remove their sense of inferiority, arouse their national pride, and liberate them from Greek bondage.

Once Bulgarian independence had been achieved, it is understandable that Bulgarians should have placed Paisi on a pedestal and ascribed to him an array of qualities and ideas which would establish him not only as the prime instigator of liberation but also as a remarkable personality for his age and environment. Essays have been written on "Paisi and Rousseau" (1890), for example, and more recently, "Paisi Hilendarski as a Philosopher of History" (1934), "Father Paisi and Bulgarian Geography" (1935), and the like. As a historian also Paisi enjoys a high reputation. To quote a Bulgarian history professor, "Father Paisi stands much higher than many first historians of other nations whose attempts to write the histories of their people stand beneath all manner of criticism on the score of invention, credulity, and ignorance."[9] Yet Bulgarians continue to find difficulty in reconciling idealized conceptions of the presumed progenitor of their country and its history with the uniform ignorance or neglect of Paisi by his successors until 1871, when he was "discovered" by the Bulgarian historian Marin Drinov and put at the head of the national revival.

The fact that Paisi had the vision to perceive the dangers of denationalization, to diagnose the causes, and to supply a remedy by compiling an ultrapatriotic history, no matter how stirring, is not in itself enough to credit him with authoring the movement which led to liberation. Paisi might perhaps be compared with Juraj Križanić, the Croat Roman Catholic priest who already in 1666 discovered the formula of the nineteenth-century Russian pan-Slavists. Yet his "Politics or Conversations on Government," composed during the author's exile in Siberia, was not published until 1859, and then anonymously and in a badly translated and incomplete Russian version.[10] Without denying Križanić's originality and foresight, one may question his contribution to modern pan-Slavism. On a smaller scale, Paisi also was the victim of isolation and of his too-prophetic foresight. Because of presumed causes and aftereffects, Paisi too has perhaps been taken out of the context of his time.

Between 1765, when the first known copy was made, and 1844, when an adaptation was printed, some forty copies or versions of Paisi's history are on record. It was copied even after it was printed (1844) as late as 1871 in Macedonia, where conditions continued to give meaning to Paisi's exhortations. Copies have been found as far apart as Macedonia and Bessarabia and continue to be found, one as recently as 1941. Until the nineteenth century it was reproduced more or less verbatim; after that almost half the copies are adaptations. It was most frequently copied in the 1830's, when Young Bulgaria was forming and the Church Question began to be raised. A contemporary reader left this reaction on a copy of Paisi: "And you, brethren, endeavor to read it for your own good, glory for Bulgarians and harm to the Greeks." Yet for the most part Paisi circulated anonymously or at least without recognition until 1852, and then he received only incidental mention until Drinov publicized him in 1871. Even the first printed version, under the title *Tsarstvennik* (Book of Kings), the name under which Paisi and similar compilations were popularly known, makes no mention of Paisi but lists a string of foreign authorities on the title page.[11]

Perhaps the anonymity with which Paisi's "History" circulated is a token of the effectiveness of his preachments. To some extent Paisi contributed to his own obscurity by his monastic modesty in disclaiming ability and credit for his "little history," which he states he collected, arranged, and translated, and in citing prominent authorities, partly no doubt to add weight to his message. Most of the personal, autobiographic element is contained in a sort of postscript, which copyists could and often did omit, some even substituting a reference to themselves. In fact, some copyists seemed more impressed with their own feat than with the manuscript. In addition, there were at least two other similar but apparently independent contemporary compilations with similar titles, based on more or less the same sources, which also passed under the general name of "Tsarstvenik" and which were also copied but not nearly to the same extent as Paisi. Both noticeably lack the patriotic fervor and nationalistic aims of Paisi's work. One is a "Short History of the Bulgaroslav People," compiled by an anonymous monk of Zograph Monastery sometime before 1785, the date of the oldest known copy; the other "Short History of the Bulgarian Slav People" was produced in 1792 by the monk Spiridon, who had left Athos in 1763 for the Moldavian monastery of Neamts.[12] Neamts had originated as a Bulgarian foundation and retained its Slavic character to the nineteenth century.

Other circumstances of a more external nature may be noted in explanation of Paisi's difficulties and relative obscurity, among them the absence of printing facilities for Orthodox Cyrillic publications. Until the latter half of the eighteenth century the only source of Orthodox religious books was Moscow. From the time of Peter and his successors textbooks and teachers also came from Russia, more or less surreptitiously, and under Elizabeth and Catherine more general works including histories were exported to the Orthodox Slavs of the Austrian and Turkish empires. The first accessible Orthodox Cyrillic press did not come into being until almost ten years after Paisi finished his work—in Vienna in 1770, for Serbian books.[13] The first book in Bulgarian was printed in 1806 in Wallachia. By a coincidence its author was Paisi's first known copyist, Sofroni Vrachanski. Paisi himself apparently had no thought of publication but begs his readers to copy or pay for copies of his manuscript. Under such circumstances and given Paisi's missionary zeal as expressed in his history, which reads like a sermon, he may have attempted to circulate his manuscript in person. In fact the Sofroni copy states that it was made when Paisi visited Kotel in 1765, but this is the only such contemporary reference although it is known that he made soliciting trips for his monastery.

Another more fundamental impediment must have been the Bulgarian

"Time of Troubles," the late-eighteenth-century period of anarchy when lawless armed bands ravaged the Bulgarian countryside and the more enterprising natives fled the country. Thus in Paisi's time there hardly could be any Bulgarian cultural or intellectual centers, and there were to be none until the nineteenth century and then mostly outside of Bulgaria. It may also be that when Bulgarians were ready for Paisi, he was no longer for them. By the second quarter of the nineteenth century, the medieval monastic tone of his work, in spite of its secular content, perhaps could not compete with the product of his successors, though some of them undoubtedly were influenced by him.[14]

To say that Paisi was something less than original, that his work circulated without adequate attribution, that it was confused with other similar manuscripts, and that it was ultimately sidetracked, is not to deny it considerable importance and influence. The existence of so many known copies and adaptations is one significant indication. Another, less measurable, is the effect on copyists and readers. When Paisi came to Kotel in 1765, the church trustees asked the young priest Stoiko Vladislavov (1739–*ca.* 1815) to make a copy, which was then chained like a holy book to a place in the church, and protected from theft by a terrifying curse. In 1781 Stoiko returned to make a second copy for himself. Later, as Bishop Sofroni of Vratsa (no mean feat for a Bulgarian in those days), he preached and wrote sermons in vernacular Bulgarian. After his escape from Vratsa and from his episcopal debts to the Greek Patriarch, he compiled and published in 1806 a formidable volume of sermons—the first printed book in Bulgarian.[15] He was also the author of the first original Bulgarian literary effort, "The Life and Sufferings of Sinful Sofroni" (1804), describing his adventures with Greeks and Turks (in which, however, there is no mention of Paisi), and spent his declining years recruiting Bulgarian volunteers for the Russians. Yet both of his Greek-educated grandsons were almost completely Hellenized.

There are also apparent instances of negative effects. For example, his first editor, Hristaki Pavlovich, after publishing Paisi's "History" in 1844, switched from the spoken eastern dialect used in the first edition of his Bulgarian grammar to a form of conservative Church Slavonic, which he considered pure Old Bulgarian, in the second.[16] Yet it was the former which was to become the basis of the literary language, though only after a die-hard struggle with the Slavonic school.

Paisi and Bulgarian History

Few of Paisi's readers became such distinguished exponents of his gospel as Sofroni, and seldom can his influence be traced so directly. Instead of looking for immediate or direct results one may consider Paisi's work in the light of his age. The most striking feature is the intensity of his Bulgarian convictions and his appreciation of the role of history in developing and maintaining national consciousness. This makes his sermon on Mount Athos a patriotic tract unique for its time and place. Five years after Paisi finished his "History," the last formal vestige of Bulgaria, the technically autonomous Bulgarian patriarchate of Ohrid, was abolished at Fanariote prompting. Twenty-five years later Bulgarian was not even included among the two-hundred-odd languages covered by Catherine's polyglot solution to knowledge, the Russian Academy's *Comparative Lexicon of All Languages and Dialects*,[17] a project originally inspired by Leibnitz. Such ignorance or confusion in Europe over Bulgarian and Bulgarians continued well into the nineteenth century until scholarly interest in "Old Bulgarian" focused attention on its modern descendant.

About fifteen years before undertaking his project, Paisi entered Hilendar, one of the four great Athos monasteries, which half a century before had led all others with eight hundred inmates. The situation which prompted Father Paisi to engage in two years of labor and provoked his patriotic outburst was brought about by the impact of reviving Greek nationalism and influence on the Athonite community. With the material and political advancement of the Fanariotes in the eighteenth century a number of previously Slav monasteries came into Greek hands. In addition, one of the prime instigators of the neo-Hellenic Greek revival, Evgenios Vulgaris, effectively preached the secular gospel as headmaster of the famous Athonite Academy until conservative religious elements forced him out in 1758.

At Hilendar, founded as a Serbian monastery in the twelfth century, the Serbian element vied with the Greeks in national boasting and with the then-Bulgarian majority for control. A famous contemporary Serbian pilgrim, Dositej Obradovich, also noted the fierce competition between Serbs and Bulgarians. To quote Paisi, "Many times have Serbs and Greeks reproached us for not having our own history." This lack Paisi was determined to remedy. On the one hand his tract is a passionate appeal to Bulgarians to wake up to their Slavic and Bulgarian heritage; on the other, it gathered together conveniently all the necessary proof to stop the carping mouths of Greeks, Serbs, or even Muscovites. Although the Greeks were his main target, a second purpose was to demonstrate historically the superiority of Bulgarians over Serbs. The short disdainful section on "Serb Kings" he included apparently to disprove the "witless" Serb contention that "from the beginning they were more famous in kings, army, and territory than the Bulgarians," whereas, says Paisi, "about the Serbs nothing is written anywhere in Latin and Greek histories." In addition to this internecine monastic rivalry, in which Paisi no doubt participated, there were squabbles over the large debt owed the Turks, all of which came to be too much for Paisi. So, although his older brother was abbot, Paisi forsook Hilendar for the more predominantly Bulgarian and perhaps solvent monastery of Zograph, a couple of hours distant. In his day, sadly notes Paisi, only Zograph was Bulgarian. There he says he found new material and completed his manuscript in 1762. Thirty years later Paisi was back in Hilendar.

Once Paisi realized what was needed it was possible for him to find models and sources for his fanciful history. For him and his audience the sources and accuracy of his Bulgarian history mattered less than that it should exist and be a source of pride. It so happens that Paisi's principal authorities were also not wholly concerned with history "as it really was." Starting with the premise that "of all the Slavic race the most glorious were the Bulgarians," Paisi was nevertheless somewhat puzzled to find so little written about them. He "used great labor to collect from various books and histories," he "read very many books and searched diligently a long time," but "in many he found nothing and in others only a little." He was particularly upset at not finding more about Bulgarian saints, fifty-eight of whom he catalogues, although he claims to have "searched through all Mount Athos monasteries, where there are old Bulgarian books and church deeds, the same in many places in Bulgaria where many old Bulgarian books are to be found." The lack of historical data Paisi attributed to the indifference and ignorance or carelessness of Bulgarians, who failed to copy and preserve their historical records, but for this he blames the Greek clergy and the Turks. Another explanation he found in "a certain Latin Mavrubir, who copied from Greek history a very short history of the Bulgarian kings, scarcely more than their names," and who accused Greek chroniclers of suppressing or distorting the glorious deeds of the Bulgarians out of

Paisi and Bulgarian History

"envy and hate." In his search for material Paisi states that he also went to "Germany" (meaning the Serbian patriarchate-in-exile at Sremski Karlovtsi in Southern Hungary), where he found "Mavrubir's history of the Serbs and Bulgarians." In his manuscript there are also a dozen references to "Baroni."

Actually most of Paisi's historical material, except for his fifty-eight saints, was taken from a 1719 Russian (Slavonic) edition of a sixteenth-century Polish condensation of Cardinal Caesar Baronius' *Annales Ecclesiastici*.[18] Although Paisi speaks of "translating" from the Russian, he often copies verbatim from Baronius, notably the general preface on "The Benefits of History," which, however, was added by the anonymous Russian translator.[19] Nor does Paisi hesitate to argue with or improve on the original where he feels that complete justice has not been done the Bulgarian side. Paisi's task was made easier inasmuch as he shared Baronius' anti-Greek point of view, and as the Orthodox Russian editor had already expurgated the more offensive Catholic elements.

If much of the content of Paisi is Baronius, the spirit is that of the Ragusan Benedictine abbot Mavro Orbini ("Mavrubir"), whose *Il regno de gli Slavi* (Pesaro, 1601) he found in a Russian version when he was sent to Karlovtsi in 1761 to bring back alms collected for Hilendar by a fellow monk who died there.[20] In Orbini, Paisi found a master. Although he may not have had time in Karlovtsi fully to exploit Orbini, he was obviously strongly influenced. There is even a parallel between Orbini's preface "to the reader" and Paisi's preface to his "readers and listeners" on the importance of having a history. Imbued with pride in his Slav ancestry ("mia natione Slava") and determined to put the Slavs on the map, the Croat Orbini literally created an ancient and glorious history for them. Paisi adopted his derivation of the Slavs from Scandinavia and identification of the Bulgars and other Asiatic peoples with Slavs, along with Orbini's genealogical tree which made Noah's son Japhet the progenitor of the Slavs. For Paisi, Orbini's Catholicism was partly offset by his ardent Slavism. Because he included non-Catholic sources, Orbini's book was put on the Index. Until the publication of the 1722 Russian version it was not generally known to South Slavs. Whereas the original edition devoted seventy-five large pages to Bulgaria, the 1722 version has only forty-five small pages; as most of this was on Catholic activity it was unsuitable for Paisi. Consequently he gives the impression of minimizing Orbini. But Paisi went the master one better. Whereas

Teachers of History

Orbini is the spiritual ancestor of a Romantic (in contrast to nineteenth-century political) pan-Slavism, Paisi is a fierce Bulgarian chauvinist. Yet at times one feels that he has not quite convinced himself of the validity of his own thesis of Bulgarian superiority. Taking a leaf out of Orbini, he falls back on the comforting thought that the Greeks must have deliberately suppressed favorable information. Nor can he refrain from pointing out that the medieval Bulgarian state succumbed to the Turks at the invitation of the Greeks.

The first Bulgarian history by a Bulgarian reflects the limitations of the author, who humbly admits he is neither a scholar nor a writer. Its ten discernible parts—on the benefits of history, preface to the reader, historical sketch of the Bulgarian people (main portion), summary of Serbian kings, continuation of the history of Bulgarian kings, names and succession of Bulgarian rulers, summary of notable Bulgarian rulers, conversion of Bulgarians (centuries before other Slavs), list of Bulgarian saints, and "postscript"—are poorly organized, repetitious, and sketchy. Except where Paisi is addressing the reader or dealing with contemporary matters from his own experience, his language is essentially the early eighteenth-century ecclesiastical Russianized Slavonic of his main sources. The fact that only after deserting Hilendar for Zograph did he discover new materials there suggests that his original search was less extensive than he implies.

Yet Paisi seems to have succeeded in accomplishing his purpose—to produce a history for Bulgarians to outmatch that of their rivals and to furnish them with convenient arguments for refuting attacks from all sides, and thus to inspire or shame his readers into acknowledging their Bulgarian nationality. As Paisi specifically addresses himself to "hearers" as well as "readers" and as most of his copyists naturally were priests and teachers, it may be assumed that the "Slavenobulgarian History" furnished texts for patriotic sermons and lessons, no doubt also by the author himself. Paisi's spirit and historical "method" characterized Bulgarian historiography, whether consciously or not, almost until the liberation. For the modern reader, however, the "History" has value mainly as a contemporary document illustrating the ebb and flow of national consciousness and rivalry in the mid-eighteenth-century Balkans.

While Paisi's manuscript was circulating from hand to mouth, a more enduring basis for Bulgarian historiography was being prepared in other quarters. The Reformation and Counter Reformation, which had extended as far as the Balkans, directed scholarly attention to the Byzantine Church and state and their successors. The resulting publication especially of documentary material, notably by Ducange and his continuators, furnished material also for Bulgarian history. The rise and fall of the Ottoman Empire also attracted scholars, particularly a string of late-eighteenth-century Hungarian and Hungarophile historians, stimulated by the prospect of the restoration of the Crown of St. Stephen. These include Georg Pray (1723–1801), Stephan Katona (1732–1811), L. A. Gebhardi (1735–1802), and especially J. C. von Engel (1770–1814). A third and perhaps most important contribution came from Germany and the "discovery" of Slavic and eastern Europe in the eighteenth century by Stritter (1740–1801), Thunmann (1746–1778), and Schlözer (1735–1809).[21] Leibnitz' suggestion for the study of historical origins through language classification was furthered by the researches of these scholars, tried out in Catherine's polyglot lexicon, and applied to the study of Russian origins by Karamzin and the pioneer Russian Slavists.[22]

Meanwhile the nationalist stimulus of Herder's *Stimmen der Völker in Liedern* (1778–1779) and *Ideen zur Philosophie der Geschichte der Menschheit* (1784–1791) and his Romantic enthusiasm for the Slavs furnished a springboard for exploration of Slavic origins and history by Father Joseph Dobrovsky and his disciples in Prague. The central issue of Bulgarian historiography from Paisi to Drinov, at home and abroad, was the Slavic as opposed to the Asiatic origin of the Bulgarians; the central problem of Slavic studies from Dobrovsky to Mikloshich was the role of Cyril and Methodius and of what eventually came to be known as "Old Bulgarian." These related problems gave Bulgaria a key place in the world of European scholarship. Because Karamzin and others had given currency to the German "Tatar" theory of Bulgarian origins, Slav as well as Bulgarian nationalists felt called upon to Slavicize not only the proto-Bulgarians but all other remotely related contemporary tribes. Thus the apparently scientific pan-Slav historians of the nineteenth century reverted to the sixteenth-century imaginative theories of Orbini, and of Paisi.[23]

The more identifiable origins of Bulgarian historiography, other than Paisi, are to be found closely linked with the beginnings of modern Serbian historiography. This is sometimes traced to Hristofor Zhefarovich, artist by profession, who in 1741 produced a book of fifty-four largely imaginary heraldic emblems and historical portraits with doggerel captions for all the "Slav" states; [24] the whole was copper-engraved for lack of Cyrillic type. Zhefarovich, an ordained monk from Doiran in Macedonia, was neither Bulgarian nor Serb but both, which was possible in the eighteenth century; he died in Moscow in 1754, labeled a Bulgarian. The author-artist states that his book was translated into "Slaveno-Serbian" (mixture of Russian, Slavonic, and Serbian), and although quite archaic it ranks as the first "Serbian" book published in the eighteenth century. The model was Paul Ritter's *Stemmatografia* published in Latin in 1701. [25] Ritter was half Croat, half German, but wholly dedicated to the "Illyrian" Slav cause promoted by Orbini, from whom he took some of his material. The graphic nature of Zhefarovich's creation, as well as its brashness, naturally appealed to Bulgarian readers, for whom it was one of the principal sources of historical lore. In 1841, Ivan Bogorov, a relative of Sofroni, published Zhefarovich's portraits of the Bulgarian kings Ivan Asen and Ivan Shishman, and his Bulgarian lion rampant, which actually became the emblem of the independent Bulgarian state. Thus patriotic fantasy got translated into reality!

The real founder of Serbian historiography, and incidentally of Bulgarian, was Jovan Rajich (1726–1801), a contemporary and possibly a fellow countryman of Paisi. His parents had emigrated to Karlovtsi in Hungarian Slavonia (Srem) from Vidin in northwest Bulgaria. After the "Great Migration" of 1690—long before the Ipek Serbian patriarchate was formally abolished in 1766—Karlovtsi became the center of Serbian religious and intellectual life. With a Jesuit elementary and Protestant secondary education, in 1753 Rajich walked to Kiev to complete his studies with three years of Orthodox theology. On his return from a second trip to Kiev, where he got the idea of writing his history, he visited Paisi's monastery for two months in 1758 in search of material and returned to Karlovtsi with some refugees from Hilendar. In 1768 he finished his principal work, an extensive and much-read history of the South Slav peoples. [26] However, it was all of twenty-six years before it was published. Although Rajich's younger and more learned contemporary, Engel, wrote that the first part (on Slavic origins) had better not have been written, Catherine liked it so well that she sent the author a gold medal and pirated the first volume, engravings and all (St. Petersburg, 1795).

It is of course possible that Rajich met and inspired Paisi at Hilendar in 1758 or at Karlovtsi in 1761, but for this there is no evidence. Yet in spite of his vastly superior education and the greater scope and scholarship of his work (he cites sixty-four authorities), Rajich and Paisi came from the same Slav Orthodox mold and used the same sources, Orbini and Baronius. In addition, Rajich either slavishly copied from Ducange or altered him when his Orthodox or Slav feelings were injured.[27] Rajich also began his work with a Biblical "preface to the amateur of history," and following established Slavic precedent, turned Goths, Vandals, Avars, etc., into Slavs. Before Rajich issued his own history, for some reason he published an annotated translation of the Serbian portion of the Catholic Gebhardi's *History of Hungary*, based to a considerable extent on Stritter.[28] However, Gebhardi's "History of Bulgaria," covering events to 1774, remained untranslated and hence inaccessible to Bulgarians.[29] This was true also of the more critical work of Engel, the Protestant rationalist historian of Hungary, who allotted about two hundred pages to Bulgarian history to A.D. 1444 in his four-volume *History of Hungary*.[30] Engel, a German who held to the Tatar theory of Bulgarian origins, had little use for Rajich's extreme Slavic eclecticism but does credit him with making a contribution to Serbian history.

The language used by Rajich was essentially Russian, with strong Slavonic influence and some Serbian and even Bulgarian traces. With the weight of considerable Orthodox prestige behind his work, it is not surprising to find the Bulgarian portion of Rajich's *History* republished in 1801 in a somewhat more popular form of "Slaveno-Serbian" by Atanas Neshkovich, a native of southern Hungary.[31] Neshkovich was commissioned to do this by certain Bulgarian merchants for the good of their people. It is possible that he, like Rajich, had Bulgarian origins. The choice of language seems odd, but the "Slaveno-Serbian" of those days differed little from the "Slaveno-Bulgarian," both being derived from Russianized Slavonic, the common literary jargon of the eighteenth century. In any case it was in this roundabout fashion that Bulgarians obtained their first published history. By a coincidence, a Bulgarian translation was made and published by Peter Sapunov in 1844,[32] the same year that Paisi's *History* first had the benefit of print.

Teachers of History

Although it was the Serb Rajich who furnished Bulgarians with a more accessible history than Paisi's manuscript, it was the Russian Venelin who not only fired the historical and national imagination of the young leaders of the patriotic revival but whose meteoric appearance completely overshadowed Paisi until his resurrection by Marin Drinov.

Stimulated by the discoveries of the founding fathers of Slavic studies in Prague and Vienna, Admiral Shishkov, president of the Russian Academy, had hoped to import the leading "Austro-Slav" scholars, including Hanka, Šafařik, and Jungmann, to occupy chairs of Slavic studies to be created in the leading Russian universities. Advised, however, to develop their own resources, the Russians found a constructive device in combining their growing political interests in the Balkans with officially sponsored field research. One of the first of these academic emissaries was a twenty-six-year-old fugitive from the medical profession, Yuri Venelin (1802–1839), whose mission was to collect historical documents in the wake of the Russo-Turkish war of 1828.

Venelin was of the stuff of which pan-Slavs were made. A Ukrainian born in Hungary, he was educated in Poland and studied medicine in Moscow, only to become an amateur archaeologist, philologist, and historian. The first product of his researches, *The Ancient and Present Day Bulgarians in Their . . . Relations with the Russians,* not only created a sensation among the Bulgarian intelligentsia of the 'thirties, but more important it started the trend which drew the center of Bulgarian intellectual and eventually political gravity from the West to Russia.[33] Though oversensitive himself, Venelin frequently indulged in vigorous, tactless, and sometimes inaccurate pontifications on Bulgarian matters of all kinds. This generated heated controversy but also healthy activity. In any event, Young Bulgaria's historical vanity was tickled, and all who saw him or his book were in turn transported by his infectious enthusiasm and the printed evidence of their almost-forgotten history. There was no exaggeration in the epitaph grateful Bulgarians placed on Venelin's grave: "He reminded the world of the oppressed but once famous and powerful Bulgarian people and passionately desired to see their rebirth. Almighty God fulfill the prayer of Thy servant."

Having stirred up the Bulgarians more than anyone before or since, Venelin's interest in Bulgarian affairs waned, partly because of publishing and other difficulties and opposition his theories encountered, partly because his pan-Slav interests were broader than Bulgaria. Aside from a study of South Slav folksongs, which had considerable influence in initiating Bulgarian interest in this field, only one other item was published before his premature death in 1839, a biographical-bibliographical survey of modern Bulgarian literature, the first contribution to writings on contemporary Bulgarian history, which greatly stimulated interest abroad as well as among Bulgarians in Bulgaria's revival.[34] However, an unpublished Bulgarian grammar is mute testimony to his failure to comprehend the essence of the Bulgarian language.

In contrast to the "History" of his unknown spiritual ancestor Paisi, Venelin's work had both an immediate and a direct effect.[35] His most ardent press agent was the former Hellenophile Odessa vodka merchant Vasil Aprilov (a Nezhin "Greek"), whom Venelin converted into a kind of nationalist Mycaenas of the Bulgarian renaissance. In addition to promoting a variety of cultural causes and championing a Russian solution for Bulgaria, Aprilov contributed to Bulgarian historiography an essay on Cyril and Methodius and a history of contemporary Bulgarian education.[36]

Although from the point of view of Bulgarian nationalism in general Venelin's influence was highly beneficial, it may also be said that his semischolarly pan-Slav enthusiasm had a retrogressive effect. It was eagerly adopted by a whole school of nationalist imitators, foremost of whom was the restless revolutionary George Rakovski (1821–1867). Under Venelin's prompting a number of Bulgarians reverted to the outmoded Slavonic literary tradition in the belief they were getting back to the genuine Bulgarian. Among them was Rakovski, antiquarian exponent of ultra nationalism. With his bad philological puns Rakovski was able to interpret history as he chose—which was for the greater glory of Bulgaria. Carried to extremes, Rakovski's method led well past Venelin's mere Slavic theory of Bulgarian origins to a theory of origin in distant Indic antiquity, as shown in the quarter-million verse invention of the Balkan McPherson, Stefan Verkovich, who foisted his *Veda Slovena* on the learned and temporarily credulous Slavic world just in time for Moscow's pan-Slav exposition of 1867.

To a surprising degree the *Veda Slovena* backed up Rakovski's historical hypotheses, notably that Bulgarian was the modern form of Sanskrit and Zend. These ideas crop up in almost everything he wrote but in particular in several half-historical, half-polemical and -philological essays. Among them was a "Guide or handbook on how to investigate and discover the oldest features of our life, language, racial origins, government, our glorious history," etc.[37] Other extravagant effusions were a "Short disquisition on the obscure and false beginnings on which is based the ancient history of all European peoples," and "Several lectures on Asen the First, the great Bulgarian king, and on his son Asen the Second," both written in Odessa but published in Belgrade in 1860 because of Russian censorship. In 1865 Rakovski published in Bucharest the first and only number of *Bulgarska Starina* (*Bulgarian Antiquity*), a periodical which was to have been devoted to the history of all the Slavic countries.

Replying to critical reviews of *Asen,* Rakovski stated that his purpose was not to write history to be taught to children.[38] Even more than Paisi and Venelin, Rakovski's object was to resurrect the past in order to create a present and future for his country. But he was much too restless and impatient to do much more than stir up historical dust. Yet he was the first Bulgarian to publish excerpts from Paisi's "History," in *Asen* and later in *Bulgarska Starina.* He also published Sofroni's autobiography in 1861.

In 1859, Gavril Krŭstevich, Paris-trained lawyer and heir to a portion of Stefan Bogoridi's exalted position, who was to be the second and last governor of Eastern Roumelia, complained that a Bulgarian history was still to be written. In actuality, midcentury Bulgarians were too preoccupied with practical issues to devote themselves to sober historical studies. Aside from the basic conflict with the Greeks over the Bulgarian Church—on the ultimate aims of which most Bulgarians were agreed though they differed violently over Orthodox, Uniate, or Protestant solutions—Bulgarian energies were absorbed in a variety of other questions of the day. These ranged from violent quarrels over spelling to the decisive issue of "Ausgleich" with the Porte as against outright revolution. Under these circumstances history served as a platform from which to preach national salvation according to the revelations of a Rakovski or of one of his opponents. A second factor retarding the development of Bulgarian historical effort was the continuing lack of a suitable and safe national cultural center and the consequent diffusion of intellectual forces in Paris, Vienna, Athens (until the Church Question became too hot), Belgrade (until Serbian nationalism became too strong), Bucharest, Odessa, and Moscow. The closest to a Bulgarian "capital," oddly enough, was Constantinople, but the Turks were not entirely unaware of

Paisi and Bulgarian History

the connection between history, books, and revolution. Until 1864 and Midhat's reforms, the Porte refused to permit a Bulgarian press outside the capital. It was in Constantinople that Gavril Krŭstevich and a few other leaders of the Bulgarian community established a sort of national society and organ, *Bŭlgarski Knizhitsi*, in 1857. Until it folded in 1862 for lack of paid subscriptions, it devoted considerable space to serious historical material, including the first Bulgarian reference to a Paisi manuscript (1859), and to criticisms of Rakovski's aberrations, as well as to translations of *Uncle Tom's Cabin*, Dickens, etc.[39]

The year 1869, however, may be taken as the date for the solid establishment of Bulgarian historical studies. The Bulgarian Literary Society founded by a young graduate of Moscow University, Marin Drinov (1838–1906), and associates, in relatively safe and centrally located Braila on the left bank of the Danube, was of great consequence for the national cultural life and eventually grew into the Bulgarian Academy of Science. Its organ, the *Periodichesko Spisanie*, furnished a much-needed outlet for historical studies, to which considerable space was devoted. In 1869 also Krŭstevich published the first and only volume of a too-ambitious *Bulgarian History*,[40] which had the remarkable number of 1,874 advance subscriptions, testimonial to the author's political position as well as to interest in the subject.

Krŭstevich, an amateur, belonged to the Slavic-origins school of Bulgarian historiography. In his maiden professional effort, *View of the Origin of the Bulgarian People*,[41] also published in 1869, Drinov took issue with Krŭstevich's theory (in which the latter followed Venelin), in favor of the Chud or Finnish origin of the Bulgarians. As the founder of professional Bulgarian history, it was fitting that it should fall to Drinov to "discover" in Father Paisi the progenitor of Bulgarian national revival and history, and thus properly to discount Venelin's "discovery" of the Bulgarians. His article, "Father Paisi, his Times, his History, and his Disciples," appeared in 1871.[42] After brief service in his liberated country Drinov returned to his adopted fatherland, where since 1873 he had been professor of history at the University of Kharkov, and his subsequent contributions in the field of history were mainly in Russian.

Professor Drinov was the first professional Bulgarian historian and the first to acquire a European reputation. Nevertheless it was left to a foreigner to write the complete history of the Bulgarians. In 1857, the Russian Academy of Sciences had decided that it was still too soon to carry out Aprilov's 1847 bequest of two thousand rubles for a complete, detailed history of the Bulgarians.[43] But twenty years later, when Bulgaria was still two years away from liberation, Šafařik's twenty-one-year-old grandson, Constantin Jireček (1854–1918), published his *Geschichte der Bulgaren;* this detailed and scholarly synthesis is not yet fully superseded.[44]

Since 1762 Bulgarian historiography had kept pace with history. Father Paisi launched his broadside against the Greek clergy just as the Fanariotes were preparing to move in on the so-called Bulgarian Patriarchate of Ohrid. At the turn of the century Bishop Sofroni's patriotic exploits put into practice what Paisi had preached, while his more famous Serbian contemporary Rajich gave the Bulgarians their first published history. Venelin's hysterical promotion of the Slav-Bulgarian cause helped those who were implementing Paisi's anti-Greek program in the 'thirties. Rakovski's fertile imagination furnished historical arguments for the revolutionary Bulgarian declaration of independence against the Greek Patriarch in 1860; Drinov's *Historical Survey of the Bulgarian Church* in 1869 was an appropriate introduction to the Porte's *firman* re-establishing a Bulgarian national church, the Exarchate, in 1870. Finally, Jireček's *History of the Bulgarians* ushered in the Russian liberation of their country.

A survey of the origins of Bulgarian historiography might end with the concluding words of the "History of the Bulgarian People, Kings, and Saints," in which its author set down most of what is known about himself, his purpose, and his methods:

I, Paisi, ordained monk and vice abbot of Hilendar, gathered together and wrote it down, turning the plain Russian speech into the plain Bulgarian and Slavonic speech. I was gradually being consumed by love and pity for my Bulgarian race because it had no collected history of the glorious deeds from the earliest times of our people, saints, and kings. Thus many times we were reproached by Serbs and Greeks for not having our own history. I saw written in many books and histories many references to the Bulgarians. On this account for two years I tried hard to collect a little from many histories. And mainly with this intention I went to Germany. There I found Mavrubir's history about Serbs and Bulgarians. Briefly about the kings, but about the saints he wrote nothing: a Catholic, he did not venerate Bulgarian and Serbian saints, who began appearing later, after the Latins separated themselves from the Greeks. But about the Serb saints he writes badly and distorts, whereas about Bulgarian saints he mentions nothing. Thus I disregarded my headaches, from which I suffered for a long time, and likewise I suffered much from stomach ache, but I ignored this out of the great zeal which I had. And I gathered together buried and forgotten things from many ages—words and speeches I wrote down. I have not had any schooling, either in grammar or in composition, but for the ordinary Bulgarians I wrote simply: I was not concerned in arranging the words according to grammar and to insert phrases but only to gather together this little history.

And I compiled it in the monastery of Hilendar, when the abbot was Lavrenti, my brother born of one mother and older than I: he was then sixty and I forty years old. At this time Hilendar was giving the Turks 3,000 grosh in taxes, and owed 27,000 grosh, and there was great brotherly unrest and disagreement. Hence I could not endure these things at Hilendar and left and went to Zograph and there I found many more accounts and writings about the Bulgarians; and I added to and completed what is said in this little history for the benefit of our Bulgarian race, for the glory and praise of our Lord Jesus Christ, to Whom is all glory, honor, and worship, and to His eternal Father and to His most holy and life giving Spirit, now and forever and ever.

AMEN.

1. Much has been written about Paisi and the national revival. For Bulgarian historiography there is M. G. Popruzhenko, "Ocherki po istorii vozrozhdeniya bolgarskago naroda. III: Istoricheski raboty," *Zhurnal Ministerstva Narodnago Prosvieshcheniya* (Oct., 1903), pp. 327–346; P. Nikov, "Zadachata na dneshnata bŭlgarska istoriografiya," *Godishnik na Sofiiskiya Universitet* (Ist.–Fil.Fak.), XVII (1920–1921), 1–95; N. Radojčić, "Raicheva bugarska istoriya," *Sbornik v chest na V. N. Zlatarski* (Sofia, 1925), pp. 353–365; and I. Duichev, "Pregled na bŭlgarskata istoriografia," *Jugoslovenski Istoriski Chasopis*, IV (1938), 40–74.

2. For example, *Speculum Veritatis*, etc. (Venice, 1725; Vienna, 1732), and *Concordia Orthodoxorum Patrum*, etc. (Tyrnau, 1730).

3. For example, the Slovene scholar and Austrian official Kopitar hoped Vienna would become the center of Slavic studies and complained about the niggardliness of the Austrian government in contrast to the generous chairs, grants, and traveling fellowships available in St. Petersburg ("Patriotische Fantasien eines Slaven," *Kleinere Schriften* [Vienna, 1857], I, 70). Actually, as imperial librarian Kopitar was also motivated by the desire to forestall the Russians in acquiring Slavic manuscripts from Mount Athos, etc., particularly at the time of Venelin's foraging expedition (see below). One may speculate on the consequences had it been an Austrian "Venelin" who "discovered" the Bulgarians.

4. In 1832 Neofit Rilski received an invitation to start a school in Plovdiv,

leading center of Grecomania, "to show that the time had come for Bulgaria to look out" (correspondence of Neofit Rilski, in *Sbornik za Narodni Umot-voreniya*, III [1890], 398). In 1835 he established the first modern Bulgarian school, in Gabrovo.

5. For example, Beron, author of the first modern Bulgarian textbook—*Bukvar* (Brashov, 1824)—signed his Latin doctoral dissertation, "Peter Beron Thrax."

6. Among his many publications were a number of translations into modern Greek, including Descartes, *Discours de la Méthode* (Kerkyra, 1824). In view of the distinguished "Greek" career of Piccolos, it is not inconceivable that Evgenios Vulgaris could have been of Bulgarian origin, as is sometimes claimed.

7. His son, Aleko Pasha, was the first governor of Eastern Roumelia.

8. "Istoriya slavenobolgarskaya o narode i o tsarei i o s'tih bolgarskih i o vseh deyania i bitia bolgarskaya." The original Paisi manuscript, now in Zograph monastery on Mount Athos, was identified in 1906 and published by Iordan Ivanov (*Istoriya Slavěnobolgarskaya* [Sofia, 1914]).

9. N. Stanev, "Paisi i bŭlgarskitě knizhovnitsi," *Sbornik v pamet na Prof. Petr Nikov* (Sofia, 1940), pp. 411–417.

10. *Politika ili razgovori o vladalaštvu* (Zagreb, 1947), a Croat translation from the 1859 edition. The complete original text—in a peculiar Slavic jargon—is still unpublished. Cf. M. B. Petrovich, "Juraj Križanić: A Precursor of Pan-Slavism," *American Slavic and East European Review*, VI (1947), 75–92.

11. *Tsarstvennik ili istoriya bolgarskaya . . . iz Mavrobira Latinskago, Baroniya, Ioanna Zonarya, Buefira Frantsuskago, Teofana Grecheskago, Svetago Dimitriya Rostovskago i drugih lyetopistsev sobrana*, edited by Hristaki Pavlovich (Budapest, 1844).

12. *Istoriya vo kratě o bolgarskom narodě slavenskom*, edited by V. N. Zlatarski (Sofia, 1900). The 1785 text of the Zograph history ("Istoria v kratě o bolgaroslovenskom narodě") is printed in I. Ivanov, *Bŭlgarski starini iz Makedoniya* (Sofia, 1908). Whether the Zograph monk or Spiridon knew of Paisi's "History" is not clear, but there is evidence that Spiridon had used the Zograph history, which might then date it before 1763.

13. The Cyrillic press in Trnava (Tyrnau) in Hungary was controlled by Uniates. The Cyrillic press in Venice, established by a Greek in 1761, issued mostly reprints of Russian liturgical books, although a history of the Serbs in Russian was printed there in 1765. An anonymous Serbian historical compilation, contemporary with and similar to Paisi's, also remained in manuscript, the oldest known copy dating from 1791 (B. Unbegaun, *Les Débuts de la langue littéraire chez les Serbes* [Paris, 1935], p. 39).

14. A copy of Paisi made not earlier than 1809, found in Bessarabia in 1932, illustrates several aspects of the Paisi problem: apparently an adaptation of Spiridon was combined with a fairly close though rearranged copy of Paisi with the last section on Saints and the autobiographical note left out,

and a few interpolations added. There is no indication of authorship in either part except a statement on the last page (which does not appear in Paisi's original) that because of the "press of monastery duties" the listing of kings had to be curtailed. The copying was done by several not always skilled hands, possibly as an exercise. Its title resembles that of the 1844 printed version.

15. *Kiriakodromion sirech: nedělnik, pouchenie,* etc. (Rimnik, 1806), 4°, 536 pp.

16. *Grammatika Slaveno-Bolgarska* (Budapest, 1836); in the second edition (Belgrade, 1845), Pavlovich refers to certain modern Bulgarianisms as unnatural "filth," like a monkey giving birth to a human. Perhaps echoing Paisi, in the Preface to his *Razgovornik Greko-Bolgarskii* (Belgrade, 1835) he begs his readers not to despise their Bulgarian race, because "Greece also gives birth to oxen and Bulgaria to philosophers."

17. *Sravnitel'nye slovari vsieh yazykov i nariechii* (St. Petersburg, 1787–1789), containing 273 words and twelve numbers in each language. A second edition (1790–1791) added seventy-nine languages, mostly American and African dialects. Vuk Karadzhich's notice (1822) of the omission of Bulgarian was the origin of Bulgarian philological studies.

18. *Dĕyaniya tsrkovnaya i grazhdanskaya ot rozhdestva Gospoda nashego Iisusa Hrista. Iz lĕtopisanii Kesarya Baronia,* etc., 2 vols. (Moscow, 1719).

19. V. Velchev, *Otets Paisi Hilendarski i Tsezar Baroni* (Sofia, 1943). While disclosing Paisi's indebtedness to Baronius, Velchev nevertheless tries hard to salvage Paisi's reputation.

20. *Kniga istoriografiya pochatiya imene, slavy i razshireniya naroda slavyanskogo,* etc. (St. Petersburg, 1722), shortened and badly translated by Sava Vladisavljevich, a fellow Ragusan, with an appendix on the conversion of the Slavs by Theofan Prokopovich, Metropolitan of Novgorod.

21. J. Thunmann, *Untersuchungen über die Geschichte der östlichen europäischen Völker* (Leipzig, 1774); A. L. Schlözer, *Allgemeine nordische Geschichte* (Halle, 1772); J. G. Stritter, *Memoriae populorum olim ad Danubium,* etc., 4 vols. (Moscow, 1770 ff.).

22. Also may be noted J. C. Adelung's *Mithridates* (1806 ff.), a comparison of five hundred languages, but with Bulgarian classed as a Serbian dialect.

23. N. S. Derzhavin, foremost Soviet historian of Bulgaria, after analyzing all the various "bourgeois" theories of Bulgarian origins, including the Tatar, Turk, Hun, Slav, Finn, Chud, Chuvash, Thracian, etc., concludes that there had been no progress since Schlözer first raised the problem—none, that is, until N. Y. Marr (Soviet arbiter of all things philological until the late Joseph Stalin deposed him) decided that Bulgarians were Bulgarians, their origins going back to Japhet—and Orbini! (*Istoriya Bolgarii* [Moscow-Leningrad, 1945], I, 176 ff.).

24. *Stematografiya,* etc. (Vienna, 1741; 2nd ed., 1745), dedicated to Arseni IV of Ipek, "Patriarch of all the Serbs, Bulgarians, Western Coastal Region, Dalmatia, Bosnia, the Danube, and all of Illyria."

25. *Stemmatografia, sive armorum Illyricorum* (Vienna, 1701). Ritter

Teachers of History

(1652–1713), also known by his translated name Vitezović, wrote in Croatian as well.

26. *Istoriya raznyh slavenskih narodov naipache Bolgar, Horvatov, i Serbov*, 4 vols. and supp. (Vienna, 1794–1795).

27. Rajich used a revision by Joseph Keglevich, *Caroli Du Fresne Domini Du Cange Illyricum vetus et novum* (Pressburg, 1746); Keglevich refers to Orbini and reproduces the lion which he had designated as the Bulgarian national emblem.

28. *Kratkaya Serblii, Rasii, Bosny i Ramy kralevstv istoriya* (Vienna, 1793).

29. First 232 pages of the fourth and concluding part of his *Geschichte des Reichs Hungarn und der damit verbündeten Staaten* (Leipzig, 1782).

30. *Geschichte des ungarischen Reiches und seine Nebenländer*, 4 vols. (Halle, 1792–1804).

31. *Istoriya slaveno-bolgarskog naroda* (Budapest, 1801), supposedly also based on Stritter but, if so, presumably via Rajich. According to Radojchich it ran through three editions, but Šafařik reported that Neshkovich's failing eyesight prevented the appearance of a second revised edition announced in 1824 (*Geschichte des Serbischen Schrifttums* [to ca. 1831], edited by J. Jireček [Prague, 1865], p. 419).

32. *Istoriata na slavenno-bolgarskiya narod iz istoriata na G. Raicha i někoi istoricheski knigi*, etc. (Bucharest, 1844).

33. *Drevnie i nynieshnie bolgare v politicheskom, narodopisnom, istoricheskom i religioznom ih otnoshenie k Rosiyanam*, I (Moscow, 1829); 2nd revised ed., 1856. Vol. II of Venelin's researches appeared in 1846 (though printing started in 1834), Vol. III in 1849; also a volume of documents collected by Venelin in Bucharest (St. Petersburg, 1840).

34. *O zarodyshě novoi bolgarskoi literatury* (Moscow, 1838); Bulgarian translations in 1842 and 1860.

35. In 1838 a copy of Paisi was made for Venelin. He had run across what may have been a Paisi manuscript in 1828 but the owner refused to sell it.

36. *Balgarskitě knizhnitsi, ili na koe slovensko pleme sobstvenno prinadlezhi kirillovskata azbuka* (Odessa, 1841); and *Dennitsa novo-bolgarskago obrazovaniya* (Odessa, 1841) and Supplement (St. Petersburg, 1842). He also published in Russian *Bolgarskie gramoty* (1845), a collection of historical documents from Mount Athos, etc. A Bulgarian colleague, Palauzov, also wrote in Russian on Bulgarian history.

37. Odessa, 1859; only part one of three projected parts was published.

38. *Dunavski Lebed* (Oct. 12, 1860), the incendiary newspaper edited by Rakovski in Belgrade, 1860–1862, and smuggled into Turkish Bulgaria.

39. The first scholar to publish a notice of Paisi and his history was the Russian V. Grigorovich, who followed in Venelin's footsteps, in *Staty kasayushchiyasya drevnago slovyanskago yazyka* (Kazan, 1852), p. 52.

40. *Istoriya blgarska*, I (Constantinople, 1869). His first literary effort was a translation from the French of *Poor Richard's Almanac* (*Mudrost dobrago Riharda* [Budapest, 1837]).

41. *Pogled vrh prois-hozhdane-to na Blgarskii narod i nachalo-to na Blgarska-ta istoriya* (Vienna, 1869). In the same year and place was published his *Istoricheski pregled na bŭlgarska-ta tsrkva.*

42. "Otets Paisi, negovoto vreme, negovata istoriya i uchenitsite mu," *Periodichesko Spisanie* (Braila), No. 4, pp. 3–26.

43. B. D. Grekov, ed., *Dokumenty k istorii slavyanovedeniya v Rossii (1850–1912)* (Moscow-Leningrad, 1948), pp. 11–14, giving the Academy's proposed project.

44. Prague, 1876, 586 pp. A not-very-successful attempt to bring it up to date was F. Hybl, *Dějiny národa bulharského*, 2 vols. (Prague, 1930).

[JOHN WHITNEY HALL]

Historiography in Japan[1]

THE recent loss of China as a place to which Americans could travel for study has turned the attention of our Oriental specialists toward the remaining friendly areas of the Far East, particularly Japan. This new focus of interest has been long overdue. In the past the tradition of Sinology has greatly overshadowed its counterpart, Japanology. It was chiefly to China and to the Chinese that the Western world looked in its search for knowledge of Oriental history and culture. As a consequence Western studies of Japan, particularly those by Americans, have been comparatively few and generally of inferior quality.

During the last few decades, however, several developments have helped to increase the prestige of Japanese studies in this country. Of chief importance have been Japan's own meteoric rise as a world power, the lengthy Pacific war, and our close association with Japan in the postwar occupation period. Another has been a marked change in the climate of our academic thinking, a shift from interest in Oriental dynasties and cultural oddities to an emphasis, stimulated by the growth of the social sciences, on social and economic development. With this change there has come a realization that the basic problems of Oriental society or economy can be studied as readily in Japan as in China. Finally there has come a recognition of the worth of Japan's own efforts in the study of her history and society. Japan, the first of the Far Eastern states to modernize herself, has been the first to produce native scholars working in the modern scientific tradition. Japanese historians, since the middle of the nineteenth century, have been extremely open to world currents of thought. In recent years they have developed a highly

284

respectable and sophisticated tradition of general historical scholarship based on sound monographic foundations. It is no accident that, while original research on Japanese history in Western languages is a fairly rare commodity, there exist a number of excellent historical surveys—works which could not have been written but for the prior effort of native historians.

The modern Japanese historian has much to offer his Western colleagues. This becomes increasingly apparent in an age when the destinies of our countries are so closely entwined and when the horizons of historical research have passed beyond the confines of the single nation to entire cultures and to world-wide patterns of development. Though much of the output of Japanese scholars will remain locked in an unfamiliar language, a substantial amount is being made available in English translation or digested in the works of Americans who have mastered the Japanese language. It behooves even the nonspecialist, therefore, to acquaint himself with the type of work being done by the Japanese in the field of history and to evaluate its quality.[2]

I

Though it is not the purpose of this study to give detailed consideration to the early historical writings of the Japanese, it must be pointed out that Japan's recent historiographical development could hardly have taken place were it not for the foundations laid in the centuries before her contact with the West. Many works compiled prior to the twentieth century remain today as standard repositories of historical fact, and much of the research of modern Japanese historians has consisted in the scientific reinterpretation of these traditional materials. We may well inquire, therefore, into the nature of Japan's early historiography, its techniques and its reliability.[3]

Before the introduction of Western historical methodology, Japanese history was set down according to three separate traditions, which we may designate as the native (or Shinto), the Chinese (or Confucian), and the Buddhist. Each of these three schools produced written histories of markedly different character and trustworthiness. The native tradition placed emphasis on the principal families and heroes of Japan, especially the emperor. The Chinese, on the other hand, centered its attention on the court and bureaucracy, while the Buddhist encouraged an otherworldly attitude toward the passage of historical events. The native and Buddhist schools, furthermore, tended to distort historical fact to political or religious ends, while the Chinese generally produced histories of a high degree of objectivity.

The earliest Japanese history still extant, the *Record of Ancient Matters* (*Kojiki*, traditionally dated 712),[4] was written in the native style. Set down as on account of the Japanese nation from its origin to A.D. 628, it appears to be based on the legendary tales preserved by the bards who were customarily attached to the leading families of early Japan. Its liberal inclusion of myth and its emperor-centered ideology made for unreliable history, but the work has stood at the head of a long line of ethnocentric writings which were revived as late as the last war to give support to Japan's ultranationalistic propaganda. Other products of the native tradition were the *Mirrors* (*Kagami*) and *Narratives* (*Monogatari*), which characterized the historical writing of the eleventh through the fourteenth centuries. These romantic works have given to Japanese history much of its color and many of its most beloved heroes. They are of limited value to the serious historian, however. Undoubtedly the most historically reliable products of the native style are the genealogies and family histories which have come down from every age. Such sources are still useful for the light they shed on the activities of the ruling groups in Japan, and they have formed the basis of Japan's modern biographical dictionaries.

Far more voluminous and significant has been the work of Japanese historians working under Chinese influence. One of the distinctive features of Chinese civilization has been a deep respect for scholarship. From early times the governments of China encouraged the keeping of records and the compilation of official histories. By the seventh century, when Japan came under strong Chinese influence, the Chinese had perfected an extremely sophisticated historiographical technology.[5] This tradition has exerted a constant beneficial influence upon Japanese historians down to the present day.

Characteristic of the Chinese style of historiography was its concentration on the central government. Most Chinese history was written for and about the bureaucracy. Its point of view, consciously or unconsciously, was that of the Confucian official who looked to the past for instruction in the task of administration.[6] At the same time Chinese historians were meticulous in the selection of their material and extremely economical in their writing. They were careful to record history with a minimum of embellishment or overt interpretation, and to maintain a scientifically devised chronological framework. It is informative to watch the Chinese-trained Japanese scholars of the eighth century at work upon the early history of Japan, to witness the attempt to authenticate and ascribe exact dates to the legends preserved in such works as the *Record of Ancient Matters*. The result was the *Chronicle of Japan* (*Nihon shoki*, 720), a work hardly more reliable than the *Record of Ancient Matters* but far more advanced in its historiographical technology. It became the first in a series of government-sponsored chronicles which form the backbone of our body of knowledge about Japan's premodern political history. Such works were, for the most part, written in formal Chinese style, and they record events in chronological order as reported to the central government. Following the direct example of the *Chronicle of Japan*, five imperially authorized histories covered in succession the course of court events down to the year 887.

With the turn into the tenth century, the Sinified court bureaucracy of Japan began to fall into political decay. While court chronicles continued to be written in the Chinese manner, these were not officially recognized nor were they of special historical significance. As the center of political gravity shifted to the headquarters of the succession of military leaders which ruled Japan after the twelfth century, the center of historical writing shifted with it. In the course of the long feudal period which followed, three chronological records of great importance were produced. The first of these, the *Mirror of the West* (*Azuma kagami*, ca. 1266), was the official history of the Kamakura shogunate. Based on the shogunate diaries and official records, it is credited with a high degree of reliability. The *Veritable Records of the Tokugawa* (*Tokugawa jikki*, 1849) was a work compiled by a committee of historians with access to official records and is the authorized record of the rule of the Tokugawa shoguns (1603–1868). Joining these two works the *Later Mirror* (*Nochi kagami*) was compiled at Tokugawa request by the great nineteenth-century historian Narushima Ryōjo (1803–1854). All three of these works were modeled after the example of the earlier chronological imperial histories. In their modern printed editions they fill twenty-one large volumes.

Histories written from a Buddhist point of view were largely a product of Japan's early feudal age. An example of this type of writing which has held the attention of later scholars is the *Fool's Miscellany* (*Gukan-shō*, 1224?). This work by the priest Fujiwara Jien (1155–1225) is considered to be the "first attempt to survey and interpret, not merely to record"[7] Japanese history. In it the author attempted to link Japanese history with that of the entire Buddhist world and to interpret his country's development in terms of the Buddhist formula of man's destiny. Few other works of this period were written with as conscious a Buddhist frame of reference. But the Buddhist priesthood had much indirect influence upon the course of Japanese historiography. Since from the twelfth through the sixteenth century the cloisters remained the chief refuge of learning, historical writings appearing during this time were largely the work of Buddhist priests. The romances of Japan's Middle Ages are liberally sprinkled with Buddhist phrases and are fully imbued with the spirit of Buddhist mysticism.

With the eclipse of the Buddhist church after the middle of the sixteenth century, the Buddhist school of historiography eventually died out. Sinified scholars replaced the priesthood as the chief literate class in Japan, and history was again written primarily in the Chinese style. The years of peace and prosperity which followed the establishment in 1600 of the Tokugawa hegemony in Japan were congenial to the spread of Confucianism and the growth of scholarship in all fields. It was largely during the following two and a half centuries that the foundations for Japan's modern historiographical development were laid. Influenced by the increasingly critical method of historical and philological research which flourished in China during the period from the sixteenth through the nineteenth century, Japanese scholars applied new insight and skills to the study of their national history.

Chief among the historical works of this age were the various products of official sponsorship, the great collaborative histories such as the *Veritable Records of the Tokugawa* referred to above. Another such work, the *Comprehensive Mirror of Japan* (*Honchō tsugan*, 1670), was compiled by members of the officially favored Hayashi school of Confucian scholars. A painstaking and rationalistic history of Japan from the country's origins to 1611, it was patterned on the style of the famous *Complete Mirror for Government* (*Tzu-chih t'ung-chien*) by China's Ssu-ma Kuang (1019–1086).

The *History of Japan* (*Dai Nihonshi*), sponsored by the Mito branch of the Tokugawa house, was the first successful attempt of the Japanese to write according to the Chinese pattern of the "dynastic history." [8] A most ambitious work, it occupied the efforts of a large compilation board from 1657 to 1906. The work is remembered particularly for its emphasis upon the position of the emperor in Japanese history, but its importance to the historian lies more in the meticulous care with which it was written and the technique of giving documentation for every quotation used. The *History of Japan* covered Japanese history from its origins only to 1393. One of the most amazing feats of scholarship of the Tokugawa period was a continuation of this history compiled single-handed by Iida Tadahiko. This work, entitled the *Unofficial History of Japan* (*Dai Nihon yashi*, 1852), was written in the same high scholarly vein as its predecessor and carried the historical coverage down to 1829. In modern edition these two works take up nineteen volumes.

Of the individual historians of the Tokugawa period none was more famous or representative of his times than Arai Hakuseki (1656–1725). Arai was not only a statesman in the Confucian sense but also a scholar of wide versatility. His historical writings showed the influence of· his studies in archaeology, philology, and the records of foreign countries. His best-known work, *Historical Commentaries* (*Tokushi yoron*, 1712), was a rationalistic attempt to explain the rise and fall of political groups and classes. In it he developed to a high point the sense of periodization in history.

The above works of compilation and interpretation would hardly have been possible had it not been for the groundwork laid by scholars who brought together historical materials into libraries and reproduced them for general use. While it is true that some of Japan's special manuscript collections antedate the seventeenth century, it is chiefly during the Tokugawa period that the origins of Japan's modern libraries are found. The contemporary Imperial Household Ministry Library Department (Kunaisho Shoryōbu) and the Cabinet Library (Naikaku Bunko) are both heavily dependent upon the Shōheiko and Momiji-yama libraries of the Tokugawa shogunate.[9] The work of Hanawa Hokiichi (1746–1821) and his son also preceded modern scholarship in the collection, classification, and publication of historical texts. Hokiichi's *Classified Texts* (*Gunsho ruiju*, 1794) became the first of many works to provide in printed form a large number of basic but inaccessible historical sources. This work and its continuation are still in use by contemporary historians. In their modern editions they comprise ninety-one volumes and include over three thousand items. Hanawa's son began the task of making an exhaustive repository of historical documents arranged chronologically from the year 887. This enterprise, taken over by the University of Tokyo, became the foundation for Japan's modern national archival publication project.

Such works represent the main core of historiographical activity during the Tokugawa period. They constitute, however, but a fraction of the total volume of writings in history and related subjects produced during that era. By the eighteenth century scholarly studies were no longer limited to a narrow court circle or to individuals sponsored by the central military government. Nearly all of the more than 250 feudal lords patronized in some way the arts, letters, and sciences. No feudal domain of worth was without its school, its library, and coterie of Confucian scholars. The result was a sharp rise in both the quantity and variety of historical writing. Particularly noteworthy were the many local histories produced for the various feudal lords and the local collections of historical materials which paralleled those gathered by shogunal order.

Another stimulus to scholarship was created by the tremendous growth of the printing industry in Japan and the consequent increase in the availability of works both ancient and contemporary. The general spread of learning among diverse groups and classes encouraged variety and specialization in many fields. By the nineteenth century there began to appear in Japan numerous specialists within the historical field as well as in those fields of scholarship ancillary to history. Antiquarians produced treatises on words and usages, court ceremonies and customs, paintings and painters. Encyclopedists, working in established Chinese tradition, produced the antecedents to Japan's modern universal encyclopedias, and bibliographers began the task of examining critically Japan's heritage in the field of letters.

One movement of particular significance was originated by specialists who took up the philological investigation of ancient works of Japanese literature. Such activity resulted in the emergence of a school of anti-Confucian scholars dedicated to the restudy of Japan's early histories and sacred literature. Men such as Motoori Norinaga (1730–1801) and Hirata Atsutane (1776–1843) not only produced the first detailed commentaries on the *Record of Ancient Matters* and other works in the native tradition, but also injected the spirit of pride into the treatment of their national history.

II

By the middle of the nineteenth century, when Japan was thrust into the community of Western powers and her intellectuals were brought face to face with the latest developments in science and the academic disciplines of the West, she had already at her disposal a mature tradition of historical scholarship, based as we have seen on the sound, though antiquated, lines of Chinese methodology and growing in nationalistic self-consciousness. With the opening of Japan to Western intellectual influence, Japanese historians rapidly absorbed the new methods and philosophies which were offered them. Within a half century Japan was to erect the whole vast framework of national libraries, universities, professorships, scholarly journals, and research institutes which have been associated with the development of academic fields in the West. In the same short period Japanese historians were able to rework their written history and to reinforce their discipline with the publication of modern collections of source materials and the preparation of adequate reference works.[10]

In our analysis of the development of Japanese historiography during the eighty-five years since the Meiji Restoration of 1868 it will be convenient to define certain phases through which this development passed. The period embracing the first thirty years of the Meiji era, roughly until 1900, was understandably a time of transition. During these years, most historians continued to write in the old Chinese style, while others experimented in the new methodology learned from abroad. Perhaps it was inevitable that later generations should have found the research in the established tradition of more lasting value.

Much of such work was done at government request. The new Meiji government which succeeded the Tokugawa shogunate was faced with the double problem of modernization and consolidation. The establishment of new departments of government and the writing of new laws could not be done without a sound knowledge of the laws and administrative practices of the past. The central government itself was quick to set up a national historiographical office, while many individual departments of the new government sponsored the compilation of histories in fields related to their activities. Among these the *History of Japanese Currency* (*Dai Nihon kaheishi,* 1876–1883) and the *History of Taxation in Japan* (*Dai Nihon sozeishi,* 1883) compiled under the auspices of the Ministry of Finance, the *History of Japanese Agriculture* (*Dai Nihon nōshi,* 1890–1891) published by the Ministry of Agriculture and Commerce, and similar works put out by the Ministries of Justice and the Army and Navy Ministries are of continued value. Perhaps the most ambitious and useful of these compilations was the *Encyclopedia of Ancient Matters* (*Koji ruien*), a monumental encyclopedia in the Chinese manner. Begun in 1879 within the Ministry of Education, it was eventually passed on to the Department of Shrines, which in 1913 completed its publication in fifty-one volumes. This work epitomizes the value, as well as the limitations, of the Chinese method of historiography for the modern historian. Compiled with great care, it is in essence a gigantic repository of quotations from past literature, classified by subject and arranged in chronological order. The editors have provided a minimum of interpretation or explanation.

Meanwhile a group of Japanese historians influenced by Western thought had made its appearance. The Japanese of the late Tokugawa and early Meiji periods had been quick to make available in translation the works of contemporary European writers. Among the first to attract the attention of the Japanese were the works of the *laissez-faire* philosophers Mill and Spencer. Historians such as Henry Thomas Buckle (1821–1865) and François Guizot (1787–1874), whose broad interpretations of civilization presented such a stimulating contrast to the narrow bureaucratic writings of the Chinese school, were of particular appeal as well. Under the inspiration of such men the Japanese made their first experiments in the writing of cultural history. Two works of the 1870's, Fukuzawa Yukichi's *A Short Account of the Theory of Civilization* (*Bummei ron no gairyaku,* 1875) and Taguchi Ukichi's *Short History of Japanese Civilization* (*Nihon kaika shōshi,* 1877), opened the modern period of Japanese historiography.

The two currents of historical study described above were brought firmly together during the 1890's by a series of developments within the University of Tokyo. In 1886 the University had begun to offer lectures in history by the German historian Ludwig Reiss (1861–1928), a student of the famous Ranke. Under Reiss the German *Geschichts-*

wissenschaft school became established at the center of Japan's academic world. In quick succession there were founded the Historical Society (Shigakkai) and its *Journal of Historical Science* (*Shigaku-zasshi*). In 1895 the government moved its Historical Bureau to the University and so completed the establishment of the University as the center of historical research in Japan. The activities of the Historical Bureau, now called the Historiographical Institute (Shiryō Hensansho), are well known. Its chief function, the compilation of the *Historical Materials of Japan* (*Dai Nippon shiryō*), carries on the work of Hanawa Hokiichi, though it should be noted that the Institute has revised its methodology along more scientific lines learned from the example of Germany's *Monumenta Germaniae Historica*. It is safe to say that the combination of the University of Tokyo professorships and the Historiographical Institute dominated Japanese historical scholarship for the next quarter century. They have continued to stand at the forefront of history as an academic discipline in Japan.

III

A second phase in the development of modern Japanese historical scholarship occupied the first forty years of the twentieth century. During these years, historiography as a science reached maturity along four broad lines: (1) the creation of a modern historical methodology, (2) the writing of specialized monographic studies of particular institutions and aspects of Japanese civilization, (3) the preparation of general historical surveys, and (4) the publication of reference works and source materials.

In the field of methodology the outstanding work of the period was Kuroita Katsumi's *Study of Japanese History* (*Kokushi no kenkyū*, 1908). Kuroita, a product of the University of Tokyo and trained in the German historical-science tradition, succeeded in formalizing the periods of Japanese historical development and supplying a definitive evaluation of the standard historical sources used by his generation. By the time Kuroita wrote, the field of history in Japan had already become divided both horizontally by periods and vertically by topics into numerous specialties. Monographic studies of political history, foreign relations, legal institutions, economic history, and the history of art, literature, and religion had made their appearance. Such works, based as they were on the old-fashioned studies of the previous generation, were not always of lasting value. The specialized work of such men as Uchida Ginzō (1872–1919) and Miura Hiroyuki (1871–1931) were especially brilliant, however, and in many instances have only recently been superseded. By the 1920's the ground had been prepared for the appearance of new and more mature historical surveys. Two works of continuing importance in this category were the *Cultural History of Japan* (*Nihon bunkashi*), published in 1922 in twelve volumes, and the *Synthetic Survey of Japanese History* (*Sōgō kokushi taikei*), published in 1926 in twenty volumes. Both of these combined the efforts of a number of recognized scholars. The latter is still unsurpassed for its factual content and excellence of documentation.

By 1900 the Historiographical Institute of the University of Tokyo had begun publication of its *Historical Materials of Japan* and its *Ancient Documents of Japan* (*Dai Nippon komonjo*). To these were later added other basic documentary series relating to the Meiji Restoration and foreign affairs. The number of volumes put out by the Institute has by now grown to over three hundred. Concurrently several private organizations took up the task of providing in modern printed form hitherto inaccessible historical materials. Two such groups warrant special attention. One of them, the Society for the Publication of Japanese Texts (Kokusho Kankōkai), has brought out over 260 volumes of premodern documentary collections, collected works, and historically significant miscellanies. The other, the Association for Japanese Historical Works (Nihon Shiseki Kyōkai), has printed some 183 volumes of materials covering the Restoration. Thus the scholars of the early twentieth century were amply provided with materials with which to work.

The academic calm which had long prevailed in the field of Japanese historical studies was eventually broken during the 1930's. Social and political problems which appeared in the backwash of the First World War began to agitate the country. Japanese scholars became more and more absorbed in ideological conflicts. Though the orthodox school of political history continued at the University of Tokyo under the leadership of Kuroita and his followers and the cultural history school was kept alive at Kyōto University by Nishida Naojirō, the initiative went into the hands of the social and economic historians. During the late 1920's and early 1930's such men as Honjō Eijirō, Ono Takeo, and Yanagida Kunio led the movement away from political and cultural history toward consideration of economic and social problems. This movement represented not only an ideological revolt against the orthodox schools of historiography but a search for new sources of documentation.

The founding of three new scholarly associations indicated the shift in interests manifested by the Japanese of the early 1930's. The first of these, the Society for the Study of Economic History (Keizaishi Kenkyūkai), was organized at Kyōto University by Honjō Eijirō in 1929. A similar group, the Social and Economic History Society (Shakai Keizaishi Gakkai), was organized in Tokyo in 1931 chiefly around Ono Takeo. Later in 1933 a group of young historians of the Tokyo area organized themselves into the Historical Science Society (Rekishigaku Kenkyūkai), in protest over what they felt had been the overly "academic" approach of historical studies up to that time. Each of these groups published its own journal. Meanwhile leaders in the field of economic and social history such as Honjō, Ono, and Takimoto Seiichi had made available numerous collections of materials both primary and secondary in the general field of social and economic history. Takimoto's fifty-four volume *Compendium of Japanese Economics* (*Nihon keizai taiten*, 1928–1930), for instance, was only the most voluminous of many such collections which provided the materials for a new approach.

The period of the 1930's produced a great deal of historical writing of living value to the contemporary historian. The journals of the above-mentioned societies contained articles of high quality based on the use of primary and sound monographic sources. The documentary footnote and index, so often absent in previous works, came into general use. The purely methodological advance made by Japanese historians of this period is well illustrated in Kurita Motoji's three-volume *General Study of Japanese History* (*Sōgō kokushi no kenkyū*, 1933). This work is a critical guide to research and literature, both premodern and modern, in the several specialized fields of history. From about this time also, the publication of annual summaries of historical research and the appearance of indexes to periodical literature in the field of history indicate the desire of Japanese scholars to keep abreast of fast-moving developments within their field and their recognition of the importance of the research monograph.

Typical of the historical production of the 1930's were several excellent general surveys and reference works compiled as joint enterprises. The *Iwanami Series on Japanese History* (*Iwanami kōza, Nihon rekishi*), published in 1933–1935, brought together 134 specialized essays covering the entire field of Japanese history. The three volumes of the *Outline of World History* (*Sekai rekishi taikei*, 1935–1936) dealing with Japanese history represent the joint efforts of a number of young specialists in cultural, political, social, and economic history. The *Outline of Japanese Cultural History* (*Nihon bunkashi taikei*), a twelve-volume work completed between 1937 and 1942, is undoubtedly the most comprehensive survey currently available. Each volume covers a single era and is written by a number of scholars each dealing with a small area of specialization.

IV

During the late 1930's, as Japan began her expansion on the continent and drifted toward war in the Pacific, her scholarly world was torn increasingly between the two forces of Left and Right. A strong Marxist influence, which had had its origin as far back as the 'twenties, had captured the minds of many of the most active writers of the period. Historians of this group placed special emphasis upon interpretations of the Meiji Restoration and the attempts to apply the Marxist formula to the general economic growth of Japan. Their most significant contribution before their eventual liquidation was the series entitled *Essays on the History of the Development of Capitalism in Japan* (*Nihon shihonshugi hattatsushi kōza*), published in seven volumes between 1932 and 1933. By this time, however, Marxists were under strong attack. After the middle 'thirties open expression of Marxist beliefs declined, though a strong underground sympathy for them continued among Japanese intellectuals.

On the other hand the drift toward nationalistic writing continued to grow. Incited by the general atmosphere of expansionism or cowed by the pressure of government and public opinion, many historians lent their energies to propagandistic purposes. The late 'thirties saw many works on Japan's national uniqueness (*kokutai*) and on her past military virtues (*bushidō*). Increasingly as we move into the period of the Pacific war, books on general historical subjects become unreliable. It is encouraging to note, however, that the major historical journals continued to publish objective and highly scholarly articles, albeit of a less-controversial nature than previously. But even these organs were obliged to cease publication as the privations of war had their effect upon the economy. By 1945, when the war came to an end, Japan had been for nearly two years virtually without publication in the historical field.

V

With the termination of the Pacific war, Japan embarked upon the slow process of rehabilitating her economic and her spiritual life.[11] The war had been extremely damaging to Japan's academic institutions, and much reconstruction was necessary before she could once again attain her prewar level of scholarly production. It soon became evident that the new Japan was to be considerably changed from that of prewar times. By 1947 the effect of SCAP policies upon Japan's educational system was becoming apparent. Some of the effects were undoubtedly unexpected. The purging of many of the old-guard scholars had brought a large number of new, young men into the universities, while the freedom of expression which the Occupation authorities permitted the Japanese encouraged a vigorous iconoclasm among Japanese intellectuals. It soon became clear that many of the new scholars were men of Marxist conviction whose desire to express themselves was doubly great owing to the long years of silence imposed upon them during the war. In the historical field the first wave of postwar activity was largely the product of such men. Infiltrating the established Historical Science Society (Rekishagaku Kenkyūkai), they took the lead in publishing the first revisionary historical works after the war.

As a whole the historical literature coming out of the early postwar period was of an ephemeral nature. Most of it was hastily written for ideological purposes. "New" histories of Japan were written by the score both by old-guard historians eager to show their democratic conversion and by Marxists equally eager to exploit the freedom of the times. Gradually, however, the academic scene began to settle down. By the end of the year 1951 Japanese historians were again producing works of excellent quality and objectivity.

A survey of the contemporary scene in Japan still shows the University of Tokyo to be the nerve center of historical research. The combination of its professorships and its Historiographical Institute is by far the strongest force in the historical field, a force which has been strengthened recently by the reorganization of the Institute into a research body. *The Journal of Historical Science* has taken on new vigor and is again at the head of the professional journals in the field. The Historical Science Society, which in its early postwar years manifested such a strong leftist tendency, is still extremely active though less aggressive in its political action. It remains the headquarters of the so-called "progressive" historians of Japan. Another of the prewar groups, the Social and Economic History Society, led by Professor Nomura Kentarō of Keiō University, has revived its activities but is still weak from the effects of the war.

A marked change in the Tokyo scene has been the establishment of a number of new libraries and archival collections, many of them with attached research bodies. The establishment of the National Diet Library (Kokuritsu Kokkai Toshokan) has co-ordinated the many scattered special libraries of prewar days. The Diet Library itself is engaged in the collection of materials on the leaders of the Restoration period in Japan. Another institution of considerable significance is the Archival Center (Shiryōkan), which is engaged in the collection of materials on the Tokugawa period. Two government research institutes attached to the Ministry of Agriculture and Forestry are also engaged in valuable, though not strictly historical, research. The National Research Institute of Agriculture (Sōgō Nōgyō Kenkyūsho) publishes not only a journal but a large number of monographs on all aspects of economic history. The Institute for the Study of the Culture of the Common People (Nihon Jōmin Bunka Kenkyūsho) is engaged in the collection and analysis of documents concerning Japan's premodern peasant and fishing population.

The second-most-important center of historical research in Japan today is Kyōto. While many of the lesser educational institutions are in bitter disagreement over the problems of historical methodology, the University of Kyōto has managed to keep above such conflicts. The Institute for the Study of Economic History is now defunct and its journal no longer published. However, Horie Yasuzō of the Department of Economics continues the tradition of the Honjō school. The reorganized Research Institute of Humanistic Science is perhaps the group most worthy of attention, both for the quality of its publications and the anti-Marxist attitude of its members. It is presently engaged in two broad lines of research. The historical subsection under Sakata Yoshio conducts a seminar on the modernization of Japan and so far has published many excellent monographs on the Meiji Restoration. Its *Journal of Humanistic Science* (*Jinbun Gakuhō*) must be placed in the first rank of historical periodicals. Another subsection engaged in research on contemporary social problems, although primarily concerned with contemporary village studies, has also produced a number of inter-disciplinary historical field studies of considerable value. These are published in its *Social Survey Reports of the Research Institute of Humanistic Sciences, Kyōto University* (*Kyōto Daigaku Jimbun Kagaku Kenkyūsho chōsa hōkoku*).

Aside from these major centers, nearly all of the prewar universities have rebuilt their facilities for historical research. Among them there is in evidence a great propensity for joint or interdisciplinary projects. The recent publication by Keiō and Ōsaka City Universities of two excellent studies of the social and economic development of Japanese villages during the feudal period is typical of the work of such groups.[12] As a result of SCAP educational reform a large number of new pre-fectural universities have been added to the prewar universities. While these institutions are still in the formative stage of their development, they have already had a striking impact upon the development of his-torical studies in Japan. The new universities, by creating local centers of research, have had the effect of causing a decentralization of scholar-ship and stimulating interest in local history. This in turn has given rise to the organization of the Committee for the Study of Local History (Chihōshi Kenkyū Kyōgikai) with headquarters in Tokyo. This group has been publishing since 1950 the journal *Studies in Local History* (*Chihōshi kenkyū*), in an effort to co-ordinate and stimulate the de-velopment of this subject. The *Manual for the Study of Local History* (*Chihōshi kenkyū hikkei*, 1952) put out by the Committee constitutes a milestone in this development. In recent years encouraging progress has been made in the discovery of new historical sources, generally at the local level, and in the gathering of such materials into local archival libraries.

Summarizing the work of Japanese historians of the postwar years, it would be safe to say that by 1952 a stage of production approaching that of the prewar 1930's had been reached. Nearly all fields have been thoroughly reworked since the end of the war and new surveys are making their appearance in great numbers. Of these the *Japanese History Series* (*Nihon rekishi kōza*, 1952–) and the *New Series on Japanese History* (*Shin Nihonshi kōza*, 1950–) are modeled on the earlier multi-volume Iwanami series. A comparison between the titles in the old and new series, however, clearly reveals the shift in interest to social and economic problems which is so strongly evident in Japan today. In contrast to the above series, which represent the work of the "progressive" historians, another series, the *New Survey of Japanese History* (*Shin Nihonshi taikei*, 1952–), is being published by more conservative historians of Tokyo and Kyōto.

Perhaps the outstanding work to come out of postwar Japan is the monumental *Encyclopedia of World History* (*Sekai rekishi jiten*, 1951–). This work is scheduled to run to nineteen volumes and devotes approximately equal space to the history of Japan, China and adjacent areas, India and the Near East, and Europe and America. Articles cover both specific items, such as persons and incidents, and broad subjects, such as historical periods and movements. They are for the most part authoritative and well documented.

Lacking as yet in the postwar years are adequate bibliographical guides. No one has yet undertaken to bring Kurita's work up-to-date.[13] And although both the Historical Society of the University of Tokyo and the Historical Science Society have published bibliographies of postwar historical literature, these works are overly selective and leave much to be desired.[14]

We are as yet too close to the end of the Pacific war to make valid prognostications for the future of current historical trends in Japan. One is struck, however, with the vigor of the present generation of Japanese historians, their sound training, and their awareness of the complex problems faced by historians the world over. Perhaps the greatest effect of war, defeat, and occupation has been to break up the formalization which had begun to take place before the war and to force a diversity and decentralization upon the Japanese academic community. Today there are vastly more students, universities, research institutes, and scholarly journals than during the most active period of the 1930's. And while quantity does not necessarily lead to quality, the present generation of historians is certainly being forced to expand its efforts in many diverse ways. The Occupation has also forcibly stimulated new thoughts and sentiments among the Japanese. The study of formerly neglected or avoided subjects, especially within the field of Japan's modern political history, is now possible. And the volume of frank studies of the emperor system or of Japan's modern diplomacy has begun to swell. Japanese historians have shown increasing interest in the development of the social sciences in this country. Interdisciplinary studies of historical problems and field expeditions which attempt to link contemporary observation and historical research are now a common occurrence. Today many historians combine in their backgrounds training in more than one discipline.

How deep-rooted these new trends are is still a matter of conjecture. In the past the Japanese have often pursued new methods merely for novelty or in an attempt to find easy techniques to accomplish difficult tasks. The tendency to let the Marxist formula take the place of sound research is still strong, but it is waning. There are encouraging signs, notably in such institutions as the Kyōto Research Institute of Humanistic Science, that Japanese scholars are aware that there is no methodological panacea for the complex problems the historian must face.

1. The writer has gathered much of the material for this study in the course of the last two years, during which he received financial support from the University of Michigan Center for Japanese Studies and the University of Michigan's Horace H. Rackham School of Graduate Studies for research in historical bibliography. The year 1952 was spent in Japan. The writer wishes to express his gratitude to Mr. Kanai Madoka and Mr. Sugiyama Hiroshi of the University of Tokyo Historiographical Institute, whose assistance during his study in Japan was most valuable.

2. Interpretive surveys of Japanese historiography are not numerous either in Japanese or in Western languages. The article by Hugh Borton, "A Survey of Japanese Historiography," *American Historical Review*, LIII (1938), 489–499, is concerned primarily with historical works rather than the philosophical or methodological development of Japanese historiography. The most recent and satisfactory survey in Japanese is the article on historiography in *Sekai rekishi jiten (Encyclopedia of World History)* (Tokyo, 1952–), VIII, 246–250. Other standard works on the subject are Izu Kimio, *Nihon shigakushi (A History of Japanese Historiography)*, revised ed. (Tokyo, 1949), a highly interpretive analysis from a Marxist point of view; Kawaguchi Hakuho, *Nihon kokushigaku hattatsushi (History of the Development of Historiography in Japan)* (Tokyo, 1936), one of the few studies to cover both the ancient and modern periods; Kiyohara Sadao, *Nihon shigakushi (History of*

Japanese Historiography), revised ed. (Tokyo, 1944), which covers in great detail the period up to 1911; and Shigakkai, *Hompō shigakushi ronsō* (*Essays on Japanese Historiography*), 2 vols. (Tokyo, 1939), the first essay of which, by Tsuji Zennosuke, gives a useful résumé of historiography in Japan from its origins to roughly the time of writing.

3. Several surveys of Japanese historical literature have appeared in Western languages. The most accessible in this country is that of Hugh Borton, mentioned in the previous note. More detailed in its coverage of the premodern period is Claude Maître, "La Littérature historique du Japon," *Bulletin de l'École Française d'Extrême-Orient*, III (1903), 564–596. Covering shorter periods of time but stimulating for their interpretations are Chitoshi Yanaga, "Source Materials in Japanese History: The Kamakura Period, 1192–1333," *Journal of the American Oriental Society*, LIX (1939), 38–55; and the introductory portions of Reischauer and Yamagiwa, *Translations from Early Japanese Literature* (Cambridge, Mass., 1951). In Japanese the classic work on early historical works is Kuroita Katsumi, *Kokushi no kenkyū* (*Study of Japanese History*), revised ed., 4 vols. (Tokyo, 1931–1936), the first volume of which deals with literature in the several branches of history. A handy reference to premodern classics in the field of history is Ōmori Kingorō's *Shiseki kaisetsu* (*Annotated Bibliography of Historical Materials*) (Tokyo, 1937). For an analytical treatment of individual works of historical writing, the previously cited work by the Shigakki is outstanding.

4. For information on the existence of translations of certain classical works of Japanese history see Borton, Elisséeff, and Reischauer, *A Selected List of Books and Articles on Japan in English, French, and German* (Washington, 1940). Those who wish to obtain access to modern printed editions of standard works of early historiography should consult Endo Motoo et al., *Shiseki kaidai* (*An Annotated Bibliography of Historical Works*) (Tokyo, 1936).

5. See Charles S. Gardner, *Chinese Traditional Historiography* (Cambridge, 1938), for a detailed study of this subject. More recent is the article on Chinese historiography in *Sekai rekishi jiten*, VIII, 232–237. The standard work in Japanese is Naitō Torajirō, *Shina shigakushi* (*History of Chinese Historiography*) (Tokyo, 1949).

6. For an interesting controversy over the degree of objectivity attained by the Chinese historian see Clyde B. Sargent, "Subsidized History," *Far Eastern Quarterly*, III (1944), 119–143, and H. H. Dubbs, "The Reliability of Chinese Histories," *Far Eastern Quarterly*, VI (1946), 23–43.

7. G. B. Sansom, *Japan, A Short Cultural History* (New York, 1943), p. 380.

8. This differed from the chronicle style in that the whole work was divided into four parts: imperial annals, tables, essays, and biographies. Tables were largely genealogies and lists of officials; essays covered ceremonies, religion, economic development, literature, etc.; biographies were of prominent offi-

cials and military figures. This section also included résumés of foreign intercourse by countries.

9. An excellent history of Japanese libraries and manuscript collections is to be found in Ono Noriaki, *Nihon toshokanshi* (*History of Japanese Libraries*) (Kyōto, 1952).

10. Several excellent surveys of the development of historical studies in post-Restoration Japan are available. In Western language the article entitled "Japon" by Serge Elisséev in *Histoire et historiens depuis cinquante ans* (Paris, 1928) presents a compact summary. More voluminous and full of much useful information is Akiyama Kenzō's "Orientation in the Study of Japanese History," in *A Guide to Japanese Studies* (Tokyo, 1937). In Japanese, two works are outstanding: *Meiji igo ni okeru rekishigaku no hattatsu* (*Development of Historical Studies since Meiji*) (Tokyo, 1933) and "Shakai keizai shigaku no hattatsu" (Social and Economic History of Japan, Its Recent Development), in *Shakaikeizaishigaku* (*Journal of the Social and Economic History Society*), X (1941), 9–10. Both these works contain articles by specialists on the development of research in a wide variety of historical fields. For information on individual works written in the post-Restoration period the standard annotated bibliographies are Kurita Motoji, *Sōgō kokushi kenkyū* (*General Study of Japanese History*), 3 vols. (Tokyo, 1935), and Honjō Eijirō, *Kaihan Nihon keizaishi bunken* (*Bibliography of Japanese Economic History, Revised*) (Tokyo, 1933) and its continuations published in 1942 and 1953.

11. No adequate survey of historical studies in the postwar period has appeared in English. Readers will find the review and news sections of the *Far Eastern Quarterly* helpful in gaining some knowledge of recent Japanese publications in the field of history. In Japanese, the Kyōto Daigaku Shimbunsha's *Gakkai no jiten* (*Dictionary of the Academic World*) (Tambaichi, 1951) is a handy guide to research groups. Annual reviews of the previous year's historical publications are published as a special issue of the *Shigaku-zasshi* (*Journal of Historical Science*) and by the Historical Science Society in its *Rekishigaku no seika to kadai* (*Historical Studies, Accomplishments, and Problems*) (Tokyo, 1950–). Perhaps the best indication of the state of current historical research in Japan is to be found in the lists of subsidized research completed or in progress which are issued periodically by the Ministry of Education. The lack of private research funds in Japan has made it inevitable that scholars should look to the government for resources to carry on their work.

12. "Kantō nōson no shiteki kenkyū" (Historical Studies on the Villages in the Kanto District), *Mita Gakkai zasshi* (*Mita Journal of Economics*, Tokyo), XLIV (1951), 2; and "Rekishi no furui nōson no shosō" (Some Aspects of a Japanese Historical Village), *Jimbun kenkyū* (*Studies in the Humanities*, Ōsaka), III (1952), 4.

13. For an attempt to do this in English see the present author's *Japanese*

History, A Guide to Japanese Research and Reference Materials (Ann Arbor, Mich., 1954).

14. See Shigakkai, *Shigaku bunken mokuroku (Bibliography of Historical Studies, 1946–1950)* (Tokyo, 1951); and Rekishigaku Kenkyūkai, *Rekishigaku no seika to kadai (Historical Studies, Accomplishments, and Problems)*, annual (Tokyo, 1950–).

PROBLEMS OF

INTERPRETATION

[ALLEN GILMORE]

Trends, Periods, and Classes

ANY historical interpretation of the past is necessarily arranged in terms of abstract concepts. The degree of abstraction will vary from the relatively high to the relatively low. Some of a historian's concepts will be close to the ground of actuality; in these cases, if need be, he can point to the thing he is discussing. A manuscript can be examined, a site explored, a constitution read, or a census taken. The circumstances are either as described, or else they are not; and you know where you stand. The pointing need not be direct, and may, indeed, be very devious, such as a reference to the bridge built by Charlemagne across the Rhine (which has since been destroyed) or to the Island of Bali (which neither historian nor reader may ever have visited). The important thing is that something either is or was there in the most obvious physical sense. The meaning of the concept can be established by pointing to the thing.

At higher levels of abstraction the meaning of historical concepts cannot be established by pointing. The "thing" may indeed be "there," but surely not in the same sense as Charlemagne's bridge. The "growth of the English constitution," the "collapse of France in 1940," or the "rule of the middle class" are not entities that can be isolated or identified as successfully as bridges and islands. The nature of their existence differs.

Some key concepts with which a historian normally works (we may take as examples the concept of a trend, the concept of a historical age or period, and the concept of a social class) are of this kind. The existence of the things to which these concepts refer is not like that of the stone that was kicked by Dr. Samuel Johnson to prove the reality of matter. Whatever may be their nature, these things are not of the sort that can be kicked or pointed at. They occupy a level on the ladder of abstraction that we may loosely say is rather high. These concepts, in other words, are relatively remote from the world of concrete physical objects.

It is not enough, however, to point out that a historian sometimes operates on the upper levels of abstraction. It is important, of course, to know how high up he is; but it is even more important to know how he got there. For one can arrive at a given level of abstraction by various means. It is necessary to recognize that the concept of a historical period is an abstraction of a fairly high order; but one wants also to know by what procedures this abstraction was constructed. In other words, one wants to know as precisely as possible what the relation is between the concept and physical actuality.

The mental processes involved in the construction of concepts may be divided into three categories. Some concepts are deductive. These are created by a systematic and logical elaboration of a given set of assumptions and premises. The concepts employed in mathematics are the best example of this category. Other concepts are inductive. In this case objective reality is deliberately and arbitrarily simplified according to a plan of analysis; this or that observed feature is abstracted from the confusion of the actual world to be used as part of a model for experimentation. These are the procedures usually described as scientific. Finally, there is a third class of concepts: those arrived at intuitively. In this case emotion, or an act of faith, or a sudden artistic insight serves as the means of simplifying observed reality. Most complex mental operations probably involve some elements from each of these three categories. The distinctions made here are extremely rough, intended to serve merely as a convenient basis for the following discussion.

The question is not what historians might or should do, but what do they do? What mental processes do they in fact employ to arrive at such concepts as trends, periods, and classes? To find out what they mean by these concepts it is necessary to consider their behavior.

The meanings of historical usage are partly the meanings of ordinary language. For many centuries history was considered a branch of literature. A very ancient tradition, with a profound influence on the behavior of present-day historians, regards history as a vehicle for artistic expression. Its primary purpose (in terms of this tradition) is to edify rather than inform. Its techniques, according to this view, are those appropriate to artistic insight rather than objective analysis. It is true that in the last hundred years this tradition has been attacked, and emphasis placed on objectivity and scientific method. But the weight of the literary tradition is nevertheless great; and this is especially the case in the area of unconscious assumption where basic conceptual habits are formed and practiced.

One sign of the continued importance of history considered as literature is the lack among historians of a professional vocabulary. In large part the terms employed by historians are those of ordinary usage. Historians, indeed, pride themselves on this, and lay claim to the ability to address and communicate with any educated audience. They make a deliberate effort to avoid what they call the "jargon" or "gobbledegook" of a specialized craft. They talk and write the way everyone else does. They do not feel the need of cutting themselves off from laymen by using an esoteric vocabulary.

The intimate connection with literature and the effort to use a non-professional vocabulary suggest that the meanings of historical concepts are often established by the same methods as the meanings of popular concepts—the meanings, that is, of everyday language. In neither case is there an explicit theory of meaning. What is meant depends not on a worked-out relationship between the word and the thing referred to, but only on usage. A historian, like the man on the street, talks like that simply because he talks like that.

This point may be illustrated first by some examples from ordinary speech. Consider the man who has just received some unexpected information and desires to describe his reaction. He might say he is "stunned" at the news. Or he might say he is "overwhelmed." He might even say that he is "literally bowled over" by the news. (In this last case he means, of course, that he is *figuratively* bowled over—precisely the opposite of what he says.) The distinctions of meaning in these phrases are not precise because they derive from the subjective feelings of the speaker rather than from the nature of the event referred to. The technique of expression employed is metaphor—a standard literary device. The man who says he is stunned means that the effect of the receipt of the news is *as if* he had been dealt a blow over the head. But there is no necessary connection between a metaphorical expression and what actually happened. There is no theory of meaning at all. The essence of metaphor would seem to be imprecision, subjectivity, and suggestion.

In spite, or perhaps because, of its lack of clarity and objectivity, metaphor as a literary device based upon usage may be useful, beautiful, or even profound. It is frequently used and understood, however, not merely as an artistic device but also as a descriptive technique. The two in fact are confused. When the figure of speech is implicit (as in the cases cited), it is often not considered a figure of speech at all. Instead it is taken as a literal description of reality—which it most certainly is not. In this sense, as a method purporting to convey an objective account of what happened, metaphor is fraught with grave dangers—especially in the field of historical writing.

These difficulties are readily apparent when popular and journalistic accounts of social events employ metaphor, as they so frequently and loosely do. The current newspaper concepts of the "cold war" and of the "iron curtain" between the East and the West are really elaborate figures of speech. Relations between the two areas are so bad it is as if they were fighting a war; we know so little about what goes on in the Soviet world it is as if we were separated from it by an impenetrable barrier. In strict fact, of course, there is no war and there is no iron curtain. The important question, then, is one of degree. How much is the reality like the thing to which it is compared? In what respects do the two elements of the metaphor overlap? In what respects are they different? My love is like a red, red rose; but she is not *exactly* like a red, red rose. For instance, she has no thorns.

The "iron curtain" metaphor, based not on theory but on usage, does not answer the important question of the relation of word to thing. On the contrary, constant repetition tends by assumption, without ever raising the question, to make of the figurative a literal expression; that is, to suggest erroneously that the degree of overlap is complete. The phrase "stunned to hear the news" is generally (but wrongly) taken as a literal phrase. The iron curtain comes in the same manner to possess an objective existence, which is emphasized as the figure is elaborated. People have to go around or under or fly over it to go from one spot on the earth's surface to another. Sounds are heard through it only faintly. A few cracks do exist in its structure, and one may hope they will some day be widened. But the barrier is "really" insurmountable;

only the Russians can remove it if they will. But who knows what they will do, or are even now doing, concealed as they are behind this thick wall? The more it is talked about and becomes established in usage, the more the iron curtain becomes a concrete thing.

Historians, if not the general public, may be counted on to recognize this popular and journalistic approach as a way of making, that is, of urging, a point. It is a rhetorical and not a descriptive device, subjective rather than objective, burdened with overtones and value judgments. To say this is not to condemn the use of metaphor for such purposes, but to point out that it is extremely important that the purpose be kept clear. To consider the examples mentioned above as more than subjective literary devices, to present them as objective descriptions of society, is misleading, inaccurate, biased, and generally in flagrant opposition to the ideals scholars uphold.

The extent to which the historian himself employs metaphor, and without a careful clarification of purpose, is something (like the nose on his face) that is constantly before his eyes but he does not see. Consider the following terms which are an everyday part of a historian's vocabulary: "fall," "collapse," "decline," "rise," "growth," "overthrow," "revolution," "revival," "renaissance." These words are not used to describe the motions of physical or even of living bodies, but of ideas, of institutions, of nations, and often of the whole complex of human affairs that we call civilization. To some extent the scholars who use these terms are dramatizing rather than describing. What they really mean is implied by the addition of an (understood) paraphrase: "In our opinion these changes, which it would be too lengthy and too dull to enumerate one by one, are comparable to the growth of a plant," or whatever thing or things they have in mind. But the difficulty remains. What does it mean to say one thing is "comparable to" something else? Without precise definition the connection between word and thing cannot be traced. The exact degree of correspondence is of crucial importance; without it, the meaning of the assertion is poetic and cannot be demonstrated.

My intent is not to disparage this kind of writing, but merely to clarify its place and purpose. When metaphors are presented to readers or understood by them as things, and not merely as words, reality assumes some very strange shapes indeed, and the gravest of misunderstandings almost necessarily follow. Perhaps historians can trust one another to appreciate the need for poetic dramatizations and to allow for the rhetorical force of figurative speech, but the same can hardly be said for the nonprofessional. What does an ordinary reader make of these "rises" and "falls," these "rebirths" (surely curious phenomena in nature) and "declines"? The best that can be said is that his picture of reality will not be nearly as full, as complete, and as accurate as the writer intended. And it remains frighteningly possible that he will understand the figure literally, and believe the world actually to be populated by these similes and metaphors, these imaginary beings and strange creatures of the mind.

There is an ever-present inclination of the uneducated to transform an allegorical allusion into a literal reality, to bring a metaphor clumsily and inappropriately to earth. Once a history student, presented with the statement that Napoleon "cut" the Austrian lines of communication in the Italian campaign of 1796, pictured the operation in its most literal sense. There had to be something physical if one was to cut as with a pair of shears. Hence he imagined railway, telephone, and telegraph lines—snip, snip, snip. When, pushed to further investigation, he discovered that humanity was blessed with none of these conveniences at the time, his picture disintegrated, leaving only a blank canvas and the conviction, which still prevailed, that something had been cut. And it is likely that he was unusual only in making further investigation. Most students never come to a position where they can hear with comfort an argument to show that there was no "Renaissance," or that the "fall" of Rome was not noticeable at the time.

Perhaps the habit of making realities out of metaphors results in no more than harmless academic misunderstanding when it is a question of Napoleon cutting the enemy to shreds or enslaving the free peoples of Europe. When, however, such figurative concepts are drawn from the more recent past and serve as a basis for men's actions, the consequences are more serious. If "labor" and "management" are to sit at a table to negotiate, it is of the utmost importance to know the relation between abstract concept and concrete thing. You can't do business with a metaphor. If "free enterprise" is to "challenge bureaucracy" successfully, the literal groundwork of these abstract figures must be known.

What ordinary people understand by the concepts historians employ is not, however, the main question. It is an important question, but somewhat irrelevant to our purpose. What we want to know is what

312

the historians themselves mean by the abstractions that are such a crucial part of their thought and expression. They, like any other observers, are faced with the chaos and infinity of human experience from which they abstract (or upon which they impose) an order. Their idea of order is not haphazard, but the product of careful professional training. Their judgments are expert judgments. But what is the nature and meaning of this order? And how is it perceived or created? Is it logical? Or inductive? Or metaphorical? Or some definable combination of the three?

There would seem to be two possibilities. It could be, on the one hand, that a historian is a man of artistic perception whose judgments are to be entrusted *as artistic judgments* partly because he is familiar with his materials and partly because he is an artist. There is nothing to do with an artist anyway, except trust him—or mistrust him. On the other hand, a historian could be an expert, familiar with his material, who is trusted because he employs a disciplined technique of conceptual analysis. In this case the technique must be one that can be critically described and defended.

In both alternatives the historian is assumed to be familiar with his materials. But it almost never helps in judging an expert to know that this is the case. The dentist or garage mechanic whose judgment you mistrust can generally be assumed to have enough professional knowledge; but that's not what you're worried about. A historian, notoriously, almost always *knows* more *about* his subject than anyone else. The question is: How does he proceed from knowledge about his material to judicious conclusions? Is this a matter of artistry or craft?

Observe first that a great many fundamental historical concepts imply the use of numbers. They suggest that a counting has taken place, or at least that a greater part has been separated from a smaller part by some kind of quantitative analysis. The "people" are said to "want" something. Public opinion is described as "deteriorating." The "proletariat" "decides" on a particular course of action. There is a "tendency" toward stability, or a "trend" toward nationalism. A "dynamic" is contrasted with a "static" economy. The eighteenth century is referred to as the "Age of Reason."

In each of these cases numbers are implied, but (and this is the important point) they are seldom given. How many individuals possessing what elements in common does it take to make a social class? How many items in what sequence to make a trend? How many repetitions of what common denominators to make an age or period? The writer says in effect, "I have here a certain number of individuals possessing certain striking characteristics in common, and I therefore imagine them to be a collective unit. This unit, or class, in turn, I can further imagine to be endowed with human attributes and to engage in various activities: it struggles, it rises, it falls, it is exploited." The trouble is that these activities are so fascinating, make such an absorbing appeal to our human emotions and sympathies, that it is all too easy for both writer and reader to lose sight of the mental steps that brought the class into existence. It is important to know whether these steps can be retraced critically, or whether they ultimately depend on imagination.

The concept of a social class has been of immense use to historians. It is a convenient symbol or shorthand that has been employed in many directions with considerable profit. As a symbol it seems neat and clear and can be used in conjunction with other symbols in useful and suggestive ways. For instance, the middle class as a ruling group in the nineteenth century can be (and often is) compared with the noble class that dominated society in the thirteenth. But the meaning of the concept itself has little of this neatness, clarity, and convenience. When the infinite details of an actual social situation are regarded with open eyes, the concept blurs and the clean picture fades tantalizingly away. It is uncertain how much weight should be given to economic or to social or to psychological factors; and it is equally uncertain how common the common denominators should be. Is a bare majority enough, or does one need a heavy preponderance of some particular factor?

These questions cannot be answered apart from particular cases. There are no abstractly "true" criteria of class. One is not so much looking for answers, in any case, as for an awareness of and concern with the problem. To employ the concept without defining some criteria puts an investigator outside the bounds of critical comment. A decision needs to be made and will, presumably, be a better decision if it is a conscious one. Its adequacy will depend on several elements: coherency, usefulness, and the point of view of the investigator. To be meaningful in a critical sense the concept of a class should have an inner logical structure and consistency. Different individuals can be grouped together only when they are judged by the same standards. The concept should be one that is relevant and applicable to the question under study. This means that it should both confirm or deny a hypothesis and be testable. At the same time it should add to one's understanding of the subject under discussion, that is, it should relate to the over-all point of view or purpose of the investigator.

Even a cursory glance at most historical writing will make it apparent what historians do when they employ the concept of a social class. Or rather what they do not do. For by tradition and inclination they shy away from what seem to them these overly subtle and abstract considerations. Discussions of the criteria of class are as infrequent in history books as accounts of the activities of classes are common. It is too often true that decisions about the meaning of the concept are unconscious. One can seldom follow step by step the mental operations historians perform when they create classes.

It is the argument of this essay that the only possible meaning of a concept like that of a social class is metaphorical when no other basis is provided for establishing meaning. A typical historian uses the concept of a class as a figure of speech, in very much the same way as the concept appears in popular usage. A number of individuals are grouped together as being "comparable to" a single entity (without explicitly establishing the basis of the comparison), and the entity then becomes a "thing" with a life of its own. It is perfectly true that a historian does observe individuals with care. (There are few who are better trained or more able to do this intelligently than he.) And he does perceive critically some features they have in common. But he then proceeds, most often, to jump intuitively to a high level of abstraction. He is very little interested in and usually says nothing of how he got there. We see the flying arrows of his imagination, but the courses of their flights cannot be followed by a critical eye.

It should be hastily added that one need not conclude because a perception is intuitive that it is necessarily bad. Such may or may not be the case. But a reader often has no means (other than his sense of artistic taste) to decide this question. The nature of the performance suddenly, but imperceptibly, changes before his eyes. At one moment a historian examining this individual and that is a scientist whose activities and assertions can be critically examined. At the next he is an artist (it may be a very good artist) whose metaphors and allegories are beyond the reach of controlled tests.

Inherently the concept of a historical period is just as fluid and slippery as that of a social class. One of the more common and successful ways for a young historian to make a reputation is to juggle this essential symbol. He may create a new period, or demonstrate that an old one has no validity. The "Renaissance" happened much earlier than is usually thought, these promising scholars will write; or they may undertake to prove that there "really" was no "Renaissance" at all. What a historian does when he consciously concerns himself with periods is to look for the existence or absence of certain common characteristics that reappear a certain number of times. What these are and how often they must reappear in order to justify the use of the symbol are matters to be determined by the writer's expert opinion. To conclude because it is opinion that the concept of a historical age has no validity, or to say that one opinion of this kind is as good as another, is a common error. It is not so common but even more of an error to conclude that something exists in nature that divides the past up into sections like those of a bamboo pole.

By and large historians are a great deal more aware what they are doing when they deal with periods than with social classes. Occasionally the "Age of Jackson" or the "Disillusioned Twenties" or the "Time of Troubles" takes on a metaphorical superexistence, becomes something more than a convenient symbol standing for a set of common elements reappearing a certain number of times. In these cases the concept is said to shape the action of individuals, rather than the other way around. But historians know—and for the most part show that they know—that not everyone who lived from 1920 to 1929 drank bath-tub gin, and they know that those who drank it did so not because they lived in a period of disillusionment but for other good and sufficient reasons. Although the concept, considered metaphysically, is just as subtle as that of a social class, historians are generally more explicit about their criteria, and can usually propound, if need be, the theory of meaning upon which it is constructed. It is more often possible to follow the operation of their minds. While this is perhaps natural enough (since one of their main activities is to place things in time), it makes all the more apparent their lack of awareness in regard to social classes.

We come finally to the historical conception of a trend, certainly one of the most characteristic and basic of all the concepts of history. The discernment of temporal patterns of change is what the historian regards as his main business. He observes and describes unique events, and at the same time he endeavors to establish their relation to one another. If we took from him such ideas as growth and decay, change and persistence, increase and decrease, rise and fall, he would be left with little to say.

There is no question but that the concept of a trend is highly abstract. One must conceptualize concrete actuality in order to perceive a trend. It is not the kind of thing that can be kicked or pointed at. When one speaks of a trend in temperature, there is nothing one can hold in one's hand and examine. Instead one must first create some measuring device, then read it at particular moments in time, and finally make a comparison of a number of readings over a given period of time. In the field of physics the meaning of a trend can be defined only in terms of some such set of operations.

In history, however, the operations are often forgotten, and trends seem to take on a separate existence of their own above and beyond the particular events which go to make them up. Thus, students in history courses are encouraged to recognize trends. They are sometimes told that factual materials are relatively unimportant; instead of memorizing these, they are instructed to concentrate on the larger currents in human affairs and tendencies of society. Trends are spoken of as "inevitable" and "irresistible." They sweep individuals along willy-nilly, and determine the course of their lives. Personalities like Napoleon's or Hitler's are said to be shaped by the trends of the age. Ultimately one approaches the conclusion (acceptable to Plato, but absurd to modern science) that the abstract determines the concrete, that the Form or the Idea is the only reality.

Few historians consciously subscribe to this conclusion. If you do not accept it (if, that is, you have some doubt that a trend belongs to a higher order of existence, a kind of supernature with an independent being of its own), then the meaning of a trend is to be determined by what a historian does. And he may do one of two things. Either he performs the sorts of operations that a physicist does in dealing with temperature trends, or he is making a literary, metaphorical, comparison.

If particular cases of a historian's use of the concept of a trend are examined, the question may be asked: Does he or does he not give the reader a definition of the meaning of the concept in terms of a set of operations that can be critically examined? The answer must be that all too frequently he does not. The reader in the vast preponderance of cases has no means of discovering a describable series of operations that would necessarily produce the concept in question. One is forced to the conclusion that the historian's mental operations were intuitive and cannot by their nature be described except as art. The process must be something like this: a number of events having been examined, a possible relationship suggests itself to the mind of the historian. He then concludes and without further ado presents to the reader the proposition that this relationship is "like" the growth of a plant, or "similar to" the decline of the sun. But in doing so the metaphor is left implicit, so that there is a strong inclination to assume that what happens is *literally* a growth, or is *in fact* a decline. His concern with a means of measuring or with the determination of a scale of frequency or intensity is negligible.

Because of this metaphorical element in his thought and method, the historian's expertness is often forgotten. Anyone can make a figure of speech about social events. Hence it is difficult for a nonhistorian to distinguish between a real expert and, say, a sports commentator who has turned into a foreign news analyst. The trained historical writer does himself an injustice in not making apparent to his reader just where this distinction lies. And the inability of the public to see the difference between a man who knows what he's talking about in this general subject area and one who does not is one of the most serious faults of our age.

Historians defend themselves by pointing out that the materials with which they work are not of the sort that can be measured quantitatively. The important judgments, they say, are not the ones that can be expressed in numbers. While this is true to some extent (although most historians are apt to neglect the very real accomplishments in this direction of the so-called policy sciences during the last decade or so), it is no real defense. The reader still wants and is entitled to know where knowledge leaves off and artistic insight begins. If metaphor is the only device that can be used, then the scholar is obliged to make it clear that that is what he is using. Up to some point no two reasonable men can differ about the validity of the statements a historian makes; beyond that point reasonable men may and do differ. In the discussion of any subject it is important to know just where this point is located.

The conclusions of this essay can easily be summarized. It was first taken as evident that historians do in fact make extensive use of abstract concepts. Then attention was focused on what historians do in the process of constructing and employing some typical concepts. It is recognized that the development of a concept is a complex matter that will involve at least three elements: deductive, inductive, and intuitive or metaphorical. The concept of a historical period seems to be largely inductive; historians operate in this respect with a more or less articulate and testable theory. Or, at least, if pressed, they can produce such a theory. In respect, however, to two other fundamental concepts, that of a social class and that of a trend, historians seem mainly to rely on intuitive procedures. The meaning of these concepts is largely a metaphorical meaning, supported by little or no theory and induced by the habit of long association with a literary tradition.

This essay is concerned with what historians do and do not do in the construction of concepts. It can fairly be said that they frequently, but for the most part unconsciously, speak a metaphorical language. It can also be said that they show a striking lack of concern with the problems that such an approach entails. They not only seldom have but do not seem to feel the need of a theory of meaning. They are reluctant to enter discussions of this subject, which make them uncomfortable and resentful. As a consequence their readers are left either naïvely to believe that their metaphors have some kind of concrete existence or to dismiss their conclusions as critically meaningless.

Having reached this point the author is tempted to step briefly from his position as cold observer and turn from what is to what ought to be. Mere awareness of a problem here and honest concern with it would make a great difference. The need is simply one of making apparent to readers where knowledge leaves off and faith or art begins. Much would be gained if historians would cease to hide their heads or act stuffily superior when these questions are raised. By avoiding or dodging the issue they do themselves a serious and unnecessary injustice. Trends, classes, periods—these complex "things" are important elements in all historical thought. And it is no use pretending their meaning is self-evident to common sense. The history profession sorely needs to do some honest worrying about the nature of its basic concepts.

[JOHN BOWDITCH]

War and the Historian

THE historian, even the historian who deals with the events of modern history, is prone to conservatism when it comes to dealing with the tools of his trade and the framework within which he constructs his image of the past. He dislikes novelty; he despises fads; he rises up in righteous anger against those younger branches of the social sciences that shamelessly break in upon his craft and, with little heed for that caution and sense of perspective in which he takes pride, take upon themselves the task of interpreting the complexities of contemporary human behavior and human society. That the historian today is somewhat on the defensive in this struggle to protect his birthright is only too evident. Society expects of its learned men that they use their knowledge of the past to throw light on the present, if not to predict the future. No doubt society always expects too much, but the historian of today may well feel disturbed, if not defensive, about the contribution he has made to solving twentieth-century man's dilemma, the problem of how to comprehend, let alone deal with, the tortured world in which he finds himself. How far, the historian may well ask himself, has he prepared his contemporaries for the phenomena of totalitarianism, for the gas chambers, for the purge trials, for—the subject which will occupy this paper— modern war?

That war has played an overwhelming role in our twentieth century is as evident to Everyman as to the professional historian. Even though it is only one of the forces that has shaped the course of recent events, war has been so powerful a force that no aspect of man's activities in the past forty years has failed to be urged on, twisted into new channels, or shattered by its impact. Everyman cannot escape war today even by relegating it to history; it lives with him daily when he opens his newspaper or turns on the radio, when he contemplates the twin phenomena of inflation and rising tax deductions from his pay checks, when he learns perhaps that a son or friend has been reported a war casualty. For if the First World War once could be popularly regarded as the war that ended wars, the Second World War, in effect, never reached a conclusion. Instead it merged into something euphemistically called "cold war," which carries with it the specter of yet a third world conflict too frightful for Everyman to contemplate. We are not merely aware of war today; we are obsessed with it.

Nor, it may be assumed, will the professional historian, if the subject is raised, dispute the assumption that war has played a prominent role throughout the modern era of Western society. If need be, statistics can be produced to show that in the period 1480–1945 there were 282 years of war, or more years of war than of peace, and that the United States alone in the period 1775–1900, when splendid isolation still had some meaning, fought nine thousand distinct battles and skirmishes.[1] One may argue the significance of such figures, but the historian can hardly blink the evidence that Western society from its inception has been an exceedingly warlike society and that the use of force has accompanied every stage of its development. If so much be conceded, then it must be granted that to discount the role of war when recording the history of that society is to act in a manner as unhistorical, as out of step with the dynamics of the modern era, as to fail to recognize the impact of Newtonian physics on Western thought or of the factory system on the economics of production. Furthermore, it exposes the professional historian to the serious charge of having betrayed his obligation to Everyman.

To what extent is the historian, and we are concerned here primarily with the historian in this country, guilty of such a charge? Obviously not entirely. There has always been at least a handful of American scholars willing to wear the unpopular label of military historian; many others can reject as unjust any accusation of having "left the wars out of history"[2] or of having been totally blind to the forces at work in our century. A distinction, too, must be made between the activities of historians in the years that separated the two World Wars, a period when concern with military questions reached a nadir in this country, and in recent years, in which serious efforts have been made to remedy the situation. Yet even when these qualifications are granted, and attention will be paid to them in the course of this paper, the complaint that Everyman can lay at the door of the academic historian is a far heavier one than is generally recognized within the profession.

To illustrate what has happened to the role of war in the hands of the American historian, let us look first at what he has done with the subject when dealing with his students in college and university classrooms, secondly at the interest he has shown in original research and the writing of monographs to enrich his own and his colleagues' understanding of the phenomenon of war, and finally at what he has produced in the way of historical literature of a general nature that transcends the monograph in scope and makes an appeal to Everyman as well as to the specialist. Admittedly these are interdependent and overlapping categories; they are introduced only for purposes of simplification.

A study of the catalogues of thirty leading American universities for the years 1935–1936 and 1951–1952 reveals that courses devoted specifically to military and naval history, if reserve-officer training programs are omitted, were virtually nonexistent in American universities before the Second World War, and today remain more the exception than the rule. Few historians in academic positions have felt competent to teach such courses or have wanted to admit the need of them, and where reserve-officer programs have been required by law, academics have been happy to leave the problem of military history to the professional military men. The fact that the latter seldom have had any historical training was once taken about as seriously as the quality of English spoken by the athletic coaches. The consequences of such neglect were made apparent with the outbreak of the Second World War, when academic historians were called upon to help with the greatly expanded military program. It then had to be recognized that something of a crisis existed because of the lack even of adequate textbooks in the field. Edward Mead Earle, assisted by a group of American historians, responded to the need with *Makers of Modern Strategy*,[3] a provocative, highly competent collection of essays which the contributors would be the first to recognize as falling short of the ideal solution. A supply of integrated, balanced works is still lacking, though the situation shows signs of improvement.

Since the Second World War it can be said that ten of the universities studied have introduced undergraduate or graduate courses on the history of land and/or naval warfare; two others offer at least courses dealing specifically with the Second World War. Princeton,[4] which today probably merits the title of the leading center of military studies in this country, aided by a grant from the Rockefeller Foundation, recently has introduced a military history course which is unique in that it is taught by members of the department of history and yet is designed to give credit to both R.O.T.C. and other undergraduate students. Should the experiment spread to other universities and colleges, the existing unfortunate dichotomy between academic and military-training programs on college campuses could be broken. Past experience would indicate that the obstacles to such an innovation would be considerable.[5] Furthermore, the above evidence of promising activity must not becloud the fact that the catalogues of eighteen of the thirty universities studied produced no evidence of systematic study of military problems. It may be assumed that the hundreds of smaller colleges and universities that normally cannot afford such specialized courses have done little or nothing in this direction.

In the case of advanced courses devoted to national histories or restricted time periods, it is more difficult to generalize. Here the personal interests and prejudices of the individual teacher come into play, and university catalogues may reveal very little about course content. In the 'thirties Laurence Packard's course at Amherst College dealing with Europe since 1870 devoted most of the second semester to a military history of the First World War, and few Amherst students graduated without at least hearing his famous lectures on the Battle of Jutland. Far more numerous were the courses bearing the title, "Europe since 1870," that devoted a similar period of time to the diplomatic background of the war and then came to an end with the assassination of Archduke Francis Ferdinand. Thousands of students of that era worked their way through the two volumes of Sidney B. Fay's *Origins of the World War* with additional selections from the works of that galaxy of able diplomatic historians including Bernadotte Schmitt, William L. Langer, and Raymond Sontag, but such writings were focused on the origins of the war and most of these same students relied on *All Quiet on the Western Front* or went to see the film *Hell's Angels* to acquire any knowledge of what happened in the war years.

It might be presumed that with the current rash of twentieth-century courses the practice of eliminating any account of the First World War would necessarily cease, but it may be doubted how far some of the generation of teachers trained in an era that was accustomed to side-stepping military questions have fundamentally altered their approach. The catalogues reveal that a number of the new courses begin in 1919 with the Versailles peace settlement, thereby escaping the first of the twentieth-century conflicts; in other cases, where the framework of the course demands a treatment of one or both of the World Wars, the very complexity of the period provides a convenient rationalization for the lecturer who finds military history unfamiliar and uncongenial ground. In such cases, it is all too easy to refer the students to a few appropriate chapters in a textbook.[6]

There is another disturbing facet to the so-called advanced course. What ground has been gained in the direction of bringing twentieth-century war into the foreground often has been at the expense of an understanding of preceding centuries. The attraction of contemporary history and politics to the average student has led to the elimination of many courses which once perforce paid some attention to the wars of a Napoleon or a Frederick the Great. Furthermore, the de-emphasis on classical languages and ancient history which began to affect the serious students of history as well as other college graduates by the 'thirties meant the partial loss of such military classics as the works of Herodotus, Thucydides, Xenophon, and Caesar, once part of the intellectual baggage of any educated man. It is a real misfortune, for the ancients, unlike many modern historians, had a full appreciation of the importance of war. Finally, the development of new specialized fields both within and without the area controlled by the historian can lead to much the same result. It is quite possible for a student to take courses in sociology, anthropology, psychology, geography, even economic history or the history of science without encountering the problem of war.

Introductory survey courses in history, designed to reach the bulk of the college student body, have to answer so many needs and encounter such insoluble problems that no generalizations may be applied to them, except possibly that most such courses and the textbooks designed to accompany them still fail to provide any real understanding of the process of war. The situation in the decade before the Second World War, when most textbooks were adding the words "social" or "cultural" to their titles, has been trenchantly, if perhaps overemphatically, put by Harvey de Weerd: "A student might finish studying any of the popular American college textbooks in recent European history on August 31, 1939, and be completely surprised at the outbreak of the most terrible war in history the following day." [7] What is more surprising is that the same charge of grossly inadequate treatment of the phenomenon of war can be laid to several recently published works. For example, a recent compendious, double-columned, thousand-page survey of Western civilization by one of the pioneers in the sociological approach to history [8] manages to dispose of the Thirty Years' War in just *two* sentences, whereas the same work allots nine times as much space to the subject of prohibition. Other writers have built textbooks on the history of ideas, telescoping brief outlines of political history between long sections on, say, eighteenth-century rationalism and nineteenth-century evolutionary thought. There has been even an attempt recently to build history around personalities with such resulting oddities as a work which describes the seventeenth, eighteenth, and nineteenth centuries in terms of Galileo, Newton, Benjamin Franklin, Napoleon Bonaparte, Darwin, and Jean Jaurès. [9] The section on Napoleon, the one military figure, emphasizes more his role as enlightened despot than his role of conqueror. These are admittedly extreme examples. The textbooks most widely in use today in major colleges and universities preserve a much better balance and by no means leave the wars out of history. The bulk of them can be criticized, however, for the failure to make clear how the character of military forces or the dynamics of warfare in any period is related to the very social and economic forces the authors go to such lengths to describe. In the case of one such text, the reader could learn more about the art of war from studying a few pictures scattered through the text than from the text itself, which makes no reference to the illustrations.

The paucity of serious research in the field of military history in this country, if measured by the output of articles and monographs, is truly amazing, particularly if one looks back to the years between the two great wars of our century. An effort to found an American journal devoted to military history in 1916 failed to survive the Armistice, [10] and the attempt was not to be repeated for another generation. An analysis of the articles printed in the *American Historical Review* in the period October, 1919, to July, 1939, may explain why. Of the 254 articles published in those twenty years, only forty-five dealt in any way with wars.

Approximately one-third of the latter were contributed by diplomatic historians interested in the political relations between states prior to the outbreak of a war or were concerned with the influence of public opinion on diplomatic relations in war time. Of the great wars of the modern era—the Thirty Years' War, the wars associated with the eras of Louis XIV, Frederick the Great, and Napoleon—there is no mention.

One of the articles, the presidential address of Dana Munro delivered at the American Historical Association Convention in December, 1926, offers an interesting exception. Professor Munro optimistically suggested as the theme of his address that the great eras of conflict of the past have both stimulated the historian to broaden his horizons and encouraged public interest in history. He ended hopefully:

> It may be interesting to note, in conclusion, that while historiography before the war had a tendency to confine its attention mainly to the description of normal life of a nation and to study its institutions and customs, *neglecting as far as possible, the portrayal of wars,* the Great War has made history more popular and may lead to its wider usefulness.[11]

Such optimism, unfortunately, seems to have been unwarranted so far as the study of military history in this country was concerned. Of the forty-five articles mentioned above, twenty-six were concentrated in the seven-year period that preceded the address; only nineteen were printed in the succeeding thirteen years and only four in the last four fateful years between the outbreak of the Spanish Civil War and the invasion of Poland.

Equally striking is the fate of the American projects to provide detailed histories of the First World War. Plans laid for an official War Department history were cut short in 1919 when the secretary of war, Newton D. Baker, recommended that the section of the staff devoted to historical work limit its activities "to the collection, indexing and preservation of records" and the "preparation of such monographs as are purely military in character." Later efforts to change this policy foundered on the indifference, and in some cases avowed hostility, of high-ranking officers to any form of critical descriptive writing of an official nature about military operations. Their attitude apparently was compounded out of a distrust for the capacity of staff officers to portray what happened on the battlefield and a fear that any account of operations at the command level would involve judgments on political issues. In the twenty years before the outbreak of the Second World War only a handful of monographs of strictly limited interest were published, a sorry record when it is remembered that foreign armies had long considered the writing of military history an integral and vital part of the General Staff functions.[12]

In the case of the elaborate 150-volume economic and social history of the war fathered by the Carnegie Endowment for International Peace, the failure of American collaborators to make an adequate contribution cannot be blamed on the army. European specialists made notable contributions, with the result that the English, French, German, Austro-Hungarian, and Russian portions of the series were substantially carried through to completion as were a number of volumes dealing with the smaller powers involved in the war. This country supplied the funds and an energetic editor in the person of James T. Shotwell, but the total contribution of American scholars amounted to a guide to government archival material,[13] a study covering the costs of the war to the American people,[14] and one on the railroads.[15] The phrase "other volumes to follow" found in the prospectus of the American series proved, in practice, no more than a pious hope.[16] That a better record is promised for the Second World War will be indicated later in the study.

To complete the record of the interwar years, it should be mentioned that in 1937 a second, and this time successful, attempt was made to launch an American journal devoted to military history. Lest too much comfort be taken from this fact, it may be advisable to say something about the checkered career of the new publication. It is a record that reveals a great deal about the vicissitudes of American military studies both before and since the Second World War.

In 1933 a group of officers at the Army War College in Washington founded the American Military History Foundation (today the American Military Institute) with membership open to all those interested in military history. Although a majority of the original membership were in the services, a small number of academic historians participated, and two years later it was possible to arrange a joint meeting with the American Historical Association at the latter's Chicago convention. Attendance at the sessions devoted to military history was not encouraging, and the experiment was not repeated until 1938, a year after the appearance of the first issue of the *Journal* of the Foundation (today *Military Affairs*). Editorial direction of the new publication for the years 1938–1942 was provided by an academic historian, Harvey de Weerd, and in those first years, despite a limited circulation, the quality of the publication was unusually high. By 1940, however, the Foundation was in debt, and the war necessarily brought complications. Through those years and until 1949 the journal continued to appear largely because the salaries of the staff and clerical expenses were borne first by the War Department Division of the National Archives and then by the new Historical Division of the Department of the Army. Of the articles submitted subsequent to the Second World War the majority came from historians working on the War Department official history, and the usefulness of the journal as a historical publication declined. When the Office of the Chief of Military History withdrew financial support in 1950, no issues were published for a year and it appeared that *Military Affairs* would go the way of its short-lived First-World-War predecessor. The crisis was overcome; in fact there are today signs of rejuvenation, but one might well ask why, five years after the Second World War, the sole American journal devoted to military history should have come so close to extinction.[17]

Articles and specialized monographs, although the lifeblood of the historical profession, cannot be expected to appeal to Everyman, nor will they reach the average historian unless they fall within the field of his interest. Mass production and division of labor have invaded the academic as well as the business world. In an age when no one can keep up with all the literature in the field of his specialty, it is all too easy to throw aside the article or monograph dealing with an unfamiliar or alien subject. It is only when prominent, mature scholars gifted with both insight and the ability to dramatize a theme—a Parkman, a Turner, a Beard—take hold of a subject, that a breach can be forced in the Chinese walls of professional prejudice and that popular interest can be aroused. Unfortunately, although America once produced a Mahan (more honored abroad than at home) and has since had a Douglas Freeman (like Mahan, not a professional historian) and a Samuel Eliot Morison (who is one), few of our best-known historians have shown a serious interest in the phenomenon of war. Until they do, it is not likely that the subject will attain the status of full respectability in academic circles.[18]

One naturally asks what accounts for the studied neglect of war by American historians. Part of the answer undoubtedly lies in a widespread misconception of what constitutes military history. Too often historians have equated the subject with the compiling of regimental histories and the moving about of brightly colored tin soldiers on mock battlefields, matters worthy of interest only to retired army and naval officers, hobbyists, and local antiquarian societies. Armed with such a narrow conception of military history, even those historians who have remained devoted to political history, as distinguished from the "new history" popularized in the interwar years, have rationalized their neglect of every aspect of war except the diplomatic. As for the protagonists of the new history, they threw out the wars simply because they chose to regard them as within the province of the old-fashioned chronicles of political events, an approach to history too antiquated to arouse the interest of a generation concerned with supposedly more fundamental economic and sociological forces.

Until recent events shattered the illusion, an equally widespread and equally pernicious notion, uncritically shared by many historians as well as laymen, held that war is essentially an aberration, an excrescence of the body politic that might have been normal in past ages of superstition and barbarism but is out of 'ace in an enlightened world. Now the assumption was made at the beginning of the essay that the Second World War, if not the First, has made even Everyman pragmatically aware of the fallacy of such a notion, but it was also suggested that historians are a conservative tribe. We want passionately to believe that war is abnormal, as well as evil, and that it can be eliminated, for not so to believe is to raise doubts about the validity of the liberal heritage of the past two hundred years. Whether tied to the tradition of the early-nineteenth-century optimists who were confident that "progress" would eliminate war or influenced by the self-styled hard-headed Marxists who were equally sure that modern war would die with the capitalist system, too many historians, when confronted with the unforeseen outbursts of mass violence of our century, have assumed the posture of ostriches.[19] Also, the course of American history, despite the nine thousand battles and skirmishes, has helped the American historian cling to such illusions longer than his European counterpart; it has helped particularly to nourish the strong antimilitaristic streak which is deeply rooted in the American tradition. If, on occasion, generals have been elected to the presidency, the armed forces in peacetime have not been popular with either historians or the public. Thus the American historian who shows an undue interest in any aspect of war runs the risk of being catalogued by his fellows as an eccentric or a militarist; and to be labeled a militarist is psychologically hard on those historians who are struggling to keep alive their own and others' faith in liberalism as a way of life.

The burden of the essay, thus far, has amounted to a negative criticism of the American historian's treatment of war. No doubt the picture has been etched out in blacks and whites with too little of the latter showing. In part to compensate for the distortion, which was deliberate, I wish now to suggest a few positive lines of action and offer a partial introduction to current research in the field. This is done with a full awareness of the extreme complexity of the subject and the limitations of my own interests which, it will be evident, lean toward economic aspects of war. In any case, the intention is not to present a bibliographical essay but to stimulate others to reassess their own approach to the subject.

Before any fundamental reorientation of thinking on the problems of military history can be achieved, a primary requisite would appear to be the overcoming of old prejudices. First, the notion that war is abnormal must be laid aside—not to prepare society for ever-larger and more-destructive wars, but in order to approach the phenomenon of war realistically. Nineteenth-century historians who lived in an age when the number and intensity of wars seemed to be declining could be pardoned for holding such a view; today it would appear more sensible to regard the nineteenth century as the "abnormal" element in the pattern. Secondly, we need a broader definition of military history to take the place of the narrow, negative one of the past. The term "total war," coined to describe the conditions of twentieth-century conflicts, carries with it the unfortunate connotation that recent wars are generically different from earlier wars, whereas the differences are probably more of degree than of kind, but the expression does have the advantage of dramatizing the evident fact that war involves not only generals and armies but every aspect of society. Historians must be willing to recognize that war is a form of human activity so deeply enmeshed in the mores and practices of the nation-state system that it cannot be treated in isolation from other forms of social activity any more than it can be ignored. When viewed in this light, the study of military history should be as useful to the historian building, say, a conceptual framework for economic history, as the special knowledge of the economic historian is essential to the proper interpretation of any war.

There is some reason to hope that the suggestion of Dana Munro in his 1926 address that great wars have always induced historians to broaden their horizons and aroused public interest in history will apply much more to the years after the Second World War than to the preceding interwar period. Hundreds of historians in the course of the last war were drawn into the armed services and the State Department, Office of Strategic Services, and other governmental agencies, where they perforce learned at first hand something of the nature and scope of modern war. Not all this experience went down the drain when the war ended, and a return to civilian pursuits and values was possible. The armed services and the government agencies profited, too, to the extent of recognizing the usefulness of historians. They learned from sad experience that accounts of how problems had been dealt with in the past, almost totally lacking at the beginning of the war, had a pragmatic value. As a result, by the time the war ended, work had started, or plans had been laid, to prepare official histories on nearly every aspect of this country's war effort. Professional historians helped to formulate and direct these plans and, in a great many cases, stayed on after the war to do the research and writing.

The form and the extent of coverage provided by such historical programs vary. The most elaborate is that of the army, which calls for nearly one hundred volumes. Unlike the divisional studies of the First World War, the tactical volumes are organized on a theater basis and exploit a mass of captured enemy as well as nearly all pertinent American and Allied documents. Furthermore, problems of over-all strategy, logistics, and the many technical services of the army are given full attention. It now appears that funds will run out before all the projected volumes are in print, but the end product, largely the work of civilian historians in or out of uniform, should offer a model of co-operative "official" history. Programs of the navy and air force, though more modest in size, are similar, with the notable exception that the tactical volumes of the navy history have been entrusted to the pen of a single historian, Samuel Eliot Morison. These programs of the armed services, when put together with the publications of many special projects such as the Air Force Strategic Bombing Survey and the output of the many government departments and wartime agencies, promise a body of printed material of unprecedented scope. Certainly no previous war has been dealt with so thoroughly or from so many points of approach.

The advantage to the historian of the official histories is immense. No individual historian, even granted full access to the records, could make a dent on the miles of filing cabinets that today house the paperwork produced by a war. Thus the official histories necessarily take on the role of primary sources once removed. On the other hand, there are problems raised by such materials. Official histories, no matter how much freedom is granted the authors in their research and writing, inevitably must adopt an impersonal tone, and the area of explicit critical judgment is necessarily circumscribed. It is to the credit of the academic historians who have participated in preparing the volumes and of the military and government officials who must bear the responsibility for what is printed that both objective and critical standards have been held to a very high level. Evidence that this studied effort to avoid overt censorship has borne fruit can be found in the favorable reception historical journals have accorded the volumes now in print. A more serious problem is likely to be the sheer bulk of these published materials, which may discourage historians as well as general readers. A simple calculation will show that to read the whole of the projected army history alone would require a year's time. It would appear that the primary contribution that the civilian historian can make toward an understanding of the American war experience may be less the search for gaps in the printed sources, of which there will no doubt be many, than the critical work of interpretation and synthesis. Otherwise what the public learns about the war may continue to be restricted to the output of novelists, journalists, self-styled military experts, and ghost writers hired to dress up the memoirs of noted public figures. Each of the latter has his place, but one need only recall the period of the mid-'thirties, when a few journalistic accounts of the First World War dominated public thinking, to recognize the damage that can be done when objective history remains unwritten or unread.

Another area of Second-World-War history that can prove rewarding to American scholars is that relating to allied and defeated foreign countries. The British program of official war history is at least as well organized as the American, but historians in other countries are confronted by many obstacles. A large part of the important records of the defeated powers are in the hands of the victors, who have only partially tapped them for the purposes of their own studies. Some of the more important documents have been or are in the process of being published, others microfilmed. Access to the unpublished materials in this country thus far has been denied to civilian historians, but efforts are being made to have the restrictions liberalized. Since many of the documents go back to the interwar period, the range of research possibilities is broad. These are rich German materials, for instance, for studies of the General Staff, the development of the Nazi war economy both before and during the war, German occupation policies in the conquered areas, and similar topics which have a bearing on military operations. In countries like France and Italy the financing of elaborate research projects is difficult to arrange. One solution would be the subsidization of foreign scholars with funds provided by an American foundation, as was done by the Carnegie Endowment for International Peace after the First World War; another would be for American historians to share in the task. Many of the French documents, including those related to the resistance movement, already are available in the Archives Nationales.

The current popular interest in contemporary history can be counted upon to keep alive the publication of works dealing with the Second World War. There is a danger, however, that preoccupation with the Second World War can perpetuate the neglect of the role war has played in previous centuries. Although recent conventions of the American Historical Association have offered a number of sessions devoted to military history, nearly all have been confined to the late war, yet at no time have historians had greater need to offer the kind of perspective that only the study of the past can provide. Each generation must reconsider the history of the past in terms of its own frame of reference. Certainly the concept of total war developed out of the twentieth-century conflicts calls for a fresh look at the wars of earlier eras. But the reverse of this process is just as important a duty of the historian. Insofar as the historian, through immersing himself in the study of a past period, is made aware of the degree to which his own frame of reference fails to fit a different set of circumstances, he is led to look more critically at some of the assumptions of his own age. To take a simple example, anyone who lived through the years of the Second World War might well carry away the firm impression that the factory production figures of which he heard so much determined the outcome of the war and, by contrast, that generals and soldiers, other than as digits, were no longer significant. Now when this economic line of approach is applied to the period of, say, Frederick the Great, two things happen. First one happily discovers that Frederick was much more "modern" in his recognition of economic factors in war than some of his biographers have recognized; then one may be dismayed to find that Frederick devoted pages of his military writings to questions of the discipline of his troops and the sense of honor of his officers, matters of secondary concern to an age preoccupied with defeating an enemy solely by producing more planes and ammunition. Is it not just possible that, on this latter score, a study of the writings of Frederick the Great would provide a useful antidote to a twentieth century that is overly prone to dwell on statistics and to forget that factors such as courage and discipline may affect the outcome of a battle?

A few of the possible lines of inquiry into the military history of the past four hundred years may be indicated by a review of a scattering of works by present-day American historians who have shown a serious interest in the problem of the relation of war to society. Two volumes in the *Rise of Modern Europe* series edited by William L. Langer will serve as starting points. The first, by Walter L. Dorn, entitled *Competition for Empire, 1740–1763,*[20] deserves special recognition if only for the fact that Professor Dorn carried through the research for the volume in a period when military history in this country was at a low point. Any student who has read the chapters entitled "The Competitive State System" and "Eighteenth Century Militarism" should be disabused of the toy-soldier caricature of eighteenth-century warfare. The second volume, entitled *The Emergence of the Great Powers, 1685–1715,*[21] by John B. Wolf, follows in the path set by Professor Dorn. It properly focuses primary attention on the vast scope and interdependence of the conflicts of the late seventeenth century and on their relation to the dynamic process of state building. Biographers of Peter the Great, for instance, have dealt with his efforts to modernize and Westernize Russia, but it is only in the context of the wars of the period, as Professor Wolf properly insists, that the driving force behind Peter's efforts is made evident.

These volumes likewise make what is virtually a pioneer effort to grapple with the economics of seventeenth- and eighteenth-century warfare. In this connection, it may be noted that Werner Sombart's *Krieg und Kapitalismus,* which in 1913 advanced the thesis that war was the primary motivating force in the early development of capitalism, went largely unchallenged in this country until the appearance in 1951 of John U. Nef's erudite *War and Human Progress.* These two studies, however, are richest for the fifteenth and sixteenth centuries, and they raise more questions than they solve. As Professor Wolf makes clear, a great deal more primary research needs to be done by economic historians before any valid generalizations can be made concerning the economics of war in the seventeenth century. Much the same can be said for the eighteenth and nineteenth centuries as well. German historians have done a good deal with the institutional history of the Prussian army, and there is the classic work of Hans Delbrück on strategy,[22] but despite the work of British and French scholars, broad gaps exist in our knowledge of the military institutions of the other European powers, and even the Germans are singularly weak on the economics of eighteenth-century warfare. The statement is also true of the French revolutionary and Napoleonic periods. Robert R. Palmer's *Twelve Who Ruled* [23] provides a fascinating study of the efforts of the Committee of Public Safety to make a war economy function in a period of revolutionary violence. One would like to see the method of approach he used applied to the Directory and to the Napoleonic period. Although a number of noted historians have shown an interest in Napoleon's Continental System, little is known about war industries and war finance in the period, including the British program of supplying munitions and subsidies to her Continental allies.

The century between the end of the Napoleonic wars and the outbreak of the First World War was as notable for the world-wide technological and social changes taking place—changes which promised to revolutionize both armies and weapons—as for the lack of major international conflicts. The American Civil War ranks among the bloodiest and most protracted of wars in any age, but it was confined to a single country and was fought under conditions sufficiently different from those prevailing in Europe for its lessons to go partially unheeded. The other wars of the period tended to be localized and of short duration. In any case, when the First World War broke out no one was prepared for the kind of struggle that ensued. One fruitful approach to the century would appear to be a search for an explanation of how this came about. Alfred Vagt's *History of Militarism* [24] and Edmund Silbener's *The Problem of War in Economic Thought* [25] suggest that much can be learned from an analysis of the attitudes toward war taken by different social groups. In this regard the material to be found in the parliamentary papers of the European countries and contemporary journals has been barely scratched. In the vast field dealing with the relation between technological change and military weapons and tactics, there is room for a host of monographs. Two studies on the role of the railroad in the Civil War [26] and another on the work of General Gorgas [27] as head of the Confederate Ordnance Department may be mentioned as examples of recent research interest by young scholars in one branch of the field, alongside the older works of James Phinney Baxter [28] and Bernard Brodie [29] on the mid-nineteenth-century revolution in naval construction in another. One would like to know more about the role of the growing armament firms and banks than appeared in the journalistic exposés of the nineteen thirties, when it was popular to blame the arms trade for the American entry into the First World War. There are also some interesting institutional problems associated with the rise of the mass, democratic army, including the bitter conflict between the adherents of the professional *versus* the militia type of army.

In the case of the First World War, as with the late war, the immediate need would appear to be for interpretive general histories, particularly in the case of American participation, histories that would deal with more than Woodrow Wilson and the Peace Conference that followed the war. An American account, treating the period as a whole, that would satisfy the canons of scholarship and also appeal to Everyman is yet to be written; since an early survey of Carlton J. H. Hayes, no prominent American scholar has grappled with the problem. [30] Monographs, too, as the paucity of American volumes in the Carnegie Series indicates, have been few and far between, yet the opportunities for new research are as rich as the nature of twentieth-century war is complex. One such line of investigation that has direct relevance to problems now confronting this country is suggested by a recent university-press publication entitled *Generals and Politicians: Conflict between France's High Command, Parliament and Government, 1914–1918.* [31] Equally timely is a forthcoming publication by one of Laurence Packard's former students dealing with the use made of scientific and technological advances as they applied to weapons and their employment in the First World War.[32] American scholars who wish to pursue their studies in this period need not be reminded that they have at their disposal the unexcelled facilities of the Hoover War Library.

The Second World War not only has delimited the period 1919–1939 as the interwar years, but it is largely responsible for posing the kinds of questions which are likely to guide the research of historians in the period. The immediate origins of the brand of total war that characterized the Second World War grew out of theories and practices developed by the totalitarian states, particularly by Germany, whence came such terms as Geopolitics, Wehrwirtschaft, Autarky, Lebensraum, Ersatz, Fifth Column, Blitzkrieg, etc., which today sprinkle the pages of literature in the field of politics. The terms themselves, and one must add the vast field of technological change, suggest some of the ramifications of modern war and the many lines of inquiry that can be pursued. Totalitarianism, somewhat belatedly, has attracted the attention of all varieties of social scientists, and the anthropologists and psychologists have already come forward—to the dismay of some historians—with explanations for totalitarian militarism. If the historian is not to find his field pre-empted by others, he will have to get over some of his conservatism and do a larger share of the delving into the roots of the Second World War.

The full record of how both the totalitarian and the democratic states prepared for the possibility of war will throw a good deal of light on the war itself. The initial advantages of the Axis powers clearly revealed the lack of adequate preparation on the part of the democracies, but the war also uncovered some surprising areas of rigidity and some fundamental errors of policy on the Axis side as well as areas of remarkable flexibility on the democratic side. Certainly no account of the Second World War can be placed in proper focus until such problems are dealt with; yet if that is to be done, a more general acceptance of the kind of approach toward military history that characterizes the studies mentioned in the latter part of the essay will be necessary. Nearly all of those few historians willing to betray any interest in the First World War and its origins channeled their efforts into what was too often a narrowly defined field of diplomatic history; this must not be permitted to happen again.

There is no intention here of making a whipping boy of the diplomatic historian. In the hands of its best practitioners, diplomatic history has been inclined to accord the phenomenon of war far more importance than was given to it by the brand of socio-economic history so popular in the interwar years.[33] Nor is the present problem one of producing fewer diplomatic historians or fewer specialized historians of any kind, but rather to meet the positive need for more than the present scattering of competently trained military historians in this country. What is of far more importance is that at every level of college and university teaching and in every variety of historical literature the role of warfare in Western society be given its proper due. The danger that American historiography will be led down a blind alley of militarism is minimal compared to the danger that the American historian will fail in his obligation to Everyman of providing a properly balanced image of the past.

1. Quincy Wright, *A Study of War* (Chicago, 1942), I, Appendix XVI; II, 685–687.

2. The expression reflects the purport of a blast directed against modern historians by Liddell Hart, *The Ghost of Napoleon* (New Haven, 1934), pp. 145–149.

3. (Princeton, 1943).

4. The Institute of Advanced Studies must be coupled with the University.

5. The fate of the course for N.R.O.T.C. students entitled, "Foundations of National Power," organized by Harold and Margaret Sprout at the instigation of Secretary Forrestal, is instructive. What was intended to be a full-year course in world politics was gradually reduced to a few hours of instruction handled by naval officers.

6. In the first years after the Second World War, when college campuses were flooded with veterans, it could be assumed that most students knew the terminology and something of the process of war. That assumption is no longer tenable. The bulk of the students today are no more prepared to digest alone an account of military operations than they are to cope with one describing the economic legislation of the New Deal.

7. "Military Studies and the Social Sciences," *Military Affairs,* IX (1945), 188.

8. Harry E. Barnes, *A Survey of Western Civilization* (New York, 1947).

9. L. B. Brown and G. B. Garson, *Men and Centuries of European Civilization* (New York, 1948), pp. 391–522.

10. *The Military Historian and Economist* (Cambridge, Mass., 1916–1918). The death in 1920 of Professor R. M. Johnston, the moving spirit behind the journal, deprived the historical profession of one who might have built up a nucleus of students interested in military problems.

War and the Historian

11. "War and History," *American Historical Review*, XXXII (1926–1927), 231. The italics are mine.

12. Histories of the record in the First World War of some twenty-eight divisions, prepared by the American Battle Monuments Commission and published by the Government Printing Office, began to appear only after the outbreak of the Second World War. They represented little more than pamphlets recording chronologically the operations of each division. The Historical Section, which was transferred in 1921 to the Army War College, utilized its small staff in the interwar years primarily for the cataloguing of materials. Part of the fruit of this clerical work finally appeared in 1948 with the publication under the aegis of the Historical Division, Department of the Army, of the *United States Army in the World War, 1917–1919,* seventeen volumes of selected documents drawn from the records of the American Expeditionary Force. In size the collection compares unfavorably with the 128 volumes of the *War of the Rebellion* documents published after the Civil War; in form it has nothing in common with the official histories produced in foreign countries. Note, for example, the many-volume, descriptive British history of the First World War: *History of the Great War Based on Official Documents by the Historical Section of the Committee of Imperial Defence* (London, 1920 ff.).

13. Waldo G. Leland and Newton D. Mereness, *Introduction to the American Official Sources for the Economic and Social History of the World War* (New Haven, 1926).

14. John M. Clark, *The Costs of the World War to the American People* (New Haven, 1931).

15. Walker D. Hines, *War History of the American Railways,* 2 vols. (New Haven, 1928).

16. The fact that Professor Shotwell was in Europe almost continuously until 1924 undoubtedly had some influence on the late start of the American series; it could hardly have been decisive, however, had this country taken a serious interest in the project.

17. Details concerning the history of the American Military Institute and *Military Affairs* may be found in an article by Jesse C. Douglas, *Military Affairs,* VIII (1944), No. 1, and in the transcript of the 1950 meeting of the Institute given *in extenso* in *Military Affairs,* XIV (1950), No. 3.

18. The economics of book publishing in a period of high costs can have a considerable influence on the number of works appearing in a field. One recent development may well encourage American historians to write works dealing at least with American wars. Since the creation of the History Book Club, the American History Book Club and, most recently, the Military Science Book Club, several authors have found studies dealing with the Revolutionary and Civil Wars to be profitable ventures. Perhaps the profit motive will succeed where others have failed.

19. For an able statement of the case against the liberal historian see Sir

Charles Oman's essay "A Defence of Military History" in his *Studies in the Napoleonic Wars* (London, 1929), pp. 24–36.

20. (New York, 1940).

21. (New York, 1951).

22. *Geschichte der Kriegskunst im Rahmen der politischen Geschichte,* 4 vols. (Berlin, 1900–1927).

23. (Princeton, 1941.) Professor Palmer's recent textbook, *A History of the Modern World* (New York, 1950), reflects admirably the seminal influence of the interest in military studies developed at Princeton.

24. (New York, 1939).

25. (Princeton, 1946).

26. Robert C. Black, Jr., *The Railroads of the Confederacy* (Chapel Hill, N.C., 1952); Thomas Weber, *The Northern Railroads in the Civil War* (New York, 1952).

27. Frank E. Vandiver, *Ploughshares into Swords* (Austin, Tex., 1952).

28. *The Introduction of the Ironclad Warship* (Cambridge, Mass., 1933).

29. *Seapower in the Machine Age* (Princeton, 1943).

30. *A Brief History of the Great War* (New York, 1920). By contrast, the British can offer the many books by the military historian Liddell Hart, Winston Churchill's classic, *The World Crisis*, 5 vols. (New York, 1923–1929), John Buchan's popular *History of the Great War*, abridged ed., 4 vols. (Boston, 1923), and several other competent works. For some reason, recent popular interest in the Revolutionary and Civil Wars has not extended to American participation in the First World War.

31. By Jere C. King (Berkeley, Calif., 1951). A comparable study of United States experience in the Second World War may be found in Louis Smith's *American Democracy and Military Power* (Chicago, 1951).

32. I. B. Holley, Jr., *Ideas and Weapons.*

33. *The Challenge to Isolation* and *The Undeclared War* (New York, 1952, 1953) by William L. Langer and S. Everett Gleason provide a brilliant case in point.

[FREDERICK S. ALLIS, JR.]

The Dred Scott Labyrinth

A TEACHER of American history who attempts to present the Dred Scott case [1] to a class of students is in for a bad time, especially if he has not specialized in constitutional history. His troubles will increase rather than diminish if he is bold enough to leave the general accounts of the case and enter the labyrinth of specialized literature on the subject, in an effort to find out what this cause célèbre was really all about. If he enters this labyrinth, not only will he be met with more than the usual amount of conflicting and contradictory material; he will soon discover that even the specialists cannot agree on just what the judges *did* say. Furthermore, since there seems to be a tendency among some of the Dred Scott specialists to approach the subject as if no one had written on it before, it is difficult to determine whether or not they are in disagreement with previous writers. The result is that a bewildering number of points have apparently been incontrovertibly established, only to be refuted, contradicted by implication, or ignored, in later writings. Unless the reader possesses unusual patience, as he attempts to thread his way through this confusion of claims and counterclaims, he is likely to become as exasperated with the judges and their utterances as were the abolitionists in the year 1857.

This state of affairs renders extremely complicated the task of a teacher who, in a survey course of American history, feels himself obliged to say *something* about Dred and his legal difficulties. It is relatively easy to discover that in the so-called "opinion of the court" Chief Justice Taney held (1) that no Negro could be a citizen of the United States; (2) that the Missouri Compromise had been unconstitutional; and (3) that the status of Negroes was a matter to be decided by state rather than by federal courts. If the teacher can cling stubbornly to the statement that most politically informed people in the United States in 1857 *thought* that this was the decision of the Court, he will be on safe ground. If, however, he is asked what the Court really *did* decide—and such a question is certainly a legitimate one—he immediately finds himself in trouble.

This paper is, in large measure, a report on one teacher's attempt to find firm ground to stand on in dealing with the problem of what the Court *did* decide in the Dred Scott case. It makes no attempt to shed any "new light" upon that case, nor does it concern itself with whether the decision was "correct" or not. It is rather an essay on what constitutional historians and lawyers have said the Court decided, written from the point of view of the teacher rather than that of the specialist.

Before a discussion of what some of the specialists have said about the Dred Scott decision is attempted, the judges themselves deserve a chance to explain what they thought they were deciding. That they were seriously concerned with the problem of just what was before them is evident from their opinions. Although nearly all the judges had something to say on this subject, it will be useful to quote briefly only from Chief Justice Taney and from Justice Curtis, since it was from the opinions of these two that most of the future disagreement stemmed. Taney went out of his way to defend himself against a charge of uttering mere *obiter dicta;* after he had held that no Negro could be a citizen within the meaning of the Constitution, he went on to say:

We are aware that doubts are entertained by some of the members of the court, whether the plea in abatement [2] is legally before the court upon this writ of error; but if that plea is regarded as waived, or out of the case upon any other ground, yet the question as to the jurisdiction of the Circuit Court is presented on the face of the bill of exception itself, taken by the plaintiff at the trial; for he admits that he and his wife were born slaves, but endeavors to make out his title to freedom and citizenship by showing that they were taken . . . to certain places . . . where slavery could not by law exist, and that they thereby became free, and upon their return to Missouri became citizens of that State.

Now, if the removal of which he speaks did not give them their freedom . . . he is still a slave; . . . no one supposes that a slave is a citizen of the State or of the United States. If, therefore, the acts done by his owner did not make them free persons, he is still a slave and certainly incapable of suing in the character of a citizen. . . .

If upon the showing of Scott himself, it appeared that he was still a slave, the case ought to have been dismissed.[3]

Taney then went on to defend the right of the Supreme Court to correct *all* the errors committed in the Circuit Court. He continued:

It has been said, that as this court has decided against the jurisdiction of the Circuit Court on the plea in abatement, it has no right to examine any question presented by the exception; and that anything it may say upon that part of the case will be extra-judicial, and mere obiter dicta.

This is a manifest mistake; there can be no doubt as to the jurisdiction of this court to revise the judgment of a Circuit Court, and to reverse it for any error apparent on the record, whether it be the error of giving judgment in a case over which it had no jurisdiction, or any other material error; and this, too, whether there is a plea in abatement or not. . . .

The correction of one error in the court below does not deprive the appellate court of the power of examining further into the record, and correcting any other material errors which may have been committed by the inferior court. . . . It is the daily practice of this court . . . to correct by its opinions whatever errors may appear on the record material to the case.[4]

Justice Curtis refused to accept Taney's position on these questions. He attacked what he called the Court's "assumption of authority to examine the constitutionality of the act of Congress commonly called the Missouri compromise act." He said:

Having first decided that they were bound to consider the sufficiency of the plea to the jurisdiction of the Circuit Court, and having decided that this plea showed that the Circuit Court had not jurisdiction, and consequently that this is a case to which the judicial power of the United States does not extend, they have gone on to examine the merits of the case as they appeared on the trial before the court and jury, on the issues joined on the pleas in bar, and so have reached the question of the power of Congress to pass the act of 1820. On so grave a subject as this, I feel obliged to say that, in my opinion, such an exertion of judicial power transcends the limits of the authority of the court, as described by its repeated decisions, and, as I understand, acknowledged in this opinion of the majority of the court. . . .

I do not consider it to be within the scope of the judicial power of the majority of the court to pass upon any question respecting the plaintiff's citizenship in Missouri, save that raised by the plea to the jurisdiction; and I do not hold any opinion of this court, or any court, binding, when expressed on a question not legitimately before it. . . . The judgment of this court is, that the case is to be dismissed for want of jurisdiction, because the plaintiff was not a citizen of Missouri, as he alleged in his declaration. Into that judgment, according to the settled course of this court, nothing appearing after a plea to the merits can enter. A great question of constitutional law, deeply affecting the peace and welfare of the country, is not, in my opinion, a fit subject to be thus reached.[5]

With these two statements the issue is joined. If, as Taney claimed, the Supreme Court could review the question of the Circuit Court's jurisdiction, not only on the plea in abatement, which claimed that *no* Negro could sue as a citizen, but also on the question of whether or not Scott were still a slave and therefore ineligible to sue, the Court might rightfully pass on the constitutionality of the Missouri Compromise. If, as Curtis claimed, the jurisdictional question could be reviewed only on the plea in abatement, the Court had no right to pass on the constitutionality of the Missouri Compromise, since a majority of the Court held that the case should be dismissed for want of jurisdiction. Thus the determination of Scott's status was, according to Taney, a legitimate part of the jurisdictional question, while, according to Curtis, his status could not rightfully be reviewed unless the Court accepted jurisdiction in the case. Since Taney's opinion was called "the opinion of the court," it might be assumed that a majority agreed with him on what he said, and that, following Chief Justice Hughes's statement about the Constitution being what the judges say it is, it would be simply a matter of counting noses to determine who was right. But it is not as easy as that. All nine of the judges handed down opinions, and only two of them concurred with the Chief Justice in virtually all he said. What, then, *did* the Court decide?

It is now time to examine what later writers have said on this question of what the Court did decide. Many of those who support the general position held by Justice Curtis dismiss much of Taney's opinion as *obiter dicta*. This is admittedly a difficult legal concept to define, and one about which there is much disagreement. For the purposes of this paper, however, it can safely be assumed that when a writer labels part or all of Taney's opinion as *obiter dicta,* he is, in effect, saying that there was no binding judicial decision on the points thus designated. Though the search for enlightenment on this question of what the Court really did decide has been conducted according to no set pattern, it

seems advisable, for the sake of orderly presentation, to adopt a chronological approach to what has been said; the various statements to be
examined will, therefore, be taken up in the order in which they were
published.

No sooner had Taney read his opinion on that fateful day in March,
1857, than a storm of criticism, much of it of a very abusive character,
arose. Most of the contemporary published material is so partisan as
to make it of historical interest only. Three studies of the case, however,
each published before the Civil War, are exceptions which are well
worth consideration. The first of these, which appeared three months
after the announcement of the decision, was entitled "A Legal Review
of the Case of Dred Scott" and was the work of the distinguished
Boston lawyers, John Lowell and Horace Gray.[6] This review is a remarkably thorough examination of the case, considering the short time
available for preparation and, in view of the climate of vituperation
in which it was produced, is remarkably fair. The authors attempt to
prove, among other things, that the Court's "decision" regarding Negro
citizenship and the Missouri Compromise was extrajudicial, and that
the only point really "decided" was "that the condition of the plaintiff,
being now an inhabitant of Missouri, must be conclusively determined
by the law of that State, as declared by its supreme court."[7] Lowell
and Gray first take up the question of the plea in abatement and, by
examining the nine individual opinions, show that only four of the
judges—Taney, Wayne, Daniel, and Curtis—believed that the Circuit
Court's decision on the plea was before the Court. Since Curtis held
that a Negro *might* be a citizen, that left only three judges supporting
the position that the Circuit Court should not have overruled the plea,
but rather should have held that Scott, as a Negro, could not be a
citizen. The authors remark on the fact that several of the judges in
their opinions speak as if a majority, rather than merely three, of the
Court supported this position and suggest that the confusion may
have arisen because the opinions, as originally read, may have been
different from those later reported by Howard.[8] Lowell and Gray go
on to point out that the judgment of the Court—which was that the
Circuit Court had no jurisdiction—was based on the fact that Scott
was a slave, but they question the right of the Court to consider this
jurisdictional point, for, as they say, "we had supposed it to be the
settled law of the supreme court, that the citizenship of the parties,

if duly averred in the writ, could not be tried except on a plea to the jurisdiction." [9] In short, they dismiss the Court's "decision" on Negro citizenship as extrajudicial and express doubt as to the validity of the judgment.

Lowell and Gray next proceed to attack the "decision" on the Missouri Compromise as unnecessary to a disposition of the case. Though they had previously accepted the fact that Taney was concerned with the jurisdictional question when he held that Scott was a slave, they now charge him with considering the case on its merits, after "holding that the decision of the first plea disposed of the cause." [10] They then attempt to show that since a majority of the Court held that the law of Missouri applied after Scott's residence in Illinois, that holding would apply equally well after his residence in the Wisconsin Territory. They put their case as follows:

> The decision, so far as the residence in Illinois is concerned, is put distinctly upon the ground, that the laws of Illinois could not operate on the plaintiff after his return to Missouri. This decision disposes equally of his residence in the Territory, for his stay in each place was for an equal time, and for similar purposes. The whole case being thus disposed of, the opinion on the Missouri Compromise Act was clearly extrajudicial.[11]

Though Lowell and Gray go on to discuss other aspects of the case, these are their strongest points. It is interesting to note that they make no distinction between the law of Illinois and an Act of Congress, believing that if Missouri law could govern the one, it would naturally govern the other.

In November, 1857, Thomas Hart Benton published his examination of the Dred Scott case,[12] the second of the three contemporary treatments of the case which merit consideration. Benton is concerned primarily with proving that the Constitution does not follow the flag; that, as he puts it, "the great fundamental error of the Court (father of all the political errors) [is] that of assuming the extension of the Constitution to the Territories." [13] Yet he finds time, in the course of his discussion, to attack the "decision" as political rather than judicial. First of all he attacks Taney's defense of his procedure in examining all possible phases of the jurisdictional question and cites part, though not the key part, of that defense. He admits that there may be times when the Supreme Court is justified in correcting all the errors committed by a lower court. The Court would be justified in so doing when "a return of the record to the Court below with errors in it, would be a silent sanction of those errors—would cause them to be repeated by the court below, and give the parties the delay and cost of another appeal; and the Supreme Court the trouble and care of a new decision." But, he insists, such is not the case in this instance:

That delay, and cost and trouble, can only be where the case is remanded for retrial, and never when it is remanded to be dismissed for want of jurisdiction. In this latter case there is no danger of a repetition of the error. In the case of such dismission there is nothing further for the Court below to do —no repetition of error for it to commit—no future trouble to be given to the Court above—nor any future cost or delay to the parties. . . . In this case, the suit was dismissed for want of jurisdiction, and that is the first step of the plaintiff in getting into court. He was turned back from the door, for want of a right to enter the court room—debarred from suing, for want of citizenship; after which it would seem to be a grave judicial solecism to proceed to try the man when he was not before the Court, and when he could take nothing from its decision if the merits had all been found in his favor.[14]

Benton was not content to charge that Taney had gone into the merits of the case after the Supreme Court had decided that the lower court had had no jurisdiction. He believed that the "decision" could be proved political because it was unenforceable. In making this point he says:

These decisions upon their face show themselves to be political, and tried by the test of enforcement, they are proved to be so. The Supreme Court cannot enforce these decisions; and that is the test of its jurisdiction. Where it cannot enforce, it cannot try. The Court is an authoritative body, acting with authority, and having power to enforce its decisions wherever it has jurisdiction. It can issue its command—(*mandamus, we command*)—and has the machinery to execute it—marshals, jails, fines, imprisonment. None of this machinery can be employed upon Congress and the people. Suasion is the only operative agent upon them; and this agent, either moral or political, is not the weapon of the Court. The pulpit and the forum persuade: a court commands. It, therefore, acted on these points [the constitutionality of the Missouri Compromise and the extension of the Constitution into the territories] without jurisdiction; that is to say, without right. . . .[15]

Neither of Benton's charges is impressive when read today. Unlike Lowell and Gray, he does not consider Taney's statement that he was dealing with the jurisdictional question when he determined that Scott was still a slave. As for the unenforceability charge, it shows how weakly established was the concept of the judicial review of acts of Congress in the period before the Civil War. Had not Scott been emancipated by his owner after the Supreme Court's decision, the Court could have "commanded" that he be held as a slave. And the presumption was that future cases in which Negroes in slave states tried to claim freedom on the basis of residence in territory north of the 36° 30′ line would be decided according to this precedent, thus giving this ruling the force of law.

Two years later, George Ticknor Curtis, brother of Justice Curtis and counsel for Scott before the Supreme Court, published a pamphlet on the case, most of which he later incorporated into his *Constitutional History of the United States*.[16] Curtis takes the same position as had Lowell and Gray, and Benton—namely, that most of the Court's "decision" was not judicial at all; but he arrives at his conclusion by very different methods. He makes a careful analysis of each judge's opinion, lists those who expressed positive opinions on each of several of the disputed points in the case, and comes to the conclusion that since on none of the disputed points had a majority of the judges arrived at the same conclusion by the same route, there was no "majority" decision at all. Curtis starts by asking how many of the judges believed that the Circuit Court's decision on the plea in abatement was rightfully before them, and agrees with Lowell and Gray that only four believed they had a right to review this point and that of these four, only three came to the conclusion that a Negro could not be a citizen and therefore could not sue. Of the five justices who held that the plea in abatement was not before the Court, not one made any specific statement as to whether or not a Negro could be a citizen. Thus, on the first point, according to Curtis, "As *three* is not a majority of *nine*, the case of Dred Scott does not furnish a judicial precedent or judicial decision."[17]

Curtis next attacks the "decision" of the Court that the Missouri Compromise was unconstitutional, using the same methods which he had adopted in his discussion of the first point. Like Benton, he believes that the question of the constitutionality of the Missouri Compromise arose on the merits of the case. He then points out that three justices— Grier, Catron, and Campbell—"who did not hold that the question of jurisdiction was to be examined and passed upon, and gave no opinion upon it" held, on the merits, that the Missouri Compromise was unconstitutional. But, in addition, three more judges—Taney, Wayne, and Daniel—who had already held that the Circuit Court should have sustained the plea in abatement and refused to hear the case, went on to give opinions on the merits. Curtis sums it up as follows:

Thus it appears that six of the nine judges expressed the opinion that the Compromise Act was unconstitutional. But in order to determine whether this concurrence of the six in that opinion constitutes a judicial decision or precedent, it is necessary to see how the majority is formed. Three of these judges, as we have seen, held that the circuit court had no jurisdiction of the case, and ought to have dismissed it, because the plea in abatement showed that the plaintiff was not a citizen; and yet, when the circuit court had erroneously decided this question in favor of the plaintiff, and had ordered the defendant to plead to the merits, and, after such plea, judgment on the merits had been given against the plaintiff, and he had brought the record into the Supreme Court, these three judges appear to have held that they could not only decide *judicially* that the circuit court was entirely without jurisdiction in the case, but could also give a *judicial* decision on the merits.[18]

Thus, before the outbreak of the Civil War, three serious reviews of the case had all reached the conclusion that the so-called "opinion of the court" on the unconstitutionality of the Missouri Compromise was extrajudicial, though each had arrived at that conclusion by a different route.[19] Two of these three had taken a similar position on the Court's "decision" regarding Negro citizenship. In all three accounts the writers accused Taney of dealing with the merits of the case after having decided that the Circuit Court had no jurisdiction. Strangely enough, in no one of these reviews of the case is the *judgment* of the Court—namely, that the case be dismissed for want of jurisdiction— carefully examined. Even if one were to believe Taney guilty of all the crimes imputed to him by the abolitionists, it is difficult to see how he would have dared to order the suit dismissed for want of jurisdiction in the lower court unless he had had a majority of the judges with him on that point.

In the period following the Civil War no significant attempt was made to re-examine the Dred Scott case from a constitutional point of view. The verdict of the war colored much of the historical writing of the time, and there gradually emerged a point of view among Northern writers which explained the war in terms of a conspiracy of Southern leaders, bent on perpetuating the institution of slavery in this country.[20] Since writers of this school considered the antislavery position "right" and the slavery position "wrong," they quite naturally treated the Dred Scott case in moral rather than constitutional terms. For example, Nicolay and Hay could write: "The slavery sentiment . . . flowed in at the open door of the national hall of justice. . . . It filtered through the very walls which surrounded the consulting-room of the Supreme Court." Under such an "insidious influence," the judges "thrust themselves forward" "in an evil hour" to "sit as umpires in a quarrel of parties and factions." Taney's decision was a

cold and pitiless historical delineation of the bondage, ignorance, and degradation of the unfortunate kidnaped Africans. . . . His unmerciful logic made the black before the law less than a slave; it reduced him to the status of a horse or dog, a bale of dry-goods or a block of stone. Against such a debasement of any living image of the Divine Maker the resentment of the public conscience of the North was quick and unsparing.[21]

James Ford Rhodes, writing a few years later, takes much the same point of view, though he is fairer to Taney. The villains in his piece are the other Southern judges, especially Justice Wayne, who "gained" Taney over to their side by offering the "bait" of settling once and for all the question of slavery in the territories. Rhodes suggests that age may have "enfeebled the will and made him [Taney] more susceptible to influences that were brought to bear upon him." Once he has made this excuse for the Chief Justice, he goes on to express surprise that "a humane Christian man" could publicly assert so "monstrous a theory" as Taney did in his opinion, and adds that "such work was demanded by slavery of her votaries." "As Douglas sinned as a statesman, so Taney sinned as a judge." [22] Nicolay and Hay do not consider at all the question of what the Court "decided"; Rhodes is content to remark that five judges "agreed with the chief justice that the Missouri Compromise was unconstitutional; and they concurred sufficiently in the other points to constitute his conclusions the opinion of the court, as it was officially called. It thus received the assent of two-thirds of the judges." He goes on, however, to blame Taney "because he allowed himself to make a political argument, when only a judicial decision was called for." [23] In both these accounts the implication is that the "decision" was extrajudicial, but both writers are so much more interested in what they consider the moral aspects of the case that they hardly bother with the constitutional and legal questions.

When, in 1895, James B. Thayer of the Harvard Law School published his *Cases on Constitutional Law,* he treated the Dred Scott case in a new way. Believing that Taney's opinion was worthy of little respect, Thayer refused to print it as the "opinion of the court," choosing instead that of Justice Nelson. He defends this choice on the ground that "this opinion alone limits itself to grounds agreed upon by a majority of the court and necessary to the disposition of the case." [24] The so-called "opinion of the court," Thayer says, "was in fact only the Opinion of the Chief Justice announcing the Judgment of the Court." [25] Thayer goes on to cite with evident approval the remarks of Lowell and Gray to the effect that the Court's "decision" on the Missouri Compromise was extrajudicial.[26] While it is true that six of the judges concurred with Justice Nelson, who had waived the question of jurisdiction and held that the judgment of the Circuit Court be affirmed, any attempt to designate the Nelson opinion as that of the Court runs into immediate difficulties. The judgment of the Court, as announced by Taney, was that the case be dismissed. How, then, could a majority also agree that the judgment of the Circuit Court should be affirmed? The answer probably lies in a statement from the opinion of Justice Grier, which may well have been the view of some of the other judges. Grier said: "The form of the judgment is of little importance; for, whether the judgment be affirmed or dismissed for want of jurisdiction, it is justified by the decision of the court, and is the same in effect between the parties to the suit." [27] In any event, it is clear that for Thayer, Nelson's opinion covered the only point really decided by the Court—namely, that Scott's status was to be determined by the courts of Missouri—and that Taney's opinion was extrajudicial. Thus, by the close of the century, it had apparently been well established that Taney's opinion was in large measure *obiter dicta,* if not actually evil. Hardly a voice had been raised in his defense.[28]

In the early years of this century two studies of the Dred Scott case appeared which sought to revise previous judgments of Taney. The first of these—a book entitled *The Legal and Historical Status of the Dred Scott Decision,* by Elbert W. R. Ewing— [29] went to the opposite extreme and praised Taney's opinion extravagantly. Ewing set out to prove that everything which Taney uttered was sound law. In the development of this thesis he engages in some very fancy special pleading. He claims, without ever really proving it, that at least six judges held the plea in abatement before the Court and concludes: "Hence, on all the points decided in the opinion as read by the Chief Justice, we have a concurrence of a judicial majority." [30] No one to date had claimed that more than two justices agreed with Taney that no Negro could be a citizen, but Ewing insists that a majority did. His most original contribution is his explanation of why the Court had to decide on the constitutionality of the Missouri Compromise. After pointing out that Scott's daughter Eliza was born "on board the steamboat Gypsey, north of the north line of the State of Missouri, and upon the River Mississippi," and that there was no way of telling whether the steamboat was on the Illinois side of the river or on the side bordering federally controlled territory, he claims that the only way of determining Eliza's status was to pass on the Missouri Compromise question.[31] Though Montgomery Blair had advanced this argument before the Supreme Court, there is no evidence that the judges paid any attention to it. Finally Ewing justifies the Court's examination of all aspects of the case on the ground that the original suit in the Missouri courts was still pending.[32] Though a defense of Taney was long overdue, it was unfortunate that this first effort was not a more competent piece of workmanship.[33]

In 1911 Edward S. Corwin published in the *American Historical Review* the first thorough examination of the constitutional aspects of the Dred Scott case since the Civil War.[34] Though he covers several phases of the case, Corwin first directs himself to the question of whether or not Taney's decision on the Missouri Compromise was *obiter dicta,* a question which he answers with an emphatic, "No." First of all, he states the conventional criticism of Taney:

What the charge of *obiter dictum* amounts to then is this: first, that the action of the Chief Justice in passing upon the constitutionality of the eighth section of the Missouri Compromise was *illogical,* as being inconsistent with the earlier part of his opinion, the purport of which, it is alleged, was to remove from the court's jurisdiction the record of the case in the lower court and, with it, any basis for a pronouncement upon the constitutional question; and secondly, that it was *in disregard of precedent,* which, it is contended, exacted that the court should not pass upon issues other than those its decision of which was strictly necessary to the determination of the case before it, and particularly that it should not unnecessarily pronounce a legislative enactment unconstitutional.[35]

In his discussion of the first charge, Corwin points out that the initial task of the Court in the Dred Scott case was to decide whether or not the plea in abatement was properly before the judges. He states that a majority "ruled decisively both that the plea in abatement was before it and that the decision of the circuit court as to its jurisdiction was subject to review by the Supreme Court." [36] This is a very significant statement for two reasons: first, Corwin accepts Taney's position that the question of the Circuit Court's jurisdiction might be reviewed both on the plea in abatement and also on any other grounds that were germane to this point; and second, Corwin disagrees with all previous writers except Ewing in saying that a majority of the Court held that the plea in abatement was before them. Having dealt with this point, Corwin goes on to cite Taney's defense of his examination of all sides of the jurisdictional question and then states:

The Chief Justice's theory was, not that he was canvassing the case on its merits, which he could have done with propriety only had he chosen to ignore the question of jurisdiction, but that he was fortifying his decision upon this matter of jurisdiction by reviewing the issues raised in the bill of exceptions, *as well as* those raised by the plea in abatement; in other words that he was canvassing the matter of jurisdiction afresh.[37]

Having disposed of the first part of the charge that Taney was uttering *obiter dicta* in passing on the constitutionality of the Missouri Compromise, Corwin goes on to the question of whether or not a judge may give an opinion on more points than those "strictly necessary to a determination of the case before it." He points out that there are differing views among the authorities as to what constitutes *obiter dictum* but insists that American constitutional law differs widely from the common law in this respect.[38] To illustrate this point he cites the decision of John Marshall in *Cohens vs. Virginia* that that suit did not violate the Eleventh Amendment, a pronouncement not "strictly necessary" to a disposition of the case and yet one which has "from that day to the present been regarded as establishing the law on the point with which it deals." [39] It follows, therefore, that the only feasible definition, historically, of *obiter dictum* in the field of American Constitutional Law would seem to be, a more or less casual utterance by a court or members thereof upon some point not deemed by the court itself to be strictly before it and not necessary to decide, as preliminary to the determination of the controversy before it.[40]

Corwin concludes:

Chief Justice Taney had therefore, it appears, a clear right to canvass the question of Scott's servitude in support of his decision that Dred was not a citizen of the United States, and he had the same right to canvass the question of the constitutionality of the Missouri Compromise in support of his decision that Dred was a slave. . . . If then the decision rendered by six of the nine judges on the bench, that the Missouri Compromise was unconstitutional, is to be stigmatized as unwarrantable, which is all that the court of history can do with it, it is not by pronouncing it to have been *obiter dictum*.[41]

When a constitutional historian of Corwin's reputation can make as categorical a statement as this, the teacher might well think that that was the end of the matter and conclude that he could safely tell his classes that the Court did "decide" that the Missouri Compromise was unconstitutional.

Corwin's article was by no means the end of the matter, however. In the first place, he did not deal with what the Court "decided" on the question of Negro citizenship. Secondly, his statement that a majority of the Court "ruled decisively both that the plea in abatement was before it and that the decision of the circuit court as to its jurisdiction was subject to review by the Supreme Court" was liable to misinterpretation. At first glance it looks as if the second half of this statement is redundant and that Corwin is simply stating that a majority of the Court considered the plea in abatement to be before them. Furthermore, since almost all previous writers had agreed that only *four* of the judges believed the plea before them, it might seem that Corwin's whole case rested on this question of how many judges considered the plea before them. A comparison of the Corwin article with those of Lowell and Gray and of Curtis reveals that there was disagreement as to the position taken by Justice Campbell on the plea in abatement. This disagreement, as will be shown below, was to be the source of future controversy.

When Charles Warren's *The Supreme Court in United States History* first appeared, in 1922, the author dismissed the whole question of what the Court decided (and incidentally this paper as well) with the following statement:

> At the present date the technicalities of the case are of no particular interest; and the interminable discussion as to whether the Court was justified in deciding on the merits of the case, after holding that the Circuit Court had no jurisdiction, is now of very slight interest. It will suffice to say that six of the judges . . . concurred in holding, not only that a negro could not be a citizen of the United States, but also that Congress had no power to exclude slavery from the Territories.[42]

Though Warren quotes from Corwin's article with approval, his remarks about "deciding on the merits of the case" show that he missed Corwin's point completely. Furthermore, he introduces a new viewpoint into the discussion when he announces that six judges held that no Negro could be a citizen. No one up to this time except Ewing had held this position.[43]

Four years later Horace H. Hagan published a most illuminating article on the Dred Scott case in the *Georgetown Law Journal*.[44] After delivering himself of some most uncharitable remarks on professors of history who attempt to deal with legal subjects,[45] Hagan addresses himself to the charge that Taney was uttering *obiter dicta* when he passed on the constitutionality of the Missouri Compromise, after having decided that the lower court had had no jurisdiction because no Negro could be a citizen of the United States. Hagan first agrees with most of the earlier writers that only a minority of the Court considered the plea in abatement to be before them and then makes this significant statement:

> *In other words, Taney in that part of his opinion dealing with the inability to be a citizen, within the meaning of the Federal Constitution, of a Negro, who had been a slave or who was descended from slaves, was in a minority and his views on this subject are not the views or the judgment of the Court.*[46]

He then proceeds to assert that the Court had a perfect right to decide that it had no jurisdiction because Scott was a slave and adds: "That it is not *obiter dicta* for a Court, after basing its judgment on one ground, to give additional reasons, arising under the issues, for its conclusion, is thoroughly established by the decisions of the Supreme Court of the United States and other Courts of the highest standing."[47]

Hagan's article is noteworthy because of the use he makes of the judgment of the Court. After pointing out that this judgment ordered the Circuit Court to dismiss the case, on the grounds that Scott was not a citizen of Missouri, he states:

> It [the Court] could rest its judgment on the one ground that Scott was a slave and therefore not a citizen or on the one ground that even if free he was not a citizen . . . or it could rest its conclusion of "no jurisdiction" on both grounds. *As a matter of fact, however, and this is the vital point so often overlooked, it was only on the contention that Scott was still a slave that a majority of the court was obtained on the jurisdictional point.* To say that its opinion on this point was dictum is equivalent to saying that in reality the Court pronounced no judgment whatever.[48]

Hagan's examination of the right of the Court to review the constitutionality of the Missouri Compromise is equally enlightening. It is worth quoting his statement on this point in full:

> In order for the Court to determine that Scott was still a slave, it was necessary for it to pass upon the validity of the Missouri Compromise. Scott had been taken by his master to the Territory of Wisconsin, where slavery was prohibited under that Act of Congress. If that Act were valid, Scott was free while in Wisconsin and free by virtue of an Act of Congress, passed under Constitutional authority. If so, could the laws of Missouri, upon his return to that state, make a slave out of a man freed by the paramount power of the Federal legislature? Some critics of the judgment of the Court impliedly replied in the affirmative by stating that this did occur under the prior decision of the Court in *Strader v. Graham* . . . and that the Court should have based its decision upon that authority alone and should have declined to consider the validity of the Congressional Act. In the Strader case, however, a Negro slave had gone with his master's consent from the State of Kentucky to the State of Ohio, where slavery was forbidden, and had then returned to Kentucky, and it was held that his status, while in Kentucky, was conclusively established by the decision of its courts that he was still a slave. But, evidently, the rule thus applied between equal sovereignties would not logically or necessarily apply where it was a question only of an apparent conflict between a law of the Federal Government and the laws of the State of Missouri. If the Federal law were constitutional, it was supreme and the laws of Missouri could not create a slave out of a man whom a valid enactment of a paramount power had declared to be free. Therefore, the vital question in the Dred Scott case, the question that could not be avoided, was the constitutionality of the Missouri Compromise.[49]

Dred Scott Labyrinth

Though Hagan never cites Corwin's article, his treatment of the question of what the Court decided is essentially an elaboration on the Corwin theme. Taken together, the two articles establish a most convincing explanation of what Taney's opinion meant and what its relationship to the other opinions was. The one basic question left unanswered is this: how was it, if only three of the judges held that no Negro could be a citizen, that five of the judges could, in their opinions, speak of this question as having been "decided" by the Court? [50] The only possible explanation for this is that some of the judges must have changed their positions between the time when the case was discussed by the full court and the time the decisions were handed down. And the chances are that if the evidence to support this presumption has not appeared by now, it never will. With this one exception, therefore, the Corwin-Hagan position gives the teacher a most persuasive explanation of the mystery of what the Court decided in the Dred Scott case.

This is, however, by no means the end of the story. In the course of the next few years two articles were published in the *Mississippi Valley Historical Review* which attacked Taney's opinion afresh and which sought to establish the opinion of Justice Nelson as the only really legitimate one. In 1929 Frank H. Hodder's article entitled "Some Phases of the Dred Scott Case" appeared.[51] This study of the case contained new material and a fresh point of view; and it immediately attracted wide attention, primarily because of the author's attempt to attribute motives of self-interest to Curtis' dissenting opinion.[52] On the question of what the Court decided, however, Hodder's treatment leaves much to be desired. Essentially, he returns to the position taken by Thayer. He speaks of Taney trying "to prove that the Court had a right to discuss the merits of the case after deciding that it had no jurisdiction" but then goes on to add that "technically Taney acted in accordance with what at that time was the practice of the Court" and cites Corwin as reference for this second statement.[53] This shows that he had missed Corwin's point about Taney's "canvassing the matter of jurisdiction afresh," for Corwin makes it clear that the Chief Justice could not have reviewed the case on its merits unless he had chosen to ignore the question of jurisdiction or held that the Circuit Court was right in hearing the case. Justice Nelson, according to Hodder, delivered the "only respectable opinion" of the Court and was "the only member . . . who thought clearly in the midst of seething political controversy." [54] While it is true that six of the judges concurred with Nelson, his opinion is based on the assumption that neither Illinois law nor an Act of Congress could have any extraterritorial effect, a point which Hodder states without elaboration.[55] This, however, ignores Hagan's statement on the *Strader vs. Graham* decision that "the rule thus applied between equal sovereignties would not logically or necessarily apply where it was a question only of an apparent conflict between a law of the Federal Government and the laws of the State of Missouri." While the Hodder article contains a great deal of interesting material on other aspects of the case, the treatment of the Taney opinion shows a basic misunderstanding both of that opinion and of the Corwin article.

In 1933 Richard R. Stenberg's article entitled "Some Political Aspects of the Dred Scott Case" appeared in the *Mississippi Valley Historical Review*.[56] Stenberg carried the Hodder thesis even further and sought to prove that unless a majority of the judges had considered the plea in abatement before the Court, there could have been no examination of either the question of jurisdiction or the constitutionality of the Missouri Compromise. Stenberg cites Corwin as arguing "that, if five justices held the plea of [*sic*] abatement to be before the court and held the Missouri Compromise unconstitutional, it cannot be said that this part of the argument was any more *obiter dictum* than any other part." He then goes on: "The argument is logical, but rests on the assumption that a majority of the court did hold the plea in abatement to be before the court." [57] Stenberg then points out that Corwin counted Justice Campbell as one of those who held the plea to be before the court. To prove Corwin mistaken on this, he quotes from a letter which Justice Catron wrote to a friend in Missouri in which it is categorically stated that Campbell did *not* believe the plea before the Court.[58] This, according to Stenberg, proves most of Taney's opinion *obiter dicta*. This conclusion betrays, again, confusion about Taney's opinion and Corwin's explanation of it. It assumes, apparently, that no jurisdictional question could be taken up by the Court unless a majority of the Court thought the plea in abatement before them. The confusion may well stem from the statement of Corwin quoted above that a majority "ruled decisively both that the plea in abatement was before it and that the decision of the circuit court as to its jurisdiction was subject to review by the Supreme Court." Apparently Stenberg considered this one and the same ruling instead of two separate ones. This mistake is the more understandable because the weight of evidence indicates that only four justices thought the plea before them, and that Corwin was wrong on that point.[59] Still, as an argument that Taney's opinion was *obiter dicta,* the Stenberg position is untenable.

Carl B. Swisher's life of Taney, published in 1935,[60] contains an unusually lucid account of the Dred Scott case, especially on the question of what the Court decided. After agreeing with everyone except Ewing and Corwin that a minority of the Court believed the plea in abatement before them,[61] he makes the following statement:

> Others [of the judges] presumably agreed with him [Taney] in private as to the inability of negroes to be citizens, but because of differences as to technical problems of procedure, or because they felt that the discussion of the first point might embarrass the discussion of the second [the constitutionality of the Missouri Compromise], in which they were more deeply interested, they did not concur in this portion of Taney's opinion. This was true in spite of the fact that Taney referred to his opinion as the opinion of the court.[62]

Though this statement leaves unanswered the problem of how so many of the judges could speak of the question of Negro citizenship as having been "decided" by the Court, it suggests that Taney expected to carry a majority of the judges with him on this point. Certainly there is no other possible explanation of this mysterious matter. Swisher goes on to point out that the critics of Taney "tended to ignore the fact that he was still dealing with jurisdiction, and claimed that, having decided that the court had no jurisdiction, Taney had gone on to a discussion of the merits as if the court had jurisdiction." [63] Swisher concludes: "Their [the critics'] characterization of Taney's discussion of his second point [the constitutionality of the Missouri Compromise] as illegitimate because delivered as *obiter dictum,* and as a treatment merely of the merits of the case after having decided against jurisdiction, is not to be accepted without the reserve which the facts justify." [64] Thus Swisher supports, essentially, the position taken by Corwin, whom he cites with approval. While the teacher might wish that the statement on the *obiter dictum* question had been more positive, and might be in doubt as to just what the phrase "without the reserve which the facts justify" means, this study of the case is clear and logical throughout.

Before 1935 all of the studies of the Dred Scott case had appeared in publications that would be likely to attract the attention of the specialists only. Swisher's life of Taney, however, was published by a nationally known commercial house in New York City and presumably received the widespread attention which it deserved. Furthermore, when Swisher published his *American Constitutional Development* in 1943, which included an account of the Dred Scott case that followed very closely that in his life of Taney,[65] his treatment of the case was given a very wide currency indeed. The teacher might think that since no fresh study of the case has attempted to challenge the Swisher position,[66] that position might gradually have become accepted as the "correct" one on the question of what the Court "decided." It is a discouraging commentary on the writing of history to report that nothing of the kind has happened. Though many accounts of the Dred Scott case have been written since 1935, the teacher has been unable to discover one which gives a really satisfactory explanation of what the Court did "decide." One example should suffice to illustrate this point. It is taken from Avery Craven's *The Coming of the Civil War,* published in 1942. In the course of his discussion of the Dred Scott case, the author makes the following statement:

> The second part of Taney's argument was designed to prove the Court's right to discuss the merits of the case after it had decided that it had no jurisdiction. It is now generally agreed that he succeeded in showing that this was the accepted practice of the Court at that time; but it is also generally agreed that the Court's opinion was nothing more than *obiter dicta* and that to give such an opinion when the public mind was so stirred over the slavery issue showed deplorably bad judgment.[67]

This whole question of what the Court decided might, however, be approached from an entirely different point of view—a purely pragmatic one. If this approach is used, the question now becomes: Was the decision of the Court binding on the country in the years following its delivery? The Republican Party certainly ignored the decision when, in their 1860 platform, they took the position of denying "the authority of Congress, of a territorial legislature, or of any individual to give legal existence to Slavery in any Territory of the United States." In 1862 Congress abolished slavery in the territories without so much as a "by-your-leave" to the Supreme Court. In short, it looks as if Allan Nevins is correct when he says, "When the Republicans took control of the government, the decision was set aside quietly, completely, and forever."[68]

If, however, the teacher should happen on an article by Morris M. Cohn entitled "The Dred Scott Case in the Light of Later Events," [69] he will begin to wonder if the decision had actually been set aside. Cohn's purpose is, as he says, "to show that the authority of that case [Dred Scott] has not been impaired in any of its legal phases." [70] He starts by citing the statement of Justice Miller in the Slaughter House cases, to the effect that the Dred Scott decision that a slave could not be a citizen was "effective to compel the adoption" of the Thirteenth and Fourteenth Amendments. [71] He then goes on to show that Taney's position on the Missouri Compromise—that it violated the Fifth Amendment—was "met with approval by later judges of the same court." [72] Though Cohn cites a large number of cases, [73] he concentrates on *Downes vs. Bidwell*—one of the so-called "Insular" cases. He points out that all the judges cited the Dred Scott decision in this case, and that Justice White, one of the majority, made extensive use of it. Admitting that Taney's refusal to distinguish between slaves and other forms of property may have been erroneous, Justice White insisted that Taney's interpretation of the Fifth Amendment was sound. [74] Cohn concludes:

> The decision in the Dred Scott case was sound in principle. When the tumult of anger and outrage, engendered by the slavery question had passed away, and the judges were confronted with the principles announced by that decision, they did not disregard it. The tribute which Mr. Justice Brown paid to the ruling, that as to property rights the decision was impregnable, shows that there was lasting quality in that decision, which, when occasion should compel, would come out. [75]

Without necessarily accepting all of Cohn's arguments, it is still clear that the Dred Scott decision *has* been cited as precedent in later cases and thus, to that extent, has not been "set aside quietly, completely, and forever." In short, the teacher can get little comfort from what he learns if he attempts to use a pragmatic approach to the Dred Scott case.

Finally, if a *coup de grâce* needs to be administered to his hopes that he may discover what the judges did "decide" in the Dred Scott case, the teacher has only to ponder the point made by James G. Randall that the controversy was not really a case at law at all. As Randall puts it:

> The Dred Scott case was hardly in essence a judicial controversy at all. In the form in which it was brought before the United States Supreme Court it was only nominally a case at law involving an immediate issue as to per-

sonal or property rights to be determined by court decree. Whatever the decree, it had been predetermined by the parties to the suit, who were not *bona fide* litigants with opposite interests, that the Negro and his family should be set free.[76]

To what extent the moot character of the case serves to invalidate the decision cannot be determined here. One thing is certain: it can only add to the already numerous perplexities that becloud the controversy and leave the teacher even more unhappy about what disposition to make of the legal tribulations of Dred Scott.[77]

After protracted wanderings in the Dred Scott labyrinth, the teacher can, however, reach a few relatively firm positions on what the Court did "decide" in this much-disputed case. He can assert with confidence that the Court did reach a judicial decision that Scott was a slave and therefore ineligible to sue as a citizen in the federal courts. He can assert with equal confidence that there was no judicial decision on the question of Negro citizenship. And thirdly, he can assert, with a shade less confidence, that the Court did decide judicially that the Missouri Compromise had been unconstitutional. As for the mystery of how five of the judges could speak of the Court's "decision" that no Negro could be a citizen when only three of them supported that position in their opinions, he can do no more than speculate. This much achieved, the teacher is now free to examine some of the other controversies which surround the case: How did the suit get started in the first place, and who was responsible for its being carried to the Supreme Court of the United States?[78] Why did the Supreme Court of Missouri reverse all previous precedents in their decision on the appeal?[79] Who was responsible for causing the Supreme Court of the United States to drop its original plan of dealing with only the narrowest aspects of the case?[80] And so forth. As he surveys these new labyrinths, the teacher is tempted to conclude that the only sensible way of handling the Dred Scott case in class is to ask—hurriedly—if there are any questions on the reading assignments which cover the subject, pray that there will be none, and then pass rapidly on to the Lincoln-Douglas debates.[81]

1. The basic source for this case is Benjamin C. Howard, *A Report of the Decision of the Supreme Court of the United States and the Opinions of the Judges thereof, in the Case of Dred Scott versus John F. A. Sandford* (New

York, 1857). It can be found in Howard's *Reports*, XIX, 393–633, and was also printed separately. It will be hereafter cited as *19 Howard*. The correct spelling of the defendant's name is Sanford.

2. When Scott first sued Sanford in the federal Circuit Court, the latter entered a plea in abatement in which he claimed that Scott had no right to sue because he was a "negro of African descent; his ancestors were of pure African blood, and were brought into this country and sold as negro slaves." If the Circuit Court had sustained this plea, they would have been ruling that *no* Negro, free or slave, was eligible to sue in the federal courts. The plea in abatement is in *19 Howard*, pp. 396–397.

3. *Ibid.*, p. 427.

4. *Ibid.*, pp. 427–429.

5. *Ibid.*, pp. 589–590.

6. This article first appeared in the *Law Reporter* for June, 1857. It was soon thereafter separately published under the title *A Legal Review of the Case of Dred Scott as Decided by the Supreme Court of the United States* (Boston, 1857). For the authorship of this review, see J. B. Thayer, *Cases on Constitutional Law* (Cambridge, Mass., 1895), I, 495.

7. *A Legal Review*, p. 57.

8. *Ibid.*, pp. 10–12.

9. *Ibid.*, p. 12.

10. *Ibid.*, p. 24.

11. *Ibid.*, pp. 25–26.

12. *Historical and Legal Examination of That Part of the Decision of the Supreme Court of the United States in the Dred Scott Case, etc.* (New York, 1857).

13. *Ibid.*, p. 26.

14. *Ibid.*, pp. 7–8.

15. *Ibid.*, p. 25. For a reiteration of this point, see p. 121.

16. *Constitutional History of the United States, etc.* (New York, 1896), hereafter to be cited as *Constitutional History*. Curtis' pamphlet was published in 1859. See *Constitutional History*, II, 266.

17. *Ibid.*, II, 268–270.

18. *Ibid.*, II, 270–271.

19. For a thorough but much more partisan review of the case by a contemporary, see Timothy Farrar's article in the *North American Review*, LXXXV (October, 1857), 392–415. Farrar takes the position that the Court decided nothing at all.

20. For a discussion of this school of historical writers, see H. K. Beale, "What Historians Have Said about the Causes of the Civil War," in *Theory and Practice in Historical Study: A Report of the Committee on Historiography*, published by the Social Science Research Council (New York, no date), pp. 59–61

21. John G. Nicolay and John Hay, *Abraham Lincoln: A History* (New York, 1886), II, 69–77.

22. *History of the United States from the Compromise of 1850, etc.* (New York, 1892), II, 253–261.

23. *Ibid.*, II, 257, 261.

24. Thayer, *op. cit.*, I, 480.

25. *Ibid.*, I, 490.

26. *Ibid.*, I, 495–496.

27. *19 Howard*, p. 469.

28. The only account favorable to Taney written before 1900 that this writer has discovered is in Samuel Tyler, *Memoir of Roger Brooke Taney* (Baltimore, 1872). After characterizing Taney's opinion as "the most comprehensive and best-reasoned politico-judicial opinion ever pronounced by any tribunal," Tyler proceeds to spend most of his time attacking the dissenting opinion of Curtis and lambasting Seward for his animadversions on Taney in his Senate speech of 1858. At no point does Tyler attempt a careful analysis of the Taney opinion. See pp. 360–391.

29. (Washington, 1909).

30. Ewing, *Legal and Historical Status*, pp. 34–44.

31. *Ibid.*, pp. 106–109.

32. *Ibid.*, p. 110.

33. Edward S. Corwin makes the following statement about Ewing's book. After acknowledging Ewing as the source for a quotation from a law encyclopedia, he says: "I may add that this is the sum total of my indebtedness to the work mentioned" (*American Historical Review*, XVII [1911], 56 n).

34. "The Dred Scott Decision, in the Light of Contemporary Legal Doctrines," *American Historical Review*, XVII (1911), 52–69. This same article, with minor revisions, was published in E. S. Corwin, *The Doctrine of Judicial Review* (Princeton, 1914), pp. 129–157.

35. Corwin, *Doctrine of Judicial Review*, p. 134.

36. *Ibid.*, pp. 134–135.

37. *Ibid.*, pp. 135–136.

38. *Ibid.*, pp. 136–138.

39. *Ibid.*, p. 138. Corwin's statement in *American Historical Review*, XVII (1911), 58, is even stronger: "It [Marshall's decision] had always been regarded as good law in all its parts and indeed was so treated and enforced, once and again, by the court over which Taney himself presided."

40. Corwin, *Doctrine of Judicial Review*, p. 139.

41. *Ibid.*, pp. 139–140. It should be pointed out that after supporting Taney on the *obiter dictum* question, Corwin went on to attack his use of the Fifth Amendment to invalidate the Missouri Compromise.

42. Charles Warren, *The Supreme Court in the United States History* (Boston, 1922), III, 22–23.

43. Three other accounts of the case which appeared during the 1920's can be dismissed briefly in passing. In 1922 B. C. Steiner's *Life of Roger Brooke Taney* (Baltimore) appeared. He attempted to sum up the Court's decision on the various points as follows (p. 372): "By a vote of seven to two (McLean

and Curtis), the Court had held that Scott was a slave. Three of the justices (Taney, Wayne, and Daniel) had said that no descendant of a slave could be a citizen, and one (Curtis) had dissented from that view. Four, and possibly five, justices (Taney, Wayne, Daniel, Curtis, and possibly Grier), had decided that the plea in abatement and the whole judgment of the Court below were before the Court on the record, two had denied this (Catron and McLean), and two (Nelson and Campbell) expressed no opinion in the matter. Nelson rested his entire opinion on reaffirming the decision of the Circuit Court, and five, including Taney, concurred with him. Four justices out of nine held the Missouri Compromise Act unconstitutional (Taney, Wayne, Grier, and Catron). The confused condition of affairs appears in these combinations."

Steiner's arithmetic adds greatly to the "confused condition of affairs." He stands alone in naming Grier as one of those who thought the plea in abatement before the Court. Six, and not five, judges concurred with Nelson in affirming the judgment of the Circuit Court. Finally six, and not four, of the justices believed the Missouri Compromise unconstitutional.

Edward Channing's account of the case, which appeared in the sixth volume of his *A History of the United States* (New York: The Macmillan Company, 1925), contains some interesting material on other aspects of the controversy, but adds little to a solution of the problem of what the judges decided. He says (pp. 194–195):

"Technically, the only thing decided was that the Supreme Court of the United States and the Federal Circuit Court of the Missouri district had no jurisdiction because Dred Scott was not and could not be a "citizen" within the meaning of the Constitution, and therefore the suit must be dismissed. As by-products, the majority of the judges in reaching this decision had incidentally rendered other decisions or quasi-decisions,—one of these was that mere residence in a Free State did not prevent a negro from returning to the condition of slavery on returning to a Slave State. Another, a third, was that Congress could not exclude slavery from the national domain by a law and therefore that the Missouri Compromise and probably the law confirming the Ordinance of 1787 were illegal."

Channing seems to imply, by his use of the words "incidentally" and "quasi-decisions," that the Court's ruling on the Missouri Compromise was extra-judicial, but his statement is not precise enough to make such a conclusion warrantable. Nowhere does he cite Corwin's article in the *American Historical Review*.

When Albert J. Beveridge published his *Abraham Lincoln, 1809–1858* (Boston, 1928), he simply followed Warren, Channing, and Steiner. He speaks of Warren's account as "full, detailed, accurate, and distinguished for impartiality, fairness, and courage." He speaks of Channing's account as "brilliant and reliable" (see II, 456 n.).

44. "The Dred Scott Decision," *Georgetown Law Journal*, XV (1926), 95–114.

45. "If the circumstances surrounding the Dred Scott case have been misconceived, the decision itself has been even more grievously mistreated. It is a shining example of the danger inherent in college professors writing on legal subjects. A degree in sociology, philosophy, or political science does not necessarily qualify even a first-rate historical mind to analyze properly a complicated legal decision or opinion." Even the lawyers "have seen fit to adopt the conclusions of New England and Ohio professors of history" (*ibid.*, pp. 106–107).

46. *Ibid.*, p. 108. Italics Hagan's.

47. *Ibid.*, p. 108, and note 22, where a long list of cases is cited to prove this point. These cases are all later than the Dred Scott case, however.

48. *Ibid.*, p. 109. Italics Hagan's.

49. *Ibid.*, pp. 109–110.

50. Taney (*19 Howard*, p. 427) says: "The court is of opinion . . . that the judgment on the plea in abatement is erroneous." And over a year later, in a supplementary statement, the Chief Justice (Tyler, *op. cit.*, p. 578) said: "It is true, that in the case of Dred Scott the decision is in express terms confined to the case of a person of the African race whose ancestors had been brought to this country as slaves. . . . And the Court deemed it to be its duty to confine the decision to the case before it, and says so in the opinion delivered." Curtis (*19 Howard*, p. 589) says: "Having first decided that they were bound to consider the sufficiency of the plea to the jurisdiction of the Circuit Court, and having decided that this plea showed that the Circuit Court had not jurisdiction . . ." McLean (*19 Howard*, p. 549) speaks of the jurisdiction of the court "against which they decided" and was apparently speaking of the plea in abatement. Wayne (*19 Howard*, p. 454) says: "The opinion of the court meets fully and decides every point which was made in the argument of the case by the counsel of either side of it. Nothing belonging to the case has been left undecided." And finally Daniel (*19 Howard*, p. 482) speaks as if a decision on the plea in abatement had made it unnecessary to go further, but justifies further discussion because "these questions are intrinsically of primary interest and magnitude, and have been elaborately discussed in argument, and . . . with respect to them the opinions of a majority of the court, including my own, are perfectly coincident."

51. *Mississippi Valley Historical Review*, XVI (1929), 3–22.

52. *Ibid.*, pp. 13–15.

53. *Ibid.*, p. 18 and footnote 46.

54. *Ibid.*, p. 12.

55. *Ibid.*, p. 11.

56. *Mississippi Valley Historical Review*, XIX (1933), 571–577.

57. *Ibid.*, p. 576.

58. *Ibid.*, pp. 576–577. This letter, dated May 31, 1857, was from Catron to Judge Samuel Treat of Missouri. The testimony is weakened, however, when Catron speaks of Curtis as also believing the plea in abatement was

not before the Court. See *19 Howard,* p. 567, for a clear statement that the opposite was true.

59. Campbell's own statement (*20 Wallace,* p. xi) is that "the plea in abatement and the questions arising upon it, in the opinion of a majority of the court, were not before the court." He lists McLean, Catron, Nelson, Grier, and himself as supporting this view. See Thayer, *op. cit.,* I, 491 n.

60. *Roger B. Taney* (New York, 1935).

61. *Ibid.,* p. 506. For some reason, Swisher does not list Curtis as one of those who believed the plea in abatement to be before the Court.

62. *Ibid.*

63. *Ibid.,* p. 508.

64. *Ibid.,* p. 509 and note 16.

65. Carl B. Swisher, *American Constitutional Development* (Boston, 1943), pp. 243–251.

66. In 1951 Father Vincent C. Hopkins' *Dred Scott's Case* (New York) appeared. This study is a very detailed examination of every phase of the case, particularly of its early stages. It includes lengthy paraphrases of each judge's opinion, and closes with a careful examination of the constitutional issues which the case presented. Though this book is an extremely useful one, the author passes few judgments on the material he discusses, and those which he does pass are not original. Father Hopkins accepts the Corwin-Hagan-Swisher position when he speaks of Taney covering all the points argued by counsel "from the viewpoint of jurisdiction" (p. 72).

67. Avery Craven, *The Coming of the Civil War* (New York, 1942), p. 383.

68. Allan Nevins, *The Emergence of Lincoln* (New York, 1950), I, 115.

69. *American Law Review,* XLVI (1912), 548–557.

70. *Ibid.,* p. 554 n.

71. *Ibid.,* pp. 548, 556.

72. *Ibid.,* p. 549.

73. *Ibid.,* p. 551 n.

74. *Ibid.,* p. 555.

75. *Ibid.,* p. 556.

76. James G. Randall, *Civil War and Reconstruction* (New York, 1937), p. 148.

77. The latest, and by far the most charming, addition to the literature on the case is an article by John Charles Hogan entitled "The Role of Chief Justice Taney in the Decision of the Dred Scott Case," which appeared in the January-February, 1953, number of *Case and Comment.* Hogan, who is identified as "First Year Student, School of Law, U.C.L.A.," attempts to prove that Taney never wrote his opinion at all but that it was the work of Justice Wayne. He bases his case (1) on Taney's known illnesses and incapacity for work during the early part of 1857; (2) on Taney's delay in

filing his opinion with the Court reporter after the decision had been read; (3) on a vocabulary and word-count analysis of the opinion and of Wayne's writings; and (4) on the fact that Wayne concurred so fully with Taney and delivered so brief an opinion of his own. The article is undocumented and unworthy of serious consideration, but the idea is an intriguing one. I am indebted to Mrs. Lucie-Lee Hancock, Librarian of the Lawrence (Mass.) Law Library, for calling my attention to this article.

78. On this question, see Hopkins, *op. cit.*, Appendix.

79. See Helen T. Catterall, "Some Antecedents of the Dred Scott Case," *American Historical Review*, XXX (1924–1925), 56–71.

80. On this question compare the treatment of F. H. Hodder, *loc. cit.*, with that in Allan Nevins, *op. cit.*, II, Appendix I.

81. I wish to record my gratitude to my former teacher, the late Professor James G. Randall of the University of Illinois; to my colleague Dr. Miles S. Malone of Phillips Academy, Andover; and to Messrs. James S. and John P. Eastham, attorneys, of Andover, for valuable assistance in connection with the preparation of this paper. Needless to say, none of the above-mentioned gentlemen should in any way be held responsible for any of my statements.

Contributors

FREDERICK S. ALLIS, JR. (A.B., Amherst, 1935; M.A., Harvard, 1940). Instructor in History, Phillips Academy, Andover. Author of "Boston and the Alien and Sedition Laws," *Proceedings of the Bostonian Society* (1951). Editor of *William Bingham's Maine Lands, 1790–1820, Publications of the Colonial Society of Massachusetts,* XXXVI and XXXVII (Boston, 1954).

JOHN BOWDITCH (A.B., Amherst, 1936; Ph.D., Harvard, 1949). Associate Professor of History, University of Minnesota. Author of *Anzio Beachhead* (Washington, 1947). Co-author of *A History of the Fifth Army,* IV and VII (Washington, 1946). Contributor to *Modern France: Problems of the Third and Fourth Republics,* edited by Edward Mead Earle (Princeton, 1951).

RALPH BOWEN (A.B., Amherst, 1940; Ph.D., Columbia, 1946). Assistant Professor of History, Columbia University. Author of *German Theories of the Corporative State, with Special Reference to the Period 1870–1919* (New York, 1947); "The Philosophy of Giambattista Vico," *Columbia Journal of Philosophy,* XLVI (1949); "La Modernité de Diderot," *Les Cahiers Haut-Marnais,* No. 24 (1951). Co-author of *Chapters in Western Civilization,* I (New York, 1948). Co-editor of *Introduction to Contemporary Civilization in the West,* 2nd edition, 2 vols. (New York, 1954).

BURR C. BRUNDAGE (A.B., Amherst, 1936; Ph.D., Chicago, 1939). Professor of History and Chairman of the Department of History and Political Science, Cedar Crest College. Author of *The Juniper Palace* (New York, 1951); "The Ancient Near East as History," *American Historical Review,* LIV (1949); "The Place of the Ancient Near East in the Study of History," *History*, New Series, XXXVI (1951). Contributor to *The Place of Feudalism in History*, edited by Rushton Coulborn (Princeton, 1954).

ROBERT F. BYRNES (A.B., Amherst, 1939; Ph.D., Harvard, 1947). Associate Professor of History, Rutgers University. Author of *Antisemitism in Modern France: I, The Prelude to the Dreyfus Affair* (New Brunswick, N.J., 1950); "Marpon et Flammarion," *Revue des Sciences Humaines*, LIX (1950); "Pobedonostsev's Conception of the Good Society," *Review of Politics*, XIII (1951). Contributor to *Modern France: Problems of the Third and Fourth Republics*, edited by Edward Mead Earle (Princeton, 1951).

JAMES F. CLARKE (A.B., Amherst, 1928; Ph.D., Harvard, 1938). Professor of History and Director, Institute of East European Studies, Indiana University. Author of "The First Bulgarian Book," *Harvard Library Notes*, III (1940); "Serbia and the Bulgarian Revival," *American Slavic and East European Review*, IV (1945). Contributor to *Essays in the History of Modern Europe*, edited by Donald C. McKay (New York, 1936).

CHARLES WOOLSEY COLE (A.B., Amherst, 1927; Ph.D., Columbia, 1931). President of Amherst College. Author of *French Mercantilist Doctrines before Colbert* (New York, 1931); *Colbert and a Century of French Mercantilism*, 2 vols. (New York, 1939); *French Mercantilism, 1683–1700* (New York, 1943); "Relativity of History," *Political Science Quarterly*, XLVIII (1933). Co-author of *Economic History of Europe* (Boston, 1941); *History of Europe* (New York, 1949). Contributor to *Redirecting Education*, edited by R. G. Tugwell and L. Keyserling (New York, 1934).

PAUL FARMER (A.B., Amherst, 1939; Ph.D., Columbia, 1942). Associate Professor of History, University of Wisconsin. Author of *France Reviews Its Revolutionary Origins: Social Politics and Historical Opinion under the Third Republic* (New York, 1944); *The European World: A Historical Introduction* (New York, 1951). Contributor to *The Modern University*, edited by Margaret Clapp (Ithaca, N.Y., 1950).

ALLEN GILMORE (A.B., Amherst, 1935; Ph.D., Harvard, 1942). Washington, D.C. Author of "Augustine and the Critical Method," *Harvard Theological Review*, XXXIX (1946); "The Methods and Concepts of History," *Journal of General Education*, VI (1952).

List of Contributors

MYRON P. GILMORE (A.B., Amherst, 1932; Ph.D., Harvard, 1937). Professor of History, Harvard University. Author of *Argument from Roman Law in Political Thought 1200–1600* (Cambridge, Mass., 1941); *The World of Humanism 1453–1517* (New York, 1952); "Authority and Property in the Seventeenth Century: The First Edition of the *Traité de Seigneuries* of Charles Loyseau," *Harvard Library Bulletin*, IV (1950). Contributor to *Problems in European History*, edited by Kenneth Setton (New York, 1954).

JOHN WHITNEY HALL (A.B., Amherst, 1939; Ph.D., Harvard, 1950). Assistant Professor of History, University of Michigan. Author of *Japanese History, A Guide to Japanese Research and Reference Materials* (Ann Arbor, Mich., 1954); *Tanuma Okitsugu, Forerunner of Modern Japan* (Cambridge, Mass., 1954); "Notes on the Early Ch'ing Copper Trade with Japan," *Harvard Journal of Asiatic Studies*, XII (1949); "Materials for the Study of Local History in Japan: Pre-Meiji Village Records," *Occasional Papers* (University of Michigan, Center for Japanese Studies), No. 3 (1953). Editor of *Occasional Papers* (semiannual).

H. STUART HUGHES (A.B., Amherst, 1937; Ph.D., Harvard, 1940). Associate Professor of History, Stanford University. Author of *An Essay for Our Times* (New York, 1950); *Oswald Spengler: A Critical Estimate* (New York, 1952); *The United States and Italy* (Cambridge, Mass., 1953); "The End of Political Ideology," *Measure*, II (1951); "The Problem of Limited Collaboration," *Confluence*, III (1954). Contributor to *Modern France: Problems of the Third and Fourth Republics*, edited by Edward Mead Earle (Princeton, 1951); *The Diplomats: 1919–1939*, edited by Gordon A. Craig and Felix Gilbert (Princeton, 1953).

MELVIN KRANZBERG (A.B., Amherst, 1938; Ph.D., Harvard, 1942). Associate Professor of Social Studies, Case Institute of Technology. Author of *The Siege of Paris, 1870–1871; A Political and Social History* (Ithaca, N.Y., 1950); "The Hitlerian Legend," *Forum*, CVI (1946); "The Humanistic-Social Studies in an Engineering Education: Some Basic Fallacies," *Journal of Engineering Education*, XXXVIII (1947).

EDWIN C. ROZWENC (A.B., Amherst, 1937; Ph.D., Columbia, 1941). Professor of History, Amherst College. Author of *Cooperatives Come to America* (Mt. Vernon, Iowa, 1941); "The Evolution of the Vermont State Board of Agriculture," *Vermont Quarterly*, XIV (1946); "Agriculture and Politics in the Vermont Tradition," *Vermont Quarterly,* XVII (1948). Editor of *Slavery as a Cause of the Civil War* (Boston, 1949); *The New Deal—Revolution or Evolution* (Boston, 1949); *Roosevelt, Wilson and the Trusts* (Boston, 1950); *Reconstruction in the South* (Boston, 1952).

ROBERT SIDNEY SMITH (A.B., Amherst, 1927; Ph.D., Duke, 1932). Professor of Economics, Duke University. Author of *The Spanish Guild Merchant* (Durham, N.C., 1940); "The Institution of the Consulado in New Spain," *Hispanic American Historical Review,* XXIV (1944); "Spanish Antimercantilism of the Seventeenth Century," *Journal of Political Economy,* XLVIII (1940). Contributor to *The Cambridge Economic History of Europe,* I, edited by J. H. Clapham and Eileen Power (Cambridge, Eng., 1941); *El Indice del Archivo del Tribunal del Consulado de Lima,* edited by Federico Schwab (Lima, Peru, 1948).

PAUL L. WARD (A.B., Amherst, 1933; Ph.D., Harvard, 1940). Professor of History and Head of the Department of History, Carnegie Institute of Technology. Author of "An Early Version of the Anglo-Saxon Coronation Ceremony," *English Historical Review,* LVII (1942); "William Lambarde's Collections on Chancery," *Harvard Library Bulletin,* VII (1953). Co-editor of William Lambarde, *Archeion* (Cambridge, Mass., to be published).